Multinationals and Corporate Social Responsibility

The 'corporate social responsibility' ('CSR') movement has been described as one of the most important social movements of our time. This book looks at what the CSR movement means for multinationals, for states and for international law. International law is often criticised for being too 'state-centred', and ill-equipped to deal with the challenges of globalisation. However, drawing from many and varied examples of state, NGO and corporate practice, this book argues that, while international law has its limitations, it presents more opportunities for the CSR regulation of multinationals than many people assume. The main obstacles to better regulation are, therefore, not legal, but political. Essential reading for anyone who wants to understand how international law works and how it can be used to further international CSR objectives.

JENNIFER A. ZERK was admitted as a solicitor in Australia in 1991 and in England and Wales in 1993. She holds law degrees from the University of Adelaide and the University of London, and a PhD in law from the University of Cambridge. Formerly an energy law specialist with a major London firm, she now works as an independent researcher and consultant, advising on the legal and regulatory aspects of 'corporate social responsibility'.

CAMBRIDGE STUDIES IN INTERNATIONAL AND COMPARATIVE LAW

Established in 1946, this series produces high quality scholarship in the fields of public and private international law and comparative law. Although these are distinct legal subdisciplines, developments since 1946 confirm their interrelation.

Comparative law is increasingly used as a tool in the making of law at national, regional and international levels. Private international law is now often affected by international conventions, and the issues faced by classical conflicts rules are frequently dealt with by substantive harmonisation of law under international auspices. Mixed international arbitrations, especially those involving state economic activity, raise mixed questions of public and private international law, while in many fields (such as the protection of human rights and democratic standards, investment guarantees and international criminal law) international and national systems interact. National constitutional arrangements relating to 'foreign affairs', and to the implementation of international norms, are a focus of attention.

The Board welcomes works of a theoretical or interdisciplinary character, and those focusing on the new approaches to international or comparative law or conflicts of law. Studies of particular institutions or problems are equally welcome, as are translations of the best work published in other languages.

A list of books in the series can be found at the end of this volume.

Multinationals and Corporate Social Responsibility

Limitations and Opportunities in International Law

Jennifer A. Zerk

CAMBRIDGE
UNIVERSITY PRESS

CAMBRIDGE UNIVERSITY PRESS
Cambridge, New York, Melbourne, Madrid, Cape Town,
Singapore, São Paulo, Delhi, Tokyo, Mexico City

Cambridge University Press
The Edinburgh Building, Cambridge CB2 8RU, UK

Published in the United States of America by Cambridge University Press, New York

www.cambridge.org
Information on this title: www.cambridge.org/9780521175203

First published 2006
Reprinted 2008
First paperback edition 2011

A catalogue record for this publication is available from the British Library

ISBN 978-0-521-84499-4 Hardback
ISBN 978-0-521-17520-3 Paperback

Contents

Preface   page ix
Table of treaties, declarations and other international
    instruments   xi
Table of cases   xvi
Table of statutes and statutory instruments   xxi
List of abbreviations   xxiv

Introduction   1

Part I Regulatory issues and problems

**1   Multinationals and corporate social responsibility: a
new regulatory agenda**   7
  Why are people so concerned about multinationals?   8
  The rise of the CSR movement   15
  Defining 'corporate social responsibility'   29
  Regulation in a deregulatory era   32
  Corporate social responsibility and human rights   42
  Designing regulatory responses: some persistent
    problems   44
  Conclusion   58

2   Multinationals under international law   60
  What is international law?   61
  Who makes international law?   62
  The concept of international legal personality   72
  Multinationals and human rights   76

The role of non-state actors   93
Conclusion   103

3   Multinationals under national law: the problem
     of jurisdiction   104
     The limits of jurisdiction under public
        international law   105
     The limits of jurisdiction under private international
        law   113
     Extraterritorial CSR regulation of multinationals:
        time for a rethink?   133
     An alternative definition of 'extraterritoriality' 140
     Conclusion   142

Part II   Home state regulation of multinationals

4   New directions in extraterritorial regulation
     of CSR standards   145
     Defining the 'home state'   146
     Why do 'home states' have an interest in the foreign
        CSR standards of multinationals?   151
     Extraterritorial regulatory techniques: recent
        state practice   160
     Home state CSR initiatives under international law 194
     Conclusion   196

5   Private claims for personal injury and
     environmental harm   198
     Tort-based claims   200
     The US Alien Tort Claims Act ('ATCA')   207
     Theories of parent company liability   216
     Parent company liability and the relevance of the
        organisational form   234
     Implications for international law   237
     Conclusion   239

Part III   International regulation of multinationals

6   Towards an international law of CSR?   243
     International CSR standards for multinationals: a
        brief history   244

Emerging legal principles   262
International CSR regulation: proposals, precedents
    and possibilities   278
Precedents in international CSR regulation   284
Conclusion   297

7   **Multinationals and CSR: limitations and
opportunities in international law**   299
The developing role of home states   300
Direct obligations for multinationals?   304
On the outside looking in: implications for less
    developed host states   306
Conclusion   309

Bibliography   311
Index   324

Preface

It was while working as an energy lawyer in a busy London firm that I first became aware of corporate social responsibility (CSR). Like many lawyers, I expect, I wasn't sure what to make of it at first. How might CSR and the law inter-relate? Were there legal implications I should be aware of? And where was this all heading? Here, some years later, I have attempted to answer these questions, from the perspective of international law. During the course of my research, I found that the prevailing negativity about the capacity of international law to address contemporary problems of 'globalisation' often flowed through into discussions about CSR law and policy. But while this volume began as a critique of international law, I now believe that, while international law certainly has its limitations, it also presents more opportunities for the international regulation of multinationals than many people assume. In this book, I have tried to explain why.

This volume is a revised, expanded and updated version of a thesis submitted for the degree of PhD from the University of Cambridge in 2002. Writing first the thesis, and then this book has been quite a challenge – not least because CSR is such a new and fast-moving area – and there are many people I would like to thank. First of all, I was extremely fortunate to have had the chance to work with Dr Christine Gray at the thesis-writing stage. As a PhD supervisor she was first-rate, and approached the task in such a generous, light-handed and constructive way. I have been grateful for her interest and support. I have also been grateful for the financial support provided by the Arts and Humanities Board of the British Academy and also the Master and Fellows of Magdalene College, Cambridge, in the form of two Leslie Wilson Scholarships (minor) and the Donaldson Bye-Fellowship in 2000–1.

Many more people have given up their time to answer my questions, and share their thoughts and experiences with me. Nick Coppin at the FCO (Global Social Responsibility Unit), Paul Hawker at the DTI, Ben Mellor and Lucia Wilde at the DFID, and Dave Allwood at the ECGD all provided useful background material on aspects of UK government CSR policy. I am most grateful to them. Of those people from further afield, I would like to thank, in particular, Imar Doornbos and Maurice Sikkel of the Netherlands Ministry of Economic Affairs, Paola Pinoargote, Joost Koojimans and Monica Evans of the ILO, Marta Seoane of the WHO's Tobacco Free Initiative, Scott Jerbi at the Office of the UN High Commissioner for Human Rights, Greg Maggio of OPIC, Sheila Logan of the FAO, Joerg Weber of UNCTAD and Richard Howitt MEP. Gabrielle Russell of the Australian Democrats was a great help to me in researching the Australian Corporate Code of Conduct Bill. I am grateful to Richard Meeran of Leigh Day and Co. for taking the time to talk to me about the *Lubbe* v. *Cape* litigation. Iain McGee and Paul Scott of Corporate Register provided some useful data on CSR reporting history and current practice. From NGOs, special thanks are due to Anne von Schaik of the Clean Clothes Campaign, Duncan McLaren of Friends of the Earth, Peter Frankenthal of Amnesty International, Mark Brownlie of the GRI, Natacha Thys of the International Labor Rights Fund, Marco Simons of EarthRights International and Halina Ward of the International Institute for Environment and Development. Many other colleagues have provided additional help, advice, insight and guidance along the way, in particular John Collier, Simon Deakin, Janet Dine, Martin Dixon, Richard Fentiman, Charles Gibson, QC, Michael Hopkins, Paul Hunt, Rob McCorquodale, Susan Marks, Peter Muchlinski, Richard Nolan, David Oliver, Ken Peattie, Phillip Rudolph, Colin Warbrick, Angela Ward. I am most grateful to all of them. I am also indebted to Anna Kirk for her comments on earlier drafts of chapters for this book.

On the home front, I would like to thank my husband, Phil Rawlins, and our daughter, Anna, for their fortitude and patience with me, especially over recent months. Phil, in particular, has lived with this project for a long time and the fact that this book was written at all is a testament to his generosity, kindness and support. Finally, I would like to pay a special tribute to three people of tremendous courage, compassion and decency. They are my parents, Melvyn and Linda, and my late grandfather, Frank. Their values and example have provided both the inspiration and purpose behind this book. This book is dedicated to them, with my admiration and thanks.

Table of treaties, declarations and other international instruments

Treaties

1945   Agreement for the Prosecution and Punishment of the Major War Criminals of the European Axis, and the Charter of the International Military Tribunal, London, 8 August 1945, 82 UNTS 280

1948   Convention on the Prevention and Punishment of the Crime of Genocide, Paris, 9 December 1948, in force 12 January 1951, 78 UNTS 277

1950   European Convention on Human Rights and Fundamental Freedoms, Rome, 4 November 1950, in force 3 September 1953, ETS, No. 5

1957   Treaty Establishing the European Economic Community, Rome, 25 March 1957, in force 1 January 1958, 298 UNTS 11 (as amended); now the Treaty Establishing the European Community, consolidated version published at OJ 2002 No. C325/33, 24 December 2002

1961   Vienna Convention on Diplomatic Relations, Vienna, 18 April 1961, in force 24 April 1964, 500 UNTS 95; UKTS (1965) 19

1965   International Convention on the Settlement of Investment Disputes Between States and Nationals of Other States, Washington, 18 March 1965, in force 14 October 1966, 575 UNTS 159, 17 UTS 1270; (1965) 4 ILM 524

1966   International Covenant on Economic, Social and Cultural Rights, adopted by UNGA Resolution 2200A (XXI), 16 December 1966, in force 3 January 1976, 999 UNTS 3

1966   International Covenant on Civil and Political Rights, adopted by UNGA Resolution 2200A (XXI), 16 December 1966, in force 23 March 1976, 999 UNTS 171

1968   Convention on Jurisdiction and Enforcement of Judgments in Civil and Commercial Matters, Brussels, 27 September 1968, in force 1 February 1973, OJ 1972 No. L299/32, 31 December 1972, 1262 UNTS 153; (1968) 8 ILM 229

1969   Vienna Convention on the Law of Treaties, Vienna, 23 May 1969, in force 27 January 1980, 1155 UNTS 331; (1969) 8 ILM 679; UKTS (1980) 58

1969   International Convention on Civil Liability for Oil Pollution Damage, Brussels, 29 November 1969, in force 19 June 1975, 973 UNTS 3; UKTS (1975) 106

1971   Convention on the Establishment of an International Fund for Compensation of Oil Pollution Damage, Brussels, 18 December 1971, in force 16 October 1978; (1972) 11 ILM 284; UKTS (1978) 95 (n.b. replaced by the 1992 Protocol, 27 November 1992, in force 30 May 1996)

1981   ILO Convention on Occupational Safety and Health and the Working Environment, Geneva, 22 June 1981, in force 11 August 1983 (No. 155)

1989   Convention on the Control of Transboundary Movements of Hazardous Wastes and their Disposal, Basel, 22 March 1989, in force 24 May 1992, 1673 UNTS 126; (1989) 28 ILM 657

1991   Convention on the Ban of the Import into Africa and the Control of Transboundary Movement and Management of Hazardous Wastes within Africa, Bamako, 30 January 1991, in force 22 April 1998; (1991) 30 ILM 775

1992   North American Free Trade Agreement, Washington, Ottawa and Mexico City, 17 December 1992, in force 1 January 1994; (1993) 32 ILM 289, 603

1993   ILO Convention Concerning the Prevention of Major
        Industrial Accidents, Geneva, 22 June 1993, in force 3
        January 1997 (No. 174)

1994   General Agreement on Trade in Services, Marrakesh, 15 April
        1994, in force 1 January 1995; (1994) 33 ILM 46

1994   Agreement on Trade Related Investment Measures,
        Marrakesh, 15 April 1994 (annex 1A of the 1994 Marrakesh
        Agreement Establishing the World Trade Organisation), 1868
        UNTS 186

1997   OECD Convention on Combating Bribery of Foreign Public
        Officials in International Business Transactions, Paris, 27
        November 1997, in force 15 February 1999; (1998) 37 ILM 1

1998   Statute of the International Criminal Court, Rome, 17 July
        1998, in force 1 July 2002, UN Doc. A/CONF.183/9, 2187 UNTS
        90; (1998) 37 ILM 1002

1998   Convention on the Prior Informed Consent ('PIC') Procedure
        for Certain Hazardous Chemicals and Pesticides in
        International Trade, Rotterdam, 10 September 1998, in force
        24 February 2004; (1999) 38 ILM 1

1999   ILO Convention Concerning the Prohibition and Immediate
        Elimination of the Worst Forms of Child Labour, Geneva, 17
        June 1999, in force 10 November 2000 (No. 182); (1999) 38
        ILM 1207

2003   Framework Convention on Tobacco Control, Geneva, 21 May
        2003, in force 27 February 2005, WHA56.1

Declarations and other 'soft law' instruments

1948   Universal Declaration of Human Rights, UNGA res. 217A (III),
        UN Doc. A/810, 71

1970   Declaration on the Principles of International Law
        Concerning Friendly Relations and Co-operation Among
        States in accordance with the Charter of the United Nations,
        UNGA res. 2625, Annex, 25 UN GAOR, Supp. (No. 28), UN
        Doc. A/5217 at 121

1976   OECD Declaration on International Investment and
        Multinational Enterprises, Paris, 21 June 1976; (1976) 15 ILM
        967

1976   OECD Guidelines for Multinational Enterprises (annexed to
        the 1976 OECD Declaration on Investment and Multinational
        Enterprises, above); (1976) 15 ILM 969

1977   ILO Tripartite Declaration Concerning Multinational
        Enterprises and Social Policy, November 1977, Geneva; (1978)
        17 ILM 422

1981   WHO International Code on Marketing of Breast Milk
        Substitutes, adopted by the WHA, Res. WHA34.2, 21 May 1981

1985   UN Guidelines for Consumer Protection, UN Doc.
        A/RES/39/248 (1986)

1985   FAO Code of Conduct on the Distribution and Use of
        Pesticides, adopted at the 25th session of the FAO
        Conference, Rome, 19 November 1985

1990   Draft UN Code of Conduct on Transnational Corporations,
        UN Doc. E/1990/94, 12 June 1990

1992   Declaration of the UN Conference on Environment and
        Development, Rio de Janeiro, 13 June 1992, UN Doc.
        A/CONF.151/26/Rev. 1, Vol. 1, Annex I; (1992) 31 ILM 874

1992   Agenda 21: Programme of Action for Sustainable
        Development, adopted by the UNGA at its 46th session, UN
        Doc. A/CONF.151/26

1996   OECD Recommendation on the Tax Deductibility of Bribes to
        Foreign Public Officials, adopted by the Council, 11 April
        1996, C(96)27(FINAL); (1996) 35 ILM 760

1998   ILO Declaration on Fundamental Principles and Rights at
        Work, adopted at the 86th session of the International
        Labour Conference, Geneva, 18 June 1998

2000   OECD Declaration on International Investment and
        Multinational Enterprises, Paris, 27 June 2000,
        DAFFE/IME(2000)/20

2000   OECD Guidelines for Multinational Enterprises (annexed to
        the 2000 OECD Declaration on International Investment and
        Multinational Enterprises, above); (2001) 40 ILM 237

2002   Declaration on Sustainable Development of the World
        Summit on Sustainable Development, UN, 'Report of the
        World Summit on Sustainable Development', UN Doc.
        A/CONF.199/20, Sales No. E.03.II.A.1

2002   Plan of Implementation of the World Summit on
        Sustainable Development, UN, 'Report of the World Summit
        on Sustainable Development', UN Doc. A/CONF.199/20, Sales
        No. E.03.II.A.1

2003   UN Norms on the Responsibilities of Transnational
        Corporations and other Business Enterprises with Regard to
        Human Rights, adopted by the UN Sub-Commission on the
        Protection and Promotion of Human Rights, 13 August 2003,
        UN Doc. E/CN.4/Sub.2/2003/12/Rev.2

Table of cases

International

ICJ

Anglo-Norwegian Fisheries Case (UK v. Norway) [1951] ICJ Reps 116
Asylum Case (Colombia v. Peru) [1950] ICJ Reps 266
Arrest Warrant Case (Congo v. Belgium), [2002] ICJ Reps 3
Barcelona Traction Light & Power Company (Belgium v. Spain) [1970] ICJ
    Reps 3
Nicaragua Case (Merits) [1986] ICJ Reps 14
*North Sea Continental Shelf Cases (Federal Republic of Germany v. Denmark;
    Federal Republic of Germany v. Netherlands)* [1969] ICJ Reps 3
Reparations for Injuries Suffered in the Service of the United Nations [1949] ICJ
    Reps 174
Right of Passage over Indian Territory Case [1960] ICJ Reps 6

Other international courts and tribunals

Bankovic and Others v. Belgium and Others, European Court of Human Rights,
    (2001) 11 BHRC 435; (2001) 41 ILM 517
*Decision Regarding Communication 155/96 (Social and Economic Rights Action
    Center/Center for Economic and Social Rights v. Nigeria)*, African
    Commission on Human and Peoples' Rights, Case No.
    ACHPR/COMM/A044.1, 27 May 2002
Osman v. United Kingdom (Case No. 2345/94), European Court of Human
    Rights, 28 October 1998, [1998] ECHR 101; (1999) 29 EHRR
    245
Velasquez Rodriguez v. Honduras, Inter-American Court of Human Rights
    (ser. C.) no. 4 (1988); (1989) 28 ILM 294

WM v. *Denmark*, European Court of Human Rights, 14 October 1992, (1993) 15 EHRR CD28

EU

Case 21/76, *Bier BV* v. *Mines de Potasse d'Alsace SA* [1976] ECR 1735; [1978] QB 708

Case C-212/97, *Centros Ltd.* [1999] ECR I-1459

Case T-219/95, *Danielsson* v. *Commission* [1995] ECR II-3051

Case T-102/96, *Gencor Limited* v. *Commission* [1999] ECR II-753

Case 170/83, *Hydrotherm Geratebau* v. *Andreoli* [1984] ECR 2999

Case C-381/98, *Ingmar GB Ltd* v. *Eaton Leonard Technologies Inc.*, TLR, 16 November 2000

Case C-281/02, *Owusu* v. *Jackson*, [2005] 2 WLR 942

Case T-585/93, *Stichting Greenpeace Council* v. *Commission* [1999] ECR 2205

UK

Adams v. *Cape Industries* [1990] Ch 433

AG for New Zealand v. *Ortiz* [1984] AC 1

Al-Adsani v. *Government of Kuwait*, Court of Appeal, 21 January 1994; (1995) 100 ILR 465

The Amoco Cadiz [1984] 2 Lloyds Rep. 304

Bank of Tokyo v. *Karoon* [1987] AC 45

Belmont Finance v. *Williams Furniture* (No. 2) [1980] 1 All ER 393

British South Africa Co. v. *Companhia de Moçambique* [1893] AC 602

Connelly v. *RTZ* [1998] AC 854

DHN Ltd v. *Tower Hamlets* LBC [1976] 1 WLR 852

Donoghue v. *Stevenson* [1932] AC 562

Gilford Motor Co. v. *Horne* [1933] Ch 935

Government of India v. *Taylor* [1955] AC 491

Re Harrods (Buenos Aires) Ltd [1992] Ch 72 (CA)

Hesperides Hotels Ltd v. *Muftizade* [1979] AC 508

Home Office v. *Dorset Yacht Club* [1970] AC 1004

Jones v. *Lipman* [1962] 1 All ER 442

Leonard's Carrying Company Ltd v. *Asiatic Petroleum Company Ltd* [1915] AC 705

Lubbe v. *Cape plc* [2000] 1 WLR 1545; [2000] 4 All ER 268 (HL) 277

Masters v. *Leaver* [2000] ILPr. 387 CA

Meridian Global Funds Management Asia Ltd v. *Securities Commission* [1995] 3 All ER 918

Midland Bank plc v. *Laker Airways Ltd* [1986] QB 689

Ngcobo and Others v. *Thor Chemical Holdings Ltd*, TLR 10 November 1995

Phelps v. *Hillingdon LBC* [2000] 3 WLR 776

R v. *Secretary of State for Foreign Affairs ex parte World Development Movement Limited* [1995] 1 All ER 611

R (on the application of B and Others) v. *Secretary of State for the Foreign and Commonwealth Office* [2005] QB 643

Saab v. *Saudi American Bank* [1998] 1 WLR 937

Sea Assets v. *PT Garuda Indonesia* [2000] 1 All ER 371

Sithole and Others v. *Thor Chemical Holdings Ltd.*, TLR 15 February 1999

Smith v. *Littlewoods* [1987] AC 241

Société Nationale Industrielle Aerospatiale v. *Lee Kui Jak* [1987] AC 871

Spiliada Maritime Corporation v. *Cansulex Ltd* [1987] AC 460

Williams v. *Natural Life Health Foods* [1998] 1 WLR 830 (HL)

Other European States

Société Fruehauf v. *Massardy* [1965] D.S. Jur. 147 (1965) JCP II 14 274 bis (Cour d'Appel, Paris); English translation, (1966) 4 ILM 476 (France)

US

Aguinda v. *Texaco*, 945 F Supp 625 (SDNY 1996)

Amlon Metals v. *FMC Corporation*, 775 F Supp 668 (SDNY 1991)

Associated Vendors, Inc. v. *Oakland Meat Co.*, 210 Cal. App 2d 825 (1962)

Babcock v. *Jackson*, 12 NY 2d 473 (1963)

Baker v. *Carr*, 369 US 186 (S Ct 1962)

Banco Nacional de Cuba v. *Sabbatino*, 376 US 398 (S Ct 1964)

Bano v. *Union Carbide Corporation*, 273 F 3d 120 (2d Cir. 2001)

Beanal v. *Freeport McMoRan*, 969 F Supp 362 (ED La 1997)

Bi v. *Union Carbide Chems. and Plastics Co.*, 984 F 2d 582 (2d Cir.) cert. denied 510 US 862, 114 S Ct 179, 126 L Ed 2d 138 (1993)

Bigio v. *Coca-Cola*, 239 F 3d 440 (2d Cir. 2000)

Borja v. *Dole Food Co.*, No. CIV.A.3:97-CV308L, 2002 US Dist. LEXIS 23234 (ND Tex 4 December 2002)

Bowoto v. *Chevron*, 312 F Supp 2d 1229 (ND Cal 2004)

Canada Malting v. *Paterson Steamships Ltd*, 285 US 413 (1932)

Doe v. *Unocal*, 963 F Supp 880 (CD Cal 1997)

Doe v. *Unocal*, 27 F Supp 2d 117 (CD Cal 1998)

Doe v. *Unocal*, 248 F 3d 915 (9th Cir. 2001)

Doe I v. *Unocal* 395 F 3d 932 (9th Cir. 2002)

Dowling v. *Richardson-Merrell, Inc.*, 727 F 2d 608 (6th Cir. 1984)

Eastman Kodak Co. v. *Kavlin*, 978 F Supp 1078 (SD Fla 1997)

Environmental Defense Fund, Inc. v. *Massey*, 986 F 2d 538 (DC Cir. 1993)

Equal Employment Opportunity Commission v. *Arabian American Oil Co.*, 499 US 244, 111 S Ct 1227, 113 L Ed 2d 274 (1991)

Filartiga v. *Pena-Irala*, 630 F 2d 876 (2d Cir. 1980)

Flores v. *Southern Peru Copper*, 343 F 3d 140 (2d Cir. 2003)

Gulf Oil Corp. v. *Gilbert*, 330 US 501 (1947)

Harrison v. *Wyeth Laboratories Division of American Home Products*, 510 F Supp 1 (ED Pa 1980), 676 F 2d 685 (3d Cir. 1982)

International Shoe Co. v. *Washington*, 326 US 310 (1945)

Iwanowa v. *Ford Motor Co.*, 67 F Supp 2d 248 (DNJ 1999)

Jota v. *Texaco*, 157 F 3d 153 (2d Cir. 1998)

Kadic v. *Karadzic*, 70 F 3d 232 (2d Cir. 1995)

Kasky v. *Nike*, 539 US 654 (2003)

Martinez v. *Dow Chemicals*, 219 F Supp 2d 719 (ED La 2002)

National Coalition Government of the Union of Myanmar v. *Unocal*, 176 FRD 329 (CD Cal 1997)

Piper Aircraft Co. v. *Reyno*, 454 US 235 (1981)

Presbyterian Church of Sudan v. *Talisman Energy*, 244 F Supp 2d 289 (SDNY 2003)

In re Richardson-Merrell Inc., 545 F Supp 1130 (1982)

Roe v. *Unocal*, 70 F Supp 2d 1073 (CD Cal 1999)

Sanyo Corp. v. *Universal City Studios*, 464 US 417 (1986)

Sarei v. *Rio Tinto*, 221 F Supp 2d 1116 (CD Cal 2002)

Sequilhua v. *Texaco*, 847 F Supp 61 (SD Tex 1994)

Sinaltrain v. *Coca-Cola*, 265 F Supp 2d 1345 (SD Fla 2003)

Sosa v. *Alvarez-Machain*, 542 US 692 (2004), 124 S Ct 2739 (2004)

In re South African Apartheid Litigation 346 F Supp 2d 538 (SDNY 2004)

Tel-Oren v. *Libyan Arab Republic*, 726 F 2d 774 (DC Cir. 1984)

In Re Union Carbide Corporation Gas Plant Disaster at Bhopal, India in December, 1984, 634 F Supp 842 (SDNY 1986)

In Re Union Carbide Corp. Gas Plant Disaster; No. MDL 626, 1992 WL 36135, 1992 US Dist. LEXIS 1909 (SDNY, 18 February 1992)

US v. *Alcoa*, (1945) 148 F 2d 416 (2d Cir. 1945)

Wiwa v. *Royal Dutch Petroleum Co.*, 226 F 3d 88 (2d Cir. 2000)

Wiwa v. *Royal Dutch Petroleum Co.*, 2002 WL 319887 (SDNY 28
    February 2002)
WS Kilpatrick v. *Environmental Tectronics Corp.*, 493 US 400 (1990)

Commonwealth

Barrow and Heys v. *CSR Ltd*, unreported, Supreme Court of WA, 4 August
    1988, Library No. 7231 (Australia)
Briggs v. *James Hardie & Co. Pty Ltd* (1989) 16 NSWLR 549 (Australia)
CSR Ltd v. *Wren* (1997) 44 NSWLR 463; [1998] Aust Tort Rep 81–461
    (Australia)
CSR Ltd v. *Young* (1998) Aust Tort Rep 81–468 (Australia)
Dagi v. *BHP* [1997] 1 VR 428 (Australia)
Oceanic Sun-Line Special Shipping Co. Inc. v. *Fay* (1988) 165 CLR 197
    (Australia)
Recherches Internationales Quebec v. *Cambior Inc.* [1998] Q J No. 2554 (QL)
    (Canada)
Renault v. *Zhang* (2002) 210 CLR 491 (Australia)
Sahu v. *Union of India* [1990] AIR (Supreme Court) 1480 (India)
Union Carbide v. *Union of India*, Decision of the Madhya Pradesh High
    Court at Jabalpur Civil Revision no 26 of 88, 4 April 1988
Voth v. *Manildra Flour Mills* (1990) 171 CLR 538 (Australia).
Wilson v. *Servier Canada* 50 OR (3d) 219 (2000) (Canada)

Table of statutes and statutory instruments

UK

Anti-Terrorism, Crime and Security Act 2001

Civil Jurisdiction and Judgments Act 1982

Civil Procedure Rules 1998 (SI 1998 No. 3132)

Companies Act 1985

Companies Act 1985 (Operating and Financial Review and Directors'
    Report) Regulations 2004 (SI 2005 No. 1011)

Companies Act 1985 (Operating and Financial Review) (Repeal)
    Regulations 2005 (SI 2005 No. 3442)

Competition Act 1998

Consumer Protection Act 1987

Control of Misleading Advertisements Regulations 1998 (SI 1998 No.
    915)

Criminal Justice (Terrorism and Conspiracy) Act 1998

Employment Rights Act 1996

Environmental Information Regulations 2004 (SI 2004 No. 3391)

Finance Act 2002

Financial Services and Markets Act 2000

Freedom of Information Act 2000

Human Rights Act 1998

Occupational Pension Schemes (Investment, and Assignment,
    Forfeiture, Bankruptcy etc.) Amendment Regulations (SI 1999 No.
    1849)

Private International Law (Miscellaneous Provisions) Act 1995

Public Interest Disclosure Act 1998

Rules of the Supreme Court of England and Wales (SI 1965 No. 1776)

Sex Offenders Act 1997

Supreme Court Act 1981

Unfair Terms in Consumer Contracts Regulations 1991 (SI 1991 No. 2083)

EU

Council Regulation 2137/85/EEC of 25 July 1985 on the European Economic Interest Groupings OJ 1985 No. L199/1, 31 July 1985

Council Directive 85/374/EEC of 25 July 1985 on the approximation of the laws, regulations and administrative provisions of the Member States concerning liability for defective products, OJ 1985 No. L210/29, 7 August 1985

Council Directive 89/391/EEC of 12 June 1989 on the introduction of measures to encourage improvements in the safety and health of workers, OJ 1989 No. L183/1, 29 June 1989

Council Regulation 2455/92/EEC of 23 July 1992 concerning the export and import of certain dangerous chemicals, OJ 1992 No. L251/13, 29 August 1992 (repealed and replaced by Council Regulation 304/2003 of 28 January 2003, see below)

Council Directive 96/82/EC of 9 December 1996 on the control of major accident hazards involving dangerous substances, OJ 1997 No. L10/13, 14 January 1997

Council Regulation 1980/2000 of 17 July 2000 on a revised Community eco-label award scheme, OJ 2000 No. L 237/1, 21 September 2000

Council Regulation 44/2001 of 22 December 2000 on jurisdiction and the recognition and enforcement of judgments in civil and commercial matters, OJ 2001 No. L12/1, 16 January 2001

Council Directive 2003/4/EC of 28 January 2003 on public access to environmental information and repealing Council Directive 90/313/EEC, OJ No. L41/26, 14 February 2003

Council Directive 2003/51/EC of 18 June 2003 amending directives 78/660/EEC, 83/349/EEC, 86/635/EEC and 91/674/EEC on the annual and consolidated accounts of certain types of companies, banks and other financial institutions and insurance undertakings, OJ 2003 No. L178/16, 17 July 2003

Council Regulation 304/2003 of 28 January 2003 concerning the export and import of dangerous chemicals, OJ 2003 No. L63/1, 6 March 2003

Council Directive 2003/87/EC of 13 October 2003 establishing a scheme for greenhouse gas emission allowance trading within the

Community and amending Council Directive 96/91/EC, OJ 2003 No.
L275/32, 25 October 2003

Europe (national legislation)

Joint Stock Corporation Act 1965 (Germany)
Nouvelles Regulations Economiques, adopted 15 May 2001 (France)

US

Age Discrimination in Employment Act of 1967, 29 USC § 621
Alien Tort Claims Act of 1789, 28 USC § 1350
Anti-Terrorism Act of 2002, 18 USCA § 2332d
Clean Air Act of 1990, 42 USC § 7604
Comprehensive Anti-Apartheid Act of 1986, 22 USC § 5001
Export Administration Act of 1979, 50 USC § 2405
Foreign Assistance Act of 1961, 22 USC § 2191
Foreign Corrupt Practices Act of 1977, 15 USC § 78dd-1
Foreign Sovereign Immunities Act of 1976, 28 USC §§ 1602
Freedom of Information Act of 1966, 5 USC § 552
Trade Act of 1974, 19 USC § 2101

Commonwealth

Bhopal Gas Leak Disaster (Processing of Claims) Act 1985 (India)
Companies Act 1993 (New Zealand)
Corporations Act 2001 (Australia)
Freedom of Information Act 1982 (Australia)
Trade Practices Act 1974 (Australia)

Abbreviations

ABTA	Association of British Travel Agents
AC	Appeal Cases
Adel LR	*Adelaide Law Review*
AIP	Apparel Industry Partnership
AIR	All India Reports
AJCL	*American Journal of Comparative Law*
AJHR	*Australian Journal of Human Rights*
ALI	American Law Institute
All ER	All England Reports
ANPED	Alliance of Northern Peoples for Environment and Development (now known as the Northern Alliance for Sustainability)
Ariz JICL	*Arizona Journal of International and Comparative Law*
ASH	Action on Smoking and Health
ASIL Proc	*American Society of International Law Proceedings*
ATCA	Alien Tort Claims Act
BHRC	Butterworths Human Rights Cases
BIT	Bilateral Investment Treaty
BITC	Business in the Community
BJIL	*Brooklyn Journal of International Law*
BUILJ	*Boston University International Law Journal*
BYIL	*British Yearbook of International Law*
CBI	Confederation of British Industries
Can YIL	*Canadian Yearbook of International Law*
CAP	Committee of Advertising Practice
Ch	Chancery Division
CJTL	*Columbia Journal of Transnational Law*
CLJ	*Cambridge Law Journal*

CLR	Commonwealth Law Reports
Comp Lab J	*Comparative Labour Law Journal*
CORE Coalition	Corporate Responsibility Coalition
CPR	Civil Procedure Rules
CSO	civil society organisation
CSR	Corporate Social Responsibility
CWLR	*Common World Law Review*
DEFRA	Department for the Environment, Food and Rural Affairs
DFID	Department for International Development
DTI	Department for Trade and Industry
EC	European Community
ECGD	Export Credits Guarantee Department
ECHR	European Convention on Human Rights
ECJ	European Court of Justice
ECR	European Court Reports
EHRR	European Human Rights Reports
EIB	*Environment Information Bulletin*
EITI	Extractive Industries Transparency Initiative
EJIL	*European Journal of International Law*
ELR	*Environmental Law Review*
EMAS	Eco-Management and Audit Scheme
EMSF	European Multi-Stakeholder Forum
ETI	Ethical Trading Initiative
ETS	Council of Europe Treaty Series
EU	European Union
Ex-Im Bank	Export Import Bank
FAO	Food and Agricultural Organisation
FCO	Foreign and Commonwealth Office
FCPA	Foreign Corrupt Practices Act
FDI	Foreign Direct Investment
FLA	Fair Labor Association
FoE	Friends of the Earth
FOI	Freedom of Information
FRS	Financial Reporting Standard
FSC	Forest Stewardship Council
F Supp	Federal Supplement
GATS	General Agreement on Trade in Services
GATT	General Agreement on Tariffs and Trade
GCAC	Global Compact Advisory Council

GRI	Global Reporting Initiative
GYIL	*German Yearbook of International Law*
Hague YIL	*Hague Yearbook of International Law*
Harv HRJ	*Harvard Human Rights Journal*
Harv ILJ	*Harvard International Law Journal*
Harv LR	*Harvard Law Review*
Hast I&CLR	*Hastings International and Comparative Law Review*
HRQ	*Human Rights Quarterly*
HSE	Health and Safety Executive
IBLF	International Business Leaders Forum
IBLR	*International Business Law Review*
ICC	International Chamber of Commerce
ICCPR	International Covenant on Civil and Political Rights
ICESCR	International Covenant on Economic, Social and Cultural Rights
ICFTU	International Confederation of Free Trade Unions
ICHRP	International Council on Human Rights Policy
ICJ	International Court of Justice
ICJ Reps	International Court of Justice Reports
ICLQ	*International and Comparative Law Quarterly*
ICSID	International Centre for Settlement of Investment Disputes
IIA	International Investment Agreement
ILA	International Law Association
ILC	International Law Commission
ILM	International Legal Materials
ILO	International Labour Organisation
ILR	International Law Reports
IMF	International Monetary Fund
IMO	International Maritime Organisation
Ind LJ	*Industrial Law Journal*
Indian JIL	*Indian Journal of International Law*
Int'l Lawyer	*International Lawyer*
Int'l L&P	*International Law and Politics*
ITS	International Trade Secretariats
JCHL&P	*Journal of Contemporary Health Law and Policy*
JPIL	*Journal of Personal Injury Litigation*
JSE	Johannesburg Stock Exchange
McGill LJ	*McGill Law Journal*
MAI	Multilateral Agreement on Investment

MD&A	Management Discussion and Analysis
Melb UL Rev	*Melbourne University Law Review*
MEP	Member of European Parliament
MFN	Most Favoured Nation
MLR	*Modern Law Review*
MNE	multinational enterprise
MP	Member of Parliament
NAFTA	North American Free Trade Agreement
NCP	National Contact Point
NEPA	National Environmental Policy Act
NGO	non-governmental organisation
NILR	*Netherlands International Law Review*
NSWLR	New South Wales Law Reports
NYIL	*Netherlands Yearbook of International Law*
NYUJIL&P	*New York University Journal of International Law and Politics*
OECD	Organisation of Economic Co-operation and Development
OFR	Operating and Financial Review
OFT	Office of Fair Trading
OHCHR	Office of the High Commissioner for Human Rights
OPIC	Overseas Private Investment Corporation
OR	Ontario Reports
PIC	prior informed consent
PPT	Permanent People's Tribunal
PR	public relations
QB	Queen's Bench
R&D	research and development
RIIA	Royal Institute of International Affairs
SRI	socially responsible investment
Tex ILJ	*Texas International Law Journal*
TLR	Times Law Reports
TNC	transnational corporation
TRIMs	Trade Related Investment Measures
UBJEL	*University of Baltimore Journal of Environmental Law*
UCC	Union Carbide Corporation
UCIL	Union Carbide India Limited
UCLR	*University of Chicago Law Review*
UDHR	Universal Declaration of Human Rights
UKTS	United Kingdom Treaty Series

UN	United Nations
UNAIDS	United Nations Joint Programme on Aids
UNCED	United Nations Conference on the Environment and Development
UNCLOS	United Nations Convention on the Law of the Sea
UNCTAD	United Nations Commission for Trade and Development
UNCTC	United Nations Centre for Transnational Corporations
UNDP	United Nations Development Programme
UNEP	United Nations Environment Programme
UNGA	United Nations General Assembly
UNICEF	United Nations International Children's Emergency Fund
UNIDO	United Nations Industrial Development Organisation
UNSC	United Nations Security Council
UNTS	United Nations Treaty Series
USC	United States Code
USCA	United States Code (Annotated)
UTLJ	*University of Toronto Law Journal*
Vand JTL	*Vanderbilt Journal of Transnational Law*
VJIL	*Virginia Journal of International Law*
VR	Victoria Reports
WEF	World Economic Forum
WHA	World Health Assembly
WHO	World Health Organisation
WLR	Weekly Law Reports
WSSD	World Summit on Sustainable Development
WTO	World Trade Organisation
WWF	World Wildlife Fund
Yale LJ	*Yale Law Journal*
YJIL	*Yale Journal of International Law*

Introduction

Multinationals are not traditional subjects of international law. Historically, the role of international law in relation to multinationals has primarily been to define the rights and obligations *of states* with respect to international investment issues. International law has been used to regulate the jurisdiction of states over multinationals, and their rights of diplomatic protection and, through treaties, has provided states with a means by which investment conditions for multinationals could be stabilised, harmonised, and generally enhanced.

But the world is changing fast. Concern about the social and environmental impacts of 'globalisation' means that new demands are now being made of international law. Can international law respond to these demands? Does international law provide an adequate framework for the regulation of the social and environmental impacts of multinationals on a global scale? Many people think not. Some have doubted that international law is even 'conceptually equipped' to perform such a role.[1] Public opinion, too, is generally sceptical as to the extent to which multinationals can be regulated effectively. Critics point out the ease with which multinationals can avoid national regulation through their mobility and flexibility of structure and organisation. While each state is entitled to regulate those parts of a multinational incorporated or operating within its territory, many states may not have the resources or political will to do so effectively, giving rise to differences in social and environmental standards between states. These differences, it is argued, are exploited by some multinationals for commercial advantage; that is, multinationals will tend to gravitate to regions in which production costs are lowest

---

[1] F. Johns, 'The Invisibility of the Transnational Corporation: an Analysis of International Law and Theory' (1994) 19 *Melb UL Rev* 893.

because of low regulatory standards and expectations. In turn, competition for inward investment is said to put further downward pressure on regulatory standards in those countries, especially the poorer countries of the world, struggling to achieve economic growth.

The international 'corporate social responsibility' ('CSR') movement has developed in response to these perceived gaps in the regulatory system. While the concerns at the heart of the CSR movement are not new, the proposition that multinationals have responsibilities as 'good corporate citizens', independent of the regulatory framework within which they operate, has been hailed as one of the 'big ideas of this new century'.[2] The 'social responsibilities' of companies, and particularly of large multinationals, are now extensively discussed in books, political debates, academic articles and the media. The past few years have seen an extraordinary proliferation of 'codes of conduct' for multinationals, as international organisations, NGOs, trade unions, national governments, and multinationals themselves, all struggle to define what CSR means in practice.

This book explores the implications of these developments for international law. Its central argument is that, while international law has its limitations, it is also capable of supporting new regulatory opportunities that have the potential greatly to improve the welfare of people and communities affected by multinational activities, particularly in less developed countries. These new opportunities are emerging as a consequence of developments at two levels: first, the growing willingness of 'home states' to consider strategies to regulate the performance of multinationals *beyond* national borders and, second, the intensification of efforts at international level to develop global ethical standards for business.

CSR covers a wide range of concerns, but this book focuses on three issues that are currently at the forefront of most CSR-related campaigns: workplace, environmental and consumer safety standards. Although it is concerned with international law, it is written from a UK perspective (in the sense that many of the examples of regulatory techniques and 'state practice' are derived from UK law and governmental policy) although examples are also drawn from other jurisdictions (particularly the common law jurisdictions) where relevant. This is not to suggest that the UK experience is necessarily representative of what is happening in other

---

[2] Mary Robinson, 'Beyond Good Intentions: Corporate Citizenship for a New Century', address given to the Royal Society for the Encouragement of the Arts, Manufacture and Commerce, London, 7 May 2002.

jurisdictions. In reality there is a good deal of variation, even among the richer 'home states', in terms of the governmental resources devoted to international CSR issues (although it is relevant to note that the UK is widely regarded as one of the leaders in this area). Moreover, different cultural and legal traditions inevitably mean that no two states will approach CSR-related issues in exactly the same way.[3] Unfortunately, there is not the space in this book to do proper justice to this diversity, but some of these differences – and also some key similarities – should be apparent from the chapters that follow.

Part I of this book is concerned with background and theory. Chapter 1 outlines the background to the CSR movement, and the relationship between CSR and the law, before discussing some practical problems relating to the design of international CSR regimes for multinationals. Chapter 2 is a discussion of the basic principles of international law-making, as they relate to CSR. (Readers familiar with international law may prefer to skip this chapter.) Chapter 3 focuses on one issue of international law that is particularly problematic as far as the regulation of multinationals is concerned. This is, of course, the problem of 'jurisdiction'.

Part II of this book is an examination of developing state practice in relation to CSR, and particularly the problem of 'double standards', that is, the practice of applying different social and environmental standards in different countries depending on prevailing regulatory conditions. Chapter 4 looks at emerging 'extraterritorial' regulatory techniques proposed, or already in use, by home states. The use of the term 'home state' in this book generally refers to the state of incorporation of the parent company of a multinational. 'Host state', on the other hand, means the state in which a particular investment is made or where activities of affiliates of the multinational take place. For convenience, 'home states' and 'host states' are often discussed as if they were two separate groups, although it is acknowledged that most 'home states' for multinationals are also important 'host states' as well. Chapter 5 considers the regulatory possibilities offered by litigation against parent companies of multinationals in their 'home courts' (often referred to as 'foreign direct liability' litigation).

Part III explores the implications of developing state practice and various international initiatives for international law. Chapter 6 considers the prospects for a new body of international law – an 'international

---

[3] M. Hopkins, 'Corporate Social Responsibility around the World' (1998) 2 *Online Journal of Ethics*, No. 2. http://www.stthom.edu/cbes/onlinejournals.html.

law of CSR'? – and the form it could take. Chapter 7 concludes this book with an assessment of the capacity of international law to support the 'new regulatory agenda' with respect to CSR; that is, greater accountability of multinationals for their social and environmental performance (particularly in countries where regulatory standards are low or, for whatever reason, unlikely to be enforced) and an end to the practice of 'double standards'. It is concluded that, while international law has its limitations (primarily its 'state-centredness'), it also offers more opportunities for the social and environmental regulation of multinationals than many people assume. The question is: are we prepared to use them?

PART I · REGULATORY ISSUES AND PROBLEMS

1   Multinationals and corporate social responsibility: a new regulatory agenda

Multinationals are among the most controversial players on the international stage today. But what are multinationals? And why are people so concerned about them? Is it possible to regulate multinationals effectively? Or are they, as many people believe, 'beyond the law'?

As this chapter will show, concerns about multinationals have developed and changed over time. Historically, public opposition to multinationals has arisen mainly from concerns about undue concentrations of power, and their implications for national sovereignty and cultures. In recent years, however, there has been a shift in emphasis away from these 'state-centred' concerns towards more 'people-centred' concerns, such as the environment and human rights. As will be seen, the CSR movement has played no small part in this.

Most, if not all, leading companies now have strategies relating to CSR. Over the past few years there has been an explosion in management, assurance and reporting standards designed to help companies become more 'socially responsible' and to measure and report on their progress. Governments, too, have been forced to re-evaluate their policies on industry and enterprise to reflect these new concerns. Already, some new regulatory proposals and initiatives have appeared at national and regional level, designed to enhance 'corporate accountability'. These will be explored further in chapter 4. Generally, though, governments of capital-exporting states like the UK and USA are reluctant to take steps which may harm the 'international competitiveness' of their industrial sector and for this reason tend to favour a 'voluntary' approach to CSR. The underlying philosophy is that the drivers for companies to act ethically and to do good, above and beyond minimum legal requirements, should come primarily from employees, investors, consumers and the general public, rather than from further governmental intervention. As will be seen, this suggests a specific set of regulatory tactics – to find ways to harness these influences on corporate behaviour, without adding significantly to the 'regulatory burden' of companies.

Whether CSR is actually 'voluntary' is open to question. Nevertheless, given the approach of most governments to CSR to date, it is not surprising that the idea that multinationals may be subject to *direct* obligations under international human rights law is currently attracting so much attention. It is important to remember, though, that while CSR and human rights do overlap to some extent, they are not the same, and it would be a mistake to confuse the two. Also, human rights law is not the only potential source of international CSR regulation. Other, more traditional, regulatory strategies are possible, but whatever approach is taken, multinationals do raise some particularly difficult practical and definitional issues when it comes to designing effective regulatory regimes. These are discussed towards the end of this chapter.

Why are people so concerned about multinationals?

Big business elicits strong reactions. In his book *The Corporation*, now a successful television series and film, the Canadian academic Joel Bakan argues that the corporation is 'a pathological institution, a dangerous possessor of the great power it wields over people and societies'.[1] The multinational corporation, because of its apparent mobility and assumed lack of loyalty to any one jurisdiction, is particularly mistrusted. But how did this mistrust come about?

In Europe, the controversy surrounding multinationals can be traced back to the post-war years.[2] This was a time of huge expansion for corporations, particularly those originating in the USA.[3] Many Europeans were beginning to resent the level of reliance by local industry on US foreign investment and worried, too, about the 'Americanisation' of culture, tastes and management methods. By the late 1960s, opposition to

---

[1] J. Bakan, *The Corporation: the Pathological Pursuit of Profit and Power* (New York: Free Press, 2004), p. 2.

[2] P. Muchlinski, *Multinational Enterprises and the Law* (Oxford: Blackwell, 1995).

[3] R. Vernon, *Sovereignty at Bay: the Multinational Spread of US Enterprise* (New York: Basic Books, 1971); C. Tugendhat, *The Multinationals* (London: Eyre & Spottiswoode, 1971), chapter 2.

US-owned multinationals was high, as evidenced by the popularity of books critical of the 'American invasion'.[4]

In the USA, on the other hand, multinationals appear to have been regarded relatively benignly by the public until the 1960s. But by this time the reputation of corporate America had begun to wane, as Hood vividly describes:

Investigative journalism became a heroic, even romantic, calling, with the name of the game being to catch greedy corporations in the act of polluting the water, selling shoddy and overpriced products, exploiting workers and families, and sacrificing the public's health, safety and welfare to make a quick buck. On television and in the movies, business executives increasingly became villains, to be challenged by heroic lawyers, policemen, reporters and activists.[5]

By the 1970s, the multinational had become synonymous, around the world, with power and wealth and, to many, a potent symbol of the economic and political dominance of the USA.[6] What is striking about much of the literature on multinationals from that time, compared with today, is the extent to which the interests of the multinational are identified with the interests of its state of origin, or 'home state'.[7] Multinationals were viewed, perhaps simplistically, as economic agents of their home states, with no particular allegiances to the states in which they chose to invest. With this mindset, the nationality of the foreign investor was of crucial importance. Foreign-owned multinationals were regarded as a threat to the sovereignty of their host states in two ways: first, because of fears that they might exercise undue influence over the host state's

[4] J. Servan-Schreiber, *The American Challenge* (New York: Atheneum, 1979) (first published in French as *Le Défi Américain* (Paris: Editions Denoel, 1967). It is worth pointing out, though, that Servan-Schreiber was not opposed to US companies as such, but argued that European authorities needed to become more proactive to ensure that European companies were able to compete with them more effectively.

[5] J. Hood, *The Heroic Enterprise: Business and the Common Good* (New York: Free Press, 1996), p. xiii.

[6] According to the findings of one survey of European public opinion carried out during the 1970s, multinationals were often assumed either to be American or to be based on American organisational models. Some European-based multinationals were wrongly attributed in questionnaires with US nationality. See G. Peninou, M. Holthus, D. Kebschull and J. Attali, *Who's Afraid of the Multinationals: a Survey of European Opinion of Multinational Corporations* (Farnborough: Saxon House, 1979).

[7] As Barnet and Muller put it, 'what really excited [Servan-Schreiber] was not the fact that a group of companies were becoming too powerful but that they were *American* companies representing the power of the *United States*'; R. Barnet and R. Muller, *Global Reach: the Power of the Multinational Corporations* (New York: Simon & Schuster, 1974), p. 75.

national policies and, second, because they helped to perpetuate inequalities *between* states. But while foreign ownership of local industry was a concern for all host states, these issues had particular significance for less developed countries.

Concerns of 'Southern' or 'less developed' countries about multinationals are usually explained against the background of the post-colonial campaign by the 'Group of 77' for a 'New International Economic Order'. Many newly independent countries were highly sensitive to the possibility that, by seeking inward investment, they might merely be replacing one form of colonialism with another. These states faced a dilemma. On the one hand, foreign investment was seen as a key to economic growth and prosperity. On the other hand, governments of these countries were reluctant to surrender control over valuable economic resources to those they saw as representatives of foreign economic interests. In addition, less developed host states were concerned about the possibility of meddling by multinationals in domestic political processes, either for their own commercial reasons or (more sinisterly) on behalf of their 'home state'.[8]

Relationships between multinationals and their 'home states' were not always harmonious either. Home states recognised the potential threat posed by multinationals to local economic, employment and security policies.[9] One of the most contentious issues within home states was the impact of overseas investment on local job markets. Unsurprisingly, it was in the USA where the 'migration' of jobs first became a significant political issue. Worried by the increasing proportion of goods destined for the US market that were being produced outside the USA, labour leaders became, through the 1970s, increasingly vocal. Not only was American 'blue collar' labour in danger of becoming 'obsolete', according to some critics, but trade unions, organised on national lines, were losing the leverage needed to protect the jobs that remained.[10] As a result, trade unions began lobbying for legislation to cut back on investment incentives, and to restrict the export of capital and technology, where American jobs might be at risk.[11]

By 1972, concerns about the implications of multinational activities had become sufficiently strong to prompt the Economic and Social Council of the UN to initiate a dedicated research project to 'study the role of

---

[8] Muchlinski, *Multinational Enterprises*, pp. 6–7.
[9] R. Vernon, *Storm Over the Multinationals: the Real Issues* (London: Macmillan, 1977), chapter 6.
[10] Barnet and Muller, *Global Reach*, chapter 11.   [11] Ibid., pp. 319–23.

multinational corporations and their impact on the process of development' and to 'submit recommendations for further action'.[12] The report
of the UN's working group, handed down in June 1974, summed up the
competing views and interests as follows:

> Home countries are concerned about the undesirable effects that foreign invest-
> ment by multinational corporations may have on domestic employment and the
> balance of payments, and about the capacity of such corporations to alter the
> normal play of competition. Host countries are concerned about the ownership
> and control of key economic sectors by foreign enterprises, the excessive cost to
> the domestic economy which their operations may entail, the extent to which
> they may encroach upon political sovereignty and their possible adverse influ-
> ence on socio-cultural values. Labour interests are concerned about the impact
> of multinational corporations on employment and workers' welfare and on the
> bargaining strength of trade unions. Consumer interests are concerned about
> the appropriateness, quality and price of the goods produced by multinational
> corporations. The multinational corporations themselves are concerned about
> the possible nationalization or expropriation of their assets without adequate
> compensation and about restrictive, unclear and frequently changing govern-
> ment policies.[13]

In the UN working group's diagnosis, the key sources of tension
between states derived from concerns about sovereignty, power and economic dependency. Host states were concerned about a loss of power to
multinationals, which, because multinationals were so closely identified
with home state interests, exacerbated fears about their own subjugation
within the international economic system. While the wealthier home
states were broadly inclined to encourage outward investment, it was
recognised that this came at the price of a loss of control over domestic
social and economic conditions.

Revisiting the UN working group's report today, it is striking how
little emphasis is given to questions concerning the social and ethical behaviour of multinationals themselves. As noted above, concerns
about corporate exploitation of the environment and people had already
started to surface by this time, particularly in the USA. Where these
issues are raised, most detailed consideration is given to the implications for capital-exporting countries (e.g. the problem of increasing

---

[12] Economic and Social Council Resolution 1721 (LIII), quoted in UN, 'The Impact of
Multinational Corporations on Development and on International Relations', UN DOC.
E/5500/Rev. 1., ST/ESA/6 (New York: UN, 1974); (1974) 13 ILM 800, p. 19.

[13] Ibid., p. 26.

unemployment owing to 'migration' of jobs off-shore).[14] In relation to
employment issues, the UN's group of experts made a number of recommendations designed to improve the quality of jobs, to manage the
consequences of unemployment caused by the mobility of multinationals and to enhance prospects for employee participation in negotiations
on wages and conditions. Importantly, though, the report's authors also
took the view that there was a need for the home states of multinationals to take a greater role in relation to the regulation of the health
and safety standards for employees of foreign subsidiaries.[15] This idea is
explored further in later chapters of this book.

If nothing else, the UN working group had highlighted the need for
more guidance on the respective roles, and responsibilities, of the major
players concerned. Work on a UN Code of Conduct on Transnational Corporations (the 'Draft UN Code')[16] began in March 1975. In the meantime,
the OECD had already begun work on its own set of 'Guidelines' for
multinationals, issued in 1976 (the 'OECD Guidelines').[17] Like the Draft
UN Code, these Guidelines were addressed to home and host states, as
well as multinationals themselves. The launch of the OECD Guidelines in
1976 was closely followed in 1977 by the ILO's Tripartite Declaration of
Principles concerning Multinational Enterprises and Social Policy (the
'ILO Tripartite Declaration')[18] which set out the ILO's expectations of
home states, host states and multinationals in relation to 'social' (particularly labour) issues. The history and legal significance of these codes,
together with their key CSR-related provisions, are discussed in more
detail in chapter 6.

The 1980s marked the start of what Vernon has described as 'a
period . . . of redemption' for multinationals.[19] Certainly, by the end of
the decade, UN agencies were adopting a more positive tone. Relations
between multinationals and their developing host states were beginning to improve, largely as a result of experience gained from greater

---

[14] See UN, 'The Impact of Multinational Corporations', n. 12 above, section VII. The
report did, however, include a section on 'Consumer Protection' (section VIII), though
not environmental protection.

[15] UN, 'The Impact of Multinational Corporations', p. 79.

[16] UN, 'Draft UN Code of Conduct on Transnational Corporations', UN Doc. E/1990/94, 12
June 1990.

[17] Annexed to the 1976 OECD Declaration on International Investment and
Multinational Enterprises, Paris, 21 June 1976; (1976) 15 ILM 967, 969.

[18] (1978) 17 ILM 422.

[19] R. Vernon, *In the Hurricane's Eye: the Troubled Prospects of Multinational Enterprises*
(Cambridge, MA: Harvard University Press, 1998), p. 5.

exposure to each other.[20] This was also a period of greater 'interna-
tionalisation' of multinational activities, resulting in a more pluralistic
economic system than had previously been the case.[21] The notion of
the 'typical' multinational (usually a US-based mining or manufacturing
giant) was becoming increasingly difficult to sustain, and the growth of
non-US-based multinationals, including some multinationals based in
developing countries, meant that it was no longer possible to view the
multinational simply as an agent of American hegemony.

At the same time, the rise of economic liberalism, as a political philosophy, was transforming relations between corporations and states. The
1980s and early 1990s saw a wave of privatisations of government-owned
utilities and infrastructure, first in the UK and, later, in other European states, Australia and Canada. In addition, the collapse of the Soviet
Union in 1991 led to extensive economic restructuring and privatisation
programmes in much of Eastern Europe as well, as these states planned
their transition from communist to market-based economies. By the mid-
1990s even the least developed countries of the world were espousing the
principles of economic competition and deregulation, although often,
it has to be said, as a result of external pressures.[22]

This was also a period of liberalisation at international level. During the 1970s and early 1980s, the international trading system was
under a considerable amount of strain. Two world recessions, oil price
shocks and the growth of competition in manufacturing from less
developed countries were creating pressures for national economies,
which resulted in a proliferation of non-tariff barriers, such as quo-
tas, voluntary export restraints and subsidies.[23] The Tokyo Round agreement, completed in 1979, was to prove less than effective as a means
of dealing with these new forms of protectionism, and by the 1982
GATT ministerial meeting there was widespread concern that the GATT
system was facing collapse.[24] But despite the tensions, and serious

---

[20] UNCTC, 'Transnational Corporations in World Development: Trends and Prospects'
(New York: UN, 1988), p. 5.

[21] R. Gilpin, *The Challenge of Global Capitalism: the World Economy in the 21st Century*
(Princeton: Princeton University Press, 2000), p. 165.

[22] P. Mosley, J. Harrigan and J. Toye, *Aid and Power: the World Bank and Policy-Based Lending*,
2nd edition, 2 vols. (London: Routledge, 1991), vol. I; R. Swaminathan, 'Regulating
Development: Structural Adjustment and the Case for National Enforcement of
Economic and Social Rights' (1998) 37 *CJTL* 181.

[23] M. Trebilcock and R. Howse, *The Regulation of International Trade*, 2nd edition (London:
Routledge, 1998), p. 21.

[24] Ibid., pp. 93–4.

economic difficulties, it was agreed in 1985 to launch the Uruguay Round of trade negotiations, which ultimately resulted in the World Trade Organisation ('WTO'), a new dispute resolution procedure, new agreements on trade in services and the protection of intellectual property rights, and significant new commitments on the reduction of non-tariff barriers.[25]

At the same time, the EC and North American states were in the process of developing their own separate regional trading arrangements. In 1986, the EC member states adopted the Single Europe Act, with the aim of establishing a single European market by the end of 1992. This was followed up in 1992 with the Maastricht Treaty, which provided for further economic and political co-operation between EC member states and also established the European Union ('EU'), a new institution. Across the Atlantic, Canada and the USA concluded in 1988 a Free Trade Agreement designed to remove tariffs between them over a ten-year period and a number of other measures including the removal of restrictions on foreign direct investment between the parties. In 1992 these arrangements were extended to include Mexico under the North American Free Trade Agreement ('NAFTA').

The removal of barriers to trade and investment between states is regarded as a significant contributing factor to the enormous growth in foreign direct investment (or 'FDI') during the late 1980s and 1990s,[26] a rate of growth that easily outstripped the growth in world trade economic output over the same period.[27] Advances in technology and communications have also played an important role, in dramatically reducing the costs of investing abroad. These developments have all helped to bring about what Gilpin has described as the transition from a 'state-centred' to a 'market-dominated' world.[28]

The policies pursued by governments through the 1980s and the 1990s had combined to produce an international economic system that was generally favourable to multinationals, and many of the tensions that had defined relationships between states (and between states and companies) through the 1970s appeared to have subsided. However, this period

[25] J. Jackson and A. Sykes, *Implementing the Uruguay Round* (Oxford: Clarendon Press, 1997), pp. 2–5.

[26] UNCTAD, 'World Investment Report 1997: Transnational Corporations, Market Structure and Competition Policy' (New York and Geneva: UN, 1997), UN Sales No. E.97.II.D.10, Overview, pp. 1, 10.

[27] Gilpin, *The Challenge of Global Capitalism*, pp. 22, 169–71.

[28] Ibid., pp. 18–19.

of 'comparative tranquillity' – which Vernon has attributed to 'a balance in a struggle among some vital forces rather than the result of a settled and unchallenged consensus'[29] – would soon be at an end. By the early 1990s, multinationals were facing up to a new set of challenges and demands, this time emerging mainly from civil society, based around ideals of 'corporate social responsibility' or 'CSR'.

The rise of the CSR movement

Most people view the CSR movement as a relatively recent social phenomenon, but this is not entirely correct. In actual fact, moral issues arising from commercial activities have occupied philosophers, writers, religious leaders and law-makers for centuries, if not millennia.[30] With industrialisation, however, the role of business in society became an issue of more than academic importance, as large-scale commercial activity began to impact on the lives of more and more people. Some industrialists began to take philanthropic obligations upon themselves,[31] inspired by religious convictions, social concern, a desire to emulate the land-owning classes, or a combination of these.

But isolated philanthropic initiatives provided no answer to the more fundamental question: did business have any *inherent* responsibilities towards society? It was in America, during the 1930s, that this debate really took off. In 1929, in an address that still sounds strikingly relevant today, the then Dean of Harvard Business School, Walter B. Donham, said: 'Businesses started long centuries before the dawn of history, but business as we now know it is new – new in its broadening scope, new in its social significance. Business has not learned how to handle these changes, nor does it recognise the magnitude of its responsibilities for the future of civilisation.'[32]

There are many individual examples of what we would today call 'voluntary CSR initiatives' that date back to the same time, or earlier. In 1914, Henry Ford announced that his Highland Park plant would pay five dollars for an eight-hour working day, substantially more than prevailing industry rates, and at a time when a nine-hour day was the

---

[29] Vernon, *In the Hurricane's Eye*, p. 60.   [30] Hood, *The Heroic Enterprise*, p. xv.
[31] The construction of the Cadbury town 'Bournville' in the English Midlands in the 1870s is a good example. For other historical examples, see Hopkins, 'Corporate Social Responsibility around the World'.
[32] Quoted in K. Peattie, 'Research Insights into Corporate Social Responsibility (Part I)' (2002) 1(2) *New Academy Review* 33, 50.

norm. As early as 1935, Robert Wood Johnson, of Johnson & Johnson, published a leaflet entitled 'Try Reality' in which he sought to define his company's responsibilities towards various groups, now generally referred to as 'stakeholders' (i.e. shareholders, employees, consumers and the community at large). This was followed in 1945 by a company-wide 'Credo', which sets out Johnson & Johnson's social and ethical aspirations in greater detail, and expresses ideas still familiar in corporate codes today.

Seven decades later, the debate about the responsibilities of business, and their scope, goes on. At one extreme is the view (prevalent in domestic company law) that companies are responsible primarily, if not solely, to their shareholders. As Milton Friedman famously argued: 'There is one and only one social responsibility of business – to use its resources and engage in activities designed to increase its profits so long as it stays within the rules of the game, which is to say, engages in open and free competition, without deception or fraud.'[33] In other words, business contributes to society through the generation of wealth and employment. How that wealth is distributed is a matter for governments, not companies.[34] On the other hand, companies do not (and should not) enjoy absolute freedom – they must still act fairly and honestly and within the law.

In another ideological camp altogether are those who regard this version of corporate rights and responsibilities as a doctrinal sleight of hand.[35] They point out that the modern corporate form – complete with limited liability[36] – is neither a historical accident nor the natural state of affairs, but reflects an ordering of principles around dominant interests, at the expense of the most vulnerable.[37] Somewhere in the middle (and probably representing the 'mainstream' position) are those who argue that, in reality, proper financial management of a company (i.e. in the interests of its shareholders) and CSR go hand in hand, as unethical companies tend to be unsustainable in the long run.[38] In other words,

---

[33] M. Friedman, *Capitalism and Freedom* (Chicago: University of Chicago Press, 1962), p. 133.

[34] 'The role of well-run companies is to make profits, not save the planet. Let them not make the error of confusing the two.' M. Wolf, 'Sleepwalking with the Enemy', *Financial Times*, 16 May 2001, p. 21. See also E. Sternberg, *Just Business: Business Ethics in Action*, 2nd edition (Oxford: Oxford University Press, 2000), p. 6.

[35] E.g. Bakan, *The Corporation*, esp. chapter 1.   [36] See further pp. 26, 54–6, 228–33 below.

[37] J. Dine, *Companies, International Trade and Human Rights* (Cambridge: Cambridge University Press, 2005), esp. chapter 2.

[38] M. Hopkins, *The Planetary Bargain: Corporate Social Responsibility Matters* (London: Earthscan Publications, 2003).

companies need to be 'socially responsible' to fulfil their obligations to their shareholders. What's more, CSR can actually increase productivity and profits in the long run.[39] These arguments are often referred to as the 'business case' for CSR.[40] But, while this argument is an attractive one, it has failed to convince a significant proportion of campaigners and critics, who have argued that explicit recognition of the interests of other 'stakeholders' is necessary.[41]

Whatever the philosophical rights and wrongs of CSR as a concept,[42] companies, particularly US companies, have long recognised that demonstrations of compassion and humanity are attractive to consumers. 'Family' and 'family values' were popular themes in advertising throughout the inter-war period. As Bakan writes:

By the end of World War I, some of America's leading corporations, among them General Electric, Eastman Kodak, National Cash Register, Standard Oil, US Rubber, and the Goodyear Tire & Rubber Company, were busily crafting images of themselves as benevolent and socially responsible. 'New Capitalism', the term used to describe the trend, softened corporations' images with promises of good corporate citizenship and practices of better wages and working conditions. As citizens demanded that governments rein in corporate power and while labor militancy was rife, with returning World War I veterans, having risked their lives as soldiers, insisting on better treatment as workers, proponents of the New Capitalism sought to demonstrate that corporations could be good without the coercive push of governments and unions.[43]

But although CSR-related themes may have been played out in corporate PR for some time, it is only relatively recently that the term 'CSR' has come to be associated with a recognisable social movement. This is not to imply that the principles underlying CSR are new: the ideological seeds of the CSR movement can be seen in environmental campaigns of the

---

[39] Ibid, pp. 14, 16–17. For a review of recent studies see M. Kelly, 'Holy Grail Found: Absolute, Positive, Definitive Proof that CSR Pays Off' (2004) 18(4) *Business Ethics* 4. Note, however, that this is by no means universally accepted. L. Roner, 'Noted Economist Says that Corporate Social Responsibility is Irresponsible', *Ethical Corporation*, 25 January 2005.

[40] For a review of literature discussing the 'business case' for CSR see Peattie, 'Research Insights (Part I)'.

[41] See further p. 169 below.

[42] For a discussion of the philosophical case *against* the idea that corporations have wider social responsibilities (i.e. to groups other than their shareholders) see Sternberg, *Just Business*.

[43] Bakan, *The Corporation*, p. 18.

1970s and 1980s,[44] and also in some other NGO-led initiatives of around the same time, such as the campaign orchestrated by the International Baby Food Action Network against Nestlé.[45] The modern CSR movement has, however, been given extra momentum by more fundamental and wide-ranging concerns about the international economic system, how it is run and the role of corporations within it.

'Anti-globalisation' and 'anti-capitalism' demonstrations have been a feature of most of the significant inter-governmental meetings on trade and investment since the Seattle trade talks of 1999. NGOs, which have long argued the linkages between the international economic system and poverty, have for some years been devoting a considerable amount of time and effort to campaigns and research relating to the impact of 'globalisation' on the world's poor. Of course, the 'globalisation' debate encompasses a wide range of concerns – about over-consumption, environmental degradation, cultural identity, poverty, human rights and democracy.[46] A recurring theme of anti-globalisation protests and campaigns, however, is the idea that there are, at present, excessive concentrations of power within the international economic system. And multinationals – viewed as both the primary architects and beneficiaries of 'globalisation' – have attracted special attention.

The idea that multinationals are overly powerful is not new, as this chapter has already explained. However, campaigners complain that the situation is worsening; that is, while inter-governmental efforts to improve trading and investment conditions for multinationals appear to be succeeding, efforts to design an international framework for social and environmental regulation of multinationals have generally failed.[47] The result, according to critics such as Korten and Bakan, is a redistribution of power 'more tightly connected to the needs and interests of corporations and less so to the public interest'.[48] As Korten puts it:

The new corporate colonialism is no more a consequence of immutable historical forces than was the old state colonialism. It is a consequence of conscious choices based on the pursuit of elite interest. This elite interest has been closely aligned

[44] The links between the CSR movement and environmental campaigning are clear from the fact that some of the most active NGOs in the CSR movement, such as FoE, have a predominantly environmental brief.

[45] M. Keck and K. Sikkink, *Activists Beyond Borders* (Ithaca, NY: Cornell University Press, 1998), p. 131.

[46] N. Klein, *No Logo* (London: Flamingo, 2000).   [47] But see further chapter 6 below.

[48] Bakan, *The Corporation*, p. 154. See also Dine, *Companies, International Trade and Human Rights*.

with the corporate interest in advancing deregulation and globalization. As a consequence, the largest transnational corporations and the global financial system have assumed ever greater power over the conduct of human affairs in the pursuit of interests that are increasingly at odds with the human interest. It is impossible to have healthy, equitable, and democratic societies when political and economic power is concentrated in a few gigantic corporations.[49]

It is not surprising, therefore, that the OECD's attempt to develop a 'Multilateral Agreement on Investment' (the 'MAI') was viewed by many environmental and human rights campaigners as a step too far. The aim behind the MAI, launched by the OECD in 1995, was a framework for the rapid liberalisation by states of their rules relating to inward investments. OECD countries were seeking to build on an existing network of Bilateral Investment Treaties ('BITs') and the progress that had already been made within the WTO with the agreement of a General Agreement on Trade in Services ('GATS')[50] and a set of Trade Related Investment Measures ('TRIMs').[51] The MAI would have introduced 'national treatment' and 'most favoured nation' standards for laws relating to foreign investment. In addition, contracting states would be subject to a number of further restrictions on performance and local purchasing requirements under their own domestic laws.

A feature of the draft MAI that particularly angered civil society groups and anti-globalisation campaigners, though, was the proposed investor–state dispute resolution mechanism. This mechanism would have given companies the right to take enforcement action against a host state alleged to be in breach of its treaty obligations. Although investor–state dispute resolution provisions were already a common feature of BITs,[52] the fact that multinationals would have no corresponding *duties* under the MAI contributed to the general impression that what was proposed was a one-sided regime primarily for the benefit of business.[53] It was feared that this mechanism would be used by multinationals to 'bully'

---

[49] D. Korten, *When Corporations Rule the World* (London: Earthscan Publications, 1995), p. 181.

[50] 1994 General Agreement on Trade in Services, Marrakesh, 15 April 1994, in force 1 January 1995; (1994) 33 ILM 46.

[51] 1994 Agreement on Trade Related Investment Measures, Marrakesh, 15 April 1994 (annex 1A of the 1994 Marrakesh Agreement Establishing the World Trade Organisation), 1868 UNTS 186.

[52] See M. Sornorajah, *The International Law on Foreign Investment* (Cambridge: Cambridge University Press, 1994); T. Brewer and S. Young, *The Multilateral Investment System and Multinational Enterprises* (Oxford: Oxford University Press, 1998).

[53] See FoE, 'The World Trade System: Winners and Losers', November 1999, Policy and Research Unit Briefing Paper, http://www.foe.co.uk/campaigns.

host states and, worse, that host state parties would be discouraged from enacting laws to tighten social or environmental standards for fear of falling foul of non-expropriation obligations.[54]

While a number of reasons can be given for why the MAI negotiations eventually collapsed,[55] Muchlinski argues that the project was flawed at a deeper level:

The principal reason [for the failure of the MAI] lies in the conception of the agreement as pure investor and investment protection instrument. This made the agreement an anachronism from the start. The MAI was based on fundamental misconceptions as to the nature of transnational economic interactions in an era of increased privatisation and deregulation at the national level. Thus, the MAI started from the false premise that governmental power to control business had to be curtailed. It lived in a world dominated by the old political agendas signified by the 'right/left' axis of Cold War politics, in which the principal concerns of foreign direct investors were to preserve existing investments in recently decolonised and/or increasingly politically assertive host countries . . . The new political environment no longer places 'right/left' issues of ownership and control at centre stage. Rather, there has been a transformation in political discourse, which challenges not the legitimacy and value of free enterprise as such, but its legitimacy as a polluter, an abuser of market power, a corruptor of state officials, an exploiter of workers, and a potential accomplice to violations of fundamental human rights. Thus the correct starting point should have been an acknowledgement that, in this new investment environment, the new regulatory issues, of the kinds listed above, emerge.[56]

Wherever the real responsibility lies, the failure of the MAI in 1998 was generally regarded within the NGO community, and by the media, as a victory for 'people power'. Working hard to maintain the momentum gained from the anti-MAI campaign, many of these groups have turned their attention to the activities of the WTO and other institutions associated with 'globalisation'. In doing so, they have been remarkably effective at mobilising public protests, culminating in the so-called 'Battle of Seattle', a series of protests which effectively derailed the opening of the Seattle Round of WTO negotiations in December 1999.[57]

---

[54] J. McDonald, 'The Multilateral Agreement on Investment: Heyday or Mai-Day for Ecologically Sustainable Development' (1988) 22 Melb UL Rev 617.

[55] See, for example, Y. Kodama, 'Dispute Settlement under the Draft Multilateral Agreement on Investment' (1999) 16(3) Journal of International Arbitration 45; R. Schlegelmilch, 'WTO: Why Still No Multilateral Rules for Foreign Direct Investment?' (2000) 6 International Trade Law and Regulation 78.

[56] P. Muchlinski, 'The Rise and Fall of the Multilateral Agreement on Investment: Where Now?' (2000) 34 Int'l Lawyer 1033, 1049–50.

[57] 'A Global Disaster', The Economist, 11 December 1999, p. 21.

The globalisation debate has revitalised public interest in multinationals. But today's critics are more likely to view multinationals as state*less* institutions, than as political and economic agents of their home states.[58] The point that the annual turnover of some multinationals exceeds the annual GDP of many of the poorer states of the world is frequently made.[59] The behind-the-scenes involvement of multinationals in law-making at both domestic and international level also generates a good deal of comment.[60] In the language of the globalisation debate, the term 'multinational' no longer implies any connections with any particular state but, instead, a virtually autonomous international actor.

The anti-globalisation movement echoes many of the concerns of NGOs active in the CSR field. Both groups (which overlap to some extent) are concerned about the lack of accountability of multinationals within the international system, and the implications of this lack of accountability for social and environmental standards world-wide. The international impact of the CSR movement has been enhanced by two further (and related) developments: first, the rise in consumer activism and, second, the huge opportunities offered by the internet to mobilise public opinion and co-ordinate campaign activities across national borders. The internet has not only increased the speed with which information can be shared, but also provided a new medium through which concerned individuals and groups can express their views. Importantly, these technological advances have allowed a public debate to take place, on an international scale, in a way that is capable of bypassing state interests and institutions.

---

[58] Bakan, *The Corporation*, p. 22.

[59] See, for example, I. Bantekas, 'Corporate Social Responsibility in International Law' (2004) 22 *BUILJ* 309, 309 comparing Coca-Cola's profits for the first six months of 2003 ($2.1 billion) with the 2002 GDP for Gambia ($370 million), Liberia ($562 million) and Eritrea ($642 million). See also Dine, *Companies, Trade and Human Rights*, pp. 10–11.

[60] Korten, *When Corporations Rule the World*, chapter 13; J. Madeley, *Big Business Poor Peoples: the Impact of Transnational Corporations on the World's Poor* (London: Zed Books, 1999), chapter 11; G. Monbiot, *Captive State: the Corporate Takeover of Britain*, 2nd edition (London: Pan Books, 2001); Bakan, *The Corporation*, pp. 24–5; N. Hertz, *The Silent Takeover: Global Capitalism and the Death of Democracy* (London: Heinemann, 2000). The involvement of corporations at the 2002 World Summit on Sustainable Development ('WSSD') in Johannesburg infuriated many NGOs and generated a considerable amount of comment in the left-wing press. See P. Brown, 'Summit Row over Big Business Plans', *Guardian*, 27 August 2002, p. 1; J. Ginsberg, 'Green Groups Say Big Firms are Trying to Hijack Forum', *Independent*, 28 August 2002, p. 4.

As will be apparent from this and following chapters, CSR is a broad and complex area, involving a wide range of different organisations and interest groups. There are, of course, national differences in the way CSR is interpreted and the extent to which these ideas have taken root.[61] But for campaigners based in the richer, industrialised countries of the world, the issue at the top of the agenda continues to be the treatment by multinationals of the most vulnerable, particularly those who live and work in less developed countries.[62] The working conditions of those employed to produce luxury goods, toys and clothing for sale in the industrialised countries have received a huge amount of media attention over the past decade. The use by multinationals of 'sweatshop' labour in the poorer countries of the world is widely criticised, not merely because of the impact on employment in industrialised countries (a longstanding concern of trade unions in the USA), but because it represents a form of exploitation. Another area of concern is that of abusive marketing practices, particularly towards consumers in poorer countries. Manipulative and cynical marketing of 'baby milk' products to the third world is probably the best-known example of this, but tobacco companies have also been accused of seeking to compensate for the diminishing demand for their products in industrialised countries through aggressive marketing in poorer states.[63]

Added to this are continuing concerns about the impact of multinational enterprise on the environment. A series of highly publicised environmental disasters, such as the *Exxon Valdez* oil spill off Alaska and the Bhopal disaster in India, raised legitimate questions about the international accountability of multinationals for serious environmental harm. The litigation brought by South African asbestosis victims against the UK parent of a group of mining companies in the late 1990s[64] provides a graphic reminder, if one was needed, of the consequences of the 'double standards' applied by some corporations in their international operations.

As noted above, concerns about the 'social responsibility' of large multinationals are not new. But attention has shifted in recent years from the failings of a few named multinationals to more fundamental issues of accountability and justice in the 'globalising' era. In other words, how can the accountability of multinationals be

---

[61] See pp. 2–3 above; Hopkins, 'CSR around the World'.

[62] See, for instance, Klein, *No Logo*, which has become an international bestseller.

[63] ASH, *Fact Sheet 21: Tobacco in the Developing World*, August 2004.

[64] *Lubbe v. Cape plc* [2000] 1 WLR 1545; [2000] 4 All ER 268 (HL) 277. See further p. 205 below.

ensured – towards workers, communities and consumers – within a political, economic and legal framework that is so skewed towards the protection of economic interests?

Overall, the CSR movement has brought about a change in emphasis in the debate about multinationals. Reflecting the shift from a 'state-centred' to a 'market-dominated world',[65] greater prominence is now given to 'people-centred' (as opposed to 'state-centred') concerns. This is not to suggest that multinationals do not continue to pose considerable political and regulatory problems for states. But while states have made great strides in the international regulation of issues such as investor protection, taxation and corruption,[66] it seems that health and safety and environmental issues have been left behind. The power of multinationals, and their apparent lack of accountability, is contributing to widespread feelings of unease and insecurity, not only in the less developed countries but in industrialised countries as well.[67] 'Globalisation' is giving rise to a new political struggle, not between states and multinationals or, necessarily, between North and South, but between 'people and corporations'.[68]

Companies have had no choice but to respond. For some, this has meant a re-evaluation of long-held positions and principles. In the case of Shell, this was brought about following the bitter controversy surrounding the death of the writer and activist Ken Saro-Wiwa. Saro-Wiwa was an outspoken critic of the operations of international oil companies in Nigeria, including BP and Shell. In 1993, following a series of protests (which, according to the Nigerian government, included acts of sabotage), Saro-Wiwa was arrested along with a number of other activists. On 10 November 1995, after what was widely regarded as a show trial, Saro-Wiwa was executed along with eight others. This incident provoked international outrage – much of which was levelled at the Shell Group. What particularly angered supporters of Saro-Wiwa was the failure of Shell to intercede with the government to try to get the death sentences commuted or reduced. However, Shell's position was that it was not the role of companies to interfere in the domestic politics of host states. Indeed, its Statement of General Business Principles at the time said:

Shell Companies endeavour always to act commercially, operating within existing national laws in a socially responsible manner, *abstaining from participation in party politics and interference in political matters*. It is, however, their legitimate right

---

[65] See n. 28 above.   [66] See further pp. 286–9 below.   [67] Klein, *No Logo*.
[68] Monbiot, *Captive State*, p. 17.

to speak out on matters which affect the interests of employees, customers and shareholders, and on matters of general interest where they have a contribution to make based on particular knowledge.[69]

The strength of public feeling over Shell's failure to intervene in the Saro-Wiwa case seemed to have caught Shell managers by surprise. As Sir Philip Watts (a former managing director of Shell Nigeria) later wrote, 'it was a timely lesson in how the underlying expectations of the societies around us had changed'.[70] In 1997 Shell published a revised Statement of Business Principles, amended, in Shell's words, 'to reflect heightened public interest in human rights issues and in the concept of sustainable development'.[71] In it, Shell companies acknowledge their 'responsibility' 'to express support for fundamental human rights in line with the legitimate role of business and to give proper regard to health, safety and the environment consistent with their commitment to contribute to sustainable development'.[72] This was a significant turnaround for Shell. Several years and several CSR reports later, Shell is now regarded – by the business community at least – as a CSR leader.[73]

Today, most leading companies devote considerable resources to activities designed to help manage, co-ordinate, measure, report upon and otherwise promote their corporate responsibility performance. With the growth of shareholder and media interest in the subject, CSR is becoming competitive. Each year, US-based *Business Ethics* magazine lists its '100 Best Corporate Citizens' and, in the UK, Business in the Community ('BITC') (a membership organisation supported by the UK government) hands out annual awards for excellence in responsible business practices and community involvement. The rise of 'socially responsible investment' or 'SRI' has created a new market for systems whereby the CSR-related performance of different companies can be measured and ranked. In support of these activities there have sprung up, on both sides of the Atlantic, numerous research initiatives and new business school training programmes, along with an army of consultants and other service providers and a bewildering array of conferences. New industry-led

---

[69] Shell, 'Statement of General Business Principles', July 1994 (emphasis added).

[70] P. Watts, 'The International Petroleum Industry: Economic Actor or Social Activist?' in J. Mitchell (ed.), *Companies in a World of Conflict* (London: RIIA, Energy and Environmental Programme, 1998), p. 26.

[71] See http://www.shell-usgp.com/gpbpmain.asp.

[72] Shell, 'Statement of Business Principles' (1997), http://www.shell.com.

[73] Hopkins, *The Planetary Bargain*, p. 23. Although some NGOs have expressed a different view. See FoE, 'Failing the Challenge: the Other Shell Report 2002', http://www.foe.co.uk/resource/reports/failing-challenge.pdf.

bodies and think tanks, such as BITC in the UK and Business for Social Responsibility in the USA, have been created to help support the efforts of businesses – and new alliances between NGOs have been forged to help co-ordinate the work of groups seeking social and legal reform.[74] In addition, companies are actively seeking to develop relationships with NGOs to help them to identify key areas of concern and suitable responses.[75]

But despite all this, the business community still has a long way to go to regain public trust. The Enron and WorldCom scandals of 2001 were particularly damaging. To many, the Enron scandal was not an isolated incident, but a direct consequence of the legal framework in which all companies operate. Responding incredulously to the group's final CSR report, Bakan writes:

Unfortunately, this paragon of corporate social responsibility . . . was unable to continue its good works after it collapsed under the weight of its executives' greed, hubris and criminality. Enron's story shows just how wide a gap can exist between a company's cleverly crafted do-gooder image and its actual operations and suggests, at a minimum, that scepticism about corporate social responsibility is well warranted.[76]

Certainly, there is still plenty of scepticism about CSR.[77] Nevertheless, for CSR campaigners in Western Europe and the USA at least, the first battle has been largely won. It is no longer necessary to persuade companies of the need to be socially responsible, at least on some level. Companies which do not acknowledge the need to address ethical issues in their corporate policies and operating practices risk being labelled 'dinosaurs'.[78] The nature of the CSR debate has now moved on – from 'why?' be socially responsible, to 'how?'

This has prompted an explosion of literature on CSR-related topics, particularly in the field of management science.[79] Surprisingly, though,

---

[74] See, for example, the work of the Corporate Responsibility Coalition in the UK ('CORE'). CORE is a coalition of around fifty NGOs, religious groups and trade unions. See further pp. 168–70 below.

[75] B. Allen and J. Zerk, 'A Partnership of Equals?' (2005) 154 *EIB* 14.

[76] Bakan, *The Corporation*, p. 58.

[77] See, for instance, Christian Aid, 'Behind the Mask: the Real Face of Corporate Social Responsibility' (Christian Aid, 21st January 2004), http://www.christian-aid.org.uk.

[78] Bakan, *The Corporation*, p. 41.

[79] For an excellent review of CSR-related literature, covering a range of different academic disciplines, see Peattie, 'Research Insights (Part I)' and K. Peattie, J. Solomon, A. Soloman and J. Hunt, 'Research Insights into Corporate Social Responsibility (Part II)' (2002) 1(3) *New Academy Review* 39.

contributions by lawyers and legal commentators, outside a few specialist areas, have been few and far between. While key elements of CSR –
environmental protection, workplace health and safety, and consumer
protection – are well-established legal disciplines, it is only recently that
legal writers have begun to address CSR as a concept in its own right. This
is partly owing to the lack of clarity about the scope of CSR (specifically
whether it refers to the 'voluntary' activities of companies over and above
minimum legal standards, or whether it extends to regulated areas)[80]
and, hence, uncertainty about the role that legal professionals should
play.[81] However, one particular legal issue has emerged as crucial: the
company law principle of 'limited liability' or 'separate corporate personality'.[82] To many CSR campaigners, this is the single greatest legal
obstacle to multinational accountability and, although criticism of this
principle is not new,[83] arguments over rationale, its appropriateness in
relation to corporate groups and its possible abuse as a means of legally
evading responsibility[84] have become central to NGO-led campaigns for
legal reform. The other main area, relevant to CSR, in which lawyers
are having an impact at domestic level is in the field of corporate governance.[85] On the other hand, there has been relatively little in the
way of legal comment, from a domestic law perspective, on the broader
social and environmental agenda, and the so-called 'voluntary' activities
of companies. However, there is growing interest in the 'legal context'
of CSR, namely, the role of the law as a driver towards greater corporate
accountability and, conversely, the potential influence of CSR, as a social
movement, on legal trends.[86]

---

[80] See further pp. 32–6 below.   [81] Peattie et al., 'Research Insights (Part II)'.
[82] See further pp. 228–33 below.
[83] See P. Blumberg, *The Multinational Challenge to Corporation Law: the Search for a New
Corporate Personality* (Oxford: Oxford University Press, 1993).
[84] J. Dine, *The Governance of Corporate Groups* (Cambridge: Cambridge University Press,
2000).
[85] The Company Law Review in the UK, the fall-out from the corporate accounting
scandals in the USA and new regulatory proposals at EU level have collectively
initiated a huge amount of legal comment. See Peattie, 'Research Insights (Part I)' and
Peattie et al., 'Research Insights (Part II)'.
[86] See H. Ward, 'Legal Issues in Corporate Citizenship' (International Institute for
Environment and Development, February 2003), http://www.iied.org/cred/pubs.html;
Sustainability, 'The Changing Landscape of Liability: a Director's Guide to Trends in
Corporate Environmental, Social and Economic Liability' (Sustainability, December
2004), http://www.sustainability.com/publications/latest/liability.asp; J. Zerk, 'Legal
Aspects of Corporate Responsibility Reporting: Panacea, Polyfilla or Pandora's Box?'
(2004) 3(3) *New Academy Review* 17; P. Rudolph, 'The Central Role of Lawyers in

So far, international lawyers have proved much more ready to engage with CSR campaigns and debates than their commercial law counterparts, especially in relation to human rights. Of course, it has been recognised for some time now that multinationals pose some significant challenges to the traditional 'state-centred' structure of international law.[87] Until fairly recently the main focus of international law scholarship on multinationals has been on economic issues and problems, such as regulation (and protection) of foreign investments, tax and transfer pricing, and jurisdictional problems arising from domestic anti-trust laws.[88] The social and environmental dimension of foreign investment received comparatively little attention until the mid-1990s,[89] by which time, as a result of a series of serious incidents involving the

Managing, Minimizing, and Responding to Social Responsibility Risks – a US Perspective' in R. Mullerat (ed.), *Corporate Social Responsibility: the Corporate Governance of the 21st Century* (The Hague: Kluwer, 2005).

[87] D. Vagts, 'The Multinational Enterprise: a New Challenge for Transnational Law' (1970) 83 *Harv LR* 739; S. Asante, 'International Law and Investments' in M. Bedjaoui (ed.), *International Law: Achievements and Prospects* (Dordrecht: Martinus Nijhoff, 1991). See also Johns, 'The Invisibility of the Transnational Corporation', 893; T. Voon, 'Multinational Enterprises and State Sovereignty under International Law' (1999) 21 *Adel LR* 219; Dine, *Companies, International Trade and Human Rights*.

[88] C. Wallace, *The Multinational Enterprise and Legal Control: Host State Sovereignty in an Era of Economic Globalisation* (The Hague: Martinus Nijhoff, 2002). For a bibliography of international law materials on foreign investment issues see C. Wallace (ed.), *Foreign Direct Investment and the Multinational Enterprise: a Bibliography* (Dordrecht: Martinus Nijhoff, 1988). See further Sornorajah, *Foreign Investment*. On issues of diplomatic protection, expropriation and 'piercing the corporate veil' for international law purposes, see I. Seidl-Hohenveldern, *Corporations in and under International Law* (Cambridge: Grotius Publications, 1987). Muchlinski, *Multinational Enterprises and the Law* represents something of a turning point in the literature on multinationals and the law. While a large proportion of this volume is devoted to the economic regulation of multinationals (e.g. tax, anti-trust and treatment of foreign investments), the author also raises a number of issues of relevance to the social and environmental regulation of multinationals, such as the prospect of 'group liability' (pp. 322–33) and social and environmental disclosure (pp. 366–71). A chapter is also included on international labour standards (chapter 12).

[89] Although articles critical of the foreign workplace health and safety performance of multinationals were beginning to appear during the mid-1980s, many of which were inspired by the tragedy at Bhopal. See the collection of essays in C. Pearson (ed.), *Multinational Corporations, Environment and the Third World* (Durham, NC: Duke University Press, 1987), especially B. Castleman, 'Workplace Health Standards and Multinational Corporations in Developing Countries'. See also the collection of papers in J. Ives (ed.), *The Export of Hazards: Transnational Corporations and Environmental Control Issues* (London: Routledge & Kegan Paul, 1985), especially B. Castleman, 'The Double Standard in Industrial Hazards'; T. McGarity, 'Bhopal and the Export of Hazardous Technologies' (1985) 20 *Tex ILJ* 333.

activities of multinationals in developing countries, defects in the international regulatory system were becoming painfully obvious.[90] In the past few years, however, there has been an explosion of academic interest in the social and environmental problems posed by multinationals and prospects for legal reform.[91]

It is clear from the amount of work being devoted to the subject that, as far as the social and environmental regulation of multinationals is concerned, international law has reached a crucial point. Reflecting a certain amount of frustration with the lack of progress on these issues by states and inter-governmental institutions, many NGOs and academic writers are examining the potential of international human rights law as a source of *direct* international law obligations for multinationals. It is widely accepted by now that direct human rights obligations are at least a theoretical possibility (as well as being justifiable in terms of international policy).[92] Less certain, though, is how human rights law, traditionally aimed at states, might be translated to the corporate context. In other words, what is the substance of these obligations, and how might they differ from the human rights obligations of states? The past few years have seen the publication of several studies which aim to clarify, not only the standards which might apply to multinationals,[93] but

---

[90] J. Cassels, *The Uncertain Promise of Law: Lessons of Bhopal* (Toronto: University of Toronto Press, 1993).

[91] Several volumes have appeared devoted specifically to problems of legal accountability of multinationals. M. Kamminga and S. Zia-Zarifi (eds.), *Liability of Multinational Corporations under International Law* (The Hague: Kluwer, 2000) contains a series of essays on developments at both international and national level relating to the legal status of multinationals and their future regulation, particularly in the area of human rights (as well as a useful set of appendices). M. Addo (ed.), *Human Rights Standards and the Responsibility of Transnational Corporations* (The Hague: Kluwer, 1999), another collection of writings, examines a range of structural, doctrinal and practical issues underlying the present regulatory system, including obstacles to legal accountability. For a series of essays on particular international initiatives, as well as different national perspectives on CSR, see R. Mullerat (ed.), *Corporate Social Responsibility: the Corporate Governance of the 21st Century* (The Hague: Kluwer, 2005).

[92] See S. Joseph, 'Taming the Leviathans: Multinational Enterprises and Human Rights' (1999) 46 *NILR* 171; S. Danailov, 'The Accountability of Non-State Actors for Human Rights Violations: the Special Case of Transnational Corporations' (October, 1998) downloadable from http://www.humanrights.ch/cms/pdf/000303_danailov_studie.pdf; ICHRP, *Beyond Voluntarism: Human Rights and the Developing International Legal Obligations of Companies* (Versoix: ICHRP, 2002), chapter 2; J. Paust, 'Human Rights Responsibilities of Private Corporations' (2002) 35 *Vand JTL* 801; D. Kinley and J. Tadaki, 'From Talk to Walk: the Emergence of Human Rights Responsibilities for Corporations at International Law' (2004) 44 *VJIL* 931. See further pp. 76–83 below.

[93] ICHRP, *Beyond Voluntarism*, chapter 3; Danailov, 'The Accountability of Non-State Actors'; Kinley and Tadaki, 'From Talk to Walk'.

also the situations in which multinationals could potentially be liable for their 'complicity' in human rights violations committed by states.[94] However, only tentative proposals have emerged so far on how these obligations might be implemented and enforced in practice.[95] To many writers and activists, the best course of action would be a new human rights treaty on corporate obligations (which should include some form of enforcement mechanism),[96] though others view this as an impossible dream, at least for the time being.[97] Of course, most writers are not so naive as to suggest that there is any one, simple solution to problems arising from 'corporate irresponsibility' and 'double standards'. As Braithwaite and Drahos show, global business regulation is already a hugely complex field – even on an issue-by-issue basis – involving a bewildering array of actors and ever-changing patterns of influence.[98] Clearly, any new regimes to emerge on multinationals and CSR must take account of past regulatory practice. Others argue, however, that reform is needed on a much more fundamental level – the very roots of company law, for instance – if justice for vulnerable groups in society is ever to be achieved.[99]

Defining 'corporate social responsibility'

Many writers have complained that CSR, as a concept, is confusing and often ill defined. This is partly because definitions are often presented with an agenda in mind. Business groups, for example, tend to adopt

[94] A. Clapham and S. Jerbi, 'Categories of Corporate Complicity in Human Rights Abuses' (2001) 24 *Hast I&CLR* 339; S. Ratner, 'Corporations and Human Rights: a Theory of Legal Responsibility' (2001) 111 *Yale LJ* 443.

[95] Although note that the possibility of enforcement of human rights obligations in national courts under national laws (and particularly under the US Alien Tort Claims Act) has generated a huge amount of literature. References are too numerous to list here, but for an excellent survey and analysis of recent case law, see S. Joseph, *Corporations and Transnational Human Rights Litigation* (Oxford: Hart Publishing, 2004).

[96] Joseph, 'Taming the Leviathans'; P. Redmond, 'Transnational Enterprise and Human Rights: Options for Standard Setting and Compliance' (2003) 37 *Int'l Lawyer* 69. The ICHRP concludes, on the other hand, that it is too early to reach a definite conclusion on the future form that human rights regulation should take. ICHRP, '*Beyond Voluntarism*, p. 155

[97] Redmond, 'Transnational Enterprise and Human Rights', p. 99.

[98] J. Braithwaite and P. Drahos, *Global Business Regulation* (Cambridge: Cambridge University Press, 2000).

[99] See esp. Dine, *Companies, International Trade and Human Rights*, who argues that law – company law and international law in particular – is used to conceal power relationships in society, and acts as a 'moral deflection device'.

definitions of CSR that emphasise its *voluntary* aspects. The Confederation of British Industries ('CBI') defines CSR as 'a catch-all title referring
to the activities of companies in areas where they impact on society
and/or the environment, as well as on companies' shareholders, customers, suppliers, employees and other players'. However, the CBI draws
a distinction between *legislative* standards and 'that additional activity
which many businesses undertake anyway to add value to the business
and build their reputation'. Only the latter, i.e. that which is 'over and
above the legal requirement', is CSR.[100] This idea of CSR as 'voluntary'
and 'over and above legal requirements' also permeates UK governmental policy on CSR. The UK government web-site on CSR issues defines CSR
as:

> the business contribution to our sustainable development goals. Essentially it
> is about how business takes account of its economic, social and environmental
> impacts in the way it operates – maximising the benefits and minimising the
> downsides. *Specifically we see CSR as the voluntary actions that business can take, over
> and above compliance with minimum legal requirements,* to address both its own
> competitive interests and the interests of wider society.[101]

The European Commission also views CSR primarily as a voluntary
activity,[102] but differs from the above definitions in that it treats compliance with the law as part and parcel of being 'socially responsible':
'Being socially responsible means not only fulfilling legal expectations,
but also going beyond compliance and investing "more" into human capital, the environment and relations with stakeholders.'[103] NGOs, on the
other hand, tend to downplay the idea that CSR is 'voluntary', focusing
instead on the ethical imperatives for companies to behave as 'good corporate citizens'. For instance, the Canadian-based group Ethics in Action
defines CSR as 'a company's obligation to be accountable to all of its
stakeholders in all its operations and activities'.[104] The source of this
obligation is not, however, explained.

The distinction – commonly made – between law and CSR is confusing and unhelpful. Apart from anything else, it wrongly assumes that
legal compliance is an absolute, whereas in reality there are degrees of

---

[100] CBI, 'Business Summaries: Corporate Social Responsibility (CSR)',
http://www.cbi.org.uk.
[101] DTI, 'What is CSR?', http://www.societyandbusiness.gov.uk (emphasis added).
[102] See European Commission, 'Communication from the Commission concerning
Corporate Social Responsibility: a Business Contribution to Sustainable Development',
COM (2002) 347, final, Brussels, 2 July 2002, p. 5.
[103] Ibid, p. 6.   [104] See http://www.ethicsinaction.com.

compliance and co-operation (as every tax adviser knows).[105] It also reflects a rather simplistic view of what regulation actually is, as will be discussed further in the next section.

More neutral definitions of CSR avoid references to legal standards but assume that there is a set of ethical principles with which all businesses should comply. CSR Wire, an on-line news service, defines CSR as an alignment of social and business values: 'CSR integrates the interests of stakeholders – all those affected by a company's conduct – into the company's business policies and actions. CSR focuses on the social, environmental and financial success of a company – the triple bottom line, with the goal being to positively impact society while achieving business success.'[106] As this definition shows, it is possible to define CSR both in terms of decision-making *processes* and in terms of social and environmental *outcomes*. The World Economic Forum ('WEF') has defined 'corporate citizenship' (a term used interchangeably with CSR) as:

the contribution that a company makes in society through its core business activities, its social investment and philanthropy programmes, and its engagement in public policy. That contribution is determined by the manner in which a company manages its economic, social and environmental impacts and manages its relationships with different stakeholders, in particular, shareholders, employees, customers, business partners, governments, communities and future generations.[107]

It is not surprising, therefore, that CSR is often confused with corporate governance, but these are actually two separate concepts. Corporate governance is generally taken to refer to issues relating to ownership and control of companies, and covers topics such as decision-making, reporting and transparency, whereas CSR, as noted above, is concerned with a wider set of relationships – with employees, suppliers, communities, consumers and interested NGOs.[108] Clearly, though, there are links between the two, as a well-run company, capable of 'institutionalising' the values it espouses, is more likely to be able to manage its social and environmental impacts effectively.[109]

---

[105] See further p. 34 below. On the relationship between CSR and taxation see M. Baker, 'Taxing Times', *Ethical Corporation*, September 2005, p. 43.

[106] See http://www.csrwire.com.

[107] WEF, 'Follow-up Questionnaire on the World Economic Forum CEO Statement: Global Corporate Citizenship: the Leadership Challenge for CEOs and Boards', (2002), http://www.weforum.org/pdf/GCCI/GCCI_CEO_Questionnaire.pdf.

[108] Hopkins, *The Planetary Bargain*, p. 1.

[109] Dine, *Companies, International Trade and Human Rights*, p. 233.

The definitional problems surrounding CSR are compounded by the emergence of some new terms – 'corporate citizenship' and 'corporate sustainability' – which cover the same or similar territory.[110] While 'corporate social responsibility' (or 'CSR') is still the most widely used term internationally, some commentators and companies prefer the term 'corporate responsibility', arguing that the inclusion of the word 'social' is limiting and misleading as it is often used to refer specifically to workplace standards. On the other hand, as Hopkins rightly points out, to delete the term 'social' makes it much easier for companies and politicians to shift the focus away from social and environmental issues and towards more business-centred concerns like corporate governance and financial reporting.[111] For these reasons, the term 'corporate *social* responsibility' ('CSR' for short) is chosen for the purposes of this book and refers to the notion that each business enterprise, as a member of society, has a responsibility *to operate ethically and in accordance with its legal obligations and to strive to minimise any adverse effects of its operations and activities on the environment, society and human health.*

This definition potentially covers a broad range of management-related topics, including corporate governance, trade practices and other business ethics issues, such as bribery and corruption. However, as noted in the introduction, the focus of this book is on the concerns at the heart of the current controversy over multinationals and globalisation, namely, treatment of workers (particularly workers in less developed countries), environmental issues and consumer protection.

Regulation in a deregulatory era

The 'voluntary versus mandatory' debate

The difficulties in defining CSR (and its relationship with the law) also reflect a lack of agreement about the role the law should play in this area in future. This is commonly referred to as the 'voluntary versus mandatory' debate. This debate continues to divide CSR professionals. On the one hand, representatives of companies and industry organisations argue that CSR should not be regulated. Regulation, it is argued,

---

[110] Most commentators regard 'corporate citizenship' as similar to CSR, although it is sometimes taken to cover issues such as corporate philanthropy as well.
'Sustainability' is often taken to refer primarily to environmental issues, but can also cover economic and social policies designed to maximise the long-term 'sustainability' of the individual company and its operations.

[111] Hopkins, *The Planetary Bargain*, pp. 11–12.

would stifle innovation and damage national 'competitiveness'. Instead, companies should be able to develop their own responses to CSR problems and, through peer pressure, collectively 'raise the bar' for industry in general.[112] Not only would new regulations be counter-productive, say those in the 'voluntarist' camp, they are also unnecessary as companies already are aware that there are financial gains to be made in being 'socially responsible'.

The so-called 'business case' for CSR has generated a huge amount of research, and a number of reports and articles have appeared which purport to demonstrate that companies which adopt socially responsible policies are better run, more attractive to investors, employees and consumers, more efficient and therefore more profitable.[113] Reviewing recent UK research on the relationship between CSR and business performance, the Work Foundation concludes: 'What appears clear is that CSR in its broadest sense does not inhibit company performance – rather as part of a comprehensive strategy it is likely to lead to performance and productivity gains, resulting in a stronger investment proposition to shareholders.'[114]

Many NGOs, on the other hand, remain unconvinced that the 'business case' for CSR is sufficient in itself as a guarantee of responsible corporate behaviour. In the UK, a number of NGOs, including Amnesty, Action Aid and Friends of the Earth ('FoE'), have formed an alliance specifically to campaign for new laws to improve corporate transparency and accountability. By 2004, membership of the CORE Coalition had grown to over a hundred, and it includes religious groups, trade unions and research institutions as well as environmental and human rights NGOs. On its web-site, CORE states: 'The CORE Coalition believes that the 'voluntary approach' to Corporate Responsibility has failed . . . We believe the only way Corporate Responsibility will succeed is through

---

[112] See, for instance, CSR Europe, 'Response to the European Commission Green Paper "For a European Framework on CSR", December 2001', http://www.csreurope.org/whatwedo/stakeholderdialogue/csreuroperesponse/printpage/.: 'Force-fitting a prescriptive or mandatory framework is liable to inhibit the creativity and wide stakeholder dialogues which have been at the heart of CSR's success to date,' p. 3.

[113] See nn. 38–40 above.

[114] S. Bevan, N. Isles, P. Emery and T. Hoskins, 'Achieving High Performance: CSR at the Heart of Business' (London: the Work Foundation (in partnership with Virtuous Circle), March 2004), http://www.theworkfoundation.com/publications/achieving-high-performance. jsp. p. 23.

new laws which make companies value people and the planet, as much as they value making a profit.'[115]

But while new regulatory ideas could and should be explored, the debate as to whether CSR should be 'voluntary' or 'mandatory' is misguided for several reasons. First, it tends to overlook the fact that many CSR-related issues are already closely regulated. In most jurisdictions, companies are subject to detailed regulatory requirements as regards issues such as workplace health and safety, environmental and consumer protection. Companies which operate negligently and without regard for human life or safety are, in principle at least, liable to their victims under civil law (e.g. the law of tort), and possibly under criminal law as well.[116]

Second, the 'voluntary versus mandatory' debate reflects an overly simplistic view of what law is, and how it guides human behaviour. As discussed in the previous section, CSR encompasses legal compliance, although it also includes an added obligation to act ethically and to take proper account of a range of other interests. This, of course, gives CSR special significance for multinationals investing in countries where legal requirements are unclear or ambiguous, or are not consistently enforced. But, even in the most sophisticated legal systems, few (if any) regulatory regimes are bullet-proof. There will still be grey areas as to how laws may be interpreted. If a legal loophole or ambiguity is discovered, the 'socially responsible' response may well be to comply with the spirit of the law, rather than to try to avoid it. CSR may also have a bearing on choices by companies as to whether to *enforce* their legal rights and, if so, how. Multinationals and their lawyers are regularly criticised for the strategies they employ in defending legal claims.[117] There may also be cases in which pursuing legal rights to their full extent may not be 'socially responsible'.[118]

---

[115] See http://www.corporate-responsibility.org. The key regulatory proposals put forward by CORE so far are discussed further at pp. 168–70 below.

[116] In practice, however, the financial, legal and practical obstacles are such that victims of corporate wrongdoing often find it very difficult to achieve redress from multinationals, particularly in cases where claimants have limited resources of their own. See further chapter 5 below.

[117] B. Dinham and S. Sarangi, 'The Bhopal Gas Tragedy 1984 to ?: the Evasion of Corporate Responsibility' (2002) 14(1) *Environment and Urbanisation* 89, 90.

[118] This is especially likely to be the case where the defendant is seen as being particularly vulnerable, or has only limited resources with which to defend the claim. Examples would include Nestlé's US$6 million lawsuit against the Ethiopian government claiming damages for alleged expropriation of assets (eventually settled

To summarise so far, the 'voluntary versus mandatory' debate is based on the mistaken impression that CSR and the law are somehow separate, whereas in reality they are intertwined. Even in its narrowest sense, CSR should, and does, have a bearing on how companies respond to and use the law; that is, how companies respond to their legal obligations and how they use the law to enforce their rights. The 'voluntary versus mandatory' debate also overlooks the progress that has already been made in many jurisdictions, not to mention internationally,[119] in the regulation of substantive CSR-related issues such as health and safety, environmental standards and consumer protection. Moreover, as more than one commentator has pointed out, even purely voluntary commitments may ultimately have legal effect, for instance in shaping standards of care, or to the extent that they are incorporated into contractual commitments, or as part of the regulatory background against which different industries operate.[120]

The third misconception underlying the 'voluntary versus mandatory' debate is the implicit assumption (by those arguing for greater use of mandatory standards in this field) that mandatory legal requirements will necessarily lead to higher standards of corporate behaviour and transparency. In reality, the law, as important as it is, is only one of a range of factors that influence corporate behaviour. In many cases – especially where the legal standards are flexible or unclear or are unlikely to be enforced – other factors, such as corporate culture or pressure from consumer groups, will be just as important, if not more so. Simply put, the fact that something is required by law does not necessarily mean it will be done well.[121]

The 'voluntary versus mandatory' debate has done little to further the debate about the appropriate regulatory responses to CSR-related problems. Not only has it helped to perpetuate a limited and unhelpful definition of CSR, it has also distracted attention away from the substantive issues that have given rise to so much international

---

for US$1.6 million in 2002) and the McDonalds 1990 libel suit against two leafleteers, Helen Steel and Dave Morris. For an account of the McDonalds libel case (from the defendants' perspective) see J. Vidal, *McLibel: Burger Culture on Trial* (New York: The New Press, 1997). See, generally, Sustainability, 'The Changing Landscape of Liability'.

[119] Braithwaite and Drahos, *Global Business Regulation*. See further pp. 284–97 below.

[120] Ward, 'Legal Issues in Corporate Citizenship'; S. Picciotto, 'Rights, Responsibilities and Regulation of International Business' (2003) 42 *CJTL* 131, esp. 145–6.

[121] P. Monaghan, 'Impacts of Reporting: Uncovering the Voluntary vs Mandatory Myth' in Accountability (ed.), *Accountability Quarterly, Does Reporting Work?: The Effect of Regulation* (September 2003), AQ21.

concern. Obviously, there is no one solution to the problems surrounding globalisation, international investment, poverty and exploitation. Many of these problems call for co-ordinated action on different levels: international and national, governmental and self-regulatory.[122] The crucial question is not whether CSR should be 'voluntary' or 'mandatory', but, in light of a particular problem, what is the best regulatory response?

Changing regulatory techniques

A further criticism that could be made of the 'voluntary versus mandatory' debate is that it fails to do justice to the range of regulatory techniques already in use. While the traditional 'command and control' style of regulation is preferred in some cases, governments are increasingly resorting to other regulatory strategies such as incentives or rewards to encourage good behaviour, or transparency initiatives (compulsory publication of pollution statistics, for example) to harness investor and consumer power.

'Command and control' refers to the imposition of a minimum legislative standard, which is then backed up by legal sanctions. In the UK, as in other parts of the world, the move away from this style of regulation has been influenced by a number of different factors. The first significant factor was the rise of economic liberalism in the 1970s, and its emphasis on 'small government' as the key to economic success. Under this theory, unnecessary governmental interventions in markets create inefficiencies that can damage productivity and competitiveness. It follows, therefore, that regulation must be both minimal and cost-effective, a principle that remains central to the way new regulatory proposals are evaluated and implemented in the UK.[123] The problem of over-regulation has been a particular concern as governments have sought to open up previously state-owned industries (such as telecommunications, gas and electricity)

---

[122] Picciotto, 'Rights, Responsibilities and Regulation', 146.

[123] Better Regulation Task Force, 'Imaginative Thinking for Better Regulation', Cabinet Office, September 2003, http://www.btrf.gov.uk/reports/imaginativeregulation.asp. Since August 1998, all UK government departments have been required to carry out 'Regulatory Impact Assessments' in respect of all regulatory proposals which potentially have an impact on businesses, voluntary bodies and charities. Note, however, that the methods and assumptions used to calculate the costs of regulation to business have been criticised. See D. Doane, 'From Red Tape to Road Signs: Redefining Regulation and its Purpose', CORE pamphlet, 2004, http:// www.corporate-responsibility.org.

to competition. Over-regulation, it was feared, could operate as a barrier to entry. Instead, the approach has been to keep sector-specific regulatory requirements such as licence conditions to a minimum, and to give a greater role to general laws on matters such as competition and consumer protection.[124]

The second factor behind the move away from 'command and control' regulation has been the realisation that in some contexts this style of regulation is ineffective or, worse, counter-productive. Certainly, its imprecision and lack of flexibility can be a disadvantage, and many business commentators claim that it stifles innovation by companies.[125] This form of regulation, it is argued, does not inspire excellence, but rather prompts a 'race for the bottom' and makes legal compliance little more than a 'box-ticking' exercise.

Further difficulties associated with 'command and control' regulation include a lack of information necessary to set minimum standards at the appropriate level, regulatory standards falling behind changing needs and expectations or technology ('regulatory lag'), problems of avoidance ('creative compliance')[126] and the costs of monitoring and enforcement. For all these reasons, governments around the world have increasingly been exploring alternative regulatory techniques.[127] These include self-regulation, use of incentives, awards and accreditation systems, market-based initiatives, disclosure obligations, publication of league tables, allocation of private statutory rights, statutory compensation schemes, publicity and government-sponsored information and education campaigns.

Self-regulation takes a variety of different forms. At one end of the spectrum, regulation can be left entirely to the companies concerned. A trade association or professional body may be given responsibility for organising and administering the self-regulatory scheme, which will frequently involve a requirement that its members adhere to a 'code of conduct'. The administering body may also be given responsibility, by its members, for investigating and taking action in response to complaints

---

[124] R. Baldwin and M. Cave, *Understanding Regulation: Theory, Strategy and Practice* (Oxford: Oxford University Press, 1999), pp. 38, 45.

[125] Ibid., p. 37.

[126] I.e. 'the practice of avoiding the intention of the law without breaking the terms of the law'. Baldwin and Cave, *Understanding Regulation*, p. 38.

[127] 'The last two decades of the twentieth century saw the rise of the "new regulatory state", where states do not so much run things as regulate them or monitor self-regulation'; Braithwaite and Drahos, *Global Business Regulation*, p. 28.

that the terms of the code have been breached.[128] Some self-regulatory systems may, however, include an element of governmental oversight.[129] This can range from guidance and approval of self-regulatory schemes,[130] to providing an organisation with a legal mandate to oversee a self-regulatory scheme.[131] Some self-regulatory schemes have the benefit of government backing in the form of 'back-stop' regulation, under which repeated breaches of the terms of a voluntary code may ultimately be punishable by legal sanctions.[132] In addition, the UK government has itself been involved in developing non-binding codes of conduct for various industries. While these government-sponsored codes of conduct may not be legally binding as such, a history of compliance may well have a bearing on whether or not a company or individual is prosecuted by the authorities for code-related offences,[133] and the damages which may be payable. As will become apparent from the survey of state practice in chapter 4, CSR regulation in the UK relies heavily on 'self-regulatory' schemes.

As a form of regulation, incentives are usually popular with companies, for obvious reasons.[134] Regulatory incentives are commonly associated with the tax system (which can either reward a company directly, or remove a financial *disincentive* associated with a socially beneficial course of action). Incentives can also take the form of preferred status in public sector procurement processes,[135] or programmes that reward good behaviour with lower administration or licensing

---

[128] See, for example, the code of conduct developed by the ABTA, http://www.abta.com.

[129] This is sometimes referred to as 'co-regulation'. See Better Regulation Task Force, 'Better Regulation', n. 123 above, pp. 45–6.

[130] See, for example, the Consumer Codes Approval Scheme, operated by the UK Office of Fair Trading ('OFT'). Under this scheme, organisations are able to apply to the OFT for approval of their self-regulatory schemes. See http://www.oft.gov.uk/business/codes/default.htm.

[131] Baldwin and Cave, *Understanding Regulation*, pp. 39–41.

[132] See, for example, the code of practice administered by the UK Advertising Standards Authority (the 'CAP' code), which is backed up by the Control of Misleading Advertisements Regulations 1988 (SI 1988 No. 915).

[133] See, for instance, Environment Agency, 'Enforcement and Prosecution Policy', 1 November 1998, http://www.environment-agency.gov.uk/business/444217/444661/112913/?version=1&lang=e, para. 28.

[134] For a more critical view of financial incentives see, however, J. Braithwaite, 'Rewards and Regulation' in S. Picciotto and D. Campbell (eds.), *New Directions in Regulatory Theory* (Oxford: Blackwell, 2002).

[135] See pp. 192–3 below.

costs,[136] or simply with praise and public recognition, such as award schemes. Market-based initiatives, such as tradable emissions permits, are another potentially useful way of encouraging companies to invest in less polluting technologies.[137] A good social and environmental record can also be rewarded through compulsory public compensation or insurance schemes. Not only do these schemes provide a basis for compensation, they can also encourage greater investment in environmental and health and safety improvements by linking premiums to past performance.[138]

Alternatively, states and their regulatory authorities can require the publication of certain health and safety, environmental or social information. While this kind of regulation does not lay down substantive standards regarding the operations of a company, the obligation to disclose certain information (or the threat of inclusion in a public list of poor performers)[139] can be a powerful incentive for a company to improve its social and environmental performance. This may only be a side-effect of legislation designed primarily to ensure that the public have the information necessary to take steps to protect themselves from risks[140] or that investors are able to make informed decisions about a company's future prospects.[141] However, there are cases where disclosure regulation has been used expressly to put pressure on companies

[136] The UK Environment Agency, for instance, operates a system whereby those companies that can demonstrate compliance with EMAS (the EU's 'Eco-Management and Audit Scheme') receive a lower risk rating under its Integrated Pollution Prevention and Control Regime than comparable companies that have not adopted EMAS procedures. As risk rating influences the fees charged to industrial operators, compliance with EMAS can help to reduce the overall fees and charges bill payable to the regulator. See further EMAS, 'An Introductory Guide to EMAS: the Pinnacle of Environmental Management', DEFRA, 2003, http://www.emas.org.uk.

[137] See, for example, the EU CO_2 emissions trading scheme operating under Council Directive 2003/87/EC of 13 October 2003 establishing a scheme for greenhouse gas emission allowance trading within the Community and amending Council Directive 96/91/EC, OJ 2003 No. L275/32, 25 October 2003.

[138] Baldwin and Cave, *Understanding Regulation*, pp. 53–5.

[139] E.g. UK Environment Agency's annual 'Spotlight on Business', a publication that highlights 'good and bad performers' over the year and also gives details of major prosecutions brought. See http://www.environment-agency.gov.uk/business.

[140] See, for example, Council Directive 96/82/EC of 9 December 1996 on the control of major accident hazards involving dangerous substances, OJ 1997 No. L10/13, 14 January 1997, under which operators of installations must notify local authorities of processes using certain chemicals and possible accident risks.

[141] E.g. Companies Act 1985 (Operating and Financial Review and Directors' Report) Regulations 2004 (SI 2005 No. 1011). See further pp. 173–4 below.

to be more 'socially responsible'. The Johannesburg Stock Exchange Listing Rules use a method known as 'comply or explain', under which
companies must state in their annual reports whether or not they comply with the 2002 King Code on Corporate Governance and if not, why
not.[142]

Socially undesirable activities, such as pollution or abusive employment practices, are criminalised in many states, and enforcement powers placed in the hands of state authorities such as regulators, tribunals
or courts. However, some states have sought to deal with these kinds of
problems through the allocation of private enforcement rights to private individuals and groups. There are plenty of examples of this kind
of regulation in US environmental law. The US Clean Air Act of 1990,[143]
for example, provides for citizen suits against polluters in violation of
emission standards. Individuals may also have the right to sue corporate
wrongdoers under the common law of tort, a form of regulation considered further in chapter 5 below. In some cases, these common law
rights have been codified and extended by statute.[144]

At the 'softest' end of the scale of alternative regulatory techniques are
public information and education campaigns. These methods are used
where it is considered that greater legal controls would be impractical,
or pose unacceptable restrictions on personal freedoms. The UK government's campaign to encourage healthy eating is an example of this kind
of approach to social problems.[145] But while public information campaigns of this kind have an impact on the behaviour of consumers (and
therefore an indirect impact on manufacturers), this approach is often
criticised for being too soft on companies that manufacture harmful
products.

As this short survey of regulatory techniques shows, it is not always
possible to characterise regulation as 'voluntary' or 'mandatory'. For
instance, while a requirement to disclose information may be mandatory as a matter of law, substantive operating standards may be left to
the individual company concerned. Similarly, while it may be mandatory

---

[142] J. Burke, 'The Reporting Implications of South Africa's King Code on Corporate
Governance' in Accountability (ed.), *Accountability Quarterly, Does Reporting Work?: The
Effect of Regulation* (September 2003), AQ21.

[143] 42 USC § 7604.

[144] See, for example, Council Directive 85/374/EEC of 25 July 1985 on the approximation
of the laws, regulations and administrative provisions of the Member States
concerning liability for defective products, OJ 1985 No. L210/29, 7 August 1985,
implemented in the UK by the 1987 Consumer Protection Act.

[145] See, for example, http://www.doh.gov.uk/fiveaday/index.htm.

to hold a permit to operate a potentially polluting facility, companies may have the flexibility to determine their own emissions targets, and to purchase additional emissions allowances if need be. In many cases, governments will decide that the optimal level and style of regulation involves a mix of these different techniques. Even so, alternative forms of regulation do not overcome all of the problems of 'command and control' styles of regulation. In the case of market-based techniques, for example, it will still be necessary to lay down rules and targets and to put in place administrative arrangements to ensure that those trying to cheat the system are detected and dealt with.[146] It is also important to note that the apparent trend away from more traditional forms of regulation has not been universally welcomed. To some critics, the rise of alternative regulatory strategies, particularly the use of economic incentives and other market-based techniques, is evidence of the extent to which states are now 'captive' to business.[147]

What is regulation?

As will be apparent from the discussion above, the term 'regulation' can have a range of different meanings and it is important to be clear about how it will be used in this book. For legal purposes, regulation is generally taken to refer to the control over private activities exercised by public authorities.[148] However, this term can also refer to more diverse sources of social control or influence, 'including unintentional and non-state processes'.[149]

Today, companies are 'regulated' (in the widest sense of the word) by a hugely diverse group of actors who may include shareholders, public authorities, inter-governmental bodies, trade unions, NGOs, insurers and consumer groups. The key to successful regulation, then, is a proper understanding of the influences and pressures guiding corporate behaviour and how they might be manipulated to achieve a particular aim. Regulation does not have to be binding and enforceable to be effective (a proposition with which international lawyers will be familiar).[150] For these reasons, this book adopts a flexible definition

---

[146] Baldwin and Cave, *Understanding Regulation*, pp. 56–62.
[147] Monbiot, *Captive State*, pp. 342–54; Doane, 'Red Tape'.
[148] Baldwin and Cave, *Understanding Regulation*: 'At its simplest, regulation refers to the promulgation of an authoritative set of rules, accompanied by some mechanism, typically a public agency, for monitoring and promoting compliance with those rules', p. 3.
[149] Ibid., p.4.   [150] See further pp. 61–2 below.

of regulation, which encompasses 'any form of social control or influ-ence',[151] regardless of its source. However, as this book is concerned with questions of *international law*, the primary focus will be on the activities of states, whether unilaterally or through international organisations, rather than other entities or groups.[152] As chapters 4, 5 and 6 will show, these activities draw from the full range of regulatory styles discussed above. The important question, for the purposes of assessing state activ-ity in the CSR field so far, is not whether regulatory initiatives are 'bind-ing' or 'non-binding', but whether they have the potential to change corporate choices and behaviour in line with a particular objective. This characteristic is referred to in the following chapters as 'regulatory potential'.

Corporate social responsibility and human rights

Might the CSR standards of multinationals already be regulated, in part, by international law? By now, companies seem to have accepted that compliance with human rights obligations is an important part of being 'socially responsible'. Most leading multinationals now have a 'human rights policy' displayed somewhere on their web-sites. Rio Tinto's state-ment that '[w]e support human rights consistent with the Universal Declaration of Human Rights and Rio Tinto respects those rights in con-ducting the Group's operations throughout the world'[153] is fairly typical. Rio Tinto's human rights policy goes on:

We seek to ensure that Rio Tinto's presence fosters sound relationships and avoids civil conflict wherever we are. Rio Tinto respects and supports the dignity, well being and rights of Group employees, our families and the communities in which we live, as well as others affected by the Group's operations . . . Where those rights are threatened, we seek to have international standards upheld and to avoid situations that could be interpreted as condoning human rights abuses. We ensure that our equipment and facilities are not mis-used [*sic*] in violation of them.[154]

Human rights commitments also feature in companies' annual CSR reports. According to BP's 2003 Sustainability Report: 'As a global busi-ness, we are sensitive to the need to respect and support human rights. We aim to ensure that we act responsibly to protect the rights of employ-ees and contractors, and we work with governments and other bodies

---

[151] Baldwin and Cave, *Understanding Regulation*, p. 2.   [152] See further pp. 62–3 below.
[153] See http://www.riotinto.com/community/humanrights/aspx.   [154] Ibid.

to promote respect for human rights wherever we work.'[155] The report then goes on to discuss BP's policy in relation to a particularly controversial project, the Baku–Tbilisi–Ceyhan Pipeline Project, claiming that 'BP and its partners have set out to establish a new benchmark in human rights and environmental standards'.[156] Barclays, in its 2003 report, goes further: 'Barclays has endorsed the UN Universal Declaration of Human Rights and we aim to run our business in accordance with both the Declaration and the International Labour Organisation (ILO) Conventions and Treaties.' This report also mentions Barclays' involvement in the Business Leaders Initiative on Human Rights 'which will explore ways in which businesses can implement the principles of the Universal Declaration of Human Rights (UDHR)'. Glaxo Smith Kline's Corporate Responsibility Principles include a commitment 'to uphold the UN Universal Declaration of Human Rights, the OECD Guidelines for MNEs and the core labour standards set out by the International Labour Organisation'.[157]

Corporate 'endorsements' of international human rights instruments are now commonplace.[158] However, most CSR reports are careful to avoid any suggestion that these human rights standards are legally binding on companies. On the contrary, if CSR is a voluntary concept, as many business representatives insist,[159] and human rights are merely an aspect of CSR, then, logically, it would seem that human rights are still regarded, by the business community at least, as comprising moral rather than legal obligations.

Although CSR and human rights are often spoken of as if they are interchangeable, they should not be confused. They are distinct concepts, with different origins and purposes, and cover different, though overlapping, subject matter. As shall be discussed further in chapter 2, the primary targets of human rights law have always been states, and it

---

[155] BP, 'Defining Our Path: Sustainability Report 2003', http://www.bp.com, p. 32.

[156] Ibid, p. 34. For an alternative viewpoint see Amnesty International, 'Human Rights on the Line: the Baku–Tbilisi–Ceyhan Pipeline Project', May 2003, http://www.amnesty.org.uk/business.

[157] Barclays plc, 'Corporate Social Responsibility Report 2003', http://www.personal.barclays.co.uk, p.10; Glaxo Smith Kline, 'Corporate Responsibility Report 2003', http://www.gsk.com, p. 3.

[158] The web-site of the Business and Human Rights Resource Centre lists seventy-two companies which expressly refer to the UDHR in their corporate policies and a further twenty-nine companies with human rights policies, but without express reference to the UDHR. See http://www.business-humanrights.org.

[159] See pp. 29–30, 32–6 above.

is only relatively recently that its potential in relation to private corporate activity has been widely discussed.[160] CSR, on the other hand, as its name suggests, was originally (and is still primarily) addressed towards corporate activity. While compliance with human rights standards is clearly part of being 'socially responsible', CSR is concerned with wider corporate citizenship issues such as good management, transparency, community investment and regeneration. Nevertheless, human rights standards – whatever their legal status vis-à-vis companies[161] – have certainly helped to shape the international corporate citizenship agenda. Many key CSR issues – environmental quality or labour standards, for example – have links to human rights and, as the corporate statements above show, companies look to these international human rights instruments for guidance as to social expectations. International human rights instruments are also used by companies and NGOs to provide indicators against which their social and ethical performance can be judged. For instance, the Global Reporting Initiative ('GRI') 2002 Sustainability Reporting Guidelines, an influential set of guidelines for companies, draws directly from international instruments such as the UDHR and various ILO Conventions for its 'key performance indicators'.[162]

At the same time, the CSR movement has helped to reinvigorate interest in human rights law, though now as a potential means of regulating multinationals. As will be discussed further in chapter 2, the proposition that companies are subject to direct obligations under international human rights law is now gaining support, notwithstanding the lack of mechanisms by which these obligations can be enforced. In the meantime, human rights campaigners have been exploring options for holding multinationals accountable for human rights violations under *national* law. In the USA, a series of lawsuits have been brought against companies under the US Alien Tort Claims Act ('ATCA')[163] claiming damages for alleged human rights violations. These developments are discussed further in chapter 5.

Designing regulatory responses: some persistent problems

Are multinationals special?

Much of the discussion above could apply, not just to the activities of multinationals, but to companies in general. The remainder of this

---

[160] See further pp. 28–9 above.   [161] See pp. 76–83 below.
[162] GRI, '2002 Sustainability Reporting Guidelines', http://www.globalreporting.org, p. 54.
[163] Alien Tort Claims Act of 1789, 28 USC § 1350.

chapter is concerned with the particular problems posed by multinational corporate activity. Obviously, CSR does not apply only to multinationals. Therefore, an important question to consider at the outset is whether multinational companies require a special *international* legal response or whether (as representatives of the business community tend to argue) they ought to be treated the same way as any other company, that is, subject only to the laws of each individual country in which they operate. In other words, are multinationals special?

Despite the level of media attention given to allegations of abuses by multinationals, there is no agreement as to whether the presence of multinationals causes the overall social and environmental standards in host states to rise, to fall or to stay the same.[164] Multinationals operating in less developed countries routinely claim to adopt higher social and environmental standards than their local competitors, in many cases exceeding local legal requirements. If this is the case, then what is the justification for additional regulatory requirements for multinationals, merely by virtue of the fact that they operate in more than one state?

Codes of conduct developed by the OECD, the ILO and the UN reveal a certain amount of ambivalence as to whether initiatives targeted specifically at multinationals (as opposed to companies in general) are appropriate or necessary. According to the OECD Guidelines, 'The *Guidelines* are not aimed at introducing differences of treatment between multinational and domestic enterprises; they reflect good practices for all. Accordingly, multinational and domestic enterprises are subject to the same expectations in respect to their conduct wherever the *Guidelines* are relevant to both.'[165] But whether or not 'differences of treatment' are

---

[164] Zarsky, for example, argues that rather than bringing about a 'race to the bottom', competition for inward investment between host states causes environmental standards to become 'stuck in the mud'. See L. Zarsky, 'Stuck in the Mud: Nation States, Globalization and the Environment', Globalization and Environment Study, OECD Economics Division, The Hague, May 1997. Redmond, on the other hand, argues that 'it is unrealistic not to acknowledge that . . . pressures [on host states] . . . will translate into like pressures upon labour conditions, environmental protection, occupational health and safety regulation and other protections that have costs imposts upon international production'; Redmond, 'Transnational Enterprise and Human Rights', 80. In practice, though, there are likely to be significant variations from country to country and from sector to sector, depending on a range of factors, e.g. the relative bargaining positions of the states and companies concerned and the domestic political situation.

[165] OECD Guidelines (2001) 40 ILM 237, Part I, para. 4. Similar provisions also appear in the Draft UN Code, n. 16 above, and the ILO Tripartite Declaration, n. 18 above.

justified actually depends upon the nature of the regulatory goals. For instance, is the goal of regulation to raise substantive social and environmental standards, to remove incentives for 'social dumping', to improve the overall accountability of companies, or to help deliver home state policies on international development? Three arguments could potentially be mounted in favour of special regimes for multinationals in the CSR field: the 'development' argument, the 'morality' argument and the 'mobility' argument. Each argument reflects a different set of regulatory aspirations, as well as a number of assumptions about multinationals and their activities.

The 'development' argument is based on the notion that multinationals, because of their size or resources, have a special role to play in the delivery of social and environmental benefits to local communities. As discussed in later chapters, the idea that companies, as well as governments, have a key role to play in achieving 'sustainable development' goals has become an important theme of international environmental policy. But this is not an entirely new idea. Many countries, including the now 'industrialised' states, have at some stage imposed special requirements on foreign investors as part of their national development strategies. It is important to note, however, that the practice of imposing discriminatory performance and local purchasing requirements on foreign investors is controversial.[166] Restrictions on these kinds of measures already exist under many BITs,[167] the GATS[168] and the TRIMs Agreement,[169] and further restrictions were proposed as part of the (ultimately unsuccessful) MAI.[170] These restrictions have obvious implications for the development policies of less industrialised host states.[171]

The 'morality' argument in favour of social regulation of multinationals is based on the idea that the benefits of 'globalisation' are not distributed fairly, and are sometimes obtained at an unacceptable cost to certain sections of society, particularly within less developed countries. Multinationals should not, for instance, be permitted to profit from weak environmental or consumer safety standards abroad by using other

---

[166] Local purchasing requirements, for example, are opposed on the basis that they create market distortions, the result of which may be higher prices for goods than would be the case in an open market.

[167] UNCTAD, 'World Investment Report 2003: FDI Policies for Development: National and International Perspectives' (New York and Geneva: UN, 2003), UN Sales No. E.03.II.D.8.

[168] See n. 50 above.   [169] See n. 51 above.   [170] See pp. 19–20 above.

[171] UNCTAD, 'World Investment Report 1999: Investment Trade and International Policy Arrangements' (New York and Geneva: UN, 1999), UN Sales No. E.99.II.D.3, p. 42.

countries as a dumping ground for their most polluting operations or for consumer products that are subject to safety restrictions or bans elsewhere. Also, unsafe labour conditions or the use of child labour are not, it is argued, a legitimate cost saving on the production of consumer goods. In other words, there is a moral 'bottom line' below which multinationals must not go, and regulation is needed to ensure that, if this line is crossed, the company concerned is held accountable.

An important assumption behind the 'morality' argument is that, while host states undoubtedly have duties towards their own citizens in relation to workplace conditions, environmental quality and consumer safety, in some cases they do not have the resources – financial, technical or institutional – to regulate their own industries effectively. Worse still, some of the least well off developing countries may regard low labour and environmental standards as a vital source of 'comparative advantage' so that, even if certain social reforms are seen as desirable, these must, for the time being at least, give way to the state's shorter-term economic needs.[172] Therefore, the 'morality' argument states that, where the host state is unable or unwilling to implement and enforce appropriate regulatory standards, human rights considerations demand that alternative means of regulation be found.

According to the 'mobility' argument, multinationals have significantly more flexibility than enterprises operating in a single state. Their ability to relocate all or part of their operations abroad allows them to play governments off, one against the other. This is not only a feature of the largest and most powerful multinationals. According to UN statistics, even smaller and medium-sized multinationals are becoming more 'internationalised'.[173]

This flexibility, coupled with their importance to host state economies, is said to put multinationals in a better bargaining position vis-à-vis host states than national companies. Their bargaining strength is used by multinationals to extract valuable investment incentives from host states, such as tax concessions, financial assistance, special infrastructure and the use of deregulated 'export processing zones'. Furthermore, host states are engaged in competition for FDI with each other, putting further downward pressure on national labour and environmental standards. Multinationals therefore require special regulatory

[172] Zarsky, 'Stuck in the Mud'.
[173] UNCTAD, 'World Investment Report 2000: Cross Border Mergers and Acquisitions and Development' (New York and Geneva: UN, 2000), UN Sales No. E.00.II.D.20.

regimes to reduce their incentives to relocate operations, to put relationships between multinationals and their host states on a more even keel and to guarantee minimum standards for employees, consumers and the general public.[174]

It will be obvious that each of the above arguments in favour of international regulatory solutions for multinationals rests on assumptions and generalisations about multinationals that will not always be correct. The 'development' argument, for example, assumes that multinationals have access to technology or other advantages not available to local companies. The 'morality' argument is based on the assumption that multinationals (more than smaller, national companies) are engaged in exploitative practices, the consequences of which either outweigh the potential benefits to host states in terms of increased employment and economic growth or raise issues of human rights. The 'mobility' argument assumes that multinationals can relocate operations from state to state with relative ease and that their locational choices are motivated primarily by production costs. Nevertheless, as the following chapters will show, each of these arguments has played, and continues to play, a vital role in shaping national and international policy on multinationals.

Generalisations, assumptions and prejudices are not a sound basis for regulatory policy. It is therefore important that preconceptions about multinationals, like those mentioned above, are questioned and, where possible, tested through empirical research. On the other hand, it is undeniable that multinationals, simply by virtue of the fact that they exist in more than one country, face a different set of CSR-related issues from those faced by enterprises which, for whatever reason, do not operate or invest abroad. These issues are inherent in questions such as 'in what countries and on what terms will we invest?'; 'what will govern whether or not we continue to invest?'; and 'to what standards should we adhere in the conduct of our daily operations (e.g. legal minimum standards, home state standards, 'best practice' or 'international' standards)?'.

Of course, multinationals are not the only enterprises potentially governed by international law. As will be seen, human rights law, to the extent that it addresses itself to corporations, does not necessarily distinguish between multinationals and smaller, national enterprises. Nevertheless international law does have a potentially vital role to play in shaping regulatory responses to *international* CSR challenges specific to

---

[174] Joseph, 'Taming the Leviathans', 202.

multinational activity. First, though, as with any regulatory regime, it is important to have a clear vision of what the particular objectives are.

What is a 'multinational'?

Once the need for further regulation has been established, the next step is to identify the types of enterprises to which the new regulatory initiative should be targeted. This is by no means straightforward in relation to multinationals, which are made up of not one but many different legal entities.

The multinational is a flexible concept, which has evolved over time to take account of developments in international investment patterns and management techniques. Initially, the term was generally understood to refer to a company that owned, directly or through its subsidiaries, assets located in the territory of more than one state.[175] Membership of the enterprise was defined by the presence of ownership links between a parent company and its subsidiaries. The other main characteristic of the enterprise was that it operated on an integrated basis, subject to the overall management of the parent company.[176] This definition reflected what was known about the management structures of the larger international commercial enterprises of the time.

Since the 1960s, however, the management structures of international commercial enterprises have become increasingly diverse. It is now well recognised that FDI is only one of a number of possible strategies that could be employed by companies to expand into new markets and

---

[175] D. Fieldhouse, 'The Multinational: a Critique of a Concept' in A. Teichova, M. Lévy-Leboyer and H. Nussbaum (eds.), *The Multinational in Historical Perspective* (Cambridge: Cambridge University Press, 1986). Commonly used variations include 'transnational', 'transnational corporation' (or 'TNC'), 'international company' and 'multinational enterprise' (or 'MNE'). These terms are generally regarded as interchangeable, although in the context of UN discussions on multinationals, a distinction has been drawn between the terms 'transnational' and 'transnational corporation' on the one hand and 'multinational' on the other. 'Transnational' and 'transnational corporation' were said best to describe the activities of a company based in one country with cross-border activities, whereas the term 'multinational' referred to enterprises owned and controlled by entities from different countries; Muchlinski, *Multinational Enterprises and the Law*, p. 13.

[176] 'The goal . . . is the greatest good of the whole unity, even if the interests of a single part of the unity may suffer'; *Business Week,* 25 April 1963, p. 63, quoted in Fieldhouse, 'The Multinational'. Hood and Young have defined the multinational as a corporation which 'owns (in whole or in part), controls and manages income-generating assets in more than one country'; N. Hood and S. Young, *The Economics of the Multinational Enterprise* (London: Longman, 1979), p. 3.

to exploit new opportunities overseas. While organisational forms are determined to a large extent by the relevant industrial sector,[177] business observers and economists have for some time now recognised the growing importance of contract-based arrangements, such as franchises, licences, joint ventures and distribution arrangements.[178]

In its everyday sense, the term 'multinational' has become a shorthand way of referring to a variety of cross-border commercial arrangements and alliances. Today, the term is as likely to refer to an international brand as to any particular organisational structure. To economic analysts like Dunning, the most important distinguishing feature of a multinational, as opposed to other forms of investment, is the presence of FDI.[179] This distinguishes the activities of a multinational from those of a 'portfolio' investor. However, for the purposes of Dunning's definition, FDI does not necessarily imply transfer of capital through a foreign subsidiary but a transfer of resources, where 'control over the use of resources remains with the investor'. FDI 'consists of a "package" of assets and intermediate products, such as capital, technology, management skills, access to markets and entrepreneurship'.[180]

It has been necessary to define the concept of the 'multinational' more closely for the purposes of data collection on multinational activities, a job presently carried out by a number of international organisations, including the World Bank, the IMF, the OECD and, of course, UNCTAD. UNCTAD, in its capacity as convenor of the UN's Programme on Transnational Corporations, publishes an annual report on international investment and production trends which includes statistics on the assets, employment and investment activities of the world's largest multinationals. For the purposes of this report, UNCTAD defines 'transnational corporations' (or 'TNCs')[181] as:

[177] For a general review of economic literature on multinationals, see R. Caves, *Multinational Enterprise and Economic Analysis* (Cambridge: Cambridge University Press, 1996), chapter 1.

[178] P. Buckley and M. Casson, *The Future of the Multinational Enterprise*, 2nd edition (London: Macmillan, 1976); J. Dunning, 'Non-equity Forms of Foreign Economic Involvement and the Theory of International Production' in J. Dunning (ed.), *Explaining International Production* (London: Unwin Hyman, 1988); J. Dunning, *Multinationals and the Global Economy* (Wokingham: Addison Wesley, 1993), chapter 1. In relation to the impact of modern management techniques on this traditional model, see also J. Birkinshaw, 'Multinational Corporate Strategy and Organisation: an Internal Market Perspective' in N. Hood and S. Young (eds.), *The Globalisation of Multinational Enterprise Activity and Economic Development* (London: Macmillan, 2000).

[179] Dunning, *Multinationals and the Global Economy*, p. 3.

[180] Ibid., p. 5.   [181] See n. 175 above.

incorporated or unincorporated enterprises comprising parent enterprises and their foreign affiliates. A *parent enterprise* is defined as an enterprise that controls assets of other entities in countries other than its home country, usually by owning a certain equity capital stake. An equity capital stake of 10 per cent or more of the ordinary shares or voting power, or its equivalent for an unincorporated enterprise, is normally considered as a threshold for the control of assets . . . A *foreign affiliate* is an incorporated or unincorporated enterprise in which an investor, who is resident in another country, owns a stake that permits a lasting interest in the management of that enterprise (an equity stake of 10 per cent for an incorporated enterprise or its equivalent for an unincorporated enterprise).[182]

This wording emphasises 'equity-based' over 'contract-based' organisational structures, but there are reasons for framing the definition of 'TNCs' in this way. In practice, there are real difficulties in evaluating the accuracy and comparability of data relating to the contributions by a 'parent enterprise' to a foreign entity with which it has only contractual links, particularly in relation to intangibles such as technology and know-how.[183] Therefore, although it is recognised that non-equity arrangements such as licensing, franchising and sub-contracting are important conduits for FDI, flows of investment through equity-based business forms are treated by data-gathering agencies as the main indicators of multinational activity.

In summary, 'multinational' is a term capable of describing a wide range of international investment arrangements. Historically, studies of multinationals have concentrated on equity-based structures. Equity-based structures are also the primary focus of statistical surveys on multinational activities. However, more recent writing on multinationals, particularly in the field of economics, has noted the growing importance of non-equity or contract-based forms. Consequently, most general-purpose definitions of the multinational now emphasise, not the presence of 'ownership' relationships between entities, but relationships of 'control'.

For convenience, this book adopts a stylised notion of the multinational that comprises a parent company, located in a home state and linked to its foreign affiliates through relationships of control (i.e. 'cross-border control relationships'). The use of the term 'subsidiary' in place of 'affiliate' implies the presence of 'equity-based' rather than other

---

[182] UNCTAD, 'World Investment Report 2000', p. 267.
[183] See Vernon's comments on UNCTAD's 'World Investment Report 1997' in (1998–9) *Economic Development and Cultural Change* 458.

(usually 'contract-based') control links. However, it must be remembered that reality is usually more complicated than this.

Constructing a legal definition: flexibility or certainty?

The flexibility of the multinational as a concept makes the formulation of a legal definition very difficult. The OECD Guidelines define multinational enterprises as enterprises that

> usually comprise companies or other entities established in more than one country and so linked that they may co-ordinate their operations in various ways. While one or more of these entities may be able to exercise a significant degree of influence over the activities of others, their degree of autonomy within the enterprise may vary widely from one multinational enterprise to another. Ownership may be private, state or mixed.[184]

In other words, there will be control relationships between different entities, located in different countries, which may or may not result from shareholdings. It is deliberately flexible, the OECD having decided that '[a] precise definition of multinational enterprises is not required for the purposes of the *Guidelines*'.[185]

Various economic theories have been advanced to explain the existence of multinationals, and where their boundaries might lie.[186] As a conglomeration of different companies, a multinational is not a 'legal person' in the same way as, say, a company, a partnership or an individual. But this does not mean that multinationals cannot be identified in legal terms. Legal definitions are capable of identifying economic structures, comprising different legal entities, and bound together by relationships of control.

The idea that assets can be 'controlled' without necessarily being 'owned' is familiar enough to commercial lawyers and managers. A company may enjoy 'control' over a foreign subsidiary notwithstanding that it only has a small equity interest in that subsidiary. The extent of control enjoyed over a part-owned subsidiary may be dependent, not on the size of the shareholding, but on the voting rights attached to

---

[184] OECD Guidelines (2001) 40 ILM 237, Part 1 (Concepts and Principles), para. 3.

[185] Ibid.

[186] For an overview of the different theories of multinational organisation and behaviour, including the most influential of these, 'transaction cost' theory, see Dunning, *Multinationals and the Global Economy*, chapter 4; J. Cantwell, 'A Survey of Theories of International Production' in C. Pitelis and R. Sugden (eds.), *The Nature of the Transnational Firm* (London: Routledge, 1991); R. Caves, *Multinational Enterprise and Economic Analysis* (Cambridge: Cambridge University Press, 1996).

the relevant shares, the size of the shareholding relative to that of other shareholders, and contractual arrangements between shareholders. Companies can also control each other in other ways. Franchising and distribution agreements will often contain very detailed provisions as to how the contracted-out business is to be run, the performance of which is closely monitored by the grantor of the franchise or distribution rights. The need to manage risks associated with a long-term supply agreement may lead to a purchaser being given rights to be consulted on and to participate in certain of its supplier's business decisions, arguably another form of 'control'. 'Control' relationships may exist even in the absence of any express provisions in a contract: relative bargaining positions, surrounding market conditions such as the availability of alternative resources or suppliers, and the practicalities of enforcing laws and agreements may all affect the dynamics of commercial relationships.

Statutory definitions of group enterprises all involve different degrees of arbitrariness and flexibility. A fairly common device is for a prescribed shareholding to give rise to a presumption of control, which is then open to rebuttal.[187] These definitions may not capture all the relevant relationships and participants in a given case, but instead reflect a choice about the need for legal certainty in a particular context, versus the need for flexibility. Where the definition of the 'group' is necessary as part of an anti-avoidance scheme, the law will seek to identify the 'control' relationships through which legal obligations might be evaded. But in some cases it may not be possible to define all of the relationships that might be relevant and still give regulated entities the certainty they require to carry on their business efficiently and in compliance with the law. Certainty is a particularly important consideration where the consequences of a breach are potentially serious for a company and its directors. In these circumstances, considerations of justice and fairness would tend to favour a simpler, though perhaps more arbitrary, definition of the relevant 'control' relationships. In other contexts, company reporting requirements for example, policy-makers and legislatures may place more emphasis on the substance of the 'control' relationship than its form. Additional considerations include practical issues such as subsequent monitoring and enforcement by regulatory authorities. Policy-makers may consider, in the particular case, that a limited regime that

---

[187] See, for example, the definitions of 'subsidiary undertaking' and 'participating interest' under the UK Companies Act 1985, section 260(2).

can be operated cost-effectively and credibly is preferable to one that is overly complex.

To summarise, although multinationals are not 'legal persons' in the conventional sense, they can be legally defined by reference to 'control' relationships. The relevance of the different 'control' relationships that make up the enterprise, however derived, will depend on the legal context, taking account of the objectives of the regulation and also other considerations, such as the practicalities of monitoring and enforcement and the need for legal certainty.

Allocating liabilities

For enforcement purposes it is necessary for regulations to prescribe, not only the *boundaries* of the enterprise, but also which of its constituent entities are to be held liable in the event of a breach and on what basis. The starting point in any discussion about the allocation of liability within group enterprises is the principle of 'separate corporate personality'. Under this principle, each member of a group enterprise is treated as legally distinct from the others (a 'separate legal person'), regardless of the links (e.g. of ownership or control) that may exist between them. It follows that, as a general rule, a parent company is not liable for claims made against its subsidiary. In the case of a claim for damages for injury or harm, the plaintiff may only claim against the entities within the multinational group that were *legally* responsible.[188] While there are grounds on which the legal distinction between a parent company and its subsidiary may be disregarded (called 'piercing the corporate veil'), the circumstances in which national courts are prepared to do so are extremely limited.[189]

A number of writers, especially Blumberg, have criticised the application of the principle of 'separate corporate personality' to corporate groups.[190] Certainly, the ability of multinationals to shift resources 'across the corporate veil' can create real regulatory problems.[191] In addition, as will be discussed further in chapter 5, the doctrine of

---

[188] See further chapter 5 below.

[189] Dine, *Companies, International Trade and Human Rights*, pp. 58–62.

[190] P. Blumberg, 'Limited Liability and Corporate Groups' (1986) 11 *Journal of Corporations Law* 573; Blumberg, *The Multinational Challenge*. See also P. Blumberg, 'The American Law of Corporate Groups' and T. Hadden, 'Regulating Corporate Groups: an International Perspective', both in J. McCahery, S. Picciotto and C. Scott (eds.), *Corporate Control and Accountability: Changing Structures and the Dynamics of Regulation* (Oxford: Clarendon Press, 1993).

[191] Dine, *Corporate Groups*, esp. chapter 5.

'separate corporate personality' can place significant obstacles in the way of those seeking to recoup their losses for personal injury or environmental harm caused by the activities of multinationals (the so-called 'involuntary creditors').[192] This has led Blumberg and others to argue that the law ought to pay greater attention to the 'economic reality' behind groups of companies and be more ready to disregard the technical legal barriers erected between different legal entities. This approach is often referred to as 'enterprise theory'.

Domestic company and insolvency laws contain a number of examples of cases where law-makers have been prepared to 'pierce the corporate veil' by legislation.[193] In the UK, for example, a parent company can be ordered to make a contribution to the assets of an insolvent subsidiary on the basis that it was acting as a 'shadow director'.[194] Under the Companies Act 1993 of New Zealand, the courts have the discretion to make orders requiring contributions from other group members based on factors such as the extent to which those other companies (usually the parent company) were involved in the management of the insolvent entity, and the extent to which their own conduct gave rise to the insolvency.[195]

While group liability regimes focus most frequently on the parent company,[196] other variations are possible. Under German company law rules,[197] known as 'Konzernrecht', the German parent company is entitled to manage the group in such a way that the subsidiaries' interests are subordinated to the interests of the group as a whole; the quid pro quo for this flexibility is that the parent may be jointly liable with its controlled subsidiaries for the subsidiary's debts. This would mean that, in the event of the insolvency of one or more of the subsidiaries, creditors of the insolvent subsidiary companies may have a claim against the assets of both the subsidiary and the parent.

This German law provides an example of a statutory framework for the recognition, for limited purposes, of group enterprises. Under this regime, membership of the enterprise is defined either up front by the enterprise itself (through a registration system), or by the regulatory

---

[192] P. Blumberg, 'Asserting Human Rights against Multinational Corporations under United States Law: Conceptual and Procedural Problems' (2002) 50 *AJCL* 493.

[193] Blumberg, *The Multinational Challenge*; Dine, *Corporate Groups*, chapter 2.

[194] UK Companies Act 1985, section 741.

[195] Companies Act 1993 (New Zealand), sections 271 and 272.

[196] K. Hopt, 'Legal Elements and Policy Decisions in Regulating Groups of Companies' in C. Schmitthoff and F. Wooldridge (eds.), *Groups of Companies* (London: Sweet & Maxwell, 1991).

[197] Joint Stock Corporation Act 1965 (Germany).

authorities on a 'case by case' basis. [198] But to suggest that innovations of this kind are part of a wider trend in favour of 'enterprise' principles (and away from traditional 'entity' principles of company law)[199] is probably an exaggeration.[200] Even if courts and legislatures were prepared to consider the possibility, using 'enterprise' principles as the rule rather than the exception poses a number of practical difficulties, not least of which concerns the definition of the 'economic entity'[201] and the legal position of minority shareholders, past and future shareholders and corporate shareholders that enter and then exit the group.[202] The concept of 'limited liability' offers significant advantages in terms of convenience, efficiency and legal certainty, making '[a] radical abandonment of the traditional approach to group liability . . . unlikely'.[203]

Ordinarily, then, the multinational does not have any distinct legal status, and each of its members is treated as legally distinct from each other.[204] Interestingly, though, there is some support for 'enterprise theory' in the definition of 'transnational corporation' used in the 'Norms on the Responsibilities of Transnational Corporations and Other Business Enterprises with Regard to Human Rights' developed by the UN Sub-Commission on the Promotion and Protection of Human Rights (the 'UN Norms').[205] In this document, the 'transnational corporation' is defined as 'an economic entity operating in more than one country or a cluster of economic entities operating in two or more countries – whatever their legal form, whether in their home country or country of activity, and whether taken individually or collectively'.[206]

---

[198] For an example of a regulatory regime that permits the registration of *non-equity* (i.e. contract-based) business forms, see Council Regulation 2137/85/EEC of 25 July 1985 on the European Economic Interest Groupings OJ 1985 No. L199/1, 31 July 1985. The legislation provides for the establishment of a business vehicle known as the 'European Economic Interest Group', a non-profit-making entity constituted by contract between its members. Upon registration it enjoys, similar to a company, a legal existence separate from its members.

[199] See Blumberg, *The Multinational Challenge.*

[200] See further Muchlinski, *Multinational Enterprises and the Law*, pp. 328–9.

[201] Ibid., p. 330.

[202] D. Prentice, 'Some Comments on the Law of Groups' in J. McCahery, S. Picciotto and C. Scott (eds.), *Corporate Control and Accountability* (Oxford: Clarendon Press, 1993), p. 372.

[203] Muchlinski, *Multinational Enterprises and the Law*, p. 329.

[204] However, as will be discussed further in chapter 5, this should not preclude parent company liability on other grounds.

[205] Adopted by the UN Sub-Commission on the Protection and Promotion of Human Rights, 13 August 2003, UN Doc. E/CN.4/Sub.2/2003/12/Rev.2 (2003). See further pp. 261–2 below.

[206] Ibid., para. 20.

Administration, supervision and enforcement

A further issue that needs to be addressed when devising international regulatory regimes for multinationals is how best to allocate supervisory and (where applicable) enforcement functions between national and international institutions. In other words, which is the most appropriate body to develop and administer a particular international regulatory regime? Should it be the home state, the host state or some other international body? Obviously, these questions raise important issues of sovereignty and international justice, themes that recur throughout this book.

As will be discussed further in chapter 2, classical international law principles give priority to 'host state' regulation of multinationals. In theory, each state has the right to regulate multinational activities within its own territory as it sees fit, subject to any overriding obligations under international law. However, as is often pointed out, many states (especially the least developed) simply do not have the necessary resources, systems or political will to regulate CSR issues effectively.[207] Given the current lack of machinery at international level to oversee the activities of multinationals,[208] it is not surprising that many CSR campaigners see home state regulation as the best short-term regulatory option.[209] However, there are definitional, political and legal problems with this approach. First, the 'home state' of a multinational is not always easy to identify.[210] And, even if a home state can be identified with a reasonable amount of certainty, why should this state, rather than any other, be responsible for regulating the target multinational? These questions are considered further in chapter 4. Second, international law imposes restrictions on the extent to which any state can regulate industrial and commercial activities outside its territorial boundaries. The nature and extent of these restrictions is considered in more detail in chapter 3.

Summary

The multi-jurisdictional nature of multinational activities, and the fact that multinationals are made up of more than one legal entity operating within often very complex organisational structures, pose real regulatory difficulties. Key practical problems include defining the target

---

[207] Joseph, 'Taming the Leviathans'.   [208] See chapter 6 below.

[209] Recent years have seen a number of new regulatory proposals for extraterritorial regulation of multinational activities by the home state. A. McBeth, 'A Look at Corporate Code of Conduct Legislation' (2004) 3(3) *CWLR* 222. See further pp. 164–70 below.

[210] See further pp. 146–51 below.

enterprise, explaining the allocation of liabilities within that enterprise and identifying (or creating) the appropriate supervisory institutions. When defining multinationals for legal purposes there will always be a tension between two competing considerations: the need for flexibility versus the need for certainty. Where a regulatory regime includes sanctions for non-compliance, it will be necessary to define which of the constituent entities of a multinational will be liable in the event of a breach, and on what basis. Should this be the legal entity (or entities) geographically closest to the breach, or the parent company, or both? Should the liability of the parent company be 'strict' (on the basis of its role as 'co-ordinator' or 'overseer' of the international operations of the group) or 'fault-based'? Finally, the jurisdictional basis of any 'home state' regulation must be clearly defined and understood. These problems, and how they have so far been approached in practice, are considered further in later chapters.

Conclusion

The CSR movement has been a hugely important social movement and has had a significant impact on the social and political landscape against which multinationals operate. Its main achievement so far has been to persuade companies, small and large, that they do have responsibilities, as 'corporate citizens', beyond mere profit creation. However, the regulatory debate – i.e. is further regulation needed and, if so, how might this be achieved? – goes on.

Unfortunately misunderstandings, about both the nature of CSR and how regulation works in practice, have threatened to derail this extremely important debate. First, and contrary to the claims of many business representatives, CSR is not purely 'voluntary' and cannot be so easily separated from matters of legal compliance. Instead, it encompasses all aspects of corporate decision-making, including the way companies interpret their legal obligations and enforce their legal rights. Second, much of the discussion on the future of regulation in the CSR field (the 'voluntary versus mandatory' debate) reflects a very limited understanding of what regulation actually is, focusing on traditional prescriptive methods and overlooking, to a large extent, the regulatory potential of other options.

Although many companies appear to be making a genuine effort to reduce their social and environmental impacts, calls for greater regulatory supervision, of multinationals in particular, have not gone away.

The past few years have seen a number of new regulatory proposals at national level, including some particularly ambitious (though so far unsuccessful) attempts to develop extraterritorial regimes specifically aimed at improving the social and environmental accountability of multinational groups. These and other initiatives will be discussed further in chapter 4. However, it is worth noting in the meantime that devising regulatory regimes for multinationals is not a simple matter. Legally speaking, the multinational is a difficult concept to pin down. In addition, the fact that an enterprise operates in more than one jurisdiction raises a specific set of legal and practical issues that need to be analysed properly if a regulatory regime is to be credible and workable.

International law has a potentially vital role to play in supporting regulatory responses to multinationals, and the health, safety and environmental inequalities exposed by their activities. However, this cannot be appreciated fully unless traditional preconceptions about the nature of 'regulation' are dispensed with. This theme will be taken up again in later chapters. First, though, it is necessary to explore the basic features of international law, its key attributes and constraints, and the implications of these for future international regulation in the CSR field.

2 Multinationals under international law

What is international law? Where does it come from? To whom is it addressed? And to what extent does international law already regulate the behaviour of multinationals?

The aim of this chapter is to explore the relevance of international law to the CSR performance of multinationals, in terms of both the creation of standards and their enforcement. As will be seen, international law, as a determinedly 'state-centred' system, does not provide ready-made solutions to the social and environmental problems posed by multinationals. Many writers point to a 'mismatch' between the international legal system – built around the notion of a society of 'sovereign equals', each with jurisdiction over a defined patch of territory – and the reality of transnational corporate activities. How can such a system provide an adequate framework for the international regulation of CSR?

Certainly, multinationals pose real challenges to the international legal system. But these challenges are by no means insurmountable. As far as future opportunities for international regulation are concerned, two developments are potentially significant: first, the growing conviction that private entities (traditionally referred to as 'objects' rather than 'subjects' of international law) are themselves subject to 'direct' obligations under international human rights law and, second, growing demands on states as regulators of private enterprise.

This chapter begins with a short explanation of how international law operates, and the main sources of its legal rules. It then considers the concept of international legal personality. In particular, how can something that seems to defy legal definition be said to be an 'international legal person'? It is important, though, not to confuse problems of definition with problems of theory. There is actually nothing *in principle* that prevents the international community from conferring some degree of international legal personality on multinationals. Indeed, many would argue that this has already occurred.

The next question to consider, then, is the extent to which multinationals may already be subject to *direct* obligations under international law. Given the staunchly deregulatory stance of most prominent home states of multinationals, it is not surprising that the question of the direct liability for multinationals under human rights law has received so much attention of late, though the law on this issue is only in the early stages of development. On the other hand, it is clear that states are required to take some steps to protect against human rights violations by private parties, which gives rise to the interesting possibility that home states may be subject to regulatory obligations under international human rights law in respect of multinationals over which they have 'jurisdiction'. However, it is far from clear to what extent home states are required to guard against human rights violations that occur *beyond* their territorial boundaries (and within the territory of other states).

Finally, the role of non-state actors in international law-making is considered. Because of the 'state-centredness' of international law, there is an understandable tendency among practitioners and academics to focus on the acts of governments and public authorities in discerning what the international law on a subject might be. However, this approach does not really do justice to the richness of activity on CSR issues at both domestic and transnational levels. A 'bottom up' approach to international law, on the other hand, offers a framework for understanding the relevance of other, self-regulatory and 'non-binding' initiatives that would otherwise (under traditional international legal theory) be accorded only peripheral status, at best.

What is international law?

International law refers to the rights and obligations that govern and emanate from relations between states. International law is often divided into two separate disciplines: 'private international law' (or 'conflict of laws') and 'public international law'. As discussed in chapter 3, private international law governs the way in which courts approach private law cases with a 'foreign element' and is, strictly speaking, a field of domestic law.[1] Public international law, referred to in this book

---

[1] See further p. 113 below.

simply as 'international law', is a separate legal system in which states are both the rule-makers and its main 'subjects'. This idea of states as both law-makers and subjects is why international law is often described as a 'horizontal' legal system, in contrast to the 'vertical' or 'hierarchical' operation of domestic law systems. This lack of an overarching legislature or enforcement mechanism (coupled with the undeniable fact that states do flout international law from time to time with apparent impunity) means that it is still common to hear international law described as a 'primitive' legal system or even 'not really law at all'. However, both of these observations reflect a rather narrow perception of what is meant by 'law'. Obviously, legal obligations do not depend on their enforcement for their *existence* and, moreover, 'no system of law depends, or can, in the last resort, depend for its authority solely on the chances of enforcement'.[2] Whether international law is viewed as a set of rules or as a decision-making 'process', [3] '[t]he real foundation of the authority of international law resides . . . in the fact that the States making up the international society recognise it as binding upon them, and, moreover, as a system that *ipso facto* binds them *as* members of the society irrespective of their individual wills.'[4]

Who makes international law?

International law is made by states, working bilaterally, multilaterally or through international organisations.[5] However, unlike most domestic legal systems, there is no central law-making authority. Moreover, the principle of 'sovereign equality' means that no one state can prescribe laws for any other without their consent. There is, however, a special set of rules in international law known as rules of jus cogens or 'peremptory norms'. A peremptory norm is defined as a rule which is 'accepted and recognised by the international community of States as a whole as a norm from which no derogation is permitted and which can be modified only by a subsequent norm of general international law having the same

---

[2] G. Fitzmaurice, 'The Foundation of the Authority of International Law and the Problem of Enforcement' (1956) 19 *MLR* 1, 8.

[3] R. Higgins, *Problems and Process: International Law and How We Use It* (Oxford: Clarendon Press, 1994).

[4] Fitzmaurice, 'The Authority of International Law', 8.

[5] But this is not to suggest that other entities, NGOs in particular, do not play a significant role in the development of new international law principles and norms. See further pp. 93–102 below.

character'.[6] Prohibitions on the use of force, slave trading and genocide are generally regarded as rules of jus cogens.[7]

As rules are derived from unwritten sources (e.g. custom, general principles of law) as well as written sources (e.g. treaties), finding the law and applying it to a particular situation is often difficult. Article 38(1) of the Statute of the International Court of Justice is generally regarded as the best and most authoritative description of the sources of international law. This provision directs the court 'whose function is to decide [disputes] in accordance with international law' to apply:

(a) international conventions [i.e. treaties] . . . (b) international custom, as evidence of general practice accepted by law; (c) the general principles of law recognised by civilised nations; [and] (d) . . . judicial decisions and the teachings of the most highly qualified publicists of various nations, as a subsidiary means for the determination of rules of law.[8]

The two most significant sources of international law in the CSR field are custom and treaties.

Custom

Custom can give rise to a rule of international law where there is 'constant and uniform usage practised by the States in question'[9] coupled with opinio juris, that is, a 'belief' by states 'that they are conforming to what amounts to a legal obligation'.[10] In other words, there must be both 'conduct and conviction'[11] from the states concerned. State practice encompasses not only executive acts, such as unilateral or multilateral statements or agreements, but an array of other state functions, documents and activities such as national legislation, judicial decisions, voting patterns within international bodies, official manuals and other policy statements. However, identifying a pattern of behaviour through state practice is one thing – proving that it has passed into international law, and is therefore legally binding upon all states, is quite another.

---

[6] Vienna Convention on the Law of Treaties, Vienna, 23 May 1969, in force 27 January 1980, 1155 UNTS 331; (1969) 8 ILM 679; UKTS (1980) 58, Article 53.

[7] M. Akehurst, 'The Hierarchy of the Sources of International Law' (1974–5) 47 BYIL 273.

[8] Article 38.

[9] *Asylum Case (Colombia v. Peru)* [1950] ICJ Reps 266, 276–7; *Anglo-Norwegian Fisheries Case (UK v. Norway)* [1951] ICJ Reps 116.

[10] *North Sea Continental Shelf Cases (Federal Republic of Germany v. Denmark; Federal Republic of Germany v. Netherlands)* [1969] ICJ Reps 3, 44.

[11] P. Birnie and A. Boyle, *International Law and the Environment*, 2nd edition (Oxford: Oxford University Press, 2002), p. 16.

First, it is necessary to demonstrate a sufficient level of international consensus around the new practice or rule.[12] But with such diversity among states in terms of cultural background, history, stages of development and vested interests, differences in approach and perspective are, of course, inevitable. How close must the consensus around a custom be? According to the ICJ in the *North Sea Continental Shelf* cases, state practice must be 'both extensive and virtually uniform in the sense of the provision invoked'.[13] However, occasional deviations by states from a particular custom do not necessarily affect the development of the law if those deviations are generally treated by other states as 'breaches of a rule, not as indications of a recognition of a new [i.e. different] rule'.[14] Then there is the question of the relative weight to be given to the views and practices of different states. In theory, the principle of 'sovereign equality' means that each state ought to have an equal say in the creation of international law through custom. However, in practice, some issues will be more relevant and pressing to one group of states than another[15] and, where this is the case, courts are likely to take particular notice of the statements and practices of those states most affected by the proposed new rule.[16]

A second area of uncertainty concerns the length of time required for state practice to become a legally binding obligation. While it has sometimes been necessary to demonstrate a long history of compliance, it is recognised in ICJ decisions that this is not an absolute requirement. Instead, as was put in the *North Sea Continental Shelf* cases, 'even without the passage of any considerable period of time, a very widespread and representative participation in the convention might suffice of itself, provided it included that of States whose interests were specifically affected'.[17] In new areas of international law – space law, for instance – it is possible for new customary rules to develop very quickly.[18]

---

[12] As a general rule, state practice must be international for a customary rule to emerge, although the ICJ has been prepared to consider the possibility of 'regional' customary law. See *Asylum Case*, n. 9 above; *Right of Passage over Indian Territory Case* (1960) ICJ Reps 6. See generally M. Shaw, *International Law*, 5th edition (Cambridge: Cambridge University Press, 2003), pp. 87–8.

[13] [1969] ICJ Reps. 3, 43.   [14] *Nicaragua Case (Merits)* [1986] ICJ Reps 14, 98.

[15] For instance, the division of resources on the continental shelf will clearly be of greater concern to those states with maritime boundaries than to landlocked states.

[16] *North Sea Continental Shelf Cases*, n. 10 above, 42; See also H. Lauterpacht, 'Sovereignty over Submarine Areas' [1950] 27 *BYIL* 376, 394.

[17] *North Sea Continental Shelf Cases*, n. 10 above, 42.

[18] B. Cheng, 'United Nations Resolutions on Outer Space: "Instant" International Customary Law?' (1965) 5 *Indian JIL* 23; Shaw, *International Law*, p. 76.

Finally, and often most problematic, is the question of opinio juris. As noted above, it is not sufficient merely to show a pattern of behaviour; states must also have indicated their consent to the new customary rule and their recognition that they are legally bound by it.[19] As the court put it in the *Nicaragua* case:

for a new customary rule to be formed, not only must the acts concerned 'amount to a settled practice' but they must be accompanied by the *opinio juris sive necessitatis*. Either the States taking such action or other States in a position to react to it, must have behaved so that their conduct is 'evidence of a belief that this practice is rendered obligatory by the existence of a rule of law requiring it'. The need for such a belief, i.e. the existence of a subjective element, is implicit in the very notion of *opinio juris sive necessitatis*.[20]

Logically, this would mean that a 'persistent objector' to a new rule would not be bound by it.[21] On the other hand, most writers take the view that it is not necessary for all states to express their positive acceptance of a new rule before it can be regarded as customary international law. Instead, it is possible for consent to be inferred from the apparent acquiescence of affected states.[22]

Clearly, the subjectivity of opinio juris makes proving a new rule of international law extremely difficult. As is often pointed out, states may have a variety of reasons for behaving as they do – convenience, diplomacy, economic and political self-interest, to name just a few – which may have nothing to do with a sense of legal obligation. It is recognised that proving the subjective motives underlying any one instance of state practice is often a difficult, if not impossible, task.[23] Determining whether or not there has been acquiescence from states in the development of a new customary rule can also be difficult: 'States fail to protest for very many reasons. A state might not wish to give offence gratuitously or it might wish to reinforce political ties or other diplomatic

---

[19] In this way, custom is distinguished from patterns of behaviour that have arisen out of mere convenience, or courtesy, to which binding legal obligation is attached.

[20] *Nicaragua Case (Merits)*, n. 14 above, 108–9.

[21] See further J. Charney, 'The Persistent Objector Rule and the Development of Customary International Law' (1985) 56 BYIL 1.

[22] I. MacGibbon, 'The Scope of Acquiescence in International Law' (1954) 31 BYIL 143. However, a state cannot be said to have 'acquiesced' in the development of a new rule of customary international law unless it has actual or constructive knowledge of the proposed new rule. See *Anglo-Norwegian Fisheries Case*, n. 9 above. See also Shaw, *International Law*, p. 85.

[23] See, for instance, the comments of Judge Tanaka and Judge (ad hoc) Sorensen in the *North Sea Continental Shelf Cases*, n. 10 above, 176, 246.

and political considerations may be relevant. It could be that to protest over every single act with which a state does not agree would be an excessive requirement.'[24]

This subjective element also makes it difficult to be clear about the point at which a claim or practice has passed from mere custom into customary international law. Often, the question of whether a novel practice is a breach of an existing rule, or the establishment of a new one, is not one that can be answered definitively.[25] In practice, international tribunals do not accept claims of new customary rules readily, and the party seeking to rely on a new legal principle will generally face an uphill struggle. There may be a long period of academic speculation about a new rule before it is eventually confirmed. However, if it is possible to show an overall picture of acceptance, commitment and compliance among states, then an international tribunal may be persuaded that a new rule of international law has emerged.

International responses to environmental problems have had a significant impact on the development of customary international law. Two propositions, in particular, are now widely believed to have achieved customary status, namely: '(i) that states have a duty to prevent, reduce, and control pollution and environmental harm, and (ii) a duty to co-operate in mitigating environmental risks and emergencies, through notification, consultation, negotiation, and in appropriate cases, environmental impact assessment.'[26] Other principles which arguably have a bearing on the scope of states' international obligations with respect to the environment include the 'precautionary principle'[27] and the

---

[24] Shaw, *International Law*, pp. 85–6.

[25] International lawyers have long been troubled by the apparent 'circularity' in the requirement for opinio juris, i.e. 'How can custom create law if its psychological component requires action in conscious accordance with law pre-existing the action?' A. D'Amato, *The Concept of Custom in International Law* (Ithaca, NY: Cornell University Press, 1971), pp. 66–8. See further O. Elias, 'The Nature of the Subjective Element in Customary International Law' (1995) 44 *ICLQ* 501. Shaw responds: 'one has to treat the matter in terms of a process whereby states behave in a certain way in the belief that such behaviour is law or is becoming law. It will then depend upon how other states react as to whether this process of legislation is accepted or rejected'; Shaw, *International Law*, p. 83.

[26] Birnie and Boyle, *International Law and the Environment*, pp. 104–5.

[27] I.e. 'Where there are threats of serious or irreversible damage, lack of full scientific certainty shall not be used as a reason for postponing cost-effective measures to prevent environmental degradation'; 1992 Declaration of the UN Conference on Environment and Development, Rio de Janeiro, 13 June 1992, UN Doc. A/CONF.151/26/Rev. 1, Vol. 1, Annex I ('Rio Declaration'); (1992) 31 ILM 874, principle 15.

principle of 'common but differentiated responsibility',[28] although these do not have the same normative force as the principles on transboundary harm.[29] On environmental matters, customary law is potentially an important source of regulatory obligations *of states* in the CSR field. However, it is doubtful at present that a home state's obligations to prevent transboundary harm impose any requirements of ongoing *extraterritorial* regulation with respect to multinationals 'based' in their respective jurisdictions.[30] As chapter 4 will explore in more detail, where states have begun to implement policies in relation to the CSR performance of multinationals abroad, there is little evidence so far that this is being done out of a sense of legal obligation. (Many would argue that the clear preference of most home states for a 'voluntary' approach to international CSR-related problems would suggest quite the opposite.) But this is not to say that new customary obligations could not develop in future. As chapter 4 will show, recent state practice in this field suggests that some home states are taking more than a passive interest in the foreign CSR performance of multinationals based in their respective jurisdictions and are showing a willingness to confront international CSR issues that would have been unimaginable only a decade ago.

As a method of law-making, custom has some important advantages over other methods. Customary legal principles, and their applications, are developed over time as needs dictate. Unlike law-making by international treaty, states do not need to negotiate a detailed regime up front, nor do they go through a formal ratification process, with all the political risks that this may entail. The (usually) gradual process of customary law-making gives states a period in which to adjust to new rules. Moreover, the lack of a requirement for any express acceptance of a new principle of law can help ensure that 'the inactive are carried along by the active'.[31] On the other hand, customary legal principles can take many years to develop and, even then, may be too vague to predict what their application in a given set of circumstances might be. Where a specific outcome is sought, within a particular time frame, or where clarity of obligations is needed, states will often move to legislate through an international treaty rather than rely on customary international law.

---

[28] Ibid., principle 7.

[29] On the 'precautionary principle', see Birnie and Boyle, *International Law and the Environment*, pp. 118–21. On the issue of 'common but differentiated responsibility', see ibid., p. 103.

[30] See further pp. 158–60 below.

[31] Birnie and Boyle, *International Law and the Environment*, p. 16.

Treaties

Treaties are agreements between states setting out their obligations towards one another.[32] They are often compared with contractual arrangements at domestic level and, indeed, many aspects of treaty law are drawn from contractual principles.[33] Treaties may be 'bilateral' (i.e. between two states) or 'multilateral' (i.e. with more than two signatories). However, unlike customary international law, a state must expressly and positively consent to treaty obligations, through a signing and ratification process, before it is legally bound by the new regime.[34]

The amount of effort invested by states in treaty-making has increased exponentially with 'globalisation'. With the growth of international commerce, communications and trade, treaties have become crucial as a means of co-ordinating state responses to cross-border issues and problems. Multilateral treaties now govern many activities taken for granted in modern life, such as international communications, post and travel. Treaties have been used to address a number of serious international environmental problems such as air and marine pollution, trade in endangered species and transboundary movements of hazardous wastes.[35] More recently, treaty regimes have emerged in relation to other CSR-related issues such as child labour and tobacco marketing.[36] Some groups, FoE in particular, have argued the need for an overarching treaty on CSR, setting out the responsibilities of directors and companies in more detail, and providing for sanctions in case these obligations are breached. These proposals are discussed in more detail in chapter 6.[37]

---

[32] The 1969 Vienna Convention on the Law of Treaties, n. 6 above, defines a 'treaty' as 'an international agreement concluded between States in written form and governed by international law; whether embodied in a single instrument or in two or more related instruments and whatever its particular designation': Article 2(1)(a). Other terms sometimes used for treaties include 'conventions', 'international agreements', 'pacts' and 'protocols'.

[33] See, for instance, the various grounds for invalidity or termination of a treaty, which include concepts such as mistake, fraud and fundamental breach. See 1969 Vienna Convention on the Law of Treaties, n. 6 above, Articles 48, 49 and 60. Unlike contract law, however, there is no requirement for 'consideration' (i.e. an exchange of obligations) for state parties to be bound.

[34] See 1969 Vienna Convention on the Law of Treaties, Article 11. Although non-parties to a convention will be bound by its provisions to the extent that they reflect customary international law. See p. 69 below.

[35] See Birnie and Boyle, *International Law and the Environment*, esp. chapters 7, 8, 10 and 12. See further pp. 292–5 below.

[36] See further pp. 289–90 and 290–1 below.   [37] See pp. 278–9 below.

Relationship between custom and treaties

Treaties and custom are regarded as separate sources of international law. As discussed above, customary international law is normally binding on all states,[38] but treaties are only capable of binding the states that choose to become party to them. Nevertheless, treaties also play a vital role in the development of customary law.

First, treaties have been widely used as a method of declaring, codifying, clarifying and amplifying existing customary law. The 1961 Vienna Convention on Diplomatic Relations[39] and the 1969 Vienna Convention on the Law of Treaties[40] are often cited as examples of treaties of this kind. Second, a treaty can cause emerging customary principles to 'crystallise'. Endorsement of a legal principle by a wide range of states through the treaty signing and ratification process may provide the evidence of state practice and opinio juris needed to confirm that a developing principle of customary international law has finally passed into law. Third, treaty obligations may come to form part of customary international law if, for instance, they are subsequently followed by a sufficient number of states (non-parties as well as parties) and this state practice has been motivated by opinio juris.[41]

Theoretically, neither of these two sources of international law – custom or treaty – is superior to the other. Instead, customary law and treaty law are said to operate in parallel. As the court put it in the *Nicaragua* case, 'customary international law continues to exist and to apply separately from international treaty law, even where the two categories of law have identical content'.[42] However, in practice, proving that a treaty obligation exists will usually be far more straightforward than proving a new principle of customary law.

'Soft law'

'Soft law' in the international law context refers to principles and policies which have been negotiated and agreed between states, or promulgated by international institutions, but which are not mandated by law

---

[38] But see n. 12 above.

[39] Vienna Convention on Diplomatic Relations, Vienna, 18 April 1961, in force 24 April 1964, 500 UNTS 95; UKTS (1965) 19.

[40] See n. 6 above.

[41] See *North Sea Continental Shelf Cases*, n. 10 above. Although note that the ICJ considered that 'it would . . . be necessary that the provision concerned should, at all events potentially, be of a fundamentally norm-creating character such as could be regarded as forming the basis of a general rule of law', 41–2.

[42] *Nicaragua Case (Merits)*, n. 14 above, 96.

or subject to any formal enforcement mechanisms. 'Soft law' instruments are given a range of titles, typically 'codes of practice', 'guidelines', 'recommendations' or 'declarations', but, whatever the terminology, the crucial distinction between a 'soft law' instrument and a treaty is that compliance with the former is 'voluntary' (at least in the legal sense). To date, states and international bodies have generally preferred to document their CSR-related policies, principles and aspirations in 'soft law' instruments rather than by way of treaties. Notable 'soft law' statements on CSR include, of course, the 1976 OECD Guidelines for Multinational Enterprises[43] (substantially revised in 2000),[44] the 1977 ILO Tripartite Declaration on the Declaration of Principles concerning Multinational Enterprises and Social Policy,[45] the UN Secretary General's 'Global Compact'[46] and, most recently, the UN Norms.[47] These and other examples will be discussed further in chapter 6.

To many commentators and practitioners, the term 'soft law' is a misnomer. Soft law is not 'law' in the sense that it is immediately binding on states, individuals or institutions. Yet it does represent a form of 'regulation' to the extent that has a bearing on choices and behaviour.[48] More than this, soft law instruments have a potentially vital role to play in the development of international law on CSR.[49]

First of all, soft law instruments can be a way of galvanising support for a particular programme or policy. Projects of this kind can help to focus thinking about certain issues, to clarify positions and to develop understanding between states. The fact that soft law instruments are not immediately binding on states can be an important advantage in areas where there may be political cost. As Birnie and Boyle have explained:

---

[43] (1976) 15 ILM 969.   [44] (2001) 40 ILM 237.   [45] (1978) 17 ILM 422.

[46] See http://www.globalcompact.org.

[47] UN Norms on the Responsibilities of Transnational Corporations and other Business Enterprises with Regard to Human Rights, adopted by the UN Sub-Commission on the Protection and Promotion of Human Rights, 13 August 2003, UN Doc. E/CN.4/Sub.2/2003/12/Rev.2.

[48] See pp. 41–2 above.

[49] On 'soft law' generally, see D. Shelton, 'Introduction: Law, Non-Law and the Problem of Soft Law' in D. Shelton (ed.), *Commitment and Compliance: the Role of Non-Binding Norms in the International Legal System* (Oxford: Oxford University Press, 2000); C. Chinkin. 'The Challenge of Soft Law: Development and Change in International Law' (1989) 38 *ICLQ* 850; T. Gruchella-Wesierski, 'A Framework for Understanding Soft Law' (1984) 30 *McGill LJ* 37; H. Baade, 'Legal Effects of Codes of Conduct' in N. Horn (ed.), *Legal Problems of Codes of Conduct for Multinational Enterprises* (The Hague: Kluwer, 1980); M. Bothe, 'Legal and Non-Legal Norms – a Meaningful Distinction in International Law?' (1980) 11 *NYIL* 65; I. Seidl-Hohenveldern, 'International Economic Soft Law' (1980) 163 *Receuil des Cours* 164.

Treaties may be a more useful medium for codifying the law, or for concerted law-making, but many either do not enter into force, or, more frequently, do so for only a limited number of parties which do not necessarily include the states whose involvement is most vital to the achievement of their purposes. This is especially true of environmental issues, whose regulation may require modification of economic policies and be perceived as inhibiting development and growth. Treaties thus present problems as vehicles for changing or developing the law.[50]

Soft law initiatives are a way of testing attitudes, and the strength of a possible consensus, in cases where the negotiation of a treaty may be impractical or premature. But they may also represent the groundwork for a future 'hard law' treaty regime. Alternatively, they can become a catalyst for the development of future customary norms, either as evidence of 'state practice' or, more loosely, as a marker of current expectations and future aspirations. As Chinkin writes:

Participants in the international arena need to be able to anticipate the action and reactions of other participants so as to make reasoned choices about their behaviour. To do this effectively, the instruments of soft law cannot be ignored. They provide for the shaping and sharing of values and so create expectations as to the restraints States will accept upon their behaviour and will urge or impose upon others within their jurisdiction. They must be assumed to have been concluded in good faith to determine some restraint upon States' economic activities.[51]

Each of the OECD Guidelines, the ILO Tripartite Declaration and the UN's Global Compact principles contains an express statement to the effect that no legal obligations are intended.[52] However, the description of an international instrument as 'non-binding' does not mean that its contents are not legally significant. The 1992 Rio Declaration,[53] for instance, though technically a 'soft law' instrument, sets out several principles that are now widely regarded as part of customary law.[54]

---

[50] Birnie and Boyle, *International Law and the Environment*, p. 25.
[51] Chinkin, 'The Challenge of Soft Law', 865–6.
[52] See, for instance, OECD Guidelines, (2001) 40 ILM 237, Part I (Concepts and Principles), para. 1.
[53] See n. 27 above.
[54] Birnie and Boyle, *International Law and the Environment*, p. 109. On questions of transboundary harm and environmental risks (and associated obligations of notification and consultation), 'the more convincing view is that the Rio Declaration is merely restating existing law', p. 105. Other principles, such as the precautionary principle (principle 15), 'reflect more recent developments in international law and state practice; their present status as principles of general international law is more

As regards what will, and will not, constitute state practice, the acts or the acquiescence of a state in relation to CSR initiatives can be at least as significant (and some would say even more significant[55]) than statements made in respect of them. While the OECD Guidelines, for example, are referred to as mere 'recommendations', successive annual reports by the OECD on their implementation[56] suggest a high level of support by most OECD members for the Guidelines and the principles they contain. The UK government has gone so far as to describe the OECD Guidelines as providing 'norms for companies investing abroad'.[57]

On the other hand, as evidence of an emerging new legal rule, the fact that an instrument is expressly 'non-binding' does tend to suggest a lack of the necessary opinio juris, at least in the early stages. It is also relevant to note that the most significant soft law instruments in the CSR field (of which the OECD Guidelines are a good example) are addressed primarily to multinationals themselves, rather than to states. But what is the significance of this in legal terms? Can multinationals be made subject to *direct* obligations under customary international law? Or must international regulatory instruments, like the OECD Guidelines, always rely on the co-operation of states for their implementation? In other words, do multinationals have international legal personality in their own right?

The concept of international legal personality

'Legal personality' refers to the extent to which an entity is recognised by a legal system as having rights and responsibilities. At domestic law, legal personality is conferred not only upon individuals but also upon abstract entities such as companies and other business forms.[58] Both types of 'legal person' are, broadly speaking, the beneficiaries of legal rights, the

questionable . . . but the evidence of consensus support provided by the Rio Declaration is an important indication of their emerging legal significance', p. 105.

[55] D'Amato, *The Concept of Custom*, pp. 50–1, 88 although this is not a widely held view; see ILA, 'Statement of Principles Applicable to the Formation of General Customary International Law', Report to the 69th Conference, London, July 2000.

[56] OECD, 'Annual Report on the Guidelines for Multinational Enterprises: 2004 edition' (OECD, 2004). This and other annual and interim reports (commencing 2001) can be downloaded from http://www.oecd.org.

[57] DFID, White Paper, 'Eliminating World Poverty: Making Globalisation Work for the Poor', Cm 5006 (2000), pp. 13–14.

[58] See chapter 1, n. 198.

subjects of responsibilities, have the capacity to enter into legal relations (such as contracts) and the ability (in theory at least) to enforce the rights that arise under them. There may well be differences between domestic systems as to the nature of rights conferred to different types or sub-groups of legal person. However, just because certain individuals may not enjoy the same legal rights as others, or may be precluded by law from entering into contracts in their own right,[59] does not mean that they are not legal persons for other purposes.

Similarly, at the international level, an entity is said to have 'international legal personality' if it is the beneficiary of rights under international law, is subject to international obligations, is able to enter into legal relations on the international plane, and has the capacity to enforce international law rights and obligations. However, as in domestic law, not all international legal persons enjoy the same legal rights and not all international legal persons will be subject to the same legal obligations. Indeed, some legal obligations may be applicable to one type of legal person, but not another. As was expressed by the ICJ in its advisory opinion in the *Reparations for Injuries Case*, 'the subjects of law in any legal system are not necessarily identical in their nature or in the extent of their rights, and their nature depends on the needs of the community'.[60]

Traditionally, participants in the international legal system have been divided into 'subjects' and 'objects' of international law. It was generally believed that only states could be 'subjects' of international law. Individuals and other legal entities recognised at domestic law, such as companies, were regarded as 'objects' of international law (or 'beneficiaries' of international legal rights and obligations), but international law was not thought to be directly applicable to them and, moreover, could not be enforced except by an interested state.[61] But are these so-called 'objects' of international law really as passive as this simple 'subject–object' model suggests? Today there is much greater recognition of the role and contribution of 'non state actors' – individuals, companies, international organisations and NGOs – within the international community.[62] Higgins argues:

---

[59] E.g. minors, or women in some Islamic countries.

[60] *Reparations for Injuries Suffered in the Service of the United Nations* [1949] ICJ Reps 174, 178.

[61] For a statement of this conservative view, see A. Cassese, *International Law in a Divided World* (Oxford: Clarendon Press, 1986), p. 103.

[62] C. Weeramantry, 'Human Rights and the Global Marketplace' (1999) 25 *BJIL* 41, 49. See also Seidl-Hohenveldern, *Corporations*, p. 1.

It is much more helpful, and closer to perceived reality, to return to the view of international law as a particular decision-making process. Within that process (which is a dynamic and not a static one) there are a variety of participants, making claims across state lines, with the object of maximizing various values. Determinations will be made on those claims by various authoritative decision-makers – Foreign Office Legal Advisers, arbitral tribunals, courts . . . Now, in this model, there are no 'subjects' and 'objects', but only *participants*. Individuals *are* participants along with states, international organizations (such as the United Nations, or the International Monetary Fund (IMF)), multinational corporations, and indeed private non-governmental groups.[63]

As will be apparent from the following sections of this chapter, the growth of human rights law and international economic law has dramatically increased the scope for participation in international law by non-state actors. Therefore, rather than dividing participants into 'subjects' and 'objects' of international law, a more useful approach would be to consider the *degree* to which international law recognises the existence of different kinds of participants in the international legal system. The idea of multinationals as 'participants' in the international system provides a much more realistic picture of the role of private commercial organisations within the international system than the traditional 'subject–object' dichotomy.[64] However, as discussed in chapter 1, these 'participants' in international law are notoriously difficult to define. For international law purposes, multinationals have historically been regarded, not as single entities, but as conglomerations of related companies, 'each corporate unit operating as a native within the country of its incorporation'.[65] The 'juristic personality' of a corporate entity under international law was regarded as 'analogous to that of an individual, that is, as a national of a state'.[66] Questions relating to recognition and nationality of companies were settled by reference to domestic law.[67] It was concluded, therefore, that the multinational had no separate status under international law, aside from that enjoyed by its constituent entities by virtue of domestic law.[68]

---

[63] Higgins, *Problems and Process*, p. 50.   [64] See further pp. 93–102 below.

[65] Vagts, 'The Multinational Enterprise', 743.

[66] Johns, 'The Invisibility of the Transnational Corporation', 894.

[67] A. Fatouros, 'National Legal Persons in International Law' in R. Bernhardt (ed.), *Encyclopaedia of Public International Law*, 5 vols. (Amsterdam: North Holland, 1997), vol. III, p. 495.

[68] D. Kokkini-Iatridou and P. de Waart, 'Foreign Investments in Developing Countries: Legal Personality of Multinationals in International Law' (1983) 14 *NYIL* 87, 101–4. See also introduction to Seidl-Hohenveldern, *Corporations*.

But the inability of economists and international lawyers to develop a comprehensive definition of a 'multinational' does not mean that multinationals do not exist. As discussed in chapter 1, it is possible to define multinationals in legal terms, however imperfectly. In any event, none of these definitional problems affects the basic point: that the attribution of international legal personality is functional, and is influenced by the area of regulation (and the role of the particular participant in it), the powers conferred upon the 'person', and the aims and needs of the international community overall. Clearly, companies (and, by extension, groups of companies) do possess *rights* under international law,[69] some of which may be enforced directly (e.g. under treaty-based dispute resolution mechanisms), and to this extent can be said to enjoy some degree of 'international legal personality'. Of course, states remain at the heart of the international legal system and, as such, will continue to possess the most extensive international legal personality of the various different categories of participants. Only states possess *all* of the classical indications of international legal personality, i.e. the ability to participate in the development of international law through custom, the capacity to enter into international treaties, the prospect of direct legal responsibility for breaches of obligations and the ability to bring legal claims.[70] Nevertheless, there is now a much greater appreciation of the role of non-state actors in international life and, correspondingly, a growing conviction in international law literature that, as well as being the possessors of rights,[71] non-state actors (and particularly individuals and companies) are also subject to some direct obligations under international law.

Individuals have long been subject to international law prohibitions in relation to piracy and slavery.[72] The international criminal responsibility of individuals for war crimes, crimes against humanity and genocide has

---

[69] Such rights include rights under international investment law, such as the right not to be discriminated against vis-à-vis national firms and a right to receive compensation in the event of expropriation. See generally Sornorajah, *Foreign Investment*, esp. chapter 9. Other rights, such as the right to a fair trial, the right to privacy and the right of freedom of expression, have been extended to companies under regional human rights treaties. See M. Addo, 'The Corporation as a Victim of Human Rights Violations' in M. Addo (ed.), *Human Rights Standards and the Responsibility of Transnational Corporations* (The Hague: Kluwer, 1999). See also ICHRP, 'Beyond Voluntarism', p. 56.

[70] Note that only states have the right to bring matters before the ICJ. See the Statute of the International Court of Justice, Article 34(1).

[71] See Kinley and Tadaki, 'From Talk to Walk', 946.

[72] Shaw, *International Law*, p. 234; Danailov, 'Accountability of Non-State Actors', p. 34.

been affirmed in a series of significant international statements including the 1945 Nuremberg Charter,[73] the 1948 Genocide Convention[74] and
the Statutes of the International Tribunals on the Former Yugoslavia[75]
and Rwanda.[76] The 1998 Rome Statute for the International Criminal
Court[77] provides for criminal jurisdiction over individuals accused of
genocide, crimes again humanity, war crimes and the 'crime of aggres-
sion'.[78] The Rome Statute does not provide for prosecution of corporate
entities.[79] Nevertheless, there is nothing inherent in international law
that prevents states from addressing obligations directly to companies
and also, in theory, to corporate groups. Indeed, some writers believe
that, in the field of human rights law, this is already beginning to take
place.

Multinationals and human rights

There are two dimensions to the human rights regulation of multinationals by states: 'direct' regulation by international law and (more
conventionally) 'indirect' regulation through obligations imposed upon
states to control private actors to ensure that human rights norms are
not breached.[80]

'Direct' regulation

It is at least a theoretical possibility that international law could impose
some human rights obligations directly on companies, although it is far

---

[73] Charter of the International Military Tribunal annexed to the 1945 Agreement for
Prosecution and Punishment of Major War Criminals, London, 8 August 1945, 82
UNTS 280, Article 6.

[74] See the 1948 Convention on the Prevention and Punishment of the Crime of Genocide,
Paris, 9 December 1948, in force 12 January 1951, 78 UNTS 277 which applies to
'constitutionally responsible rulers, public officials or private individuals', Article 4.

[75] 1993 Statute of the International Criminal Tribunal for the Former Yugoslavia, 25 May
1993, annexed to and adopted by UNSC No. Resolution 827, UN Doc. S/RES/827; (1993)
32 ILM 1159.

[76] 1994 Statute of the International Criminal Tribunal for Rwanda, 8 November 1994,
annexed to and adopted by UNSC Resolution No. 955, UN Doc. S/RES/955; (1994) 33 ILM
1598.

[77] 1998 Statute of the International Criminal Court, Rome, 17 July 1998, in force 1 July
2002, UN Doc. A/CONF.183/9, 2187 UNTS 90; (1998) 37 ILM 1002.

[78] Article 5.

[79] This was a result of concern over the practicalities of prosecuting corporate
defendants, rather than doubt as to whether international criminal law actually
applies to companies. See A. Clapham, 'The Question of Jurisdiction under
International Criminal Law over Legal Persons' in M. Kamminga and S. Zia-Zarifi (eds.),
Liability of Multinational Corporations under International Law (The Hague: Kluwer, 2000).

[80] Joseph, 'Taming the Leviathans'; ICHRP, 'Beyond Voluntarism'.

less clear what these duties might entail. The usual starting point is the Preamble of the 1948 UDHR,[81] in which it is stated that '*every individual and every organ of society*, keeping this declaration constantly in mind, shall strive by teaching and education to promote respect for these [i.e. UDHR] rights and freedoms and by progressive measures, national and international, to secure their universal and effective recognition and observance'. The italicised wording excludes 'no one', in the words of Henkin, 'no company, no market, no cyberspace'.[82] On the other hand, the wording of this particular passage (to 'strive') is not particularly strong. There are slight indications in the substantive provisions that non-state actors (including corporations) have a role to play in further-ing human rights. Article 29, for instance, provides that '[e]veryone has duties to the community in which alone the free and full development of his personality is possible' and Article 30 provides that 'Nothing in this Declaration may be interpreted as implying for any State, group or person any right to engage in any activity or to perform any act aimed at the destruction of any of the rights and freedoms set forth herein.' However, it is not clear that these provisions have customary status[83] and, in any event, Article 30 is not so much an injunction to 'do no harm'[84] as an 'avoidance of doubt' provision, to clarify how the remain-der of the substantive provisions of the UDHR may and may not be used.

There are, of course, strong arguments as to why human rights law *should*, in principle, be applied directly to companies. Central to these arguments is the notion that 'power must be balanced by responsibil-ities'. The first point to make here is that multinationals can and do affect enjoyment of human rights[85] and, as they already enjoy con-siderable rights and benefits under international law, it is only proper that they should also be subject to some obligations.[86] The second point arises from the fact that the privatisation policies pursued at domestic level have meant that many tasks traditionally performed by government have now been handed over to private operators.[87] Logically, 'if human rights were historically granted to individuals to shield them against the State's abusive action, and some States' functions are taken over by

[81] 1948 Universal Declaration of Human Rights, UNGA res. 217A (III), UN Doc. A/810, 71.
[82] L. Henkin, 'Keynote Address: The Universal Declaration at 50 and the Challenge of Global Markets' (1999) 25 *BJIL* 17, 25.
[83] Kinley and Tadaki, 'From Talk to Walk', 949.   [84] ICHRP, 'Beyond Voluntarism', p. 60.
[85] Joseph, *Corporations and Transnational Human Rights Litigation*, pp. 1–4.
[86] ICHRP, 'Beyond Voluntarism', pp. 12–13.
[87] Danailov, 'Accountability of Non-State Actors', pp. 37–8.

other entities susceptible to violate those rights, we can then argue that these entities should be called upon to respect human rights obligations towards . . . individuals.'[88] In other words, although human rights law may traditionally have been devised to protect individuals from abuses by states, international law must now respond to shifts in power in the international system away from states and in favour of large corporations.[89] While noting that the obligations of multinationals may not necessarily be the same as states, Kinley and Tadaki nevertheless argue that:

> there is simply no reason why TNCs [i.e. transnational corporations] should not be obliged to take steps along the lines of . . . typical governmental functions to provide for and promote human rights, when such steps are in their power and jurisdiction . . . The improvement of the overall human rights situation of the population may indeed be . . . a central purpose of government, but we would add that TNCs not only can, but must, provide collateral and sometimes crucial collateral support to that end.[90]

These arguments are compelling. But how far should they be taken in practice? Although there may be some blurring at the edges, states and companies do perform different roles in society. Companies are fundamentally profit-creating institutions, whereas states' functions are essentially governmental. While jurisdiction over territory is a key attribute of statehood, the lack of any 'analogous jurisdictional claim'[91] for companies makes it rather more difficult to identify, first, those individuals to whom the human rights obligations of companies may be owed[92] and, second, those entities for which a company should be responsible. Also, it is easy to overlook the fact that companies, unlike states, are private parties with rights of their own. Inevitably, the extent to which companies will be required to pursue human rights goals will reflect a judgement about how this balance of rights and responsibilities (the obligation to disclose information versus the right to privacy, for example) should be struck.[93] Finally, it is necessary to face up to the unpleasant fact that protecting and promoting human rights has financial consequences for

---

[88] Ibid., p. 6.

[89] P. Alston, 'The Myopia of the Handmaidens: International Lawyers and Globalisation' (1987) 80 *EJIL* 435; Joseph, 'Taming the Leviathans', 186; ICHRP, 'Beyond Voluntarism', pp. 9–10.

[90] Kinley and Tadaki, 'From Talk to Walk', 966.   [91] Ibid., 961.

[92] Although note that the human rights obligations of states are not strictly territorial; see further pp. 86–9 below.

[93] Joseph, 'Taming the Leviathans', 199. See, for instance, the US case of *Kasky* v. *Nike*, 539 US 654 (2003) in which Nike sought to argue that its potential liability under

companies. The lengths to which a company must go to comply with its human rights obligations will, therefore, reflect a trade-off between its obligations to its shareholders on the one hand and its obligations to individuals and society on the other. While some 'fundamental' or 'core' rights – the right to life, liberty and physical integrity, for example – should always receive higher priority than mere profits,[94] it may be difficult for a tribunal to exclude financial considerations altogether (e.g. where it is necessary to determine whether a company has acted 'reasonably' in the circumstances, and so discharged the standard of 'due diligence').

Clearly, if human rights law obligations are extended to corporate actors they will need to reflect the different roles and capacities of companies vis-à-vis states. In 'translating' human rights obligations for companies, there are two key questions to answer: first, what is the legal nature of human rights obligations for companies and, second, what, practically speaking, does this entail? Kinley and Tadaki take, as their starting point, the proposition that the overarching duty to 'protect' human rights entails three more specific obligations: to 'prevent' human rights violations, to 'provide' the means to ensure human rights compliance and to 'promote' understanding regarding the application of human rights standards.[95] These obligations can be further divided into duties that apply to the actor's own conduct (referred to as a 'self-reflexive' duty) and duties which relate to the behaviour of others (e.g. subsidiaries, contractors, suppliers and government agencies). Kinley and Tadaki postulate that there is a minimum duty of 'do no harm', plus possible additional obligations to take positive steps to protect and promote human rights depending on the level of 'proximity' between the company and those affected (i.e. 'the greater the proximity of the TNCs [i.e. multinationals] to human rights bearers, the greater will be the duties of the TNCs towards them').[96]

Californian trade practices law (arising from statements it had made about its CSR credentials) was inconsistent with the company's own right to 'free speech'.

[94] Kinley and Tadaki, 'From Talk to Walk', 968. See also Joseph, 'Taming the Leviathans', who argues that 'an individual's freedom from bodily harm instinctively outweighs a corporation's right to trade at ultra-competitive levels', 199.

[95] Elsewhere this has been expressed in terms of a 'tripartite' set of obligations to 'respect, protect and fulfil' human rights standards. See M. Craven, *The International Covenant on Economic, Social and Cultural Rights* (Oxford: Clarendon Press, 1995); Joseph, 'Taming the Leviathans' ('respect, protect and ensure'), 175.

[96] Kinley and Tadaki , 'From Talk to Walk', 963–4. On the issue of 'proximity', see also ICHRP, 'Beyond Voluntarism', pp. 136–9 and Ratner, 'A Theory of Responsibility'.

A particularly difficult issue of topical interest concerns the extent to which a company should be held liable for the human rights violations of its host governments. The problem is well illustrated by the case of Shell in Nigeria, discussed in chapter 1 above,[97] and recent litigation in the USA concerning the activities of Unocal in Burma. This case, which is discussed in more detail in chapter 5,[98] concerns allegations of collusion by Unocal in alleged human rights violations by government security forces employed in connection with the construction of an oil pipeline. There is growing support in academic writing for the idea that companies ought to be responsible under international human rights law when they contribute to human rights violations committed by states, although these ideas have yet to be tested properly in court.[99] Whatever the legal position, there are plenty of recent cases in which multinationals have found themselves implicated in human rights abuses by host states, and the list of 'danger areas' is growing. For instance, a company may have entered into a contract with its host government whereby the host government agrees to provide security services in connection with a project,[100] or the company may have agreed to make available certain facilities for the government to use.[101] A company may have provided funds to a host government that it knows or suspects are being used to fund human rights abuses.[102] In some cases companies have been criticised merely for failing to speak out against human rights violations by governments of countries with which they have relationships[103] or for choosing to invest in certain 'blacklisted' countries at all.[104]

The liability of companies for the human rights violations of host states is a developing area in international human rights law. It may be that more concrete legal principles will eventually emerge out of litigation currently taking place in the US courts under the Alien Tort Claims

---

[97] See pp. 23–4 above.   [98] See pp. 203–4 below.

[99] For suggestions as to how these theories of responsibility might be applied in practice, see ICHRP, 'Beyond Voluntarism', pp. 139–42; Kinley and Tadaki, 'From Talk to Walk', 964; Ratner, 'A Theory of Responsibility'.

[100] See *Doe* v. *Unocal*, 963 F. Supp 880 (CD Cal 1997).

[101] Kinley and Tadaki cite the example of coffee companies storing arms and equipment for those responsible for crimes of genocide in Rwanda. See Kinley and Tadaki, 'From Talk to Walk', 970.

[102] E.g. *In re South African Apartheid Litigation*, 346 F Supp 2d 538 (SDNY 2004), 544–5.

[103] See pp. 23–4 above in relation to Shell in Nigeria. See also *Sarei* v. *Rio Tinto*, 221 F. Supp 2d 116 (CD Cal 2002); *Bowoto* v *Chevron*, 312 F Supp 2d 1229 (ND Cal 2004).

[104] Joseph, 'Taming the Leviathans', 188. See also *In re South African Apartheid Litigation*, 346 F Supp 2d 538 (SDNY 2004).

Act, discussed further in chapter 5.[105] But what is the position where no state action is involved? Do multinationals have any 'stand-alone' obligations under human rights law? Although it is too early to say categorically that this is the case, there is emerging consensus, among NGOs and academics at least, as to what the human rights obligations of companies could potentially be.[106] Clues are to be found in a range of international law materials, from treaties to declarations and other 'non-binding' instruments. Human rights instruments, such as the International Covenant on Economic, Social and Cultural Rights (ICESCR)[107] and the 1966 International Covenant on Civil and Political Rights (ICCPR),[108] for instance, set out standards relating to workplace health and safety and the environment, which could conceivably be extended to multinationals. The ICESCR refers to a 'right of everyone to the enjoyment of just and favourable conditions of work, which ensure, in particular . . . safe and healthy working conditions'.[109] The ILO has developed treaties dealing directly with the subject of workplace health and safety.[110] In addition, the ILO adopted, in 1998, a Declaration on Fundamental Principles and Rights at Work[111] in which it is declared that all member states of the ILO, 'even if they have not ratified the Conventions in question', have an obligation to work for the realisation of certain key worker rights.

The UN Norms project, sponsored by the UN Sub-Commission on the Promotion and Protection of Human Rights,[112] is built upon the idea that there are indeed human rights obligations that can be applied directly to companies. These 'norms' include a number of provisions that tap into key concerns of the CSR movement. For instance, on the issue of

[105] See pp. 207–15 below.

[106] See N. Jägers, *Corporate Human Rights Obligations: In Search of Accountability* (Antwerp: Intersentia, 2002); Kinley and Tadaki, 'From Talk to Walk'; ICHRP, 'Beyond Voluntarism'.

[107] 1966 International Covenant on Economic, Social and Cultural Rights, adopted by UNGA Resolution 2200A (XXI), 16 December 1966, in force 3 January 1976, 999 UNTS 3.

[108] 1966 International Covenant on Civil and Political Rights, adopted by UNGA Resolution 2200A (XXI), 16 December 1966, in force 23 March 1976, 999 UNTS 171.

[109] ICESCR, n. 107 above, Article 11.

[110] 1981 ILO Convention on Occupational Safety and Health and the Working Environment, Geneva, 22 June 1981, in force 11 August 1983 (No. 155); 1993 ILO Convention on the Prevention of Major Industrial Accidents, Geneva, 22 June 1993, in force 3 January 1997 (No. 174). See further 295–6 below.

[111] Adopted at the 86th session of the International Labour Conference, Geneva, 18 June 1998.

[112] See further pp. 261–2 below.

workplace health and safety, it is stated that 'Transnational corporations and other business enterprises shall provide a safe and healthy working environment as set forth in relevant international instruments and national legislation as well as international human rights and humanitarian law.'[113] What this might mean, in detailed practical terms, is not yet clear, although it potentially covers issues such as access to healthcare facilities, provision of adequate nutrition, clean water and air (all of which must be made available without discrimination), and respect for reproductive health.[114]

The existence of a right to a 'decent' or 'healthy' environment as a 'freestanding' human right is still controversial.[115] Nevertheless, environmental rights are undoubtedly part of wider well-established human rights, such as the 'right to life', the 'right to health',[116] the rights of indigenous or minority groups or the 'right to non-discrimination'.[117] Again, it is only possible to speculate what would be required of companies in practical terms. The UN Norms proposed a mix of procedural and substantive obligations, such as carrying out proper environmental impact assessments,[118] sharing information about environmental risks, ensuring that the views of those affected are heard and taken into account,[119] applying 'best practice' in environmental management[120] and, finally, respect for the precautionary principle in corporate decision-making.[121]

Consumer protection rights, like environmental rights, could also be derived from wider human rights, such as the 'right to health' or a 'right to life'.[122] Although stopping short of invoking human rights, the UN Guidelines for Consumer Protection[123] list a number of 'legitimate needs' which governments should strive to meet, including 'the

[113] UN Norms, n. 47 above (emphasis added).
[114] ICHRP, 'Beyond Voluntarism', pp. 35–6.
[115] Birnie and Boyle, *International Law and the Environment*, pp. 252–7; Kinley and Tadaki, 'From Talk to Walk', pp. 983–4: Joseph, 'Taming the Leviathans': 'it would seem that the right to a healthy environment is a mere aspiration, rather than a legal obligation . . .', 196.
[116] A. Kiss, 'Concept and Possible Implications of the Right to Environment' in K. Mahoney and P. Mahoney (eds.), *Human Rights in the Twenty-First Century: a Global Challenge* (The Hague: Kluwer, 1993).
[117] ICHRP, 'Beyond Voluntarism', p. 41; Kinley and Tadaki, 'From Talk to Walk', 983.
[118] UN Norms, n. 47 above, commentary on para. 14 , sub-paras. (c) and (d).
[119] Kinley and Tadaki, 'From Talk to Walk', 986
[120] UN Norms, n. 47 above, commentary to para. 14, sub-para. (g).
[121] UN Norms, para. 14. See further pp. 271–2 below.
[122] Joseph ,'Taming the Leviathans', 198.
[123] Adopted by UNGA Resolution 39/248, 9 April 1985.

protection of consumers from hazards to their health and safety', 'access of consumers to adequate information to enable them to make informed choices' and 'availability of effective consumer remedies'.[124] According to the UN Norms, the human rights responsibilities of multinationals require that they

act in accordance with fair business, marketing and advertising practices and shall take all necessary steps to ensure the safety and quality of the goods and services they provide, including observance of the precautionary principle [and should not] produce, distribute, market, or advertise harmful or potentially harmful products for use by consumers.[125]

In summary, the idea that multinationals may be subject to some 'direct' obligations under international human rights law is slowly gaining momentum, but it is not yet clear where this will lead in relation to CSR. In the absence of effective enforcement mechanisms, multinationals are likely to continue to regard human rights principles, at best, as moral rather than legal obligations. Also, because of the lack of human rights instruments applying directly and expressly to companies, it is still only possible to speculate as to what might actually be required of multinationals in practice, based on existing human rights obligations of states, 'soft law' instruments, judicial decisions[126] and other state practice. It should not be assumed, though, that the human rights obligations of states are readily translatable to the corporate context. While the power and financial resources of some multinationals may now approach (or even exceed) those of some states, their different roles and responsibilities mean that their human rights obligations will not be the same, nor should they be.

'Indirect' regulation

The section above discusses the possibility of 'direct' responsibility of multinationals under human rights law. This is not to suggest, however, that human rights obligations for companies are a new development in international law. Companies have long been subject to human rights obligations, as implemented and enforced under domestic and regional law.[127] Under this more traditional, 'state-centred' framework, human rights standards are imposed on companies at national level only, but

---

[124] Paragraph 3.   [125] UN Norms, n. 47 above, para. 13.
[126] See further chapter 5 below.
[127] See A. Clapham, *Human Rights in the Private Sphere* (Oxford: Oxford University Press, 1996).

states may be held responsible for human rights violations if these result from their failure to regulate corporate activity effectively.

Each state is obliged to take steps to protect against human rights violations by private actors operating under or within its jurisdiction.[128] The required standard is one of 'due diligence' to guard against, and to provide adequate remedies for, the consequences of the acts of third parties.[129] As the Inter-American Court of Human Rights explained in *Velasquez Rodriguez* v. *Honduras*:

> An illegal act which violates human rights and which is initially not directly attributable to a State (for example, because it is the act of a private person . . .) can lead to international responsibility of the State, not because of the act itself, *but because of the lack of due diligence to prevent the violation or to respond to it* . . . This duty to prevent [human rights violations] includes all those means of a legal, political, administrative and cultural nature that promote the protection of human rights and ensure that any violations are considered and treated as illegal acts.[130]

These obligations may be referred to as part of the 'international regulatory responsibilities' of states.[131] In practice, though, not all states have the same capacity to regulate companies effectively. Developing host states, highly dependent on foreign investment, face a particular set of problems. First, in sectors where there is competition for inward investment with other states (e.g. clothing manufacture), host states may

---

[128] H. Steiner and P. Alston, *International Human Rights in Context: Law, Politics and Morals*, 2nd edition (Oxford: Oxford University Press, 2000), p. 1349. See also *Velasquez Rodriguez* v. *Honduras*, Inter-American Court of Human Rights (ser. C.) no. 4 (1988), (1989) 28 ILM 294, and *Decision Regarding Communication 155/96 (Social and Economic Rights Action Center/Center for Economic and Social Rights* v. *Nigeria)*, African Commission on Human and Peoples' Rights, Case No. ACHPR/COMM/A044.1, 27 May 2002, http://www.umn.edu/humanrts/Africa/comcases/allcases.html; see (2002) 96 *AJIL* 937 for a case-note of this decision. See further F. Coomans, 'The *Ongoni* Case before the African Commission on Human and Peoples' Rights' (2003) 52 *ICLQ* 749.

[129] R. Pisillo-Mazzeschi, 'The Due Diligence Rule and the Nature of International Responsibility of States' (1992) 35 *GYIL* 9; ICHRP, 'Beyond Voluntarism', p. 52.

[130] *Velasquez Rodriguez* v. *Honduras*, n. 128 above, paras. 172–5 (emphasis added).

[131] See ICESCR, n. 107 above, Article 2(1) under which each state party undertakes to take steps 'to the maximum of its available resources . . . to achieving progressively the full realization of the rights [recognised in the ICESCR] by all appropriate means *including particularly the adoption of legislative* measures' (emphasis added). For a discussion on the regulatory responsibilities of states regarding the activities of multinationals operating within their territories, see *Decision Regarding Communication 155/96*, n. 128 above, para. 53. For discussion of further possible *extraterritorial* regulatory responsibilities of states under international law prohibitions on transboundary harm, see pp. 158–60 below.

find themselves in a relatively weak bargaining position, and their governments may be concerned about the potential effect of higher regulatory standards on the country's attractiveness as a foreign investment destination. Second, governments of poorer states may simply lack the technical and financial resources to monitor and enforce standards effectively. According to Joseph, 'where such disparity of power exists, it seems unrealistic to depend exclusively on host states to hold MNEs accountable for human rights violations'.[132] Joseph goes on to suggest that the more developed home states (the 'states of incorporation' of multinationals) should shoulder more of the responsibility for human rights regulation of multinationals, as

the developed home state is more likely to possess the requisite technical expertise to impose adequate safety standards, and to have a legal system able to cope with the proper attribution of responsibility within the complex corporate arrangements . . . Indeed it is common for developed nations to demand higher standards of behaviour from MNEs within their jurisdictions than do developing nations.[133]

While this may be an over-generalisation, the regulatory potential of 'home states' of multinationals is certainly worth exploring further. The definitional and jurisdictional issues raised by 'home state regulation' of multinationals are considered in more detail in the following chapters. It is argued in chapter 3 that home states are indeed permitted (albeit to a limited extent) to regulate the social and environmental standards of multinationals abroad. There are those who would go further, and argue that not only do home states have *rights* to regulate multinationals extraterritorially, they also have *obligations* to do so. But is there any basis for holding a home state responsible under human rights law for a failure to protect against *extraterritorial* human rights violations by multinationals?

Clearly, multinational activity has the potential to impact on the enjoyment of human rights. Because of this, it has been argued that the obligation to *protect* against human rights violations does indeed create positive duties for home states to regulate multinationals.[134] The Maastricht Guidelines on Violations of Economic, Social and Cultural

---

[132] Joseph, 'Taming the Leviathans', 177.   [133] Ibid., 177–8.

[134] M. Sornorajah, 'Linking State Responsibility for Certain Harms Caused by Corporate Nationals Abroad to Civil Recourse in the Legal Systems of Home States' in C. Scott (ed.), *Torture as Tort: Comparative Perspectives on the Development of Transnational Human Rights Litigation* (Oxford: Hart Publishing, 2001).

Rights, produced at a conference of human rights lawyers held in 1997 at Maastricht University, had this to say about the relationship between states and multinationals:

The obligation to protect includes the State's responsibility to ensure that private entities or individuals, *including transnational corporations over which they exercise jurisdiction*, do not deprive individuals of their economic, social and cultural rights. States are responsible for violations of economic, social and cultural rights that result from their failure to exercise due diligence in controlling the behaviour of such non-State actors.[135]

This statement begs two questions. First, to what extent is a multinational actually 'subject to the jurisdiction' of its home state and, second, to what extent are international law duties owed by home states to individuals in other countries (i.e. non-residents of the home state)?

Although the home state would clearly have 'nationality' jurisdiction over a parent company incorporated within its territory,[136] the presence of 'control relationships' between the parent company and foreign affiliates tends to be disregarded for jurisdictional purposes. To put it another way, the fact that a company incorporated in the home state controls a foreign affiliate will not ordinarily bring the foreign affiliate within the jurisdiction of the home state. These issues are discussed in more detail in chapter 3.

However, even if the home state does not have jurisdiction over the foreign affiliate as such, the home state is still potentially in a position of influence by virtue of its jurisdiction over the parent company. To what extent might it still be required to exercise its jurisdiction over the parent company to prevent human rights abuses by multinationals *beyond* territorial boundaries? Sornorajah suggests that the control relationships that form the basis of diplomatic rights under BITs may also justify the imposition of extraterritorial regulatory responsibilities on home states, at least in relation to violations by multinationals of norms of jus cogens.[137] International human rights instruments, on the other hand, take differing approaches to the question of how far, geographically speaking, the human rights obligations of home states might extend. Some of these instruments contain express limitations on the territorial scope of human rights obligations. Under the ICCPR, for

---

[135] Maastricht Guidelines on Violations on Economic, Social and Cultural Rights, para. 18 (reproduced at (1998) 20 *HRQ* 691) (emphasis added).
[136] See further pp. 106–9 below.
[137] Sornorajah, 'Linking State Responsibility', pp. 494–5.

example, each state party undertakes to 'respect and ensure to all individuals *within its territory and subject to its jurisdiction* the rights recognised in the present Covenant'.[138] But these restrictions are not confined to instruments relating to civil and political rights. Article 34 of the European Social Charter, for example, states that the Charter 'shall apply to the metropolitan territory of each Contracting State'.

The ICESCR, on the other hand, is more ambiguous about the territoriality of obligations and could be read to imply the involvement of state parties in a project to improve realisation of these rights on a wider scale. Article 2(1) of the ICESCR provides, for example:

Each State Party undertakes to take steps, *individually and through international assistance and co-operation, especially economic and technical, to the maximum of its available resources,* with a view to achieving progressively the full realization of the rights recognized in the present Covenant by all appropriate means, including particularly the adoption of legislative measures.[139]

There are indications, too, in various General Comments of the UN Committee on Economic, Social and Cultural Rights that obligations under the ICESCR are not owed exclusively to persons within that state's territorial boundaries. The idea of the 'extraterritoriality' of human rights obligations is implicit, for example, in the remarks of the Committee on the relationship between economic sanctions and economic, social and cultural rights.[140]

The 'territoriality' of human rights obligations has been considered in a series of court cases under the European Convention on Human Rights ('ECHR')[141] and the UK Human Rights Act 1998. The ECHR requires state parties to 'secure to everyone *within their jurisdiction* the rights and freedoms set out in the Convention'.[142] Both the European Court of Human Rights and the British House of Lords have held that this wording does indeed give rise to extraterritorial obligations in exceptional cases where a contracting state has effective control over territory or individuals in other states[143] or, through its diplomatic staff abroad, has assumed

---

[138] ICCPR, n. 108 above, Article 2 (emphasis added).

[139] ICESCR, n. 107 above, Article 2(1) (emphasis added).

[140] Committee on Economic, Social and Cultural Rights, 'General Comment No. 8 on the Relationship between Economic Sanctions and Respect for Economic, Social and Cultural Rights', UN Doc. E/1998/22, which suggests that states are required to take account of human rights implications in other countries when designing sanctions regimes (see para. 12).

[141] European Convention on Human Rights and Fundamental Freedoms, Rome, 4 November 1950, in force 3 September 1953, ETS, No. 5.

[142] Article 1 (emphasis added).

[143] *Bankovic and Others* v. *Belgium and Others*, (2001) 11 BHRC 435; (2001) 41 ILM 517.

responsibility for the welfare of individuals.[144] But 'jurisdiction' for these purposes is narrowly defined, and certainly would not, based on these decisions, extend to non-residents merely by virtue of the regulatory influence enjoyed by a home state over a multinational.

However, there are indications in General Comments of the UN Committee on Economic, Social and Cultural Rights that home states may have some extraterritorial regulatory obligations in respect of multinationals. In relation to the 'right to health' the Committee has stated as follows:

> To comply with their international obligations in relation to article 12, State parties have to respect the enjoyment of the right to health in other countries, and to prevent third parties from violating the right in other countries, *if they are able to influence these third parties by way of legal or political means*, in accordance with the Charter of the United Nations and applicable international law.[145]

The Committee then goes on to state that '[a] State which is unwilling to use the maximum of its available resources for the realization of the right to health is in violation of its obligations under article 12'[146] and, further, confirms that '[v]iolations of the right to health can occur through the direct action of States *or other entities insufficiently regulated by States*'.[147] On the other hand, when commenting specifically on the stronger obligation to *protect* the human right to health, the Committee only refers to the need for states to safeguard the human rights of persons *within their jurisdiction*.[148]

The Committee on Economic, Social and Cultural Rights has yet to give detailed attention to the question of home state obligations in respect of multinationals directly in its General Comments.[149] However, if the obligation to *protect* against human rights violations is only owed to

---

[144] *R (on the application of B and Others)* v. *Secretary of State for the Foreign and Commonwealth Office* [2005] QB 643. See also *WM* v. *Denmark* (1993) 15 EHRR CD28.

[145] Committee on Economic, Social and Cultural Rights, 'General Comment No. 14 on the Right to the Highest Attainable Standard of Health', UN Doc. E/C. 12/2000/4 at para. 39 (emphasis added).

[146] Ibid, para. 47.

[147] Ibid, para. 48 (emphasis added). See also 'General Comment No. 12 on the Right to Adequate Food', UN Doc. E/C.12/1999/5, para. 19.

[148] General Comment No. 14, n. 145 above, para. 51.

[149] Although a reference to multinationals can be found in General Comment No. 14, n. 145 above, which states that the obligation to *respect* human rights would require states to take account of their legal obligations 'when entering into bilateral or multilateral agreements with other States, international organisations *and other entities, such as multinational corporations*' (emphasis added), at para. 51.

those *within the jurisdiction* of the home state, then it seems likely that any extraterritorial human rights obligations of home states would be limited to softer duties to *respect* and *promote* human rights in the formulation and implementation of home state policies on CSR. In general, the extraterritorial role of states envisaged in these General Comments is a supporting one – as providers of aid, for example – rather than as a potential regulator.[150] The European Multi-Stakeholder Forum ('EMSF')[151] seems to share the view that there is a difference in the nature of the obligations owed by home states towards their own citizens and residents, compared with citizens and residents of other countries. In order to fulfil the 'clear responsibility of national governments to promote democracy and human rights', the EMSF recommended that 'governments provide [first] the appropriate legal framework for protecting human, social and economic rights *of citizens*, and [second] a climate conducive to economic, environmental and social progress particularly in developing countries'.[152]

Human rights law is, however, continually under development. Given the current level of international interest in CSR, and the developing state practice discussed in later chapters, it is possible that the obligations of home states could yet evolve to include positive obligations to regulate the extraterritorial CSR performance of multinationals 'based' in their respective jurisdictions. As noted in the 2001 EU Green Paper on CSR, '[c]orporate social responsibility has a strong international human rights dimension, particularly in relation to international operations and global supply chains'.[153] But protecting human rights via this route is not without its own difficulties. Even if such obligations were to develop as a matter of theory, proving that a home state had breached its extraterritorial regulatory obligations vis-à-vis multinational activities would be extremely difficult in practice, for a number of reasons. The first difficulty is the lack of clarity in the normative substance of the basic standards to be achieved. This is a particular problem in relation to economic, social and cultural rights, which are presented in the

---

[150] See General Comment No. 14, n. 145 above, para. 39. See also P. Alston and G. Quinn, 'The Nature and Scope of State Parties' Obligations under the International Covenant on Economic, Social and Cultural Rights' (1987) 9 *HRQ* 156, 186–92.

[151] This Forum was established pursuant to the recommendations set out in European Commission, 'Communication concerning Corporate Social Responsibility: a Business Contribution to Sustainable Development', COM (2002) 347 final, 2 July 2002.

[152] EMSF, 'Final Report and Recommendations', 29 June 2004 (emphasis added).

[153] European Commission, 'Green Paper on CSR: Promoting a European Framework for Corporate Social Responsibility', Employment and Social Affairs, July 2001.

ICESCR as standards to be progressively achieved, in accordance with the available resources of the relevant state.[154] The greater flexibility in the language employed in the ICESCR, compared with that of the ICCPR, has led some observers to suggest that economic, social and cultural rights either are of lower status than civil and political rights, or are not actually human rights at all.[155] While uncertainty about the scope of state obligations in respect of economic, social and cultural rights should not deprive those rights of status *as human rights*,[156] the progressive nature of the rights provided for in the ICESCR means that the determination of whether (and at what point) a right has been violated may not be straightforward. Moreover, how do duties to investigate, punish and provide legal redress for breaches of human rights[157] apply to possible violations by companies beyond state boundaries? To what extent, for instance, should a home state be responsible for the extraterritorial monitoring and enforcement of social standards? Should a home state necessarily be obliged to provide access to legal remedies for foreign plaintiffs? If so, to what extent would the home state be obliged to facilitate such claims, for example, through legal aid? As will be discussed further in chapter 5,[158] it is doubtful that these are legal obligations for home states at present.

The second set of difficulties concerns issues of proximity and causation. It would be necessary to show, not only that the conduct or omissions of the home state resulted in human rights violations, but that these violations were reasonably foreseeable and therefore that the home state had failed to meet the requisite standard of due diligence. Where the human rights violations occurred in another state, however, the culpability of the home state would have to be measured against that of the host state. It would be necessary to ask, for example, whether the host state, as the state *primarily* responsible for the regulation of

---

[154] ICESCR, n. 107 above, Article 2(1).

[155] See Dine, *Companies, International Trade and Human Rights*, pp. 170–3. Shaw describes the regime envisaged by the ICESCR as 'an evolving programme . . . depending on the goodwill and resources of states, rather than an immediate binding legal obligation with regard to the rights in question'; Shaw, *International Law*, p. 286. However, the ICESCR does impose some immediately binding obligations on states (see Craven, *The International Covenant*, chapter 3), albeit 'less demanding than a guarantee' (Alston and Quinn, 'State Parties' Obligations', 166). Note, also, that the distinction between 'civil and political' and 'economic, social and cultural' rights has been criticised (see Craven, *The International Covenant*, pp. 7–16), as has the notion that rights classed as 'civil and political' necessarily have primacy over others (see Higgins, *Problems and Process*, pp. 99–100).

[156] Higgins, *Problems and Process*, p. 100.

[157] See *Velasquez Rodriguez v. Honduras*, n. 128 above, paras. 172–5.   [158] See pp. 237–9 below.

industrial activities within its jurisdiction, had itself failed to discharge its international law obligations towards its own citizens and, if so, whether the host state's omissions were not a more immediate cause of the abuse.[159]

In summary, it seems extremely doubtful that home states of multinationals are presently under any positive obligations under international human rights law to regulate the social and environmental performance of multinationals beyond territorial boundaries (although this does not preclude the theoretical international law responsibility of a home state which was 'complicit' in human right abuses, e.g. on the basis of support or encouragement given for a project that was clearly in violation of human rights norms). Even if such obligations did exist, state responsibility would still only attach where the conduct or omissions of another state (e.g. the host state) could not be regarded as intervening factors, thus limiting the potential liability of home states under international human rights law to rare and extreme cases. However, developing state practice in the extraterritorial regulation of the CSR standards of multinationals has the potential to expand the human rights responsibilities of home states, as will be discussed further below. In addition, recent litigation against the parent companies of multinationals at national level has focused attention on the role and responsibilities of home states in respect of access to justice for victims of human rights abuses in other countries. These questions will be explored further in chapter 5.

Implementation and enforcement of 'direct' and 'indirect' obligations

At present there are only very limited means at international level whereby the human rights performance of companies (or states in relation to the activities of companies) can formally be challenged, let alone enforced. Of course, this does not mean that companies are not subject to human rights law; nor does it mean that human rights law lacks 'regulatory potential'.[160] It does mean, however, that those monitoring cases of human rights abuses by companies have had to be

---

[159] See ILC, Commentary on the ILC Articles on the Responsibility of States for Internationally Wrongful Acts, i.e. 'causality is in fact a necessary but not a sufficient condition for reparation. There is a further element, associated with the exclusion of injury that is too "remote" or "consequential" to be the subject of reparation. In some cases, the criterion of "directness" may be used, in others "foreseeability" or "proximity"'; ILC, 'Report of the International Law Commission on the Work of its Fifty-third Session', UNGA, Supplement No. 10 (A/56/10) (New York: UN, 2001), pp. 227–8 (citations omitted). See also Danailov, 'Accountability of Non-State Actors', p. 25.

[160] See pp. 41–2 above.

innovative in their approach. Some have tried to fill this gap with informal unofficial or ad hoc inquiries and hearings;[161] others, as shall be discussed further in chapter 5, have turned their attention to the national courts.

A number of suggestions have been made as to how existing international institutions and procedures might be adapted to make human rights central to, rather than merely a peripheral part of, the international regulatory environment for business. The ICRHP, for instance, suggests a greater role for the various existing bodies presently charged with monitoring compliance with human rights instruments; these can (and in some cases do) hear complaints by individuals relating to the activities of private companies.[162] The UN Commission on Human Rights, too, has tangentially dealt with CSR-related issues in various resolutions and reports,[163] and would seem well placed to take a greater (and more formal and proactive) role in relation to the human rights monitoring of multinationals. Kinley and Tadaki argue that, although

it would be conceptually difficult and practically impossible to require all TNCs themselves to submit human rights reports to the various UN committees . . . it would be possible for the Committees to become more insistent on states providing them with the details of corporations' compliance and non-compliance with relevant human rights treaty provisions, and further, on the strength of such reports, be expected to answer for the actions of corporations operating in their respective jurisdictions.[164]

New international monitoring institutions, specifically devoted to the activities of multinationals, remain a possibility.[165] This was one of the aims of the UN Norms,[166] although the vagueness of the Norms in relation to some crucial concepts – not least the definition of 'transnational corporation'[167] – highlights some of the difficulties involved in achieving effective implementation. These definitional problems are compounded by the prevalence of the notion of 'supply chain responsibility', that is, the idea that CSR-related obligations are owed not only to those affected

---

[161] See n. 189 below.

[162] ICHRP, 'Beyond Voluntarism', pp. 83–5. For an example of such a complaint see *Decision Regarding Communication 155/96*, n. 128 above, concerning the activities of oil companies in Ongoniland. In 2002, the African Commission on Human and Peoples' Rights handed down their decision which included the finding that the Nigerian government had failed in its human rights obligations to its citizens by failing to regulate private actors (and particularly international oil companies) effectively.

[163] ICHRP, 'Beyond Voluntarism', p. 86.   [164] Kinley and Tadaki, 'From Talk to Walk', 997.

[165] Redmond, 'Transnational Enterprise', 102. See further pp. 279–80 below.

[166] See n. 47 above. See further pp. 261–2 below.

[167] See p. 56 above.

by companies under a parent company's direct managerial control, but throughout the 'supply chain'. It is natural to work from the presumption that international law obligations in the CSR field would fall primarily on the parent company, although international codes of conduct suggest a case-by-case approach. The OECD Guidelines (which refer to human rights standards) state, for example, that 'different entities are expected to co-operate and to assist one another' in accordance with 'the actual distribution of responsibilities among them'.[168] While this may be a satisfactory approach for a 'non-binding' instrument like the OECD Guidelines, greater certainty will be needed – of the type of obligations owed, and who they are owed by – if a more adversarial approach is adopted.[169] Assuming the doctrine of separate corporate personality is here to stay, theories will need to be developed to explain how, and on what basis, different elements of the corporate group (and particularly parent companies) are to be held legally responsible. While international law may lack the necessary tools at present, there are precedents to draw upon in domestic law. Criminal law theories such as 'functional liability', 'complicity' or 'conspiracy' are all potentially useful as bases for attributing legal responsibility within complex corporate groups.[170] In the tort law field, new theories of 'parent company liability' are being developed in support of legal claims in national courts relating to alleged human rights abuses by subsidiaries abroad. These are explored further in chapter 5.

The role of non-state actors

It is stated above that international law is made by states. This is really just a shorthand way of saying that the consent of states is needed before a rule can become part of international law. In reality, though, acceptance by states of a new rule (whether by treaty or through custom) is only the last stage in a 'complex' and 'extended' process of international law-making.[171] As traditionally constructed, international law exists to regulate an international society made up, not of people, but of states which, as 'sovereign equals', collectively negotiate and apply the law that governs relations between them. This model of international law

---

[168] OECD Guidelines (Revision 2000), n. 52, Part I (Concepts and Principles), para. 3.

[169] I am grateful to Anna Kirk for her insights here. See also pp. 52–4 above.

[170] See J. Clough, 'Not-so Innocents Abroad: Corporate Criminal Liability for Human Rights Abuses' (2005) 11 *AJHR* 1.

[171] J. Johnson, 'Public–Private Convergence: How the Private Actor Can Shape Public International Law Labour Standards' (1998) 24 *BJIL* 291, 350, 354–5.

(which Slaughter has referred to as the 'billiard ball' model[172]) has the advantage of simplicity. Its disadvantage, however, is that it tends to obscure the role played by other non-state actors – people, NGOs, companies and other organisations – in developing, communicating and entrenching norms.[173] As Slaughter notes, '[v]oluntary codes of conduct adopted by transnational enterprises, for instance, simply do not fit into a state-centric, top-down framework'.[174] Slaughter proposes, instead, an alternative, 'liberal' theory of international law that 'assumes that international order is created from the bottom up' and 'identifies multiple bodies of rules, norms and processes that contribute to international order, beginning with voluntary codes of conduct adopted by individual and corporate actors operating in transnational society and working up through transnational and transgovernmental law to traditional public international law'.[175] This approach has important consequences for our understanding of how international law is developed and maintained:

In addition to identifying and integrating these different types and levels of law within a unified framework, the Liberal approach *reorders their relative priority as sources of international order*. If the sources of state behaviour lie in the formation and representation of individual and group preferences, then the key to international order lies in shaping those preferences and regulating the individual and collective ability to achieve them.[176]

This is something human rights and CSR campaigners seem instinctively to understand. NGOs have long recognised that mobilising grass-roots support for a point of view is often key to international law reform.[177] Where individuals and national groups are unable to make their claims to their own governments directly, NGOs have been able to provide the transnational links necessary to lobby other states and international organisations, and so bring pressure to bear from outside.[178] But NGOs do not merely co-ordinate and manage external pressures for change; they also play a key role in the 'socialisation' of new norms at the

---

[172] A. Slaughter, 'A Liberal Theory of International Law' (2000) 94 *ASIL Proc* 240.
[173] See Keck and Sikkink, *Activists Beyond Borders*, esp. at pp. 212–17.
[174] Slaughter, 'A Liberal Theory', 242.   [175] Ibid, 242.
[176] Ibid, 242. For a case study of how non-state actors have helped create international policy in the area of labour standards, see Johnson, 'Public–Private Convergence'.
[177] Keck and Sikkink, *Activists Beyond Borders*. See also Braithwaite and Drahos, *Global Business Regulation*, p. 31.
[178] Keck and Sikkink refer to this pattern of influence as the 'boomerang pattern'. See Keck and Sikkink, *Activists Beyond Borders*, pp. 12–13.

domestic level.[179] This has important implications for international law, as the success of this 'socialisation' process will ultimately determine which norms then become binding (whether by virtue of customary or treaty law).

If there is an outstanding example of 'bottom up' consensus-building, then CSR is probably it. As discussed in chapter 1, the transformation of CSR from a fringe concern to a 'mainstream' policy issue has largely been a result of the efforts of a diverse group of determined NGOs and trade unions. While most of the leading campaigning organisations have a human rights, anti-poverty or environmental brief,[180] there are also a host of specialist NGOs, networks and research institutions dedicated exclusively to CSR-related issues.[181] These organisations have devised codes of conduct,[182] established social and environmental labelling schemes,[183] documented cases of alleged abuse by multinationals,[184] developed detailed guidance on CSR reporting principles and techniques,[185] lobbied politicians, governments[186] and international organisations,[187] mobilised public demonstrations, called for

---

[179] T. Risse and K. Sikkink, 'The Socialization of International Human Rights Norms into Domestic Practices: Introduction' in T. Risse, S. Ropp and K. Sikkink (eds.), *The Power of Human Rights: International Norms and Domestic Change* (Cambridge: Cambridge University Press, 1999).

[180] E.g. Amnesty International, FoE, Christian Aid, the World Wildlife Fund ('WWF').

[181] E.g. Clean Clothes Campaign (Netherlands), Fair Labor Association (USA), Transparency International (USA) and the Global Reporting Initiative. There are also a number of business-led organisations and charities dedicated to CSR, such as the BITC (UK) and Business for Sustainable Development (USA).

[182] E.g. Amnesty International, 'Human Rights Principles for Companies', available from http://www.amnesty.org. For an example of a sectoral code of conduct see Clean Clothes Campaign, 'Code of Labor Practices for the Apparel Industry', http://www.cleanclothes.org. See also the ICFTU/ITS, 'Basic Code of Conduct Covering Labour Practices', http://www.icftu.org. In relation to consumer safety and marketing issues see Consumers International, 'Charter for Global Business'. http://www.consumersinternational.org. See further http://www.codesofconduct.org for links to other codes developed by NGOs and labour organisations.

[183] Examples include the 'green labelling' scheme operated by the Forest Stewardship Council and the 'Rugmark' scheme operated by a German-based charity, designed to enable consumers to identify rugs produced without the use of child labour.

[184] E.g. FoE, 'Failing the Challenge: the Other Shell Report 2002'.

[185] See, for example, the work of the GRI on CSR reporting, http://www.globalreporting.org.

[186] See, for example, the work of the WWF and FoE in relation to the UK system for awarding export credits for overseas projects (see pp. 189–90 below) or the work of the UK-based CORE Coalition in seeking to develop new laws on CSR (see pp. 168–70 below).

[187] See, for example, the work of Babymilk Action in relation to the development of a code of conduct on the marketing of breastmilk substitutes (eventually adopted by

consumer boycotts,[188] conducted inquiries into allegations of misconduct by multinationals,[189] provided advisory, liaison and information-
gathering services,[190] and acted as both official and unofficial monitors of multinational behaviour.[191] They are highly influential, too, in
terms of 'issue selection' (that is, determining the relative priority to
be given to different issues in terms of resources and international
profile).

Already, NGOs have been instrumental in the development of a number of flagship governmental and inter-governmental initiatives, such as
the Kimberley Process on Conflict Diamonds,[192] the Extractive Industries
Transparency Initiative ('EITI'),[193] the UK-based Ethical Trading Initiative
('ETI')[194] and the Voluntary Principles on Security and Human Rights.[195]

the WHO and UNICEF in 1981). There are presently around 2,000 NGOs registered
with the Economic and Social Council to lobby at the UN; J. Mertus, *The United
Nations and Human Rights: a Guide for a New Era* (New York: Routledge, 2005), p. 65

[188] The boycott of Nestlé products orchestrated by the charity Babymilk Action is a
well-known example (see http://www.babymilkaction.org). FoE regularly organises
consumer boycotts against companies targeted in specific environmental campaigns,
e.g. Esso (for lobbying against the Kyoto Protocol and for 'failing to invest in
renewable energy') and suppliers of tropical hardwoods. For a list of current boycotts
relevant to UK consumers see
http://www.ethicalconsumer.org/boycotts/boycotts_list.htm.

[189] E.g. the series of hearings convened by the Permanent People's Tribunal ('PPT') into
the Bhopal disaster in London in late 1994. See further
http://www.pan-uk.org/Internat/indhaz/hazindex.htm.

[190] E.g. the Netherlands-based Clean Clothes Campaign, a coalition of around two
hundred separate organisations, including NGOs, unions and other institutions in
countries where clothes are produced.

[191] E.g. The Fair Labor Association (a coalition of NGOs, US colleges and universities)
arranges independent verification of the workplace standards of participating
companies (and their suppliers) and publishes an annual report which describes 'the
compliance programs of Participating Companies; common compliance issues in
countries of manufacture; and efforts by Participating Companies to address them'.
See further http://www.fairlabor.org.

[192] An international certification scheme aimed at curbing trade in 'conflict diamonds'.
See further http://www.kimberleyprocess.org.

[193] A project to improve transparency of payments by extractive industries to
governments around the world, launched by British Prime Minister Tony Blair at the
WSSD in Johannesburg in September 2002. See further pp. 178–9 below.

[194] 'An alliance of companies, NGOs and trade union organisations working to promote
and implement the implementation of corporate codes of practice which cover supply
chain working conditions'; http://ethicaltrade.org, 'About the ETI'. The ETI is
part-funded by the UK government. See further pp. 99, 163 below.

[195] A code of conduct to govern the use by multinationals of security firms in
connection with their international projects, devised by the governments of the UK
and USA, in conjunction with companies working in the extractive and energy
industries and interested NGOs. See further www.voluntaryprinciples.org.

Increasingly, governments and international organisations look to NGOs for advice and draw upon their research on CSR-related issues. For instance, the work of the GRI, an organisation working to standardise reporting techniques in relation to social and environmental issues, has been endorsed by a number of national governments in the context of their own national policies on CSR reporting[196] and is explicitly referred to in the Plan of Implementation adopted at the World Summit on Sustainable Development ('WSSD') in September 2002.[197] NGOs are actively recruited to international initiatives such as the Global Compact[198] and the EMSF, and are now routinely given a formal role at international conferences on business-related issues,[199] consultations and other policy-making processes.[200] Under the revised OECD Guidelines, for instance, the OECD's Committee on Investment and Multinational Enterprises is now expressly required to include NGOs as part of its follow-up consultation procedures.[201] In addition, the National Contact Points or 'NCPs' (appointed by governments pursuant to the Guidelines)

[196] The Australian government's guide to environmental reporting, for instance, describes the GRI Guidelines as 'the internationally accepted framework for sustainability reporting'. Environment Australia, 'Triple Bottom Line Reporting in Australia – a Guide to Reporting against Environmental Indicators', June 2003.

[197] 2002 Plan of Implementation of the World Summit on Sustainable Development, in UN, 'Report of the World Summit on Sustainable Development', UN Doc. A/CONF.199/20, Sales No. E.03.II.A.1, paragraph 18(c).

[198] The Global Compact treats NGOs as 'equal partners' in the project, along with business organisations, recognising that 'such organizations have a crucial role to play in helping to foster partnerships and produce substantive action'; http://globalcompact.org, 'Frequently Asked Questions'. 'Participation' in the Global Compact project involves access to policy dialogue organised by the Global Compact office, and a right to attend its annual meetings. In addition, representatives of the ICFTU and Amnesty International are members of the Global Compact Advisory Committee, described as the 'first UN advisory body composed of both public and private sector leaders'; UN Press Release, 'Secretary-General Convenes First Meeting of Global Compact Advisory Council', 8 January 2002.

[199] E.g. the WSSD included several 'multi-stakeholder' sessions, to which NGOs were invited.

[200] E.g. the decision to give a formal role to NGOs in the development of the revised OECD Guidelines. 'Once negotiations began, there were CSO [i.e. civil society organisation] consultations on the occasion of every negotiating session, involving joint participation of government, business, labour and CSOs . . . As they were developed, drafts of the revised Guidelines were also placed on the OECD Web for public comments'; OECD, 'Civil Society and the OECD', OECD Policy Brief Series, 2001, p. 4. NGOs singled out as having played a particularly active role were ANPED (the Northern Alliance of Sustainability), FoE, Oxfam and the WWF.

[201] OECD, 'Decision of the OECD Council on the OECD Guidelines for Multinational Enterprises', C(2000)96/FINAL, adopted by the Council at its 982nd session, 26–27 June 2000, Part I, para. 2.

are directed to respond to inquiries by NGOs and 'where relevant' to consult with NGOs and 'relevant experts' in relation to compliance issues.[202]

But NGOs and trade unions are not the only non-state actors involved in 'bottom up' rule-making on CSR. Increasingly, multinationals themselves are engaging publicly in debates about the role of business in society, the standards to which they should operate and the relevance of human rights. This is an extremely important development in cultural terms. As Risse and Sikkink have observed, an important milestone in the 'socialisation' of human rights norms is reached when those accused of human rights violations stop denying the accuracy of claims (and denouncing their critics) and start engaging in a dialogue with their accusers.[203]

As noted in chapter 1, multinationals are devoting huge resources to understanding and influencing the developing CSR agenda at both national and international level. On the self-regulatory front, multinationals have developed their own (company-specific) 'codes of conduct'[204] and 'human rights guidelines',[205] created new 'sustainability' management posts, and have teamed up with governments to develop strategies to deal with specific issues of international concern such as security arrangements for industrial sites,[206] conflict diamonds[207] and corruption in the extractive industries.[208] In their CSR reports, multinationals are keen to present themselves as being in touch with the views of their critics, as these passages from recent CSR reports illustrate:

---

[202] OECD, 'Decision of the Council', ibid., 'Procedural Guidance on Implementation Procedures of the OECD Guidelines for Multinational Enterprises', para. C2(a).

[203] Risse and Sikkink, 'The Socialization of International Human Rights Norms', pp. 23–4, 27–8. Although denials are significant too. As Risse and Sikkink put it, '[w]e count the denial stage as part of the socialization process because the fact that the state feels compelled to deny changes demonstrates that a process of international socialization is already underway', p. 23.

[204] E.g. BP, 'Ethical Conduct Policy: Guidelines on Business Conduct', http://www.bp.com; Rio Tinto, 'The Way We Work', April 2003, http://www.riotinto.com; Nike, 'Code of Conduct', 1991, http://www.nike.co/nikebiz. See further http://www.codesofconduct.org/company.htm for links to corporate codes of conduct of a number of other prominent multinationals including Levi Strauss, The Body Shop and Unocal. See further OECD, 'Codes of Conduct – Explaining their Economic Significance', Report of the Working Party of the Trade Committee, 11 May 2001, TD/TC/WP (2001)10/FINAL.

[205] E.g. Rio Tinto, 'Human Rights Guidance', October 2003, http://www.riotinto.com.

[206] See n. 195 above.   [207] See n. 192 above.   [208] See further pp. 178–9 below.

We [BP] conduct dialogue with specialist stakeholders, such as NGOs, multilateral organisations and academics, to help us develop specific guidelines. For example, we worked with the Global Business Coalition and the Joint UN programme on HIV/AIDS to develop procedures now being applied across BP. We avoid resettlement wherever possible, but have developed a set of guidelines in partnership with a major economic and social rights NGO to ensure that, if people must be relocated, they are treated with respect and compensated fairly. In 2003, this helped decision-making in Angola, Indonesia and China.[209]

One of the primary means by which Rio Tinto relates to civil society is through partnerships with environmental, educational and indigenous non government organisations (NGOs) under our global partnership programme. We recognise that many voluntary organisations and NGOs have a serious interest in what we do and how we do it. The Rio Tinto global partnership programme currently involves 15 organisations.[210]

We [Nike] plan to work with industry counterparts to encourage broader disclosure of supply chains, and we plan to seek out and support effective coalitions of companies, trade unions, NGOs, multilateral agencies and governments to raise standards for our supply chain and our industry.[211]

The past decade has seen the creation of a number of new initiatives designed to aid 'engagement' between multinationals, NGOs and trade unions. The ETI in the UK, mentioned briefly above, presently numbers around thirty corporate members, four trade union organisations and sixteen NGOs. Its activities include training for members, conferences, research and other experimental projects designed to 'provide our corporate, trade union and NGO members the opportunity to work together to identify and promote good practice in specific aspects of code implementation, often in collaboration with their suppliers and partners'.[212] The Fair Labor Association ('FLA') in the USA arose out of the 'Apparel Industry Partnership', an initiative of the Clinton administration. It describes itself as 'a non-profit organization combining the efforts of industry, non-governmental organizations (NGOs), colleges and universities to promote adherence to international labor standards and improve working conditions worldwide'.[213] Like the UK's ETI, the FLA's work revolves around a code of conduct which members are expected

---

[209] BP, 'Defining Our Path: Sustainability Report 2003', April 2004, http://www.bp.com, p. 31.
[210] Rio Tinto, '2004 Sustainable Development Review', http://www.riotinto.com.
[211] Nike, 'FY04 Corporate Responsibility Report', http://www.nike.com/nikebiz, p. 48.
[212] See http://www.ethicaltrade.org.   [213] See http://www.fairlabor.org.

to abide by. (Although, unlike the ETI, compliance with the FLA's code is expected to be independently verified.) The FLA's web-site currently lists twenty 'leading brand' companies as corporate members, including Adidas, Liz Claiborne, Puma and Reebok.[214] Similar initiatives have also sprung up at international level. The UN Global Compact is a good example. Today, the Global Compact has grown into a network of over 1,400 companies together with six key UN agencies,[215] a large number of NGOs (both transnational and national), trade unions, academic institutions and industry associations. This initiative, launched by Kofi Annan in mid-2000, also operates around a code (the 'Ten Principles'), but is designed primarily to facilitate dialogue between the UN, 'world business', civil society and trade unions in relation to the social issues arising from 'globalisation'.[216]

NGOs, trade unions and businesses are forging links with each other in many different ways. In addition to forming and participating in broad-based 'coalitions' and 'think tanks', companies and NGOs are also forming 'partnerships' to tackle specific problems, such as access to HIV/AIDS drug treatments,[217] poverty[218] or environmental degradation.[219] However, at this stage it is still extremely difficult to tell how far the core ideals of the CSR community have become embedded in corporate culture. There is still plenty of scepticism within 'civil society' about the level of commitment of multinationals to self-regulatory schemes and to social and environmental reform in general. Some multinationals have seen their environmental initiatives dismissed as 'greenwash',[220] while others have been accused of using CSR-related initiatives as a

---

[214] Ibid.

[215] UN 'core partner agencies' are the Office of the UN High Commissioner for Human Rights (OHCHR), the United Nations Environmental Programme (UNEP), the United Nations Development Programme (UNDP), the United Nations Industrial Development Organisation (UNIDO) and the UN Office on Drugs and Crime.

[216] See http://www.unglobalcompactorg, 'What is the Global Compact?'.

[217] E.g. the announcement by Coca-Cola in 2001 that it would be working with the UN's Joint Programme on AIDS ('UNAIDS') on various initiatives to combat the spread of HIV/AIDS in Africa.

[218] E.g. a microfinance initiative in Uganda developed by a 'public–private consortium' comprising a range of organisations including Hewlett Packard, Freedom from Hunger and the US Agency for International Development. See R. Cowe, 'Business–NGO Partnerships – What's the Payback?', Ethical Corporation, April 2004, p. 14.

[219] E.g. the Marine Stewardship Council, a charity created by the WWF and Unilever to promote responsible fishing practices. See http://www.msc.org.

[220] The US NGO Corporate Watch has given out periodic 'greenwash awards' to 'corporations that put more money, time and energy into slick PR campaigns aimed

way of diverting attention away from bad press elsewhere[221] or as a tactical concession to avoid more stringent legislation at some later stage.[222]

Neither should the claims of home states as regards their own CSR-related initiatives and programmes necessarily be taken at face value. As noted in chapter 1, most governments remain committed to the (rather simplistic) idea that CSR is 'voluntary'. Clearly, 'non-binding' forms of regulation are generally much less costly – in both political and financial terms – than regimes carrying formal legal sanctions. Nevertheless, self-regulation can be an important first step in the development of subsequent 'hard law':

> Whether or not corporate self-regulation is largely an effort to fend off binding state and interstate regulation, it has the distinct advantage by virtue of its very non-bindingness, of having out a small army of Trojan horses onto the field of ideological struggle over corporate social responsibility, an army which NGOs are rapidly becoming adept at pushing through corporate gates.[223]

Multinationals are facing up to a changing set of moral and social expectations. Whatever the reasons behind their different contributions, their involvement in the CSR debate is undoubtedly helping to shape future international law on CSR. First and foremost, this involvement is contributing to the 'socialisation' of new ideas and norms at national level. Although multinationals have so far staunchly resisted calls for tighter regulation (at domestic or international level) in relation to international CSR issues, their support for these new principles and standards in their codes of conduct and other programmes may ultimately make tighter regulation more likely, if only to help create a 'level playing field' for CSR leaders and 'laggards' alike.[224] Obviously, introducing new regulation is a much less daunting prospect when the regulatory targets

at promoting their eco-friendly images, than they do to actually protecting the environment'. For details of past recipients see http://www.corporatewatch.org.

[221] M. Lopatin, 'Can Coke Deliver more than Fizzy Publicity?', *Observer*, 1 December 2002, p. 7.

[222] C. Williams, 'Civil Society Initiatives and "Soft Law" in the Oil and Gas Industry' (2004) 36 *NYUJIL&P* 457, 466. See also Christian Aid, 'Behind the Mask', p. 15.

[223] C. Scott, 'Translating Torture into Transnational Tort: Conceptual Divides in the Debate on Corporate Accountability for Human Rights Harms' in C. Scott (ed.), *Torture as Tort: Comparative Perspectives on the Development of Transnational Human Rights Litigation* (Oxford: Hart Publishing, 2001), p. 60.

[224] Mary Robinson, 'Beyond Good Intentions: Corporate Citizenship for a New Century', address given to the Royal Society for the Encouragement of the Arts, Manufacture and Commerce, London, 7 May 2002.

have already expressed their commitment to the principles and standards concerned. And '[s]takeholders who participate in the drafting of norms that govern their behaviour are more likely to feel a commitment to the norms adopted'.[225] At the very least, these non-state actors 'play an important role in how norms are socially constructed [and] . . . through their interpretations and behaviour, they give meaning to legal laws and norms'.[226]

Furthermore, interaction between NGOs, multinationals and trade unions, both at national level and under the auspices of the various different international institutions and initiatives described above, may well represent the early stages in the development of new 'global' regulatory regimes. Braithwaite and Drahos have described this process thus:

> [D]ialogue builds regimes through defining issues as a concern, creating contracting spaces where complex interdependency can induce cooperation, constituting normative commitments, nurturing habits of compliance that are then institutionalised into bureaucratic regimes, communicating informal praise and shame that are then institutionalised, and building capacity. When many different types of actors use many dialogic mechanisms of this sort, both impressive regime-building and impressive compliance have been repeatedly demonstrated.[227]

In summary, while non-state actors are closely involved – and in many cases have taken a leading role – in the development of international CSR principles for multinationals, their activities are not, traditionally, regarded as a source of customary norms.[228] Nevertheless, they still have a significant role to play in the 'bottom up' development of international law. In the formation of new customary rules, it is not the original source of an idea or principle that matters, but state practice in relation to it. Non-state actors can (and do) propose new norms which, if then taken up and reflected in state practice, can eventually become new (binding) customary norms.

---

[225] Shelton, 'Law, Non-Law and the Problem of Soft Law', p. 16.

[226] J. Mertus, 'Considering Nonstate Actors in the New Millennium: Towards Expanded Participation in Norm Creation and Norm Application' (2000) 32 Int'l L&P 537, 562. See also H. Charlesworth and C. Chinkin, *The Boundaries of International Law* (Manchester: Juris Publishing/Manchester University Press, 2000), pp. 88–95.

[227] Braithwaite and Drahos, *Global Business Regulation*, p. 32.

[228] For criticism of this position, see further I. Gunning, 'Modernising Customary International Law: the Challenge of Human Rights' (1991) 31 VJIL 211; Mertus, 'Considering Nonstate Actors'. See also Alston, 'Myopia'.

Conclusion

International law does not provide easy solutions to the social and environmental issues posed by multinationals. Nevertheless, its structures are capable of supporting a range of international regimes on CSR. Most obviously, states could enter into a treaty under which they each commit to regulate the activities of companies within their jurisdiction along pre-agreed lines, or to consult and share information relating to multinational activities, or to create and support new international regulatory institutions. In the meantime, state practice in the CSR field is capable of generating new customary law. Customary law, as discussed above, has the potential both to expand the obligations of 'home states' to regulate and control multinationals effectively, and arguably to impose new direct obligations on multinationals to protect and promote human rights.

The primary obstacles to effective international CSR regulation of multinationals are, therefore, not legal but political. Whether international law on CSR now moves forward, or languishes in its present state, depends on how states respond to changing social, environmental and moral expectations of companies and the new regulatory demands. So does state practice provide any indication that new norms of international law are currently under development? This question is the main focus of Parts II and III of this book. Part II looks at the progress that has been made so far at national level, in the UK and elsewhere. Part III is concerned with recent CSR-related initiatives and proposals emerging from international institutions, and the extent to which these are helping to shape the future direction of international law on CSR. First, though, it is necessary to explore one further theoretical issue that has very real implications for the future of international regulation of multinationals in the CSR field: the problem of 'jurisdiction'.

3 Multinationals under national law: the problem of jurisdiction

International law constraints on the jurisdiction of states have always posed difficulties for the regulation of multinationals. As discussed in chapter 2, international law is concerned fundamentally with relations between states. Multinationals are not traditional subjects of international law, and the extent to which international law now imposes obligations directly upon them is still controversial. This focus on *states* as the primary subjects of international law has led more than one commentator to doubt whether international law, as presently constructed, is properly equipped to deal with the challenges posed by international business.[1] As multinationals span national boundaries, no one state has rights and obligations in respect of them. For these reasons, multinationals are often said to 'fall through the cracks' of the international regulatory system.

The aim of this chapter is to examine in more detail the concept of jurisdiction, as it applies to the social and environmental regulation of multinationals. As will be seen, different branches of law approach jurisdictional problems differently depending on whether the law is called upon to enforce public law or private law rights and obligations. Both are dominated by notions of 'territoriality'. However, public international law (generally referred to in this book simply as 'international law'), which governs the geographical scope of state power, tends to view jurisdiction in spatial terms, whereas in private international law jurisdiction is generally justified in terms of 'connecting

---

[1] Johns, 'The Invisibility of the Transnational Corporation'; Bantekas, 'Corporate Social Responsibility in International Law', 310–11; Kinley and Tadaki, 'From Talk to Walk', 935, 937–9; Dine, *Companies, International Trade and Human Rights*, pp. 68–76.

factors' between the particular dispute and the 'forum state'. Clearly, these two different areas of law are designed to do two different jobs. However, this distinction should not be allowed to obscure the fact that, in deciding private law disputes, judges also perform a *regulatory* role.

Unfortunately, public international law rules on jurisdiction reflect a rather simplistic (not to mention outdated) notion of what regulation is. These international law rules are focused almost exclusively on the more traditional 'command and control' forms of regulation and have little to say about the use of the alternative forms of regulation discussed in chapter 1. This makes the legality of the subtler forms of regulation used in the CSR field (further examples of which are given in chapter 4) difficult to assess. These alternative methods of 'extraterritorial regulation' rely on the jurisdiction enjoyed by a 'home state' of a multinational over the parent company and are referred to in this chapter as 'parent-based'[2] methods of extraterritorial regulation. The conclusion is that, so far as social and environmental regulation is concerned, indirect or 'parent-based' forms of extraterritorial regulation are generally permitted, provided they do not violate the international law duty of 'non-intervention'.

The limits of jurisdiction under public international law

It is a basic principle of international law that each state has exclusive jurisdiction to regulate the activities of individuals, corporations and other entities within the limits of its territory. This is known as the 'territorial' principle. However, with respect to activities taking place *outside* the territorial limits of a state, the position is more complicated. Assertions of 'extraterritorial' jurisdiction are generally prohibited, unless they can be justified by reference to one or more established customary principles. These include the 'nationality principle', the 'universality' principle and, more controversially, the 'effects doctrine'. The 'effects doctrine' is derived from the 'territorial' principle and claims extended jurisdiction for a state in cases where activities taking place *outside* territorial limits (usually in another state) have an adverse effect *within* the regulating state.

---

[2] See n. 6 below.

The 'nationality' principle

International law has developed rules to help determine the nationality of corporations.[3] States are entitled to regulate the activities of companies incorporated under their laws, on the basis of the 'nationality' principle. However, states do not, as a general rule, prescribe laws for foreign subsidiaries of locally incorporated parent companies. The US position, as set out in the American Law Institute's 1987 Third Restatement on Foreign Relations Law[4] (the 'US Third Restatement'), is as follows:

A state may not *ordinarily* regulate activities of corporations organised under the laws of a foreign state on the basis that they are owned or controlled by nationals of the regulating state. However . . . it may not be unreasonable for a state to exercise jurisdiction for limited purposes with respect to activities of affiliated foreign entities:

  (a) by direction to the parent corporation in respect of such matters as uniform accounting, disclosure to investors, or preparation of consolidated tax returns of multinational enterprises; or

  (b) by direction to either the parent or the subsidiary in exceptional cases, depending on all relevant factors, including the extent to which
    (i) the regulation is essential to implementation of a program to further a major national interest of the state exercising the jurisdiction;
    (ii) the national program of which the regulation is a part can be carried out effectively only if it is applied also to foreign subsidiaries;
    (iii) the regulation conflicts or is unlikely to conflict with the law or policy of the state where the subsidiary is established.

  (c) *In the exceptional cases referred to in paragraph (b), the burden of establishing reasonableness is heavier when the direction is issued to the foreign subsidiary than when it is issued to the parent corporation.*[5]

In this statement, a distinction is drawn between legal obligations enforced through the parent company and obligations made directly applicable to and enforced against the foreign subsidiary itself. However, even though only one of these legislative strategies actually involves extraterritorial *enforcement*, both are treated in the US Third Restatement

---

[3] See *Barcelona Traction Light & Power Company* [1970] ICJ Reps 3, esp. at para. 70. The issue of corporate nationality is revisited at pp. 146–51 below. For the remainder of this chapter the use of the term 'home state' in respect of a multinational refers to the state of incorporation of the parent company of that multinational group.

[4] ALI, 'Restatement of the Law, Third, Foreign Relations', 1987 § 213.

[5] Ibid., § 414 (emphasis added).

as methods of 'extraterritorial regulation'. These two different methods are referred to in this chapter as 'parent-based' and 'foreign-prescriptive' extraterritorial regulation.[6]

US export control law provides examples of extraterritorial regulation of both kinds. Under the Export Administration Act of 1979,[7] the president was given the power to place 'foreign policy controls' on exports 'of any goods, technology or other information subject to the jurisdiction of the United States or *by any person subject to the jurisdiction of the United States*'.[8] In 1982, this provision was invoked by President Reagan to issue export controls on equipment and technology destined for a natural gas pipeline construction project in the Soviet Union. This particular set of controls were important because they included, for the first time, measures addressed directly to foreign subsidiaries of US companies. In addition, these regulations also imposed restrictions on non-US companies on the basis that the technology involved had been licensed from the USA. These measures were, however, extremely controversial and the European Commission disputed the idea that export controls could be extended to foreign subsidiaries of US companies on the basis of the 'nationality' principle.[9]

The measures used against the Soviet Union in 1982 represent the most extensive interpretation of the 'nationality' principle under US sanctions laws so far.[10] In contrast, the sanctions against Libya in 1986 were applied to 'US persons', defined to include overseas branches, but to exclude foreign corporations operating outside the USA.[11] Similarly, the US Anti-Terrorism Act,[12] which became effective in November 2002, applies to US citizens and residents and US-incorporated companies, but not to overseas subsidiaries of those companies.

---

[6] While these different types of regulation may also be referred to as 'direct' and 'indirect' forms of extraterritorial regulation, the terms 'parent-based' and 'foreign-prescriptive' are used here to avoid confusion with the terminology used in the discussion above (pp. 76–91) on multinationals and human rights.

[7] 50 USC § 2405.

[8] 50 USC § 2405, para (a)(1) (emphasis added).

[9] European Commission, 'Comments on the US Regulations Concerning Trade with the USSR', 12 August 1982; (1982) 21 ILM 891.

[10] Note, however, that extensive claims of jurisdiction over foreign subsidiaries of US companies have been made under other legislation. See further C. Buys, 'United States Economic Sanctions: the Fairness of Targeting Persons from Third Countries' (1999) 17 *BUILJ* 214.

[11] See further B. Carter, *International Economic Sanctions: Improving the Haphazard US Regime* (Cambridge: Cambridge University Press, 1988), p. 195.

[12] 18 USCA § 2332d.

'Parent-based' extraterritorial regulation involves subjecting foreign subsidiaries to extraterritorial regulation by the home state *through* the parent. For example, the parent can be placed under a legal obligation to ensure that a subsidiary follows a certain course of conduct, which can then be enforced against the parent company. While seemingly less contentious, parent-based extraterritorial regulation through the parent company is also capable of creating tensions between companies and between states. The French case of *Société Fruehauf* v. *Massardy*[13] concerned directions given by the US government under 'trading with the enemy' legislation to a US company to prevent its French subsidiary from providing equipment to a French purchaser destined for China. This put the parent company's legal obligations in direct conflict with the contractual obligations of the subsidiary. Ultimately, the solution adopted by the French courts was to place the French subsidiary under administration.[14]

But, while these few claims of 'nationality' over foreign subsidiaries have generated a great deal of attention, the USA's general approach has been more cautious. In relation to 'foreign corrupt practices', for example, an early proposal to apply legislation directly to foreign subsidiaries of US-owned companies was rejected because of concerns about 'the inherent jurisdictional, enforcement and diplomatic difficulties raised by the inclusion of foreign subsidiaries of US companies in the direct prohibitions of the bill'.[15] This was despite concerns that a failure to extend the law to foreign subsidiaries would create a 'massive loophole through which millions of bribery dollars would continue to flow'.[16] A form of parent-based regulation of foreign companies is used instead: US parent companies can themselves be held liable under the Foreign Corrupt Practices Act[17] ('FCPA') for the acts of foreign subsidiaries outside the USA where the US parent company has authorised or directed 'corrupt payments' to be made.

The UK has traditionally been much more reluctant than the USA to extend its laws beyond territorial boundaries. As a general rule,

---

[13] [1965] D. S. Jur. 147 [1965] JCP II 14 274 bis (Cour d'Appel, Paris); English translation, (1966) 4 ILM 476.

[14] Muchlinski, *Multinational Enterprises and the Law*, pp. 127–9.

[15] See 'House of Representatives Report No. 94–831 on the Foreign Corrupt Practices Act', at http://www.usdoj.gov/criminal/fraud/fcpa.html.

[16] See 'House of Representatives Report No. 95–640, on the Unlawful Corporate Payments Act of 1977' (subsequently enacted as the Foreign Corrupt Practices Act of 1977), at http://www.usdoj.gov/ criminal/fraud/fcpa.html.

[17] 15 USC § 78dd-1.

individuals (even UK nationals) will not be subject to UK criminal jurisdiction in relation to acts taking place outside UK territory. However, there are signs that the UK is moving towards more extensive use of 'nationality' jurisdiction. A number of new extraterritorial offences have entered the UK statute books in recent years. The Anti-Terrorism, Crime and Security Act 2001, for example, extends UK criminal jurisdiction to cover corruption offences committed by UK nationals abroad.[18] For companies, however, liability is limited to 'bod[ies] incorporated under the law of any part of the United Kingdom', meaning that foreign subsidiaries of UK companies, even if wholly owned, are outside the scope of these provisions.

The 'territorial' principle and the 'effects doctrine'

Clearly, each state has the jurisdiction to regulate activities taking place within its territorial boundaries. This principle (the 'territorial' principle) has been extended, under the doctrines of 'subjective' and 'objective' territoriality, to give states a degree of extraterritorial jurisdiction over criminal offences that have been commenced in one jurisdiction and concluded in another. For instance, a state may legitimately claim jurisdiction over criminal activity that was planned or directed from that jurisdiction, notwithstanding that the offences were completed elsewhere.[19] The USA has developed the idea of 'extended territoriality' even further, asserting extraterritorial jurisdiction over activities taking place overseas merely on the basis that those activities produced prohibited 'effects' within the USA.[20] According to the US Third Restatement, 'a state has jurisdiction to prescribe law with respect to . . . conduct outside its territory that has or is intended to have *substantial effect* within its territory'.[21] The application of the 'effects doctrine' in practice has, of course, been controversial.[22]

---

[18] Section 109. This legislation was introduced to fulfil the UK's obligations under the 1997 OECD Convention on the Combating of Bribery of Foreign Officials, see further pp. 286–9 below. See also the Sex Offenders Act 1997 (which extends UK criminal jurisdiction in respect of sex offences committed by UK nationals abroad) and the Criminal Justice (Terrorism and Conspiracy) Act 1998 (which extends UK criminal jurisdiction over UK nationals and UK companies in relation to acts taking place outside the UK that amount to conspiracies to commit terrorist offences within the UK).

[19] See, for example, UK Criminal Justice (Terrorism and Conspiracy) Act 1998, section 5.

[20] *US* v. *Alcoa* (1945) 148 F 2d 416 (2nd Cir. 1945), 443.

[21] US Third Restatement, § 402 (emphasis added).

[22] P. Roth, 'Reasonable Extraterritoriality: Correcting the Balance of Interests' (1992) 41 *ICLQ* 245.

Nevertheless, there are signs that the effects doctrine is now achieving greater international acceptance, at least in the area of competition law.[23]

But could the 'effects doctrine' be used to justify extraterritorial regulation in the CSR field? Labour regulation is one area in which it has been argued that the economic 'effects' of the migration of jobs and industry to countries with lower standards may justify the imposition of extraterritorial labour standards on home state multinationals.[24] Effects may be even less tangible. In the course of the US hearings on the FCPA, for example, it was suggested that there may be a case for extraterritorial regulation of bribery based on the 'effects' doctrine. Participation in corrupt practices abroad, it was argued, tarnishes the reputation of the USA and US-based industry and so jeopardises US foreign policy.[25] Similar arguments have been made in relation to the social standards of multinationals abroad. For instance, in 2001, an Australian Parliamentary Committee considered whether Australia's reputation as a 'home state' for industry justified extraterritorial regulation of the social standards of Australian-based multinationals[26] (before ultimately deciding to reject that particular regulatory proposal).[27]

But any attempt to stretch the effects doctrine this far would never be tolerated by other states. Even if the effects doctrine were widely accepted as a *general* basis for extraterritorial jurisdiction (i.e. with application beyond the confines of competition law), it would only be in the rarest of cases that the activities of a foreign subsidiary would rebound on the home state to such an extent as to justify extraterritorial

---

[23] See Case T-102/96, *Gencor Limited* v. *Commission* [1999] ECR II-753. See also the UK Competition Act 1998, section 2. For an example outside the field of competition law, see the UK Financial Services and Markets Act 2000, section 397, which prohibits misleading statements, promises or forecasts for the purposes of inducing a person to deal in securities. Sub-section 397(7) makes it clear that this provision applies both to acts done in the UK and to acts done elsewhere which create a 'false or misleading impression' in the UK.

[24] J. Zimmerman, *Extraterritorial Employment Standards of the United States* (Westport, CT: Quorum Books, 1992), pp. 164–7.

[25] H. Brown, 'The Extraterritorial Reach of the US Government's Campaign against International Bribery' (1999) 22 *Hast I&CLR* 407, 448–9.

[26] Commonwealth of Australia (Parliamentary Joint Statutory Committee on Corporations and Securities), 'Report on the Corporate Code of Conduct Bill', June 2001.

[27] See further p. 166 below.

application of social or environmental standards on this basis. However, a degree of extraterritorial jurisdiction could potentially be exercised on the basis of 'subjective' or 'extended' territoriality in cases where it could be shown that criminal activity had been planned or directed from that jurisdiction. This is relevant to offences of conspiracy and complicity involving parent companies of multinationals.[28]

The 'universal' principle

Some activities are regarded as having such serious implications for international peace and stability that they have been 'criminalised' under international law. All states are regarded as having an interest in their prevention and, therefore, each state is given criminal jurisdiction in respect of these offences, no matter where, by whom or against whom they are committed.[29]

Universal jurisdiction can derive from treaties, or from customary international law. The group of offences presently subject to universal jurisdiction is small: piracy, war crimes, torture, crimes against humanity, terrorism, genocide and slavery all potentially attract 'universal jurisdiction', although, with the exception of piracy, the extent to which universal jurisdiction derives from *customary* (as opposed to *treaty*) law is still controversial.[30] It is conceivable that a limited number of very serious abuses by multinationals may already attract universal jurisdiction under existing rules[31] and, as human rights law continues to expand in scope, it is quite possible that new categories of offences of 'universal jurisdiction' will develop. For the time being, however, universal jurisdiction could only be invoked to justify extraterritorial regulation of foreign corporations in the most extreme cases, such as where a

---

[28] Clough, 'Not-so Innocents Abroad'. Note, however, that this kind of regulation could also be justified under the 'nationality' principle.

[29] Higgins, *Problems and Process*, p. 58.

[30] See *Arrest Warrant Case (Congo v. Belgium)*, [2002] ICJ Reps 3.

[31] Universal jurisdiction was the legal justification for a 1993 Belgian law that, until recently, permitted prosecutions for serious human rights violations regardless of the nationality of the offenders or the victims or the location of the crimes. The French multinational TotalFinaElf had been the subject of an investigation under this law in relation to its alleged complicity in the use of forced labour by the Myanmar military. However, the law was amended in July 2003 to permit prosecutions only of Belgian nationals or residents, or where victims are Belgian. See further Joseph, *Corporations and Transnational Human Rights Litigation*, pp. 13–14.

multinational was implicated in crimes of torture, terrorism, genocide[32] or (possibly) forced labour.[33]

Summary

None of the three principles discussed above gives very much scope for 'foreign-prescriptive' extraterritorial regulation of multinationals in relation to social or environmental matters. Under the 'nationality' principle, any state has the right to impose social and environmental standards on companies having the nationality of that state with respect to activities inside and, theoretically, outside that state's borders. However, this does not give home states of multinationals the right to impose environmental or social standards directly on foreign incorporated subsidiaries operating entirely outside the borders of that home state, as companies are generally treated for these purposes as having the nationality of the place of incorporation, not that of its shareholders. Even the USA, much criticised in the past for its exorbitant claims of jurisdiction in relation to its national sanctions and trade controls laws, does not claim that the 'nationality' principle supports a *general* right to regulate foreign subsidiaries of US companies.[34]

It is doubtful that social and environmental regulation could be justified by reference to the 'effects doctrine' or the 'universality principle' either. While the 'effects doctrine' may be gaining acceptance in relation to competition law, it is untested in other areas. As yet, the 'universal' principle could only justify extraterritorial regulation in extreme cases, involving serious human rights violations. It certainly could not be used to support routine regulation of social and environmental concerns.

But while home states may not be able to impose social and environmental standards on foreign subsidiaries directly, they still possess

---

[32] Note that companies have been accused of involvement in 'genocide' in several claims brought under the US Alien Tort Claims Act, 28 USC § 1350. See, for example, *Wiwa v. Royal Dutch Petroleum Limited* 226 F 3d 88 (CA (NY) 2000), a claim launched by the family of Ken Saro-Wiwa under the US Alien Tort Claims Act in which 'genocide' is alleged against the oil company. See also *Presbyterian Church of Sudan v. Talisman Energy* 244 F Supp 2d 289 (SDNY 2003). Note, however, that in *Beanal v. Freeport McMoRan* 969 F Supp 362 (ED La 1997), the plaintiffs' allegations of 'genocide' were rejected by the court. These and other ATCA cases are discussed further in chapter 5.

[33] See *Doe v. Unocal* 963 F Supp 880 (CD Cal 1997), in which the judge held that '[t]he allegations of forced labour in this case are sufficient to constitute an allegation of participation in slave trading'.

[34] According to the US Third Restatement, n. 4 above, this is a right only exercisable 'in exceptional circumstances', § 414.

a considerable amount of potential regulatory influence in these areas, based on their jurisdiction over parent companies incorporated in their respective jurisdictions. This is discussed in more detail later in this chapter and also in chapter 4, where examples of state practice in this area are considered in more detail. First, though, it is necessary to compare the *public* international law rules on jurisdiction with those arising under *private* international law.

The limits of jurisdiction under private international law

The relationship between 'private' and 'public' international law

Despite the similar terminology, 'private' international law and 'public' international law are actually quite different. Whereas public international law concerns relations between states, private international law is the branch of domestic law that governs how national courts should approach private disputes to which there is a 'foreign element'. Private international law deals with questions such as whether or not it is appropriate for the court to take jurisdiction in a given case and, if so, the laws to be applied to determine the rights and liabilities as between the parties. As a result, courts have a tendency to approach jurisdictional questions differently depending on whether a rule derives from public law (e.g. a legal obligation not to engage in anti-competitive conduct), or from a private relationship between parties (e.g. based on contract, or a duty of care in the case of a tort). Broadly speaking, whereas the scope of public law tends to be understood in spatial terms, civil jurisdiction in the private law sphere tends to be defined by reference to connecting factors between the parties, the subject matter of the dispute and the state.[35]

But the relationship between 'public' and 'private' law is actually much more complex than the conventional distinctions imply. The extent to which 'private law' relationships (e.g. under contract) are now regulated by statute,[36] the use of civil mechanisms to enforce legal

---

[35] This concern with the spatial limits of public law (as opposed to private law) is what underlies the domestic law principle that national courts will not enforce the penal or revenue laws of another state. See Private International Law (Miscellaneous Provisions) Act 1995, section 14(3)(a)(ii). To do otherwise would, according to the English courts, amount to 'an assertion of sovereign authority by one state within the territory of another'; *Government of India* v. *Taylor* [1955] AC 491 at 511. See also *AG for New Zealand* v. *Ortiz* [1984] AC 1.

[36] See, for example, the UK Unfair Terms in Consumer Contracts Regulations 1991 (SI 1991 No. 2083). See also Case C-381/98, *Ingmar GB Ltd* v. *Eaton Leonard Technologies Inc.*,

standards and the increasing codification of 'private law' rights and obligations,[37] have all helped to blur the traditional boundaries between 'private' and 'public' law.[38] Moreover, the exercise of judicial discretion in private law matters cannot be so easily insulated from its social, political, economic and regulatory contexts. Even when public policy issues are not alluded to directly (or are excluded from consideration, as was the case in the English approach to forum non conveniens),[39] they are still there in the background, as Cassels explains:

> the way in which discretion is exercised is largely a product of one's perspective. This perspective is, in turn, a function of the way in which facts are filtered and constructed, and is based on an understanding of the purposes and values underlying legal principles. Facts and laws are not pregiven. They must be interpreted; and the process of interpretation incorporates a host of personal, political, moral and economic commitments.[40]

Harlow goes further: 'the "public/private" classification is part of another, more insular tradition. It is nothing more than an attempt by the judiciary to conceal the political issues behind a formalist façade and to shield from public criticism some highly executive-minded decisions.'[41]

Superficially, a court may only be deciding a dispute between private parties. In reality, though, judicial approaches to problems posed by multinationals in the private law sphere will reflect a set of principles and assumptions, conscious or unconscious, about the appropriate distribution of risk, reward and responsibilities between the different actors involved. But, as well as having a regulatory *context*, case law on matters of private international law also has regulatory *consequences* to the extent that it affects the balance of risks and rewards against which the investment decisions of multinationals are subsequently made. In this sense, even the act of deferring to the jurisdiction of the courts of another state, for whatever reason, is a 'regulatory' act, as Paul explains:

TLR, 16 November 2000 in which the ECJ held that European law rights would apply to an agency agreement, notwithstanding that the agreement was governed by the laws of a non-member state.

[37] See, for example, the UK Consumer Protection Act 1987.

[38] I. Brownlie, *Principles of Public International Law*, 5th edition (Oxford: Clarendon Press, 1998), pp. 302–3; C. Harlow, '"Public" and "Private" Law: Definition without Distinction' (1980) 43 *MLR* 241.

[39] See further pp. 124–5 below.   [40] Cassels, *The Uncertain Promise of Law*, p. 138.

[41] Harlow, 'Public and Private Law', 265.

By allowing transnational business to choose between legal systems imposing a lower regulatory burden than the United States, US courts have effectively lowered regulatory standards. By refusing to exercise jurisdiction in a case like *In re Union Carbide*, a court effectively allows a US manufacturer to avoid US tort liability and encourages other manufacturers to locate plants abroad.[42]

Though theoretically distinct, private international law and public international law can and do have an influence on each other. Like all areas of domestic law, private international law may be influenced by rules derived from public international law, although precisely how this occurs will depend on domestic constitutional arrangements of the relevant state. In the UK, as in other European states, the content of private international law has been affected by treaty arrangements designed to harmonise the rules governing jurisdiction, choice of law and the enforcement of foreign judgments.[43] Customary international law considerations also have the potential to affect outcomes in the field of private law, for example, as grounds for not taking jurisdiction over certain parties,[44] or as 'public policy' grounds for not applying foreign law to a dispute.[45] Similarities have also been observed between the principle of 'international comity' in public international law and the way the notion of 'comity' is used in the private law sphere (e.g. as a basis for declining jurisdiction in favour of another state),[46] although most writers reject the idea that 'international comity', as used in private law cases, is actually mandated by customary international law.[47]

[42] J. Paul, 'Comity in International Law' (1991) 32 *Harv. ILJ* 1, 72. The author is referring, here, to *Re Union Carbide Corporation Gas Plant Disaster at Bhopal, India in December, 1984*, 634 F Supp 842 (SDNY 1986). See further pp. 201–2 below.

[43] See, for example, 1968 Convention on Jurisdiction and Enforcement of Judgments in Civil and Commercial Matters, Brussels, 27 September 1968, in force 1 February 1973, OJ 1972 No. L299/32, 31 December 1972; 1262 UNTS 153; (1968) 8 ILM 229 (the '1968 Brussels Convention'). This treaty was implemented in the UK by the Civil Jurisdiction and Judgments Act 1982, although note that it has now been replaced by Council Regulation (EC) No. 44/2001 of 22 December 2000 on jurisdiction and the recognition and enforcement of judgments in civil and commercial matters, OJ 2001 No. L12/1, 16 January 2001 (the 'Brussels Regulation').

[44] For example, under the 'act of state' doctrine, or the principle of sovereign immunity. See further pp. 211–14 below.

[45] See further G. Born, *International Civil Litigation in the United States Courts*, 3rd edition (The Hague, Kluwer, 1996), pp. 629, 651–2. For the UK position, see the UK Private International Law (Miscellaneous Provisions) Act 1995, section 14(3).

[46] See further Joseph, *Transnational Human Rights Litigation*, pp. 46–7.

[47] C. McLachlan, 'The Influence of International Law on Civil Jurisdiction' (1993) 6 *Hague YIL* 125, 126. See also O. Kahn-Freud, 'General Problems of Private International Law' [1974] 3 *Recueil des Cours* 139, 165–96. In relation to the application of 'comity' principles by US courts, see Paul, 'Comity'.

But this influence is not just a one-way process. As well as being influenced *by* public international law, private international law at domestic level also has the potential to shape the development of customary rules. As noted in chapter 2, judicial decisions, including those on private jurisdictional and choice of law issues, form part of 'state practice' used to determine whether a new principle has passed into customary international law. One area of international law where judicial decisions may be expected to have a real influence is in relation to the scope of home state obligations to provide 'access to justice' to those harmed by multinational activities abroad.

Access to justice as an international law obligation of 'home states'

The availability of legal remedies is regarded as a key aspect of the effective implementation, by a state, of its human rights obligations.[48] But how far, and to whom, do these obligations extend? Clearly, states are under an obligation to ensure that legal remedies are available for violations of human rights occurring within national boundaries. As noted above, it has been suggested that this obligation ought also to extend to extraterritorial harm caused by multinationals where the home state has failed in its duties to supervise the activities of that multinational effectively.[49]

The obligation to provide legal remedies for harm has been interpreted to encompass civil (i.e. tort-based) as well as criminal law remedies.[50] However, the application by national courts of the private international law principle of 'forum non conveniens' (discussed in more detail below) casts doubt on the idea that home states of multinationals are legally obliged, as a matter of customary *public* international law, to ensure that victims of harm caused by the foreign activities of those multinationals necessarily have access to their national courts.[51] Under this principle, the national courts of some common law countries have the discretion to stay proceedings, notwithstanding that jurisdiction does exist,

---

[48] *Velasquez Rodriguez* v. *Honduras*, Inter-American Court of Human Rights (ser. C.) no. 4 (1988), para. 176. See also Committee on Economic, Social and Cultural Rights, 'General Comment No. 3 on the Nature of States Parties' Obligations', UN Doc. E/1991/23, para. 5; Craven, *The International Covenant*, pp. 127–8.

[49] Sornorajah, 'Linking State Responsibility', p. 511.

[50] *Osman* v. *United Kingdom* (Case No. 2345/94), European Court of Human Rights, 28 October 1998, [1998] ECHR 101; (1999) 29 EHRR 245. See further A. Clapham, 'Revisiting Human Rights in the Private Sphere: Using the European Convention on Human Rights to Protect the Right of Access to the Civil Courts' in C. Scott (ed.), *Torture as Tort: Comparative Perspectives on the Development of Transnational Human Rights Litigation* (Oxford: Hart Publishing, 2001).

[51] See further pp. 237–9 below.

because the forum chosen by the plaintiff is not the most 'convenient' or 'appropriate' venue for hearing the claim.

Jurisdiction of courts in civil cases against multinationals

To what extent do national courts have jurisdiction over disputes between individuals and multinational groups of companies? This question is an important one given recent attempts, discussed in more detail in chapter 5, to hold multinationals accountable for their actions in national courts.

The laws on civil jurisdiction vary from country to country. In the EU these rules have been harmonised, first by treaty[52] and, subsequently, by EU Regulation.[53] The jurisdictional rules in the UK are complicated, first by the fact that the UK is actually made up of three separate jurisdictions[54] and, second, because of the different layers of national and EU law. (For convenience, the EU jurisdictional arrangements are referred to in this chapter as the 'Brussels regime' and the core piece of legislation as the 'Brussels Regulation'.) Essentially, though, where the Brussels regime does not apply, UK courts can apply their traditional rules for determining jurisdiction.

National courts of EU states enjoy personal jurisdiction 'as of right' over companies 'domiciled' in their jurisdiction. Under the Brussels Regulation, the 'domicile' of a company is defined flexibly as the place where a company has its statutory seat, or its central administration or its principal place of business.[55] Within the EU, it is also possible to serve proceedings directly upon a foreign corporation 'out of the jurisdiction' in relation to claims over which the relevant court has subject matter jurisdiction.[56] This includes tort cases where (a) the damage was sustained within the jurisdiction or (b) the damage resulted from an act committed within the jurisdiction.[57] Therefore, in a case involving negligence resulting in injuries in France (e.g. a defective design for machinery), an

---

[52] 1968 Brussels Convention, n. 43 above.

[53] Brussels Regulation, n. 43 above, which replaced the 1968 Brussels Convention.

[54] See schedule 5 to the UK Civil Jurisdiction and Judgments Act 1982.

[55] Brussels Regulation, n. 43 above, Article 60(1).

[56] N.b. provided the Brussels regime applies. Where the Brussels regime does not apply (e.g. the proposed defendant is not located in another EU member state), permission of the court is required under the Civil Procedure Rules 1998 (SI 1998 No. 3132) ('CPR').

[57] See 1968 Brussels Convention, Article 5(3), as interpreted in Case 21/76, *Bier BV* v. *Mines de Potasse d'Alsace SA* [1976] ECR 1735; [1978] QB 708. Note that 'damage sustained within the jurisdiction' may include damage sustained elsewhere, which continued or worsened within the jurisdiction. See *Al-Adsani* v. *Government of Kuwait*, Court of Appeal, 21 January 1994; (1995) 100 ILR 465. See now Brussels Regulation, Article 5(3).

English company could potentially be sued in either the English or the French courts.

Under English common law rules, proceedings may be served on foreign companies where they have a 'presence' within England, e.g. a branch office,[58] premises in England from which or at which business is carried on,[59] or a local agent. 'Presence' in the jurisdiction can also be established through an English subsidiary, provided that the subsidiary is not merely a subsidiary but also an 'agent' of its parent.[60] It may also be possible to serve process on a foreign company out of the jurisdiction, with the permission of the court, on the basis that the foreign company is a proper co-defendant to the proceedings. However, permission will only be granted on this basis if there is at least an arguable case against the first defendant (i.e. the proceedings were not commenced against the first defendant purely to obtain 'long arm' jurisdiction over the second).[61]

US rules on personal jurisdiction vary from state to state, but generally jurisdiction over corporate entities is based on the presence of 'minimum contacts' between the entity and the relevant jurisdiction, provided that the taking of jurisdiction would not offend notions of 'fair play' or 'substantial justice'.[62] Companies incorporated in the USA are clearly subject to the jurisdiction of the US courts, and jurisdiction may be exercised over foreign companies too, to the extent that they 'do business' in the relevant state.[63] Under Federal Civil Procedure Rules, a foreign corporation can be served with proceedings through a local officer, manager or agent.[64] The question of whether a foreign subsidiary can be regarded as an agent or 'alter ego' of a foreign parent for the purpose of establishing jurisdiction over the parent has been raised in numerous cases. *Doe* v. *Unocal* involved a claim against a number of parties including two parent companies, Unocal Corporation (a Californian company) and Total SA (a French company). The plaintiffs argued that the court ought to have jurisdiction over the French parent company on the basis that the local Total subsidiary was

---

[58] UK Companies Act 1985, sections 690A, 694A, 695 and schedule 21A; *Saab* v. *Saudi American Bank* [1998] 1 WLR 937.

[59] CPR 6.5(6). *Sea Assets* v. *PT Garuda Indonesia* [2000] 1 All ER 371.

[60] 'Agency' usually requires the power to enter into contracts on behalf of the parent; it will not be implied merely by virtue of the parent–subsidiary relationship. *Adams* v. *Cape Industries plc* [1990] Ch 433.

[61] See Brussels Regulation, n. 43 above, Article 6(1); CPR, 6.20(3).

[62] *International Shoe Co.* v. *Washington*, 326 US 310 (1945).

[63] Joseph, *Transnational Human Rights Litigation*, p. 83.

[64] Rule 4(h)(1). See *Wiwa* v. *Royal Dutch Petroleum Co.* 226 F 3d 88 (2d Cir. 2000).

the 'alter ego' of its French parent or, in the alternative, acted as its agent. However, it was eventually held that the level of control exercised by Total SA over its US subsidiary was not so great that the US subsidiary could be regarded as the 'alter ego' of its French parent,[65] and neither was the subsidiary the 'agent' of Total SA for these purposes.[66] Therefore, the proceedings could not proceed against the French company.

Claims for environmental damage often fall into a special category for jurisdictional purposes. At common law, English courts did not have the jurisdiction to determine disputes relating to rights over foreign land. The rationale behind this rule was that, as rights concerning foreign immovable property only arise under the law of the place where that property is situated, they can only be litigated under the laws of that state. Until fairly recently, this rule was interpreted to include cases concerning damage to foreign land.[67] In other words, an English defendant could not be sued in the English courts for environmental damage to land located in another state. The common law position has, however, been altered by statute. Section 30(1) of the UK Civil Jurisdiction and Judgments Act 1982 confirms the jurisdiction of UK courts over proceedings 'for trespass to, or any other tort affecting, immovable property' outside England and Wales 'unless the proceedings are principally concerned with a question of the title to, or rights of possession of, that property'.[68] This means that English courts could have jurisdiction in respect of a claim against an English company for environmental damage occurring in another state.[69] The position is similar in other common law jurisdictions.[70]

As the discussion above shows, national courts can provide a venue for tort-based litigation against multinationals. Although the methods of establishing jurisdiction may differ, domestic rules on civil procedure do allow courts to exercise personal jurisdiction over foreign companies,

---

[65] *Doe v. Unocal*, 27 F Supp 2d 1174 (CD Cal 1998) 1184, 1188.

[66] Ibid., 1189. See, however, *Wiwa v. Royal Dutch Petroleum Limited* 226 F 3d 88 (2d Cir. 2000) in which it was held that jurisdiction could be exercised over the Royal Dutch Petroleum Company (incorporated in the Netherlands) and the Shell Transport and Trading Company (incorporated in the UK) on the basis that it had agents in New York in the form of an Investor Relations Office and its manager; Joseph, *Transnational Human Rights Litigation*, p. 86.

[67] *British South Africa Co. v. Companhia de Moçambique* [1893] AC 602; *Hesperides Hotels Ltd* v. *Muftizade* [1979] AC 508.

[68] Section 30(1).

[69] Although where the property is located in another EU member state, jurisdiction is governed by the Brussels Regulation, n. 43 above, Article 22.

[70] *Dagi v. BHP* [1997] 1 VR 428.

provided the foreign company has a 'presence' in the jurisdiction. 'Subject matter' jurisdiction will usually exist in cases that involve events taking place, or damage sustained, within the jurisdiction, regardless of the nationality of the defendant company. Domestic courts will also usually have extraterritorial jurisdiction in respect of torts taking place in other countries where at least one of the defendants is a locally incorporated company. However, the fact that jurisdiction exists does not mean that it will always be exercised.

Forum non conveniens

The prospect of a claim against a parent company of a multinational in its home state may be a significant advantage to a potential claimant. This will certainly be the case where the subsidiary no longer exists, or has ceased operations[71] or has only limited financial resources of its own. Other reasons why a litigant may prefer a foreign court to his own include the possibility of a higher award for damages, or where there is a risk that local proceedings could become bogged down in endless delays. However, where it is possible to do so, proceedings involving foreign loss or damage will almost always be challenged by the defendant parent company on grounds of forum non conveniens (i.e. that the plaintiff has chosen the wrong forum). Essentially, this doctrine enables a court to decline jurisdiction in favour of another (i.e. foreign) legal system. Although this doctrine is only recognised in common law countries, these include some key multinational 'home states'. The USA is one such country, as was, until recently, the UK.

The US approach

The use of the doctrine of forum non conveniens by US courts dates back to the 1930s.[72] While each state has developed its own version of the test to be applied,[73] the basic approach remains as set out in *Gulf Oil Corp. v. Gilbert*.[74] The first question for the court is whether the alternative forum is 'adequate'. If so, the court must then decide whether or not to exercise its discretion to stay the proceedings in favour of

---

[71] As was the case in *Lubbe v. Cape plc* 1 WLR 1545; [2000] 4 All ER 268 (HL) 277. See H. Ward, 'Securing Transnational Corporate Accountability through National Courts: Implications and Policy Options' [2001] *Hast I&CLR* 451, 463.

[72] *Canada Malting v. Paterson Steamships Ltd*, 285 US 413 (1932).

[73] Note also that some states, such as Texas, have codified the relevant rules under legislation.

[74] *Gulf Oil Corp. v. Gilbert*, 330 US 501 (1947).

that alternative forum. In making this decision, the court starts with the presumption that the plaintiff's choice of forum is the most convenient one for the trial of the action. This presumption is only displaced if there are sufficient and weighty 'private' and 'public' considerations pointing towards the alternative forum. 'Private' considerations include access to evidence, logistics, relative costs and availability of witnesses. 'Public' considerations concern wider issues of public policy, in particular whether the burden of hosting the litigation is justified, given the relative 'interest' in the subject matter of the claim.[75]

Unfortunately for those wishing to sue in respect of non-US activities of US-based multinationals, the initial presumption that the plaintiff has chosen the most appropriate forum for the trial of the action is treated as less strong where the plaintiff resides outside the USA.[76] A further difficulty for foreign plaintiffs seeking access to the US courts is the use of 'public interest' considerations as grounds for declining jurisdiction. This has particular implications for a foreign litigant considering a personal injury or product liability claim against a US parent company. The US courts have repeatedly held that, in matters of public safety, 'public' considerations will generally favour the jurisdiction with the greatest 'regulatory interest' in the matter, which is invariably held to be the place where the injury was sustained.[77] This is said to apply with even more force in relation to 'regulated industries', 'such as pharmaceuticals . . . and passenger aircraft'.[78]

The decision of the court in Re Bhopal[79] provides a good illustration of how this balancing process can work against the interests of foreign litigants in practice. This case, which arose out of the tragedy at Bhopal in 1984, concerned claims by many thousands of plaintiffs for damages arising from injuries, death and damage to property following a disastrous gas leak. The leak originated from an industrial facility owned by a (50.9 per cent) subsidiary of a US company, Union Carbide Corporation ('UCC'). Predictably, UCC applied to have the US proceedings stayed on

---

[75] Ibid.

[76] *Piper Aircraft Co.* v. *Reyno*, 454 US 235 (1981), 255–6. For further discussion on this point see D. Mayer and K. Sable, 'Yes! We Have No Bananas: Forum Non Conveniens and Corporate Evasion' (2004) 4 *IBLR* 130.

[77] *Harrison* v. *Wyeth Laboratories Division of American Home Products*, 510 F Supp 1 (ED Pa 1980), 676 F 2d 685 (3d Cir. 1982); *Dowling* v. *Richardson-Merrell, Inc*, 727 F 2d 608 (6th Cir. 1984).

[78] *Dowling* v. *Richardson-Merrell, Inc.*, ibid., p. 616.

[79] *In Re Union Carbide Corporation Gas Plant Disaster at Bhopal, India in December, 1984*, 634 F Supp 842 (SDNY 1986).

grounds of forum non conveniens. In relation to the first stage of the test, the court held that India was an 'adequate' alternative forum for the action. The court then went on to weigh up the competing 'private' and 'public' considerations. The 'private' interests, according to the court, pointed to India as the more convenient forum. It remained only to consider the balance of 'public interests'. The plaintiffs argued that the USA did indeed have an interest in retaining jurisdiction over the matter, that subjecting US-based multinationals to US jurisdiction in relation to foreign activities would enhance the reputation of US industry, and, rather creatively, that by tackling the problem of 'double standards' in this way, the US courts would be helping to counteract downward pressure on health and safety standards within the USA, as well as abroad. Whatever the merits of these arguments, they were found in *Re Bhopal* to be outweighed by other concerns. In particular:

> The Indian government, which regulated the Bhopal facility, has an extensive and deep interest in ensuring that its standards for safety are complied with. As regulators, the Indian government and individual citizens even have an interest in knowing whether extant regulations are adequate. This Court, sitting in a foreign country, has considered the extent of regulation by Indian agencies of the Bhopal plant. It finds that this is not the appropriate tribunal to determine whether the Indian regulations were breached, or whether the laws themselves were sufficient to protect Indian citizens from harm. It would be sadly paternalistic, if not misguided, of this Court to attempt to evaluate the regulations and standards imposed in another country . . . India no doubt evaluated its need for a pesticide plant against the risks inherent in such development . . . The court is well aware of the moral danger of creating the 'double standard' feared by the plaintiffs and *amicus curiae*. However, when an industry is as regulated as the chemical industry is in India, the failure to acknowledge inherent differences in the aims and concerns of Indian, as opposed to American citizens, would be naïve and unfair to the defendant . . . The Indian interest in creating standards of care, enforcing them or even extending them, and of protecting its citizens from ill-use is significantly stronger than the local interest in deterring multinationals from exporting allegedly dangerous technology.[80]

The court's position on the 'public interest' question was ironic, given that the Indian government had assumed responsibility for the presentation of the plaintiffs' claims and was therefore clearly party to the decision to prosecute them in the USA.[81] The judgment extract quoted above also pays scant regard to the fact that negligence was alleged, not

---

[80] Ibid., 864–5.
[81] Although note that the Indian government had changed its position on appeal. See A. Seward, 'After Bhopal: Implications for Parent Company Liability' (1987) 21 *Int'l Lawyer*

only against the Indian subsidiary, but against its US parent company, UCC, as well. As Cassels points out, 'the plaintiff was not urging the US courts to regulate Indian industries or to change Indian law, but to set standards for US-based multinationals operating abroad – standards that could not effectively be policed by other than the multinational's home jurisdiction'.[82]

The decision of the court in *Re Bhopal* is a strikingly state-centred one, especially given the scale of human misery involved. In the final analysis, the court in *Re Bhopal* decided to put US interests first. Of course, the availability of strict liability for tort, contingency fee arrangements, jury trials and the prospect of very high damages in some jurisdictions make the USA, for plaintiffs, an extremely attractive venue for litigation. As a result, US courts are sensitive to the problem of 'forum shopping' and the financial and administrative burden and cost that this entails. The message that can be taken from the judgment in *Re Bhopal* is that, as far as the US courts are concerned, foreign host states cannot have the benefits (in terms of 'comparative advantage') of low workplace, environmental and consumer standards *and* recourse to the US courts when things go wrong.

However, recent US decisions suggest a more plaintiff-friendly attitude on the part of some US courts.[83] Although the basic formula has not changed, some courts are adopting a more critical approach to the question of whether the alternative forum is indeed 'adequate' for the purposes of the first part of the forum non conveniens test. In the ATCA-based cases[84] of *Eastman Kodak Co.* v. *Kavlin*[85] and *Wiwa* v. *Royal Dutch Petroleum*[86] the courts took account of US State Department human rights reports in determining that the alternative forums could not be treated as adequate because of the risk of corruption.[87] Similarly in *Martinez* v. *Dow Chemicals*[88] (a tort-based claim), the court found that there was no adequate alternative forum for the dispute for the Filipino plaintiffs

---

695, 699. For more detailed criticism of the court's interpretation of the 'public' interests see Cassels, *Bhopal*, chapter 6.

[82] Ibid., p. 137.

[83] Mayer and Sable, 'Bananas'; Joseph, *Transnational Human Rights Litigation*, pp. 87–99; Blumberg, 'Asserting Human Rights', 503.

[84] I.e. cases brought under the US Alien Tort Claims Act, 28 USC § 1350. See further pp. 207–15 below.

[85] 978 F Supp 1078 (SD Fla 1997).

[86] 2002 WL 319887, (SDNY 28 February 2002).

[87] Joseph, *Transnational Human Rights Litigation*, pp. 91–2.

[88] 219 F Supp 2d 719 (ED La 2002).

after consulting a Department of State Report detailing problems of corruption in the Filipino courts.[89] In one case, *Sarei* v. *Rio Tinto*,[90] the court went so far as to refuse an application to dismiss ACTA-based claims on the basis that similar rights of action were not available in the alternative state, Australia.[91] Courts may also be changing their view of the 'public interests' involved. In *Bowoto* v. *Chevron*, and in stark contrast to the decision in *Re Bhopal*, the judge took account of the interest of the state of California in 'regulating the conduct of corporations that are headquartered [t]here, even if the conduct of the corporation . . . is overseas'.[92] In addition, even when an action for dismissal is successful, courts are now quite likely to impose conditions on the decision to stay the US proceedings, which could open the door for their reinstatement at a later stage.[93]

The English approach

As discussed further below, a recent decision by the ECJ[94] effectively puts an end to the use of the forum non conveniens doctrine by UK courts on the grounds of its incompatibility with the Brussels regime. However, the English approach to forum non conveniens in past cases is still worth discussing for the purposes of comparison with other jurisdictions, and for understanding the implications of this doctrine for international law obligations regarding 'access to justice'.[95]

The English courts had developed a 'two-stage' formula under which the onus was on the defendant, first, to demonstrate that there is another 'available' forum which is clearly more appropriate for the trial of the claim. If there was such an available forum, the courts would decline jurisdiction by granting a stay of the action, unless the plaintiff could show that there were 'circumstances by reason of which justice requires that the stay should nevertheless not be granted'.[96] It is at this second stage that the English approach differed most from the US

---

[89] US Department of State, 'Country Report on Human Rights Practices, Philippines, 2001', 4 March 2002, http://www.state.gov/g/drl/rls/hrrpt/2001, quoted in Mayer and Sable, 'Bananas', 160.

[90] 221 F Supp 2d 1116 (CD Cal 2002).

[91] But this may not have been correctly decided. See Joseph, *Transnational Human Rights Litigation*, p. 89.

[92] Case No. C 99–2506 (ND Cal 7 April 2000), unreported decision of Legge J (ND Ca 16 June 2000), quoted in Joseph, *Transnational Human Rights Litigation*, p. 92.

[93] Mayer and Sable, 'Bananas', 157–8.

[94] Case C-281/02, *Owusu* v. *Jackson* [2005] 2 WLR 942.   [95] See further pp. 237–9 below.

[96] *Spiliada Maritime Corporation* v. *Cansulex Ltd* [1987] AC 460, 478.

approach, in that 'substantive justice' (not other 'public interest' considerations) would determine whether the jurisdiction was retained or declined.

Not surprisingly, the doctrine of forum non conveniens has been raised by defendants in a series of cases involving allegations of negligent supervision by English parent companies of their foreign subsidiaries.[97] Many of the factors taken into account by the courts in assessing whether there is another 'clearly more appropriate' forum – availability of witnesses, need for site inspections, relative expense – have tended to point towards the courts of the country in which the damage occurred, even if the English parent company is the primary (or only) defendant.[98] In a class action, a large number of claimants residing in a foreign jurisdiction would tend to tip the balance further in favour of the alternative forum.[99]

The English courts could, however, be persuaded *not* to exercise their discretion to stay the proceedings (notwithstanding that there is another more appropriate forum available), if that alternative forum was not one in which the action could be tried 'more suitably for the interests of all the parties and the ends of justice'.[100] The fact that the alternative jurisdiction posed disadvantages to the plaintiff compared with the preferred jurisdiction would not necessarily be relevant; the general approach was that the plaintiff should take the alternative jurisdiction as she finds it.[101] However, where the practical effect of those disadvantages meant that a stay would effectively prevent the plaintiff from prosecuting any claim at all, the courts have retained jurisdiction.[102]

But while the English courts continued to develop the case law on forum non conveniens, other experts were raising concerns that the doctrine may not actually be consistent with the UK's treaty obligations under the Brussels regime.[103] It was accepted that, if the English courts

---

[97] See *Sithole and Others* v. *Thor Chemical Holdings Ltd*, TLR 15 February 1999; *Connelly* v. *RTZ* [1998] AC 854; *Lubbe* v. *Cape plc*, n. 71 above. For further discussion on this potential cause of action see pp. 216–34 below.

[98] *Connelly* v. *RTZ* [1998] AC 854; *Lubbe* v. *Cape plc* [2000] 4 All ER 268 (HL), 277.

[99] E. g. *Lubbe* v. *Cape plc* [2000] 1 Lloyd's Rep. 139, 143. But see further p. 205 below.

[100] *Spiliada* v. *Cansulex*, n. 96 above, at 476.

[101] Ibid., at 482; *Connelly* v. *RTZ* [1998] AC 854, 872.

[102] *Spiliada* v. *Cansulex*, per Lord Goff at 473; *Lubbe* v. *Cape plc* [2000] 4 All ER 268 (HL), 277. This has been extended to cases where the claim could not be brought without financial assistance (e.g. in the form of legal aid or contingency fee arrangements). See *Connelly* v. *RTZ* [1998] AC 854; *Lubbe* v. *Cape plc* [2000] 4 All ER 268 (HL), 277.

[103] J. Collier, *Conflict of Laws*, 3rd edition (Cambridge: Cambridge University Press, 2001), p. 166.

did have jurisdiction under the Brussels Regulation, the courts could not stay proceedings on the grounds of forum non conveniens where the alternative forum was also an EU state, but the position with respect to non-contracting states was unclear.[104] Although *Lubbe* v. *Cape plc* concerned the possibility of a stay in favour of a non-contracting state (South Africa), the decision of the House of Lords *not* to stay the action meant that the question of the legality of the doctrine of forum non conveniens under the Brussels Convention was not considered.[105] However, it has recently been confirmed by the ECJ that Article 2 of the Brussels Regulation does indeed prevent stays of proceedings on grounds of forum non conveniens, regardless of the domicile of the plaintiff and whether the alternative forum is an EU member state or not.[106] This effectively puts an end to the English law doctrine of forum non conveniens in negligence cases, and thus removes a significant hurdle for claimants seeking to bring claims against UK parent companies in the UK courts.

Forum non conveniens in other jurisdictions

By and large, the courts of other common law jurisdictions – Canada and New Zealand, for example – have broadly followed the English *Spiliada* approach.[107] Australia, however, is an exception. In Australia the defendant has to persuade the court, not that there is a more appropriate forum elsewhere, but that the Australian forum is 'clearly inappropriate'.[108] The difference between the two approaches is that 'the mere fact that a tribunal in some other country would be a more appropriate forum for the particular proceeding does not necessarily mean that the local court is a clearly inappropriate one'.[109] If the Australian approach seems out of step with prevailing standards of 'international comity',[110] the Australian High Court makes no apology for this:

---

[104] In *Re Harrods (Buenos Aires) Ltd* [1992] Ch 72 (CA), the Court of Appeal, overruling two earlier cases at first instance, held that the courts *would* be entitled to stay proceedings on grounds of forum non conveniens where the alternative forum was not a contracting state. The point was referred to the ECJ, but the case was settled before the issue was finally determined.

[105] R. Fentiman, 'Stays and the European Conventions – End Game?' (2001) 60 *CLJ* 10.

[106] *Owusu* v. *Jackson*, n. 94 above.

[107] See *Recherches Internationales Quebec* v. *Cambior Inc.* [1998] QJ No. 2554 (QL).

[108] *Voth* v. *Manildra Flour Mills* (1990) 171 CLR 538; *Renault* v. *Zhang* (2002) 210 CLR 491.

[109] *Oceanic Sun-Line Special Shipping Co. Inc.* v. *Fay* (1988) 165 CLR 197.

[110] P. Brereton, 'Forum Non Conveniens in Australia: a Case Note on Voth v. Manildra Flour Mills' (1991) 40 *ICLQ* 895, 900.

if one turns from what is praised as judicial comity to what is condemned as judicial chauvinism, it seems that the broader *forum non conveniens* discretion is liable to bring with it the notion that 'citizens or residents deserve somewhat more deference than foreign plaintiffs' see *Piper Aircraft* ... At least, any judicial chauvinism which might, in earlier times, have been implicit in the traditional principle was well intentioned towards the foreign plaintiff.[111]

The great advantage of the Australian approach, from the plaintiff's perspective, is that it allows little space for the kinds of state-centred concerns that played such a significant part in the outcome of *Re Bhopal*. As Prince points out:

As *Bhopal* and *Piper Aircraft* show, international comity has been used – ironically – to promote chauvinistic outcomes. This results from the mistaken belief, first, that 'comity' is merely equivalent to 'international respect' and, second, that 'international respect' should be narrowly defined as 'non-interference' in the legal processes of another country.[112]

As a result, the chances of an Australian company being able to persuade an Australian court to dismiss a claim on these grounds are small. In *Dagi* v. *BHP*,[113] a case concerning environmental damage in Papua New Guinea (allegedly caused by a majority-owned subsidiary of an Australian-based multinational), the issue of forum non conveniens was not even raised.[114]

Choice of law

Although there are circumstances in which national courts will have jurisdiction over a foreign company in a private claim,[115] it by no means follows that the law of the forum state will be applied to determine the case. Within the EU, the general rule in tort cases is that the liability of the defendant should be judged according to the law of the place where the injury or damage occurred unless there are strong reasons for applying the laws of some other country. According to Article 3(1) of the proposed Regulation on the Law Applicable to Non-Contractual

---

[111] *Oceanic Sun-Line Special Shipping Co. Inc.* v. *Fay*, n. 109 above, 254.
[112] P. Prince, 'Bhopal, Bougainville and Ok Tedi: Why Australia's *Forum Non Conveniens* Approach is Better' (1998) 47 *ICLQ* 573, 580.
[113] [1997] 1 VR 428.
[114] See further S. Seck, 'Environmental Harm in Developing Countries Caused by Subsidiaries of Canadian Mining Corporations: the Interface of Public and Private International Law' (1999) 37 *Can YIL* 139; Joseph, *Transnational Human Rights Litigation*, p. 124.
[115] See pp. 119–20 above.

Obligations ('Rome II'),[116] 'The law applicable to a non-contractual obligation shall be the law of the country in which the damage arises or is likely to arise, irrespective of the country in which the event giving rise to the damage occurred and irrespective of the country or countries in which the indirect consequences of the event arise.' However, under subparagraph (3): 'where it is clear from all the circumstances of the case that the non-contractual obligation is manifestly more closely connected with another country, the law of that other country shall apply'.[117]

In the UK, the choice of law to be applied in an international tort-based claim is governed primarily by sections 11 and 12 of the Private International Law (Miscellaneous Provisions) Act 1995. Section 11 lays down a general rule that 'the applicable law is the law of the country in which the events constituting the tort or delict in question occur'. This is clarified further by section 11(2), which provides that 'where elements of those events occur in different countries', the applicable law for a personal injury claim is taken to be 'the law of the country where the individual was when he sustained the injury'. In cases involving damage to property, the applicable law is 'the law of the country where the property was when it was damaged', and in any other case 'the law of the country in which the most significant element or elements of those events occurred'.[118] The legislation does, however, allow the courts some flexibility where there appear to be good reasons for applying some other law to the dispute. Section 12(1) provides:

If it appears, in all the circumstances, from a comparison of –

    (a) the significance of the factors which connect a tort or delict with the country whose law would be the applicable law under the general rule; and

    (b) the significance of any factors connecting the tort or delict with another country,

that it is substantially more appropriate for the applicable law for determining the issues arising in the case, or any of those issues, to be the law of another country, the general rule is displaced and the applicable law for determining those issues or that issue (as the case may be) is the law of the other country.

---

[116] 'Proposed Regulation on the Law Applicable to Non-Contractual Obligations', COM (2003) 427 final 2003/0168 (COD).

[117] Article 3(3) goes on to specify that '(a) manifestly closer connection with another country may be based in particular on a pre-existing relationship between the parties, such as a contract that is closely connected with the non-contractual obligation in question'.

[118] Section 11(1), (b) and (c).

In the case of *Lubbe* v. *Cape plc*, the plaintiffs argued (in the context of an application by the defendants for a stay on grounds of forum non conveniens) that the action, which concerned the liability of a UK parent company for injuries sustained in South Africa, ought to be governed by English law. The Court of Appeal was unpersuaded on this point, Pill LJ being of the opinion that there was a 'strong case' that 'the obligations to South African workmen employed by South African companies and the obligations of the defendants to other residents of South Africa affected by operations there . . . are to be determined according to South African law'.[119] However, at that stage in the proceedings the issue of whether the claim should be governed by English or South African law was still regarded by the court as 'an open question', which should not have a bearing on the choice of forum. A problem in transnational tort cases, as Joseph points out, is that 'the identification of the site of the tort may not be easy'.[120] It is relevant to note that '[i]n both [the *Lubbe* and *Connelly*] cases, the claimants' arguments largely targeted the policy decisions regarding work practices made in boardrooms in England, rather than the actual implementation of working practices in Southern Africa'.[121] In the end, neither the *Lubbe* nor the *Connelly* case reached trial on the substantive issues,[122] which meant the issue of choice of law was never finally determined.

Even if the governing law is that of some other state, the English courts still have the option, in rare cases, to refuse to apply foreign law on grounds of 'public policy'. Under section 14(3)(a)(i) of the 1995 Act, foreign law is not to be applied in the adjudication of a tort-based claim 'in so far as to do so . . . would conflict with principles of public policy'.[123] On this basis, foreign law ought not to be applied if its effect would be to permit a defendant to escape liability for serious human rights violations (although, as Joseph points out, this may not be of assistance to 'claimants in tort cases involving occupational health and safety such as *Connelly* and *Lubbe*').[124]

Different US courts have different approaches to the problem of choice of law and, unlike the English courts, not all start with an explicit presumption in favour of the place of injury.[125] In international tort cases,

[119] *Lubbe* v. *Cape plc* [2000] 1 Lloyd's Law Reports 139, 161.
[120] Joseph, *Transnational Human Rights Litigation*, p. 120.   [121] Ibid.
[122] See further pp. 204–5 below.   [123] See also Rome II, n. 116 above, Article 6(1) and 22.
[124] Joseph, *Transnational Human Rights Litigation*, p. 120.
[125] Although a 'significant number' of US state courts do. Joseph, *Transnational Human Rights Litigation*, p. 74.

the most widely followed rule is that the 'proper law' of the tort is the law of the state having the most 'significant relationship' to the case and the parties.[126] Under this method, courts are expected to take account of a range of public and private concerns including the needs of the international system, the regulatory policies of interested states, expectations of the parties, certainty, predictability and uniformity.[127] Another approach involves 'interest balancing' in which the policies behind competing legal principles and approaches are examined and weighed to reveal the state with the greatest interest in the particular matter. Where different legal systems would yield different results, the 'interest balancing' approach considers the reasons behind these differences and weighs up the competing policy considerations. Where a rule does not appear to be relevant to a case, e.g. because of the nationality of the parties or the particular situation involved, some other system of law, with closer connections to the case, will be applied instead. This means that, while the place of injury will in most cases provide the natural choice of law, there may be cases in which the facts of the case (e.g. the nationality of the parties) point more strongly to another legal system.[128]

But even where there is no explicit presumption in favour of the law of the place of injury, this is often the practical result. In the case of *In re Richardson-Merrell Inc.*,[129] for example, a case involving the liability of a company for pre-birth injuries suffered by British residents from a drug ingested by their mothers during pregnancy, the court thought it 'virtually certain that substantive tort law of the United Kingdom would govern'.[130] In *Re Bhopal* it was concluded that each of the possible 'choice of law' tests which could be applied (lex loci delicti, 'most significant relationship test' or the 'weight of contacts' test) favoured Indian law as the correct choice of domestic law to apply to the claim.[131]

Nevertheless, as with the UK, US courts do possess a certain degree of flexibility on this point. If the 'interest-balancing' approach described above seems somewhat *state*-centred, this may be ameliorated to some

---

[126] *Babcock v. Jackson*, 12 NY 2d 473 (1963). ALI, 'Restatement of the Law, Second, Conflict of Laws', 1971 § 145. Although note that different states within the USA apply different 'choice of law' rules to actions made under state law. See *Re Bhopal*, 634 F Supp 842 (SDNY 1986), 866.

[127] Second Restatement on Conflicts of Laws, § 6.

[128] *Babcock v. Jackson*, 12 NY 2d 473 (1963).

[129] *In re Richardson-Merrell Inc.*, 545 F Supp 1130 (1982).

[130] Ibid., 1136.   [131] *Re Bhopal*, n. 126 above, 866.

extent by the ability of the courts to apply a 'public policy' exception, under which foreign law (which would otherwise apply) may be excluded where it contravenes 'public policy'.[132] The idea that public policy encompasses international human rights considerations was confirmed in *Doe* v. *Unocal*, in which the California Superior Court Chaney J held that Myanmar law would not be applied to the extent that it might preclude the plaintiffs' claims relating to forced labour.[133]

Resolving jurisdictional conflicts

The international activities of multinationals mean that there will inevitably be cases where more than one state can legitimately claim jurisdiction over the parties and subject matter. In a product liability case, for example, there may be potential causes of action against not only the parent company, but any number of international subsidiaries and distributors as well. Furthermore, injuries may have been suffered in more than one state. Clearly, the possibility of a class action, involving many plaintiffs from a number of different jurisdictions, adds a further level of complexity.

There is a range of methods that states can use to help deal with jurisdictional conflicts such as these: some co-operative, some more confrontational. First, states can agree amongst themselves when and how jurisdictional rights may be exercised, and when they must be declined.[134] Where the connections between the chosen jurisdiction and the case seem tenuous, the defendant may be able to obtain an 'anti-suit' injunction from the courts of its home state, preventing the plaintiff from commencing or proceeding with the foreign lawsuit.[135] Finally, it is possible for a national court to refuse to recognise a foreign judgment on the grounds that to do so would be contrary to public policy or

---

[132] Born, *International Civil Litigation*, pp. 629, 651–2.

[133] Joseph, *Transnational Human Rights Litigation*, p. 75.

[134] See, for example, Article 2 of the Brussels Convention, n. 43 above, which provided that where proceedings involving the same cause of action are brought in two or more different courts, the court in which the proceedings were first commenced shall retain jurisdiction and proceedings commenced in any other courts shall be stayed in favour of the first. Note, however, that the Brussels Convention has now been superseded by the Brussels Regulation, see n. 43 above. For the equivalent provision, see, now, Brussels Regulation, n. 43 above, Article 27.

[135] Under English law, such an injunction may be granted where the proceedings in the foreign state are 'vexatious', 'unconscionable' or 'oppressive'. See *Société Nationale Industrielle Aerospatiale* v. *Lee Kui Jak* [1987] AC 871; *Midland Bank plc* v. *Laker Airways Ltd* [1986] QB 689 (although note that this case concerned a cause of action which did not exist under English law, meaning that the action could not be pursued in the UK).

'substantial justice'. In the case of *Adams* v. *Cape Industries*,[136] for example, the Court of Appeal refused to recognise or enforce a judgment of a Texan court because the method of calculating damages awards for plaintiffs was not consistent with English notions of 'substantial justice'.[137]

Summary

There are two dimensions to state jurisdiction, one deriving from public international law and one deriving from domestic law (i.e. 'private international law' or 'conflicts of law'). The former defines the geographical limits of the regulatory power of the state; the latter defines the scope of jurisdiction of national courts over private law matters such as contractual or tort-based disputes. However, both are relevant to the regulation of multinationals by 'home states'.

Public international law does not generally permit the direct imposition of regulatory standards on the activities of multinationals abroad. The activities of foreign-incorporated companies are generally outside the scope of home state jurisdiction, except in the (very rare) cases where either the 'effects' doctrine or the 'universal principle' may apply. As discussed above, none of these principles authorises direct or 'foreign-prescriptive' extraterritorial regulation of the CSR standards of foreign-incorporated companies.

On the other hand, national courts can, in some circumstances, take jurisdiction over foreign companies in the context of a private law dispute and may even (in rare cases) apply local law to determine rights and liabilities, notwithstanding that the activities giving rise to the dispute may have occurred, in whole or in part, within the territory of another state. In a tort case, for instance, foreign companies may find themselves subject to the jurisdiction of English courts, if the tort was committed wholly or partly in England, or as co-defendants in a case already involving an English defendant. Under European law, the law governing a tort-based dispute is normally the law of the place of injury. However, national courts may apply some other system of law (including, of course, the law of the forum state) where, in the words of the proposed EU Regulation, the case is 'manifestly more closely connected' with that other country.[138]

---

[136] [1990] Ch 433.
[137] This decision is open to criticism. See Collier, *Conflict of Laws*, p. 121. Nevertheless, it was applied in *Masters* v. *Leaver* [2000] ILPr. 387 CA.
[138] See n. 116 above, Article 3(3).

Private international law rules on jurisdictional and choice of law matters represent the balance struck at national level between public policy considerations on the one hand, and the need to do justice between private parties on the other. Of course these two objectives are not mutually exclusive, and in many cases they will yield the same result. Inevitably, though, different states will have different solutions for reconciling the two. Outwardly, English courts give only limited scope to public policy considerations in jurisdictional and choice of law matters,[139] and have preferred not to discuss public policy issues at all in the context of forum non conveniens proceedings. Even so, there can be little doubt that wider political issues do have a significant influence on how judges approach private law jurisdictional issues, if only on an unconscious level.

This distinction between public international law and private international law is built upon the conceptual distinction between the different roles of the courts in the public and private spheres. In the private law sphere, the courts are said to act, not as regulators, but as arbitrators of private rights. But the impact of a court case can extend far beyond the two parties to a dispute. Judicial decision-making in the private law sphere not only draws from, but also contributes to, the international social, political and regulatory environment in which multinationals operate. In so far as they identify legal obligations and guide future behaviour, decisions on private law matters will nevertheless have 'regulatory potential'.[140] The role of domestic courts as potential regulators of international CSR standards will be taken up again in chapter 5.

Extraterritorial CSR regulation of multinationals: time for a rethink?

The presence of multinationals makes jurisdictional conflicts between states inevitable. Public international law allows each state a degree of extraterritorial jurisdiction in respect of multinational groups of companies, but the extent to which states may resort to 'parent-based' regulation of multinationals (i.e. through the parent company) in relation to CSR issues is unclear. So far, the bulk of academic discussion on extraterritorial jurisdiction under public international law has taken

---

[139] P. Carter, 'The Role of Public Policy in English Private International Law' (1993) 42 *ICLQ* 1.
[140] See p. 42 above.

place against the background of controversial assertions of extraterritorial jurisdiction in two main areas – competition (or 'anti-trust') laws and export controls (or 'sanctions').[141] But while it has been acknowledged that other areas of regulation may need a different approach,[142] more consideration needs to be given to what the appropriate legal criteria might be. It is argued here that greater account should be taken of the distinctive features of regulatory initiatives in the CSR field, specifically, the regulatory techniques used by home states and the mix of state and private interests involved.

Regulatory techniques

What makes a legislative initiative 'extraterritorial'? The public international law principles discussed above are concerned with the geographical scope of *state* authority, i.e. the extent to which laws can be applied to (and enforced against) persons, entities or activities outside the territorial jurisdiction of the regulating state. But states can (and do) exert subtler regulatory pressures on multinationals in relation to their foreign social and environmental performance, short of actually prescribing and enforcing standards. Take, for instance, a requirement imposed on a parent company to publish information relating to extraterritorial workplace health and safety standards, or an offer by the home state of incentives in exchange for improvements in environmental standards in certain specified foreign countries. Are such initiatives not 'extraterritorial'? Unfortunately, the traditional 'permissive' jurisdictional principles, discussed above, with their preoccupation with 'command and control' type regulatory structures, do not provide an adequate framework for assessing the legality or otherwise of the 'softer' or 'alternative' regulatory techniques. Changes in the regulatory methods employed by states are in many ways reflective of the growing diversity of sources of regulatory pressure,[143] but international law has so far been slow to adapt.

---

[141] D. Rosenthal and W. Knighton, *National Laws and International Commerce: the Problem of Extraterritoriality* (London: Routledge & Kegan Paul and Chatham House, 1982); Roth, 'Reasonable Extraterritoriality'; D. Lange and G. Born (eds.), *The Extraterritorial Application of National Laws* (Deventer: ICC/Kluwer, 1987); A. Lowenfeld, *International Litigation and the Quest for Reasonableness: Essays in Private International Law* (Oxford: Clarendon Press, 1996); Muchlinski, *Multinational Enterprises and the Law*, chapter 5.

[142] F. Francioni, 'Extraterritorial Application of Environmental Law' in K. Meessen (ed.), *Extraterritorial Jurisdiction in Theory and Practice* (The Hague: Kluwer, 1996).

[143] Braithwaite and Drahos, *Global Business Regulation*; S. Picciotto, 'The Regulatory Criss-Cross: Interaction between Jurisdictions and the Construction of Global Regulatory Networks' in W. Bratton (ed.), *International Regulatory Competition and Coordination* (Oxford: Clarendon Press, 1996), p. 97.

Mix of state and private interests

The human rights dimension of CSR regulation[144] raises further questions about the appropriateness (as well as the applicability) of conventional jurisdictional principles. While state-centred principles such as 'nationality' and 'territoriality' may provide an adequate framework for the protection of state interests, international human rights law is built upon the premise that the interests of individuals and the interests of states are not always the same. As Higgins puts it:

> if the classic content of international law is directed to stabilizing and facilitating interstate relations, how are we to guarantee that the needs of the individuals who comprise those states are not ignored? The amelioration of interstate relations is largely directed towards other ends – ends that are important and may not necessarily be inimical to the needs of the citizen but are essentially different. The problem is not only that the norms underpinning interstate relations are rarely addressed in any direct sense to the needs of the individual, but that it is to his own government that the individual will look for his most basic needs. At the same time, it is from his own government that an individual often most needs protection.[145]

Traditional jurisdictional principles are designed to protect, not human rights, but the territorial sovereignty of states. Generally speaking, the public international law rules on jurisdiction draw no real distinction between the rights and interests of states and the rights and interests of their nationals – thus, an attempt to regulate a foreign national extraterritorially undermines the sovereignty of his home state and is therefore prohibited. But there are difficulties with this approach. First, it takes little account of the fact that individuals too have rights under international law that may be opposed to the interests of their own state (e.g. the right of an employee to safe and healthy working conditions versus the home state's interests in protecting its 'comparative advantage' as a foreign investment destination). Where human rights are involved, the privileged status given to state interests over those of the rights of the individual becomes problematic. (Universal jurisdiction may go some way towards addressing this problem but, as discussed above, the range of human rights abuses to which the principle applies is very limited.) Second, it should not *automatically* be regarded as a case of infringement of a host state's sovereignty for a home state to regulate extraterritorially, through the parent company, to ensure that a multinational respects international human rights, as there should be no conflict between the interests of the two states

---

[144] See pp. 42–4, 76–91 above.   [145] Higgins, *Problems and Process*, p. 95.

(even though there may be arguments about how the regulatory objectives are to be achieved). All in all, the new regulatory agenda for multinationals calls for a much more sophisticated and flexible set of rules on extraterritorial jurisdiction, especially where human rights are at stake.

CSR standards and the duty of non-intervention

All state action is subject to the overriding obligation that it does not amount to an unlawful 'intervention' in the domestic affairs of other states. Most states would regard CSR issues within their own territories as matters for their own domestic jurisdiction. According to the US Third Restatement,[146] for instance, extraterritorial jurisdiction cannot, as a general rule, be exercised over 'predominantly local activities, such as industrial or labour relations, health and safety practices, or conduct related to the preservation or control of the local environment'.[147]

There are, however, different views on how the international law principle of non-intervention is to be applied, particularly as regards 'regulatory' interference by one state in the affairs of another. International statements on the subject[148] are deliberately 'woolly'[149] and, in the context of globalisation, near impossible to interpret. Practically speaking, the scope of this duty depends on the answers to two questions: first, which issues are reserved as part of a state's domestic affairs and, second, what constitutes unjustifiable 'intervention' or 'interference' by one state in the domestic affairs of another?

The extent to which a particular subject is part of a state's 'domestic affairs' (and therefore an area over which a state has exclusive competence) depends on the state of international law at the time. Logically, once an issue becomes the subject of international law norms or obligations, there is a corresponding loss or 'shrinkage' of exclusive domestic jurisdiction.[150] The second half of the last century saw a dramatic expansion of international law into fields that would once have been regarded

---

[146] See n. 4 above.   [147] See commentary to § 414, (c).

[148] See, for example, the 1970 'Declaration on the Principles of International Law Concerning Friendly Relations and Co-operation Among States in accordance with the Charter of the United Nations', UNGA res. 2625, Annex, 25 UN GAOR, Supp. (No. 28), UN Doc. A/5217 at 121.

[149] Cassese, *International Law in a Divided World*, p. 147.

[150] R. Higgins, *The Development of International Law through the Political Organs of the United Nations* (Oxford: Oxford University Press, 1963); A. Trindade, 'The Domestic Jurisdiction of States in the Practice of the United Nations and Regional Organisations' (1976) 25 *ICLQ* 715.

as part of the exclusive domestic competence, or 'reserved domain', of states.[151] Through the ILO, states have negotiated and developed monitoring systems for numerous international treaties on the rights of workers.[152] The past three decades have also seen significant developments in the field of international environmental law, giving rise to new customary principles.[153] Through the WHO, states have begun to develop treaties on consumer protection issues also.[154] The implications of these international activities for an 'International Law on CSR' are discussed further in chapters 6 and 7. The important point, for present purposes, is that the more these areas become subject to international norms and obligations, the less susceptible home state regulatory initiatives will be to charges of unlawful 'interference' in another state's domestic affairs.

The second question is even more difficult to answer. There are no clear criteria in international law by which to distinguish 'lawful' from 'unlawful' regulatory intervention. One approach, suggested in relation to economic sanctions, is to focus on the intentions of the 'regulating state'.[155] Damrosch suggests, for example, that non-military forms of intervention should be regarded as lawful, provided that 'the influencing states respect the rights of the target's people to exercise free political choice'.[156] But the motives of the regulating state are rarely (if ever) pure, and even the best-intentioned regulatory gestures in the CSR field may not necessarily be greeted with enthusiasm by other states.[157] For example, a home state initiative aimed at protecting 'international worker rights' might equally be viewed by a developing host state as an unwelcome interference in domestic labour policy, with 'protectionist' aims.[158]

---

[151] S. Ratner, 'International Law: the Trials of Global Norms' (1998) 160 *Foreign Policy* 65.

[152] The ILO currently administers more than 150 international treaties on labour standards in a range of different fields. In addition it has promulgated close to 200 non-binding recommendations.

[153] See pp. 66–7 above.

[154] E.g. WHO Framework Convention on Tobacco Control, Geneva, 21 May 2003, in force 27 February 2005, discussed at pp. 290–2 below.

[155] See O. Elagab, 'Coercive Economic Measures against Developing Countries' (1982) 41 *ICLQ* 682; D. Bowett, 'International Law and Economic Coercion' (1976) 16 *VJIL* 245; T Farar, 'Political and Economic Coercion in Contemporary International Law' (1985) 79 *AJIL* 405.

[156] L. Damrosch, 'Politics across Borders: Non-Intervention and Non-Forcible Influence over Domestic Affairs' (1989) 83 *AJIL* 1.

[157] See further pp. 306–9 below.

[158] Dine, *Companies, International Trade and Human Rights*, p. 198.

The duty of 'non-intervention' is an important guiding principle, although its precise content in relation to extraterritorial regulation of CSR standards is unclear. On the one hand, the principle is often invoked by states as a reason for exercising regulatory restraint in a particular area, and by courts in favour of a 'territorial' interpretation of the scope of a particular regulatory regime. On the other hand, the principle of non-intervention has not prevented industrialised states from introducing a wide range of measures, such as preferential trade arrangements or import bans, to put economic pressure on other states to strive for higher social and environmental standards. In other words, it is a principle that is often invoked, or ignored, as needs dictate.

How this duty develops in the context of international CSR initiatives will depend on the kinds of extraterritorial initiatives developed by home states, and the level of international consensus about the principles they are designed to support. As Scott puts it:

assessing competing claims to jurisdiction is not neutral as to the subject matter being regulated, and some subject matter attracts louder cries of 'extraterritoriality!' than others. The more that one moves away from areas of common criminality, the more states become sensitive when other states seek to regulate the conduct of their nationals, notably their corporate nationals in the economic realm.[159]

The US Third Restatement lays down a framework for resolving jurisdictional problems that takes account of the nature and subject matter of the regulation proposed, as well as the interests of those the regulation is designed to protect. Under § 403, the 'reasonableness' of an exercise of extraterritorial jurisdiction 'is determined by evaluating all relevant factors' including 'the character of the activity to be regulated, the importance of regulation to the regulating state, the extent to which other states regulate such activities, and the degree to which the desirability of such regulation is generally accepted'.[160] Other considerations include 'the importance of the regulation to the international political, legal or economic system', 'the extent to which the regulation is consistent with the traditions of the international system', 'the extent to which another state might have an interest in regulating the activity' and 'the likelihood of conflict with regulation by another state'.[161]

Anticipating calls for greater use of extraterritorial legislation in future, the UK government has proposed a set of guidelines to assess the appropriateness of extraterritorial legislation (based primarily on

[159] Scott, 'Translating Torture into Transnational Tort', p. 53.
[160] US Third Restatement, n. 4 above, § 403(c).   [161] Ibid., § 403(e), (f), (g) and (h).

the 'nationality' principle) in a given set of circumstances.[162] Factors in favour of the use of extraterritorial jurisdiction include:

> where there is international consensus that certain conduct is reprehensible and that concerted action is needed involving the taking of international jurisdiction . . . where the vulnerability of the victim makes it particularly important to be able to tackle instances of the offence . . . [and] . . . where there is a danger that such offences would not otherwise be justiciable.[163]

An 'interests-balancing' approach to public law jurisdiction, which takes account of private as well as state interests, is potentially significant in the context of extraterritorial CSR regulation. In this way, the interests and rights of individuals and the attitudes of the international community are all relevant factors in an assessment as to whether a particular social initiative is legitimate or not. As Lowenfeld argues:

> the issues of jurisdiction to prescribe can and should be addressed by reference to contacts, interests, and expectations – that is to say, meaningful contacts, genuine interests, and justified expectations – rather than by reference to the traditional vocabulary of public international law, focused on the over-used concept of sovereignty.[164]

Summary

International law does not yet offer a satisfactory basis on which to assess the legitimacy of extraterritorial home state initiatives to improve the health, safety and environmental performance of multinationals. While a rigid approach to the issue of corporate 'nationality' may be a useful indicator of the limits of extraterritorial jurisdiction in the economic and foreign policy spheres, it does not necessarily follow that the same principles should be applied in the same way to other areas of regulation, particularly where the aims are to give effect to human rights. On the contrary, the health and safety of foreign workers, communities and consumers justifies a more flexible approach to jurisdiction, under which the 'duty of non-intervention' would become the guiding principle. In other words, the legitimacy of an extraterritorial home state initiative (of whatever kind) would be assessed primarily by reference to its aims, its extraterritorial impacts and its overall reasonableness, rather than by the rigid application of state-centred principles. This is not to suggest that the 'nationality' of a company would be irrelevant, but that

---

[162] Home Office, 'Review of Extraterritorial Jurisdiction; Steering Committee Report', July 1996.
[163] Ibid., para 2.21.   [164] Lowenfeld, *International Litigation*, p. 17.

the presence of 'control relationships' between a parent company and its foreign affiliate ought to be one of the factors taken into account in deciding whether a particular home state initiative is justified.

An alternative definition of 'extraterritoriality'

What are the rights and obligations of states with respect to CSR regulation? How might these rights and obligations develop in future? As explained in chapter 2, customary international law obligations do not usually appear overnight, but are nurtured and developed over time. State practice is both the means by which a customary obligation develops and the proof that it exists.

Unfortunately, most writing on international jurisdictional issues reflects the same preoccupation with traditional 'command and control' forms of regulation that underlies the 'voluntary versus mandatory' debate on CSR.[165] The extent to which other, alternative forms of regulation (discussed in chapter 1 above) might legitimately be used to bring about changes in multinational behaviour abroad has not received much attention at all. At the same time, these alternative forms of regulation are just as much a part of state practice in the CSR field as other more traditional methods. For these reasons, the definition of 'extraterritoriality' used in the survey of state practice in the next chapter is a less formalistic one than that normally used by international lawyers. It takes, as its criterion, not the place where laws are applied or enforced, but their potential extraterritorial *impact*. The impact of home state regulation of CSR standards can be felt beyond territorial boundaries in three different ways: through the imposition of extraterritorial *responsibilities*, through the grant of extraterritorial *rights* and, finally, through the offer of extraterritorial *benefits*.

Extraterritorial responsibilities

Extraterritorial responsibilities can be imposed both directly and indirectly. As discussed above, 'foreign-prescriptive' (direct) extraterritorial regulation refers to legal obligations that are addressed directly to overseas entities, such as foreign subsidiaries or contractors. Failure by these foreign entities to comply with these obligations would subject them to the risk of criminal or other sanctions under home state law. But these are of dubious legality under international law. 'Parent-based' (indirect) extraterritorial regulation refers to the use of jurisdiction enjoyed by

---

[165] See pp. 32–6 above.

the home state over the parent (i.e. on the basis that the parent is a 'national' of the home state) and relies on the ability of the parent to control, in turn, the behaviour of overseas constituents of the multinational group. For example, the parent may be required under domestic legislation to 'ensure' that its overseas affiliates conform to certain standards of behaviour, or refrain from certain conduct. Alternatively, the parent may be subject to CSR reporting requirements, on behalf of itself and its foreign affiliates. These requirements may be backed up by the threat of civil, criminal or other sanctions against the parent for non-compliance. In some cases, the risk of exposure to criminal sanctions under theories of conspiracy may of itself be sufficient encouragement to parent companies to ensure that foreign subsidiaries do not breach home state standards.[166] Alternatively, the parent could be offered financial incentives to encourage it to ensure compliance by foreign affiliates with minimum social standards. Each 'parent-based' method represents a form of extraterritorial regulation via the local (usually parent) company.

Extraterritorial rights

Extraterritorial 'rights' exist where rights created under domestic law – such as rights to enforce regulatory standards, or to participate in or to challenge the decisions of regulatory authorities, or to gain access to information – are extended to people, organisations or legal entities located in other states. Chapter 4 provides some examples of extraterritorial 'public law' rights relevant to CSR. The rights of individuals to bring private law actions against parent companies of multinationals in home state courts are discussed separately in chapter 5.

Extraterritorial benefits

Laws can also have extraterritorial reach in terms of the benefits they confer. One example would be laws that require warnings to be given in respect of product risks regardless of whether those products are destined for consumption within the territory of the home state or not. In this way, home states can extend some of the benefits of local regulation (access to product safety information, for example) to overseas workers, consumers, communities and governments. While measures such

---

[166] See, for example, sections 108 and 109 of the UK Anti-Terrorism, Crime and Security Act 2001. While jurisdiction is not extended to foreign subsidiaries directly, UK parent companies could nevertheless be held responsible for corruption offences committed outside the UK by foreign subsidiaries where the UK parent company has been 'complicit' in the offence.

as these may not produce any legally enforceable 'rights' in the sense described above, they often reflect a desire on the part of the home state to take account of extraterritorial concerns in domestic legislative policy. For example, under UK laws designed to protect 'whistleblowers',[167] it is immaterial whether disclosures relate to failures (e.g. health and safety breaches or environmental damage) taking place in the UK or abroad. The protections afforded by this legislation do not extend to employees working outside the UK.[168] Nevertheless, in so far as the legislation helps to promote transparency with respect to the foreign activities of multinationals, it is clearly of benefit to foreign workers and communities.

Conclusion

Public international law does impose limits on the extent to which one state can regulate the international CSR performance of a multinational group. Simply put, no one state has the right to enforce its laws against foreign-incorporated companies in respect of activities outside its territory, even where the foreign incorporated company is wholly owned by a locally incorporated parent. However, this is not to say that all extraterritorial regulatory initiatives are prohibited – far from it. As has been argued in this chapter, the public international law rules on home state jurisdiction are aimed at only a limited range of regulatory tactics. There are still plenty of opportunities for 'parent-based' regulation by the home state, based on the jurisdiction it enjoys over the parent company. These kinds of initiatives – generally permitted provided they comply with the international law duty of non-intervention – are explored in more detail in the next chapter. In addition, national courts enjoy a degree of extraterritorial jurisdiction in respect of tort-based claims against members of multinational groups. The potential of these kinds of proceedings, as a means of holding multinationals accountable for breaches of CSR standards, is considered further in chapter 5.

---

[167] Employment Rights Act 1996, Part IVA (inserted by the Public Interest Disclosure Act 1998).
[168] Ibid., section 196(3A).

PART II · HOME STATE REGULATION OF MULTINATIONALS

4   New directions in extraterritorial regulation of CSR standards

Extraterritorial jurisdiction over CSR standards has attracted relatively little academic attention to date. There are two reasons for this. First, overt assertions of extraterritorial jurisdiction by states in relation to social and environmental issues have so far been extremely rare. The social and environmental standards of companies are traditionally regarded as matters for the host state, in which the home state should not, as a general rule, interfere. Second, while attempts by states to influence social and environmental standards beyond their territorial boundaries may sometimes be controversial, they have so far tended not to provoke the same level of political conflict as has been generated by claims of extraterritorial jurisdiction in other regulatory areas, such as competition (or 'anti-trust') and economic sanctions.

But the rise of the CSR movement is causing home states to reassess their role in relation to the foreign activities of multinationals based in their respective jurisdictions. There is now a significant degree of public and NGO support for the idea that these states should take much greater interest in the social and environmental performance of multinationals in poorer countries. The previous chapter discusses the jurisdictional principles that limit the powers of home states to regulate the activities of multinationals in other states. However, it is suggested that, while there may be restrictions on 'foreign-prescriptive' regulation, there is still scope for other forms of 'parent-based' regulation, provided this is done sensitively, and does not infringe the principle of 'non-intervention' (i.e. that no state has the right to legislate or enforce its laws in such a way that this interferes in the domestic affairs of another state).

The aim of this chapter is to explore in more detail the techniques that are currently in use and under consideration by home states to address current CSR-related concerns, and particularly the problem of

'double standards' (i.e. the practice of applying lower workplace, environmental or consumer standards in poorer countries, where social expectations may be lower and regulation less stringent). First, though, it
is necessary to revisit some definitional and policy issues introduced
in earlier chapters, namely, what are home states? (i.e. can the 'home
states' of multinationals be readily identified?) and, second, why might
home states have a regulatory interest in the social and environmental
standards of multinationals abroad? The answer to the first question
is important in terms of the feasibility of home state regulation as a
framework for international CSR regimes. The second question needs to
be asked because, as discussed in chapter 2, it is only when states act
out of a sense of legal obligation that new customary rules can be said
to have emerged.[1]

Defining the 'home state'

Do multinationals have 'nationality'? Different experts give different
answers to this question. It will be apparent from the previous chapter that 'nationality' has important consequences in international law.
Outside the legal context, the term is used, more loosely, to refer to
the various special ties – historical, cultural, political or psychological –
that exist between a multinational and a particular state. As noted in
chapter 1, the idea of the multinational as 'stateless' is a recurring theme
in more recent literature about multinationals. To some writers, the
concept of the 'home state' is increasingly irrelevant in today's 'globalising' society.[2] But others continue to defend the concept of 'nationality' in connection to multinationals as vital to a proper understanding of their behaviour and, in particular, relations between business
and states. Dismissing the idea of 'placeless' multinationals as 'a myth',
Dicken contends that '[a]ll TNCs [i.e. multinationals] have an identifi-
able home base, which ensures that every TNC is essentially embedded
within its domestic [i.e. home state] environment'.[3] This 'embeddedness'
is manifested in a variety of ways, including the internal culture of the

---

[1] See pp. 63–7 above.
[2] R. Reich, *The Work of Nations* (New York: Alfred A. Knopf, 1991), p. 137; Korten, *When Corporations Rule the World*, p. 125.
[3] P. Dicken, *Global Shift: Transforming the World Economy*, 3rd edition (London: Paul Chapman Publishing, 1998), p. 193. See also J. Stopford and S. Strange, *Rival States, Rival Firms: Competition for World Market Shares* (Cambridge: Cambridge University Press, 1991).

multinational, management systems and philosophy, the nationality of senior company officers and staff, and the multinational's own political ties.

In its everyday sense, the 'home state' of a multinational usually refers to the state from which that group of companies originated. The 'state of origin' of a multinational very frequently (although not always) continues to be the state in which the parent company is incorporated and the state from which financial and administrative control is exercised.[4] Identifying the 'home state' of such a multinational is relatively straightforward. The position becomes more complicated following mergers between multinationals of different 'home states' or a transfer (or 'hive-off') of a part of one multinational to another. This may be complicated further by the increasing use of collaborative arrangements *between* components of different multinationals.[5] What, for example, is the 'home state' of a joint venture between three companies (each incorporated in different countries: A, B and C) established in country Z?

Although international law does not offer a comprehensive definition of a 'multinational', it does offer some insights into how the 'home state' of a multinational might be identified. Various international law rules rely on the fact that nationality *can* be attributed to companies. 'Corporate nationality' is relevant, for example, to the issue of state jurisdiction over corporate entities (as discussed in the previous chapter), the rights of states to exercise diplomatic protection over corporate entities and the international standards that must be observed by states in relation to 'foreign' corporate entities.

There are at least three factors that could be used to attribute 'nationality' to a corporation for public international law purposes:[6] the place of incorporation, the place from which control over the corporation's activities is primarily exercised and, finally, the nationality of owners or those having substantial 'control' over the activities or operations of the corporation.[7] The choice of factors relevant to nationality is influenced by the context and appears, as Brownlie has put it, 'more as a functional

---

[4] Blumberg, 'Asserting Human Rights', 494. In UNCTAD, 'World Investment Report 2001: Promoting Linkages' (New York and Geneva: UN, 2001), UN Sales No. E.01.II.D.12 the 'home state' is identified by reference to the place of ownership of 'FDI flows and stocks' and the location of corporate headquarters, p. 5.

[5] See Reich, *Work of Nations*, chapter 10; S. Ghoshal and C. Bartlett, 'The Multinational Corporation as an Inter-Organisational Network' in S. Ghoshal and D. Westney (eds.), *Organisational Theory and Multinational Corporations* (London: Macmillan, 1993).

[6] As opposed to private international law, on which see pp. 117–19 above.

[7] Brownlie, *Principles*, p. 426.

attribution or tracing and less as a formal and general status of the kind relating to individuals'.[8]

At the level of domestic law, a difference in state practice exists between 'common law' states (e.g. UK and USA) which favour the 'place of incorporation' test[9] and some 'civil law' states (e.g. Germany and France) which have traditionally referred to the place of control (variously referred to as the *siège social*, *siège réel* or 'real seat' theory) to determine nationality.[10] However, common law countries do, on occasion, 'look behind the corporate veil' and attribute nationality on other bases, for example in the context of wartime controls on 'trading with the enemy' and property ownership.[11]

At the international level, rights of diplomatic protection are based on a link of 'nationality' between the state bringing an international claim and the person alleged to have suffered a wrong under international law. In *Barcelona Traction*, the ICJ favoured the 'place of incorporation' test of corporate nationality, although noting that 'in the particular field of the diplomatic protection of corporate entities, no absolute test of "genuine connection" has found acceptance'.[12] Instead, '[s]uch tests as have been applied are of a relative nature, and sometimes links with one state have had to be weighed against those with another'.[13] In *Barcelona Traction*, the

---

[8] Ibid., p. 426.

[9] ALI, 'Restatement of the Law, Third, Foreign Relations' 1987 § 213: 'For purposes of international law, a corporation has the nationality of the state under the laws of which the corporation is organised.'

[10] But see Case C-212/97, *Centros Ltd* [1999] ECR I-1459, which appears to endorse the 'place of incorporation' test for the purposes of freedom of establishment rules under EU law.

[11] G. Schwarzenberger, *International Law*, 3rd edition, 4 vols. (London: Stevens & Sons, 1957), vol. I, p. 389; Clapham, 'The Question of Jurisdiction', 185–7. Note, however, that the US Third Restatement, n. 9 above, takes a slightly different view, arguing that this is not an attribution of nationality as such – instead, certain ownership structures are treated as 'analogous to nationality'. See § 213, comment d: 'Significant connections other than nationality'.

[12] *Barcelona Traction Light & Power Company (Belgium* v. *Spain)* [1970] ICJ Reps 3, at para. 70.

[13] Ibid. According to the US Third Restatement, a state 'is entitled to represent and afford diplomatic protection to corporations having its nationality', but then goes on to point out that this discretion may not be exercised in practice 'where that state [i.e. the state of incorporation] was chosen solely for legal convenience, for example as a tax haven . . .'; see § 213, Reporters' Notes, para 2. Differences in state practice are discussed by the court in *Barcelona Traction*, n. 12 above, from para. 70: 'Indeed it has been the practice of some States to give a company incorporated under their law diplomatic protection solely when it has its seat (*siège social*) or management or centre of control in their territory, or where a substantial proportion of the shares has been owned by nationals of the State concerned . . .'

court considered the fact that the company had been incorporated in Canada for some fifty years, and that it maintained its registered office, accounts and records there, which, together with international recognition for the relevant company's 'Canadian nationality', settled the question. In another context, though (e.g. where the state of incorporation had been chosen specifically to avoid liabilities), it is quite possible that the courts would look past the state of incorporation to a more 'genuine' connection.[14]

There is, as yet, no universal test for 'corporate nationality' under international law. International Investment Agreements ('IIAs') apply a range of different tests for corporate nationality, but these are said to be too varied to give rise to any customary rules.[15] In practice, the attribution of corporate nationality depends on the context (taking account of considerations of international policy and justice and any applicable treaty provisions), although the state of incorporation is regarded as a strong indicator for diplomatic protection purposes. Not surprisingly, therefore, there is no single international law test for ascribing nationality to multinational groups either. Consistent with the idea that they do not enjoy any independent legal status,[16] it is said that multinationals do not possess any 'nationality' separate from their constituent entities. Instead, they are viewed as an aggregate of separate entities, each with its own nationality.[17] How the nationality of each of these separate entities is determined depends on the particular domestic or international law context.

There is some recognition of the concept of the 'home state' in international 'soft' law instruments relating to multinationals, although the

---

[14] See Clapham, 'The Question of Jurisdiction', pp. 183–4.

[15] Sornorajah, *Foreign Investment*, pp. 248–9. Under ICSID, a 'place of incorporation' test will apply, unless the company has been incorporated in the state with which it is in dispute, in which case 'because of foreign control' the parties may agree that it will be treated as a national of another contracting state. See 1965 International Convention for the Settlement of Investment Disputes between States and Nationals of Other States, Washington, 18 March 1965, in force 14 October 1966, 575 UNTS 159, 17 UTS 1270; (1965) 4 ILM 524, Article 5(2)(b).

[16] See pp. 49–52 above.

[17] For a US definition see the US Third Restatement, note 9 above § 213, comment '*f*: *Multinational Corporations*': 'The multinational enterprise or corporation . . . is an established feature of international economic life, but it has not yet achieved special status in international law or in national legal systems. A multinational corporation generally consists of a group of corporations, *each established under the law of some state*, linked by common managerial and financial control and pursuing integrated policies' (emphasis added).

concept is not defined with any precision. The Draft UN Code[18] defined the 'home country' of a multinational as 'the country in which the parent company is located'. The ILO Tripartite Declaration also contains provisions addressed to 'home countries',[19] but no further explanation was thought to be necessary. Perhaps in recognition of the difficulties involved, the OECD Guidelines play down the idea of special relationships between certain 'home states' and multinationals. The Guidelines are addressed, instead, to all OECD members. These states have made a commitment to 'promote and encourage' the use of the Guidelines and to 'encourage . . . [multinationals to] . . . observe the Guidelines wherever they operate, while taking into account the particular circumstances of each host country'.[20] According to Part 1 of the Guidelines, these requirements apply in respect of all enterprises 'operating in [adherent states'] territories'. This raises the possibility that more than one state could have responsibilities under the Guidelines in relation to a single multinational. In practice, however, OECD member states have tended to focus on those multinationals with which they have special links. The UK NCP, for example, in 'promoting' the Guidelines, has concentrated on multinationals which are 'British', either because they have a parent company incorporated in the UK or because they have substantial British involvement or connections. Also, the idea of the 'home state' is implicit in a guidance note issued by the DTI regarding the procedure for making complaints under the Guidelines. Where the complaint concerns the behaviour of a multinational in a non-adhering state (and where there is no local NCP), it is to be directed to 'the NCP from the country where the Multinational Enterprise is based'.[21]

Because of the sheer diversity of international business forms, it is often not possible to point to a single home state for a multinational group. But, despite the difficulties in formulating definitive legal criteria, the idea of the 'home state' is nevertheless influential in the way home states design and target their extraterritorial regulatory initiatives. In practice home states do (however vaguely and informally) attribute 'nationality' to multinationals, as shall be seen from the examples of state practice discussed below. The criteria for this attribution

---

[18] 1990 Draft UN Code of Conduct on Transnational Corporations, UN Doc. E/1990/94, 12 June 1990.
[19] (1978) 17 ILM 422, para. 12.
[20] OECD Guidelines (2001) 40 ILM 237, Part 1 (Concepts and Principles), para. 10.
[21] DTI, 'OECD Guidelines for Multinational Enterprises'
http://www.dti/gov.uk/worldtrade/ukncp.htm#3.

are roughly similar, and take into account the various links between the multinationals and the state, the relative strength of these links vis-à-vis other states, the attitude of multinationals themselves towards issues of nationality and the purposes for which 'nationality' over multinationals is being asserted or claimed.

Why do 'home states' have an interest in the foreign CSR standards of multinationals?

Political self-interest means that the regulatory policies of home state governments are unlikely to put the health and safety of foreign workers and communities ahead of local jobs and prosperity. It would be wrong to suggest, however, that home states are unconcerned about the social and environmental performance of multinationals abroad. While the rhetoric of home state governments continues to emphasise the importance of principles of 'competitiveness' and 'sovereignty', this is increasingly qualified by the idea that international competition between multinationals has a social and environmental 'bottom line'. To help translate this new ideology into action, home state governments are giving political, logistical and financial backing to a range of new 'voluntary' initiatives aimed at improving the foreign social and environmental standards of multinationals. Increasingly, for example, access to government-sponsored overseas investment assistance is being linked (albeit loosely) to compliance with minimum social, environmental and human rights standards. It is difficult to say at this stage how successful these early attempts at extraterritorial CSR regulation will ultimately be. While some have been welcomed, even embraced, by the business community, others are more controversial. What is clear, though, is that richer home states, like the UK and the USA, do appear to have accepted that they have a role to play in 'encouraging' and 'promoting' (if not enforcing) CSR abroad. What is causing this change in attitude? Is it purely a result of political pressure from activist groups? Or are there other reasons too?

Political self-interest?

The desire of some home states to influence the CSR standards of multinationals abroad may stem, in part, from the realisation that the activities of these enterprises represent a potential source of political embarrassment. Most home states identify strongly with the multinationals their domestic policies have helped to create. Although no longer viewed as political agents,[22] multinationals do still act as ambassadors for their home states in other ways. Poor CSR standards by a multinational can adversely affect, not just the prospects of the multinational in question, but subsequent investors in that country, and the international standing of the state from which that multinational originated. Australia's reputation as a 'home state' for multinationals was raised as a possible justification for the introduction of legislation to impose an enforceable 'code of conduct' on Australian-based multinationals (although this private member's bill ultimately failed to achieve sufficient political support to become law).[23] In some cases a government may feel that there are political gains to be made within the international community by being seen to take a tough stance in relation to a particular issue, as was the case with US policy on the extraterritorial regulation of bribery and corruption.[24]

The political repercussions for a home state, both domestically and internationally, can be even worse where the home state has provided financial support to a foreign project, for example, in the form of export-credit guarantees. The UK government, for example, was heavily criticised by environmental and human rights NGOs for the support it was planning to give (through the DTI's export-credit guarantee scheme) to the Ilisu Dam project in Turkey. Opponents of the new dam argued that it would result in serious environmental and cultural damage and that the human rights of the local population had not properly been taken into account.[25] This caused acute embarrassment to the Blair government, particularly in light of earlier commitments, following the 1997 election, that UK foreign policy would henceforth have an 'ethical' dimension.[26]

Economic self-interest?

If, as seems likely, there is a 'business case' for CSR[27] – that is, if CSR does have a positive impact on the long-term productivity and sustainability

---

[22] See pp. 9–10 above.

[23] Commonwealth of Australia (Parliamentary Joint Statutory Committee on Corporations and Securities), 'Report on the Corporate Code of Conduct Bill', June 2001, paras. 3.169–3.183. This bill is discussed in more detail at pp. 165–7 below.

[24] US Foreign Corrupt Practices Act of 1977, 5 USC § 78dd-1. For further discussion of the policy background to this legislation see Brown, 'Extraterritorial Reach'.

[25] See further p. 190 above.

[26] P. Brown and K. Maguire, 'Ethics Policy in Shreds as Dam Approved', *Guardian*, 22 December 1999, p. 8.

[27] See pp. 17, 33 above.

of companies – then home states clearly have an economic self-interest in promoting it, not just locally but internationally as well. The European Commission has recognised this possible link, and sees CSR as having an important contribution to make towards achieving the EU's strategic goal, laid down at the Lisbon Summit of 2000, of becoming, by 2010, 'the most competitive and dynamic knowledge based economy in the world, capable of sustainable economic growth with more and better jobs and greater social cohesion'.[28] However, while a connection between CSR and competitiveness seems intuitively correct, little is known about what the precise relationships might be, and how they can best be managed. With this in mind, the European Commission's 2002 communication on CSR calls for more research into 'how and under which circumstances enterprises adopting CSR can contribute to the objective of enhanced competitiveness and a more sustainable society'.[29] In an attempt to demonstrate the correlation between CSR and competitiveness, a 'Responsible Competitiveness Index' was launched at the UN Global Compact Conference in Brazil in 2003. The first index covered fifty-one states, and identified twenty-two (including the USA and China) as having a 'responsibility deficit'.[30] This has been followed by the launch of a new programme: the 'UN Global Compact Policy Dialogue on Responsible Competitiveness'. In the same year, the UK government (together with the UK-based think tank Forum for the Future) hosted a workshop 'to debate the links between competitiveness, productivity and the increasingly important role of intangible assets, as well as sustainability and CSR'. It came to the 'broad conclusion – with some qualification' that 'sustainability makes a positive contribution to business success. The key was to look at this as an investment in a strategic asset or distinctive capability rather than as an expense.'[31]

But research by UK-based organisation Accountability suggests that governments have so far failed to 'understand and exploit the potential synergies between economic growth and competitiveness'. This failure, it is argued, could ultimately have the effect of discrediting both the CSR movement ('for delivering too little') and the drive for competitiveness

---

[28] European Commission, 'Communication from the Commission concerning Corporate Social Responsibility: a Business Contribution to Sustainable Development', Brussels, 2 July 2002, COM (2002) 347, final, p. 3.

[29] Ibid., p. 9.

[30] Accountability, 'Responsible Competitiveness', Briefing Paper (2004), copy available from http://www.accountability.org.uk.

[31] DTI, 'Corporate Social Responsibility: a Government Update' (DTI, May 2004), copy available from http://www.societyandbusiness.gov.uk, pp. 10–11.

('for creating unacceptable negative externalities').[32] What is needed, according to this particular piece of research, are 'enabling public policies as well as business innovation', most obviously 'policies that support competition that advantages those companies adopting responsible practices. This includes advancing frameworks and standards that level the playing field as well as raising the floor.'[33]

A second, more traditional, economic justification for extraterritorial CSR regulation by home states stems from concerns about 'migration of jobs'. As discussed in chapter 1, the governments of wealthier home states have long been concerned about the ability of multinationals to move production operations from one part of the world to another. The so-called 'migration of jobs' receives almost daily press attention in the UK and elsewhere. The UK textile industry has been particularly affected with a series of job losses and closures in recent years blamed on the inability of local producers to compete with cheap imports. In February 2002, questions were asked in the UK parliament following the announcement by British vacuum cleaner manufacturer Dyson that it would be moving its production operations from Wiltshire to Malaysia, with the expected loss of around 800 jobs. The picture is similar across the EU. Early 2004 saw several announcements from international companies, including Samsung and Philips Novalux, that they would be closing down some operations in Spain, in favour of countries such as Poland and Slovakia, where labour costs are cheaper. This trend is also spreading to the services industry. In 2003, the UK House of Commons Trade and Industry Select Committee launched an inquiry into the relocation of call centre jobs to Asia, following predictions that 100,000 jobs could be lost to the UK industry by 2008.

The apparent ease with which multinationals are able to relocate operations, coupled with the dependency of towns and regions on these companies for jobs and economic prosperity, can place home states in a poor bargaining position. Huge competition between states for inward investment, it is feared, places downward pressure on labour and environmental standards, not just for host states but for home states as well (the so-called 'race to the bottom'). As a result, the governments of these wealthier, industrialised states are under pressure from local worker groups and trade unions, which argue that competition from goods originating from countries with low social and environmental standards is 'unfair'.[34] While these concerns have not led

[32] Accountability, 'Responsible Competitiveness', n. 30 above, p. 3.   [33] Ibid., pp. 1–2.
[34] ICFTU, 'Building Workers' Human Rights into the Global Trading System', 1999, http://www.icftu.org.

to direct regulation by home states of the social and environmental standards of multinationals abroad (undoubtedly because of the difficult sovereignty and jurisdictional issues involved),[35] they are nevertheless reflected in national trade policy and investment assistance programmes.

One way of exerting economic pressure to improve social and environmental standards in other states (leaving aside the more controversial 'protectionist' measures such as trade barriers and tariffs) is through preferential trading arrangements. Essentially, development assistance in the form of preferential trading relationships is conditioned on the observance by the beneficiary country of certain standards, for example a prohibition on forced or child labour. Over time, labour standards and (to a much more limited extent) environmental standards have come to form part of the assessment criteria for US and EU schemes. The scheme operated by the US government under the 1974 Trade Act,[36] for example, provides that beneficiary status will not be given to a developing country that 'has not taken or is not taking steps to afford internationally recognized worker rights to workers in the country . . .'[37]

Similar concerns are reflected in the legislative constraints imposed upon the US Overseas Private Investment Corporation ('OPIC'). OPIC's primary purpose is to facilitate foreign investment by US corporations in less developed countries by providing insurance against political risks.[38] The US government was, however, keen not to be seen to be assisting 'capital flight' from the USA.[39] For this reason, OPIC is directed under its founding legislation not to assist projects which may result in the investor significantly reducing the number of its US employees, or which 'is likely to cause a significant reduction in the number of employees in the United States'.[40]

To summarise, competition from suppliers and contractors in countries with lower social and environmental standards suggests a further rationale for extraterritorial CSR regulation by home states, although

---

[35] See pp. 105–13 above.   [36] Trade Act of 1974, 19 USC § 2101.

[37] Ibid, § 2462, subparagraph (2)(G). For criticism of the way these provisions have been used in practice see J. Perez-Lopez, 'Conditioning Trade on Foreign Labor Law: the US Approach' (1987–8) 9 *Comp Lab LJ* 253; H. Mandel, 'In Pursuit of the Missing Link: International Workers Rights and International Trade' (1989) 27 *CJTL* 443; P. Alston, 'Labour Rights Provisions in US Trade Law: "Aggressive Unilateralism?"' in L. Compa and S. Diamond (eds.), *Human Rights, Labour Rights and International Trade* (Philadelphia: University of Pennsylvania Press, 1996).

[38] See Foreign Assistance Act of 1961, 22 USC § 2191.

[39] Zimmerman, *Extraterritorial Employment Standards*, p. 59.

[40] Foreign Assistance Act, n. 38 above, § 2191(k), (l) and (n).

it must be remembered that there may be economic disadvantages to this type of regulation too (such as increased prices of consumer goods). There is also the risk that any legislation introduced for this reason may be open to accusations of 'disguised protectionism' by other states.

Development goals?

'The modern development agenda', according to British prime minister, Tony Blair, 'goes far wider than resource transfers, to embrace issues of trade, investment, conflict, governance and the environment.'[41] In the years since the 1992 Rio Summit, governments have become increasingly aware of the potentially pivotal role of private companies in strategies to combat poverty and promote sustainable development.[42] At the very minimum, as business leaders like to point out, companies help to reduce poverty by providing jobs, skills and training, by paying taxes and thereby contributing to economic growth.[43] In addition, the privatisation programmes pursued by many countries mean that multinationals are already engaged in supplying public goods:

The operations of business now have increased their developmental impact. They have moved into areas previously viewed as the public domain in some parts of the world e.g. healthcare and education provision, supply of power and telecommunications. Multinational companies are supplying materials, goods, labour and services to and from developing countries. The socially responsible business operations of export-focussed domestic companies of these countries can therefore be influenced through those international businesses, as well as directly.[44]

Other supporters of greater public–private partnership in the delivery of development strategies point to the greater efficiency of the private sector (claimed to be a result of the disciplines of competition) and the level of innovation and professionalism typically found within large, successful companies.[45] Companies can also provide an important point of contact between home states and the governments and authorities of developing states.[46]

---

[41] Tony Blair, Speech given to Ghanaian parliament, 8 February 2002.
[42] F. Calder and M. Culverwell, 'Following Up the World Summit on Sustainable Development Commitments on Corporate Social Responsibility' (Royal Institute of International Affairs, Final Report, February 2005), p. 19.
[43] DFID, 'DFID and Corporate Social Responsibility', http://www.dfid.gov.uk.
[44] DFID, 'Socially Responsible Business Team Strategy: April 2001–March 2004'.
[45] Calder and Culverwell, 'Following Up the World Summit', pp. 19–20.
[46] European Commission, 'A Business Contribution to Sustainable Development', n. 28 above, p. 9.

The idea that business has a central role to play in delivering international sustainable development goals became an issue of key importance at the 2002 WSSD in Johannesburg. In their final declaration and 'Plan of Implementation',[47] participating states made a number of commitments to step up their efforts with respect to CSR, which are discussed in more detail in chapter 6. This theme was taken up again at the 2004 UNCTAD conference in São Paulo.[48] The UK government, for its part, has recognised the links between CSR and development issues in a series of policy documents on CSR, and has pledged itself to 'foster an enabling environment for responsible business practice to maximise the positive contribution that businesses can make to the UK's objectives on international sustainable development – including human rights, trade and investment, poverty eradication, environmental protection and corruption'.[49]

Ethical concerns?

Home state politicians may, of course, be motivated to act out of a sense of moral obligation, though this is a difficult proposition to test. As discussed in chapter 1, many writers and civil society campaigners make the case that home states of multinationals are in a unique position of responsibility, as the key architects and beneficiaries of 'globalisation'. On the other hand, richer home states may be sensitive to accusations of 'paternalism'. This was a common theme in the submissions made to the Australian parliamentary committee established in 2000 to examine the Corporate Code of Conduct Bill[50] and to the European Commission in response to its recent Green Paper on CSR.[51] The European Parliament

---

[47] 2002 'Declaration on Sustainable Development' and 'Plan of Implementation of the World Summit on Sustainable Development' in UN, 'Report of the World Summit on Sustainable Development', UN Doc. A/CONF.199/20, Sales No. E.03.II.A.1. See further pp. 268–9, 278 below.

[48] UNCTAD, 'São Paulo Consensus', adopted at the 269th plenary meeting, 18 June 2004, UN Doc.TD/410, 25 June 2004, para. 58.

[49] DTI, 'Corporate Social Responsibility: International Strategic Framework', 1 March 2004, http://www.societyandbusiness.gov.uk, p. 2.

[50] Commonwealth of Australia, 'Report on the Code of Conduct Bill', n. 23 above, para. 4.49.

[51] 'Any . . . model based on European values would be unacceptable to the rest of the world; for the US and other western nations it might be deemed arrogant, intrusive, expensive and unnecessary, while for developing countries it could also smack of protectionism, paternalism or even colonialism.' European Round Table of Industrialists, 'Response to European Commission Green Paper on CSR Promoting a European Framework'. A copy of the original Green Paper (European Commission,

has, however, expressed a different view. Calling on the European Commission to 'ensure that European firms apply the same safety measures in their subsidiary companies abroad . . . as within the Community', 'The European Parliament . . . takes the view that the sovereignty of developing countries is in no way impaired thereby and that, on the contrary, firms based in the Community have a duty to ensure the highest safety standards in their foreign subsidiaries.'[52]

A legal case?

There is no real evidence, yet, that home states are introducing extraterritorial measures in the CSR field out of any sense of legal obligation. However, the possibility that some legal obligations already exist (or are currently under development) is certainly worth exploring. The idea that home states may have some 'extraterritorial regulatory responsibilities' under international human rights law is discussed in chapter 2.[53] There is another possible source of legal obligations for home states (also alluded to in chapter 2)[54] which derives from the obligation not to cause or permit transboundary harm. Could this obligation create any additional regulatory responsibilities for home states vis-à-vis multinationals?

The obligation to prevent transboundary harm is concerned with more than just the activities of state authorities. It also entails, like the human rights obligations discussed in chapter 2, an obligation to regulate private activities effectively to ensure that serious transboundary harm does not occur.[55] According to the 1992 Rio Declaration:

States have in accordance with the Charter of the United Nations and the principles of international law the sovereign right to exploit their own resources pursuant to their own environmental and developmental policies and the responsibility to ensure that activities within their jurisdiction or control do not cause

---

'Green Paper on CSR: Promoting a European Framework for Corporate Social Responsibility', Employment and Social Affairs, July 2001) and responses (including this) can be viewed at http://www.europa.eu.int/comm/employment social/ soc-dial/csr/index.htm.

[52] European Parliament, 'Resolution on the Poisonous Gas Catastrophe in India', [1985] OJ C12/84, para. 3.

[53] See pp. 85–91 above.   [54] See p. 84 above, n. 131.

[55] See ILC, 'Articles on the Responsibility of States for Internationally Wrongful Acts' in ILC, 'Report of the International Law Commission on the Work of its Fifty-third Session', UNGA, Supplement No. 10 (A/56/10), (New York: UN, 2001), Article 3; Pisillo-Mazzeschi, 'The Due Diligence Rule', 38.

damage to the environment of other states or of areas beyond the limits of national jurisidiction.[56]

As noted above, this is widely regarded as a statement of customary international law.[57] The standard required of states in this area is generally thought to be one of 'due diligence'.[58] 'Due diligence' in this context entails the use of legislative and administrative means to protect other states and the global environment; generally 'the conduct to be expected of a good government'.[59] These customary obligations certainly require the regulation of physical sources of pollution originating from within a state's territory or subject to its jurisdiction.[60] In addition, states engaged in the exporting of hazardous wastes and technologies may be under customary international law obligations to warn recipient states of potential dangers associated with those exports.[61] These obligations are amplified and extended in treaty regimes governing international trade in wastes and other hazards. The 1989 Basel Convention,[62] for example, establishes an international regime for the regulation of trade in hazardous wastes which relies on the principle of 'prior informed consent'.[63] The 1991 Bamako Convention,[64] which governs exports of hazards to African state parties, also regulates trade in substances banned or withdrawn in the country of manufacture for health or environmental reasons.

Of course, there is a significant difference between an obligation to warn (which attaches to an export of a hazard from the territory of the regulating state) and an obligation of ongoing regulation. While states may be under international obligations to give notice and consult

---

[56] 1992 Declaration of the UN Conference on Environment and Development, Rio de Janeiro, 13 June 1992, UN Doc. A/CONF.151/26/Rev. 1, Vol. 1, Annex I; (1992) 31 ILM 874, Principle 2.

[57] Birnie and Boyle, *International Law and the Environment*, pp. 109–12.

[58] See ILC, 'Articles on State Responsibility', Article 3, commentary, para. 7.

[59] Birnie and Boyle, *International Law and the Environment*, p. 112. See also G. Handl, 'State Liability for Accidental Transnational Environmental Damage by Private Persons' (1980) 74 *AJIL* 525.

[60] Birnie and Boyle, *International Law and the Environment*, p. 109.

[61] M. Bothe, 'The Responsibility of Exporting States' in G. Handl and R. Lutz (eds.), *Transferring Hazardous Technologies and Substances* (London: Graham & Trotman, 1989).

[62] 1989 Convention on the Control of Transboundary Movements of Hazardous Wastes and their Disposal, Basel, 22 March 1989, in force 24 May 1992, 1673 UNTS 126; (1989) 28 ILM 657.

[63] See further pp. 292–4 below.

[64] 1991 Convention on the Ban of the Import into Africa and the Control of Transboundary Movement and Management of Hazardous Wastes within Africa, Bamako, 30 January 1991, in force 22 April 1998; (1991) 30 ILM 775.

with other states prior to the export of certain hazards, home states of multinationals do not presently appear to be under any requirement, by virtue of their obligations to prevent transboundary harm, to continue regulating the operation and management of those hazards once they are within the jurisdiction of another state. On the contrary, the ILC's Commentary to the Articles on State Responsibility confirms that state responsibility is based on *territorial* jurisdiction.[65] This means that, as far as international law is concerned, any ongoing regulatory responsibilities of a state with respect to, say, a hazardous industrial process, would cease once it became subject to the jurisdiction of the host state, regardless of the actual regulatory capabilities of that state. Nevertheless, as discussed in chapters 6 and 7, it is quite possible that emerging trends in extraterritorial CSR regulation, not to mention new treaty regimes, could expand the regulatory responsibilities of home states in future.[66]

Extraterritorial regulatory techniques: recent state practice

Extraterritorial social and environmental regulation of multinationals is not new. States have long sought to influence social standards in other countries through their trading relationships. Later, home states recognised that the cross-border control relationships that existed between members of groups of companies provided further opportunities for extraterritorial social regulation. The steps taken by EC member states, Canada and the USA in the 1970s and 1980s against the apartheid regime in South Africa included, for example, guidance to parent companies in relation to the employment policies of their South African subsidiaries.[67]

However, recent policy statements from home state governments suggest a growing commitment to CSR as an ethical position, and a growing willingness to use their influence to help improve the CSR performance of multinationals, particularly in poorer, less developed countries. This is partly as a result of political pressure; as discussed in previous chapters, the past few years have seen a huge amount of activity among NGOs

---

[65] ILC, 'Articles on the Responsibility of States', n. 55 above: 'For the purposes of these articles, *territorial jurisdiction* is the dominant criterion. Consequently, when an activity covered by the present articles occurs within the *territory* of a State, that state must comply with the *obligations of prevention*. "Territory" is, therefore, taken as conclusive evidence of jurisdiction. Consequently, in cases of competing jurisdictions over an activity covered by these articles, the territorially based jurisdiction prevails'; commentary to Article 2, para. 8.

[66] See also Sornorajah, 'Linking State Responsibility'.

[67] See further pp. 161–2 below.

and other CSR campaigners aimed at translating concerns about the social and environmental accountability of multinationals into legislative action. So far, actual legislative changes have been few. But CSR regulation is still only in its early stages. Within Europe, the development of EU policy on CSR is currently taking place against the background of the policy set out in the 2002 European Commission Communication on CSR.[68] In the USA, Australia and the UK, the question of extraterritorial CSR regulation of multinationals has been forced onto the regulatory agenda by the introduction of ambitious private member's bills, discussed below. In addition, ongoing dialogue – between NGOs, unions and governments – has produced various other new and innovative regulatory proposals.

The remainder of this chapter sets out some examples of some different extraterritorial regulatory techniques recently considered by home states (though this is by no means a comprehensive survey). Some of these techniques have been implemented, some are still under consideration and some, although unsuccessful thus far, are nevertheless included as an indication of other, possible, regulatory options. The direct application of home state standards (referred to in chapter 3 as 'foreign-prescriptive' regulation) does not seem to be on the regulatory agenda of any of the leading home states at present. As discussed above, most (if not all) states would consider 'direct' regulation of CSR standards of foreign subsidiaries to be beyond the scope of jurisdiction permitted under international law. Nevertheless, other 'softer' forms of regulation are already in use. For reasons explained in the previous chapter,[69] an expanded definition of extraterritoriality is used here, which encompasses not only initiatives that impose extraterritorial obligations, but also those that are capable of conferring extraterritorial rights and benefits.

'Parent-based' and 'foreign-prescriptive' regulation, governmental 'codes of conduct' and monitoring schemes

The 'code of conduct' is a frequently used means of communicating CSR standards to multinationals, although these standards are rarely backed up by conventional legal sanctions such as fines. In the late 1980s and early 1990s, US companies with subsidiaries in South Africa were subject to a 'code of conduct' in relation to their employment practices in

---

[68] See European Commission, 'A Business Contribution to Sustainable Development', n. 28 above.

[69] See pp. 140–2 above.

that country under the US Comprehensive Anti-Apartheid Act of 1986.[70] Each US company subject to the legislation was required to register with a US government authority and give periodic reports on compliance. This scheme operated through US jurisdiction over the parent company and, as such, can be regarded as a form of 'parent-based' extraterritorial regulation[71] (although standards were not formally enforced, merely 'monitored').[72]

A similar scheme was put in place in Canada in 1985 and in the UK (as well as in other EC member states) in 1977 following a decision of EC foreign ministers.[73] Under this scheme UK companies with a greater than 50 per cent shareholding in a South African subsidiary were obliged to report annually to the UK government on steps taken to implement a 'code of conduct'.[74] In addition, companies were asked to refer to their reports on 'code of conduct' activities in their annual reports. The EC Code of Conduct was concerned in particular with discriminatory work practices, collective bargaining and pay. In addition, it was stated that 'undertakings should concern themselves with the living conditions of their employees and their families' and suggested that funds be set aside for a range of matters including 'implementing medical services . . . adopting programmes of insurance against industrial accidents . . . and . . . other measures of social welfare'.[75]

A more recent example of extraterritorial regulation through a 'code of conduct' can be found in the implementation arrangements made by OECD member states in relation to the OECD Guidelines. Each member state of the OECD is required, under an OECD Council Decision of

---

[70] 22 USC § 5001. (Note that this legislation was repealed in 1994 following the holding of 'free and fair' elections in South Africa.)

[71] US companies employing more than twenty-five persons in South Africa were required to 'take the necessary steps to insure that the Code of Conduct is implemented with respect to the employment of those persons', see 22 USC § 5034. Under subsequent regulations, this requirement was extended to US companies with a controlling interest in South African employers; see Zimmerman, *Extraterritorial Employment Standards*, pp. 94–101.

[72] For a description of the monitoring procedure see ibid., pp. 98–101.

[73] See Department of Trade, Code of Conduct for Companies With Interests in South Africa: Government Guidance to British Companies on the Code of Conduct Adopted by the Governments of the Nine Member States of European Community on 20 September 1977; Cmnd 1–7233 (1978).

[74] Ibid., section 7. Companies having only a 'minority' interest in a South African subsidiary (i.e. less than 50 per cent interest), while not required to submit compliance reports, were nevertheless 'encouraged' to submit a report under the scheme 'wherever possible'.

[75] Ibid., section 5.

June 2000, to establish a 'National Contact Point' (or 'NCP') responsible for 'promoting' the OECD Guidelines and handling inquiries relating to them.[76] The background to this particular initiative is discussed in more detail in chapter 6. Separately from this, some home states have also been active in schemes (frequently in collaboration with NGOs) to develop further non-binding codes for multinationals. The UK-based ETI[77] is one example. The ETI board (on which the UK government has observer status) administers a scheme whereby UK-based multinationals are encouraged to signify their commitment to a 'Base Code of Conduct', covering matters such as working conditions, wages and child labour, and to ensure that their suppliers work towards achievement of these standards as well. The UK government was also instrumental in developing the Voluntary Principles on Security and Human Rights[78] and the Extractive Industry Transparency Initiative ('EITI'), under which participating states and companies agree to work together to increase transparency in relation to payments made to foreign governments by mining, oil and gas companies (including royalties, taxes and signature bonuses).[79]

The US government has also sponsored 'corporate codes of conduct' with extraterritorial reach. In 1996 the Clinton administration issued a set of 'Model Business Principles' for US business 'that wish to play a positive role in upholding and promoting adherence to human rights'.[80] The areas covered in the Model Business Principles include workplace health and safety, and 'responsible environmental protection and environmental practices'. The Model Business Principles were administered by the Department of Commerce under its 'Best Global Practices programme'. This programme included an award system for US-based multinationals able to demonstrate a 'high level of commitment' to the applicable standards. Following on from this, the Clinton administration also established, in August 1996, the 'White House Apparel Industry Partnership' ('AIP'), an association of manufacturers, consumer groups, unions and human rights organisations. The AIP had two broad aims: first, to raise international social standards (including standards relating to workplace health and safety) within the clothing manufacturing industry and, second, to provide consumers with more information about product

---

[76] See further pp. 251–4 below.   [77] See pp. 96, 99 above.
[78] See http://www.voluntaryprinciples.org.
[79] The EITI is overseen in the UK by the DFID. See further
http://www2.dfid.gov.uk/news/files/extractiveindustries.asp.
[80] US Department of State publication 104846, June 1997.

origins. This, in turn, led to the establishment of the Fair Labor Association (or 'FLA') in 1999 to administer a 'workplace code of conduct' for US-based multinationals in the clothing sector and to operate an accreditation scheme for 'independent' monitors.[81] The 'workplace code of conduct' includes prohibitions on the use of forced or child labour and an obligation to provide a 'safe and healthy' working environment. In addition, companies are required to establish internal monitoring procedures extending to contractors and supplies, as well as their own factories. Like the UK-based ETI, participation in the FLA is voluntary. Unlike the ETI, however, there is no representative of the US government on the FLA board, although its activities are funded, in part, by grants from US state sources.

Ensuring compliance with voluntary codes of conduct is problematic. Most voluntary codes rely for their efficacy on the 'reputational risk' posed by media claims of non-compliance, or, where possible, suspension from a particular scheme.[82] However, recent years have seen an intensification of efforts by CSR campaigners to place codes of conduct for multinationals on a more formal legislative footing. New bills of legislation have been introduced in Australia, by Senator Vikki Bourne, and in the USA, by Congresswoman Cynthia McKinney, with the aim of introducing tougher sanctions for breaches of workplace, environmental and consumer safety standards by foreign affiliates.[83] In 2003, a Corporate Responsibility Bill was tabled in the UK parliament, calling for changes to directors' duties and a statutory obligation upon companies to pay damages in cases where management failures have resulted in physical injury or harm to the environment, regardless of where in the world that harm or injury had occurred. Although none of these bills achieved sufficient support to become law,[84] their workability as models of extraterritorial CSR regulation is nevertheless worth considering. The European Parliament has also expressed its concerns about the problem

---

[81] See FLA Charter, http://www.fairlabor.org.

[82] For example, membership of the scheme administrated by the ETI 'is on an annual basis and will not be renewed for those members who have not demonstrated a commitment to the ETI process'. ETI, 'Introducing the Ethical Trade Initiative', http://www.ethicaltrade.org.

[83] For further information about the background to these pieces of draft legislation, and a comparison of their main provisions, see McBeth, 'Corporate Code of Conduct Legislation'.

[84] An Australian Joint Statutory Committee on Corporations and Securities published its decision not to support the legislation in June 2001. See Commonwealth of Australia, 'Report on the Corporate Code of Conduct Bill', n. 23 above.

of 'double standards', and in 1999 passed a Resolution calling for the establishment of a body responsible for monitoring compliance with a code of conduct which, though 'voluntary', would be enforced through withdrawal of certain incentives for non-compliant 'European companies'.

Australian Corporate Code of Conduct Bill

The objects of the 'Corporate Code of Conduct Bill', introduced into the Australian Senate in September 2000, were described as follows:

(a) to impose environmental, employment, health and safety and human rights standards on the conduct of Australian corporations or related corporations which employ more than 100 people in a foreign country; and
(b) to require such corporations to report on their compliance with the standards imposed by this Act; and
(c) to provide for enforcement of those standards.[85]

Significantly, this draft legislation was stated to apply *directly* to foreign companies related to Australian companies.[86] Obligations imposed on these foreign companies under this statutory 'code of conduct' included obligations to 'take all reasonable measures to prevent any material adverse effect on the environment in and around the place of [its] activity',[87] to 'take all reasonable measures to promote the health and safety of its workers',[88] to refrain from using or benefiting from forced or child labour,[89] to 'pay all its workers a living wage',[90] to adopt equal opportunity policies[91] and to 'ensure that any goods or services which it provides satisfy the required standards for consumer health and safety for those goods in Australia and in any other country in which it undertakes activities'.[92] Compliance with these general standards could be enforced either by civil penalties instituted by Australian regulatory authorities[93] or by civil actions for damages which may be brought by 'any person who suffers loss or damage' ('whether resident in Australia or elsewhere') as a result of their contravention.[94] Furthermore, the

---

[85] Section 3.
[86] As drafted, the legislation would also have applied to foreign *holding companies* of Australian subsidiaries, but this was identified in the report of the Parliamentary Joint Statutory Committee as a probable drafting error. See Commonwealth of Australia, 'Corporate Code of Conduct Bill', paras. 3.17–3.19.
[87] Section 7(1).   [88] Section 8(1).   [89] Section 9(1) and (2).   [90] Sub-section 9(3)(a).
[91] Section 10.   [92] Section 12.   [93] Section 16.   [94] Section 17.

Federal Court of Australia would be given the power to issue injunctions 'to prevent further loss or damage'[95] as a result of a contravention of these standards.[96]

Following a series of hearings on the proposed legislation through 2000 and 2001, a Statutory Committee eventually recommended that the legislation not go forward for a number of reasons. These included its extreme extraterritorial scope (and therefore concerns about its legality under international law), the vagueness of the obligations to which foreign companies would be subjected, concerns about its potential impact on Australian industry and also that Australia, in seeking to regulate social standards in other countries, might be accused by host states of 'arrogance' and 'paternalism'.[97] In addition, the committee questioned the need for such legislation, i.e. did the few, well-publicised instances of human rights abuses by Australian-based multinationals justify such a drastic response? The committee concluded that it did not.[98]

The Corporate Code of Conduct Bill, in the form originally presented to the Australian parliament, had other practical shortcomings. Not only were the basic legislative obligations vague, they were incorporated in the body of the bill itself, and therefore would have been difficult to amend to reflect changes in practice and gains in experience in the regulation of multinationals in CSR-related areas. Moreover, the decision to address obligations directly to foreign companies and their officers raises obvious enforcement difficulties. The possibility of enforcing obligations 'indirectly' through Australian parent companies (i.e. 'parent-based' methods of regulation) appears not to have been considered. Finally, the legislation would not extend to regulate the practices of foreign contractors to Australian companies directly, which, as was pointed out by a number of participants in the committee hearings, is where some of the most serious human rights abuses of workers might be expected to be found. Nevertheless, the bill does raise some interesting possibilities, notably the regulation of the foreign activities of multinationals through private causes of action or 'extraterritorial rights'. These are discussed further below.[99]

---

[95] Sub-sections 17(3) and (4).

[96] The bill also sought to introduce a system of social reporting for Australian-based multinationals, discussed further at p. 175 below.

[97] Commonwealth of Australia, 'Report on the Corporate Code of Conduct Bill', n. 23 above.

[98] Ibid, at para. 4.44.   [99] See pp. 182–7 below.

Despite their lack of success the first time around, the Australian Democrats did not give up on their campaign for tough extraterritorial regulation of the CSR and human rights performance of Australian-based multinationals overseas. A revised version of the Corporate Code of Conduct Bill was tabled by Australian Democrats Foreign Affairs spokesperson Natasha Stott Despoja in June 2004.[100] This new version takes broadly the same approach as its predecessor, with some additional provisions designed to give extraterritorial effect to existing Australian laws relating to human rights (e.g. discrimination) and internationally protected sites and species. Like the previous version, the 2004 exposure draft is overtly extraterritorial in that it 'applies *only* in respect of the overseas operations of such corporations' (emphasis added).[101] Unfortunately, though, it does not really address any of the more fundamental legal and practical issues identified in the course of the Statutory Committee hearings on the previous version. It is also, like its predecessor, extremely prescriptive,[102] which means that there is the danger that the legislation could quickly become out of step with developing international standards and practice. The provisions on reporting are, however, more reflective of a general trend and these are discussed further below.

The McKinney Bill

Like the Australian Corporate Code of Conduct Bill, the US Code of Conduct Bill (known as 'the McKinney Bill')[103] is aimed specifically at multinationals. This piece of draft legislation, first tabled with the US Congress on 7 June 2000 by Democratic Representative Cynthia McKinney, would apply to all US nationals[104] that employ more than twenty persons in a foreign country 'either directly or through subsidiaries, subcontractors, affiliates, joint ventures, partners or licensees'.[105] The basic obligation imposed on US parent companies was to 'take the necessary

---

[100] A copy of the bill may be viewed at http://www.democrats.org.au.

[101] Corporate Code of Conduct Bill 2004 (exposure draft), section 4.

[102] See, for instance, section 8(2)(c) which states that employers must not require their employees to work for more than five consecutive hours without a break of at least twenty minutes. Or section 9(2) which states that '[a]n Australian corporation must not use or obtain the benefit of the labour of any child under the age of fourteen years'.

[103] Bill No. HR 2782.

[104] US nationals would be defined to cover citizens and permanent residents of the USA, or 'a corporation, partnership or other business association formed under the laws of the US', see section 3(c)(5).

[105] Sub-section 3(a).

steps to implement the Corporate Code of Conduct . . . with respect to the employment of those persons'.[106]

In its application to US parent companies (rather than their foreign affiliates) the McKinney Bill was an attempt to introduce a form of 'parent-based' extraterritorial regulation. The 'code of conduct' sought to be imposed by the legislation comprised a set of standards and objectives including obligations to provide a healthy workplace, the entitlement of workers to a living wage, 'responsible environmental protection and environmental practices', compliance with international human rights standards and the establishment of monitoring and implementation procedures.[107] In an attempt to deal with the problem of 'double standards', the environmental standards imposed by the bill included 'compliance with all internationally recognised environmental standards and with all Federal environmental laws for similar operations that would be applicable to the national of the US if the operations of the national were located in the US'.[108]

Like the Australian Code of Conduct Bill, the McKinney Bill provided for civil enforcement by persons affected by failures of multinationals to live up to their statutory obligations.[109] However, there are important differences between the two bills, first, in the choice of regulatory targets,[110] second, in its references to international (rather than national) standards and, third, in the range of non-traditional sanctions provided for in the US version. In addition to the civil remedies provided for, the McKinney Bill also proposed that compliance with the code of conduct be rewarded by preferential treatment under US investment schemes,[111] with withdrawal of that preferential status as a possible sanction against non-compliance.[112] Also, unlike the Australian Code of Conduct Bill, some attempt had been made to deal with CSR-related problems arising from the activities of contractors (suppliers and distributors). Under clause 3(b)(7)(B), corporations would be required to incorporate workplace, environmental and human rights standards in their contractual arrangements.

The 'CORE' Bill

The Corporate Responsibility (or 'CORE') Bill is part of a wider campaign by a number of prominent environmental and human rights NGOs for

---

[106] Ibid.   [107] Sub-section 3(b).   [108] Sub-section 3(b)(5).   [109] Sub-section 8(b).
[110] The US Code of Conduct Bill sets out the standards that US parent companies are required to implement within the relevant enterprise, whereas the Australian bill sought to impose regulatory obligations directly upon foreign companies.
[111] Section 4.   [112] Section 6.

tighter regulation of the CSR performance of UK-based multinationals overseas.[113] So far two separate bills developed by the CORE Coalition have been introduced as private member's bills into the UK parliament: the first by Linda Perham MP in 2003 and the second (the Performance of Companies and Government Departments (Reporting) Bill) by Andy King MP in 2004. The earlier version (the 'Corporate Responsibility Bill') had three main aims: greater transparency by companies in relation to CSR issues (to be achieved by mandatory reporting provisions, a duty to consult affected 'stakeholders' about new projects, and a right of access to information),[114] an extension of directors' duties to take account of the environmental and social impacts of their operations[115] and a statutory obligation to pay compensation to those injured or harmed as a result of group management failures.[116] Like the McKinney Bill, this bill proposes a 'parent-based' method of extraterritorial regulation. In this draft legislation, obligations are only imposed on and enforced against companies incorporated in or operating in the UK[117] and their directors. However, parent companies (of 'corporate groups') would be under a duty to ensure that their subsidiaries comply with the provisions of the Act relating to transparency and consultation, and would also be liable in respect of harm and damage caused by failures to control the activities of subsidiaries adequately.

This bill, in the form presented to parliament, had no realistic prospect of becoming law. By the time it was introduced, UK governmental policy on two of its three key proposals (mandatory CSR reporting and extension of directors' duties) was already fairly well settled.[118] Also, the provisions on parent company liability do not sit well with existing civil liability and conflicts of laws principles.[119] A further shortcoming was its limited definition of 'corporate groups' which, as with the Australian Code of Conduct Bill, would exclude non-equity-based relationships (arguably the relationships most in need of regulation) from coverage by the Act. Not surprisingly, the more problematic of these proposals (relating to parent company liability) were dropped from CORE's next legislative proposal – the Performance of Companies and Government Departments (Reporting) Bill – which focused primarily on

---

[113] A copy of this bill can be viewed at http://www.publications.parliament.uk.
[114] See sections 3, 4 and 5.   [115] Section 7.   [116] Section 6.
[117] See definition of 'company' in section 12.
[118] See DTI, 'Final Report of the Steering Group to the Secretary of State', 26 July 2001. On mandatory reporting of social and environmental issues see pp. 173–4 below. On policy concerning directors' duties see Company Law Reform Bill, clause B3, and its accompanying consultation document, DTI, Company Law Reform, Cm 1–6456 (2005).
[119] See pp. 127–31 above. On civil liability principles, see pp. 216–34 below.

mandatory reporting of social and environmental impacts.[120] This was followed in 2004 with another legislative proposal, the Companies (Impact on Communities Abroad) Bill which would require the UK government to 'complete a 12 month investigation and review into UK companies' negative impacts abroad' and 'recommend legal changes on how this can be addressed, in a report to Parliament'.[121]

European Parliament Resolution on a Voluntary Code of Conduct for European Enterprises Operating in Developing Countries

In 1999, the European Parliament passed a Resolution setting out its proposals for a code of conduct for 'European enterprises operating in developing countries'.[122] In this Resolution, the European Parliament

Reiterates its request to the Commission and the Council to make proposals, as a matter of urgency, to develop the right legal basis for establishing a European multilateral framework governing companies' operations worldwide and to organise for this purpose consultations with the companies' representatives, the social partners and those groups in society which would be covered by the code.[123]

In terms of the substance of the 'voluntary code', the 1999 Resolution expresses its belief that 'European companies should comply with EU environmental, animal welfare and health standards' wherever they operate, while also recommending the inclusion of 'minimum applicable international standards' such as the ILO Tripartite Declaration, 'the ILO core Conventions', the UDHR, the ICESCR and the ICCPR. This 'code of conduct', though 'voluntary' in character, would be subject to external monitoring (by a 'European Monitoring Platform'). In addition, it was proposed that compliance be rewarded through various incentive mechanisms (discussed further below).

These recommendations were never formally implemented, and are only referred to in passing in the Commission's 2002 Communication on CSR.[124] However, the Commission did go on to establish a 'European

---

[120] See p. 175 below. Although, as with the previous CORE Bill, provisions were included to extend the scope of directors' duties to take account of wider social and environmental issues.

[121] See http://www.corporate-responsibility.org.

[122] European Parliament, 'Resolution on EU Standards for European Enterprises Operating in Developing Countries: Towards a European Code of Conduct', 15 January 1999, OJ 1999 No. C104/180, 14 April 1999.

[123] Ibid, para. 11.

[124] European Commission, 'A Business Contribution to Sustainable Development', n. 28 above, p. 5.

Multi-Stakeholder Forum' (or 'EMSF'), not to monitor multinationals as such but to facilitate dialogue between different interest groups (companies, employer organisations, civil society and trade unions) and with a view to formulating some more concrete proposals at a later stage. The EMSF reported its findings in June 2004[125] and a further Commission Communication on CSR was published in March 2006. In the meantime, the European Parliament, on its own initiative, has held a series of hearings on topical issues concerning multinationals and CSR, as discussed further below.

Transparency and access to information

Transparency and access to information has been described as a 'frontier battleground' in CSR campaigning.[126] As noted above, mandatory reporting is central to the campaign run by the UK-based CORE Coalition for tighter regulation of the CSR-related performance of multinationals. In the USA, the International Right to Know Coalition has also developed legislative proposals in support of an 'international right to know' which would oblige US-based companies to report on the social, environmental and human rights performance of overseas subsidiaries.[127]

In this area, CSR campaigners can claim some success. Many of the most significant home states for multinationals (the USA, Australia, Canada, UK and other European states, as well as the European Union itself) now support of the idea of greater transparency in relation to the CSR performance of multinationals, at home and abroad, and some have introduced legislative changes in support of this. In October 2000 the British prime minister, Tony Blair, issued a 'general challenge' to all FTSE 350 companies to produce reports on their environmental performance by the end of 2001. Since then, the UK government has been monitoring voluntary CSR reporting by companies and has supported various award schemes.[128] The European Commission's 2002 Communication on CSR lists the 'need for credibility and transparency of CSR practices' as one of the key principles underlying future EU strategy on

---

[125] European Multi-Stakeholder Forum on CSR, 'Final Results and Recommendations', 29 June 2004.

[126] H. Ward, 'Transparency and Information: a Frontier Battleground' in Accountability (ed.), *Accountability Quarterly, Does Reporting Work: The Effect of Regulation* (September 2003), AQ21.

[127] International Right to Know Coalition, http://www.globalexchange.org/campaigns/irtk.html.

[128] DTI, 'A Government Update', n. 31 above, p. 21.

CSR.[129] At both European and domestic levels, various legislative changes have been made to encourage (and in some cases require) the production of greater and more detailed information about the so-called 'non-financial' performance of corporate groups. This pattern is repeated with other, similar initiatives around the world. In addition, in an attempt to help tackle the problem of corruption, the UK and US governments have given their support to the Extractive Industries Transparency Initiative (or 'EITI'), a project designed to achieve greater transparency in relation to payments made by companies to foreign governments and other public authorities.

CSR reporting

The first EU state to make the publication of social or environmental information a formal legal requirement was Denmark, with its 'Green Accounting Law' introduced in 1995.[130] Under this law, companies whose activities have a 'significant impact' on the environment must publish annual information regarding their environmental impacts and their efforts to mitigate them. Similar laws also apply in the Netherlands. By the end of the 1990s, Norway and Sweden had also enacted laws requiring companies to disclose information relating to environmental impacts as part of their financial reports. In 2001, France followed with a new set of economic regulations, under which all French corporations listed on the French Stock Exchange would be required to include information on their social and environmental performance in the annual reports (commencing with the year 2003).[131] Importantly, these regulations require disclosures relating to the environmental impacts of foreign subsidiaries and, though to a much more limited extent, social impacts.[132] Companies are also required to report on compliance by foreign subsidiaries with 'fundamental' ILO Conventions.[133] Detailed information about the operating standards of contractors is not required, although 'reporting companies are required to disclose the importance of subcontracting to their operations and the methodology by which the

[129] European Commission, 'A Business Contribution to Sustainable Development', n. 28 above.

[130] L. Dhooge, 'Beyond Voluntarism: Social Disclosure and France's Nouvelles Regulations Economiques' (2004) 21 *Ariz JICL* 441, 446.

[131] France, Nouvelles Regulations Economiques, adopted 15 May 2001, Article 116. See further Dhooge, 'Beyond Voluntarism'.

[132] For a critique of the social disclosure requirements in relation to foreign subsidiaries, see Dhooge, 'Beyond Voluntarism', 476.

[133] European Commission, Employment and Social Affairs, 'Corporate Social Responsibility: National Public Policies in the European Union', January 2004, p. 19.

compliance of subcontractors with the fundamental conventions of the ILO is ensured'.[134]

This trend towards greater regulation of social and environmental disclosures by companies is not confined to Europe. The Australian Corporations Act 2001, for instance, now requires companies to include, in their annual directors' report, information relating to the performance of the company under Australian (federal or state) environmental regulations.[135] In South Africa, companies listed on the Johannesburg Stock Exchange ('JSE') are subject to the King Code of Corporate Governance, which recommends 'Triple Bottom Line' reporting. While these reporting requirements are, technically speaking, voluntary, JSE listing rules now include a 'comply or explain' provision, under which companies must state in their annual reports the extent to which they have taken the King Code recommendations into account and, if these recommendations have not been fully complied with, companies must explain why this has not been done.[136] In the USA, publicly traded companies are subject to quite detailed requirements regarding the disclosure of environmental information. They are specifically asked to disclose, for instance, the costs of complying with environmental regulations and whether or not there is material environmental litigation pending. This includes information about the costs of compliance with foreign laws, or the costs of foreign litigation where this is material to the company's financial condition.[137] Companies are also required to disclose information on environmental contingencies in their Management's Discussion and Analysis ('MD&A') document, which appears in the company's annual report.[138]

The UK government has, for some time now, been exploring different ways to encourage greater transparency by companies in relation to social and environmental issues. As part of a wider project to update and modernise company law, regulations were passed in early 2005 making the publication of an annual 'Operating and Financial Review' (or 'OFR') mandatory for all publicly listed companies.[139] Essentially,

---

[134] Dhooge, 'Beyond Voluntarism', 477.   [135] Corporations Act 2001, section 299(1)(f).
[136] See further Burke, 'South Africa's King Code'.
[137] See items 101 and 103 of Regulation S-K, 17 CFR § 229 (2004).
[138] Item 303, Regulation S-K. See further D. Monsma and J. Buckley, 'Non-Financial Corporate Performance: the Material Edges of Social and Environmental Disclosure' (2004) 11 *UBJEL* 51.
[139] The Companies Act 1985 (Operating and Financial Review and Directors' Report etc.) Regulations 2005 (SI 2005 No. 1011). Repealed in part by the Companies Act 1985 (Operating and Financial Review) (Repeal) Regulations 2005 (SI 2005 No. 3442).

these regulations required directors to provide much more background information on the company's performance, past and future, including 'to the extent necessary':

    (a)   information about environmental matters (including the impact of the business of the company on the environment),

    (b)   information about the company's employees, and

    (c)   information about social and community issues.[140]

The legislation had an international dimension in that parent companies subject to the legislation (and whose directors prepare group accounts) would be required to prepare the OFR on a consolidated basis, that is, a 'group operating and financial review', which covered the parent company and all of its subsidiary companies, whether located in the UK or elsewhere. However, as it turned out, this particular regulatory requirement was short-lived. In November 2005, less than eight months after its coming into effect, Chancellor Gordon Brown announced that the OFR would be repealed on the basis that it amounted to unnecessary 'gold-plating' of EU reporting requirements.[141] Legislation repealing the OFR came into effect on 12 January 2006. However, 'enhanced non-financial reporting' remains a legal requirement for company directors under EU law. Under legislation implementing the EU Accounts Modernisation Directive, directors of large and medium-sized companies are required to produce an annual Business Review which must include, as well as financial key performance indicators 'to the extent necessary for an understanding of the development, performance or position of the business of the company ... where appropriate, analysis using other key performance indicators, including information relating to environmental matters and employee matters'.[142] For corporate groups, the Business Review (as was the case under the OFR) must be prepared on a consolidated basis by parent companies, where the parent company produces group accounts.

---

[140] See Regulation 9 (Paragraph 4 of new schedule 7ZA to the Companies Act 1985).

[141] See Council Directive 2003/51/EC of 18 June 2003 amending directives 78/660/EEC, 83/349/EEC, 86/635/EEC and 91/674/EEC on the annual and consolidated accounts of certain types of companies, banks and other financial institutions and insurance undertakings, OJ 2003 No. L178/16, 17 July 2003.

[142] Ibid., implemented in the UK by the Companies Act 1985 (Operating and Financial Review and Directors' Report etc.) Regulations 2005 (SI 2005 No. 1011). See Companies Act 1985 (as amended), section 234ZZB. At the time of writing, the UK government had just announced a fresh consultation as to whether further provisions on non-financial reporting should be included in the Company Law Reform Bill.

Mandatory CSR reporting has been a key feature of the various private member's bills discussed above, with which CSR campaigners have tried to change domestic law. Under the original version of the Australian Corporate Code of Conduct Bill, each foreign subsidiary of an Australian company would have been responsible for its own annual 'compliance report',[143] although the bill was silent as to whether the social or environmental performance of contractors or suppliers would also need to be covered. The McKinney Bill took a different approach, addressing reporting obligations to the US parent company. However, the parent company would report, not only on its own behalf, but also on behalf of each of the foreign contributors to the enterprise (whether subsidiaries, sub-contractors, affiliates or joint venturers). In the UK, the Performance of Companies and Government Departments (Reporting) Bill was effectively an attempt to transform the OFR regime described above into a mandatory CSR reporting regime by UK-based companies by placing information about environmental and social impacts on the same footing as financial information (rather than merely issues which must be reported on 'to the extent necessary' to provide an accurate picture of a company's financial performance and prospects). However, as mentioned above, this bill lacked sufficient political support to proceed to committee stage.

There is an observable trend in domestic government policies towards greater transparency by companies about their international social and environmental performance. However, apart from information that is necessary to assess the *financial* position and prospects of the corporate group, these disclosures are still largely voluntary. So far, only a handful of European states have enacted laws requiring disclosures on environmental and social impacts for their own sake. On the other hand, governments remain under a significant amount of pressure from NGOs on this issue and it is possible that experiences gained from reporting regimes like the UK's OFR could pave the way for more direct and formal regulation of social and environmental disclosures. In the meantime it is recognised, of course, that the lack of benchmark criteria for social and environmental reporting does pose a challenge to its credibility as a regulatory technique. To this end (and to assist companies with their

---

[143] See section 14. (The term 'subsidiary' was not defined.) These reporting obligations would have been enforced by fines leviable against either the corporation itself or certain corporate officers (see sections 14(4) and 14(5)). The revised 'exposure draft' (n. 100 above) appears to require reporting only by the Australian parent company on behalf of its overseas subsidiaries (see Part III) but the drafting is not entirely clear.

voluntary efforts) NGOs and CSR think tanks have been active in the development of workable reporting standards, notably the AA1000 series (developed by the UK-based Institute of Social and Ethical Accountability, or 'Accountability' for short)[144] and the GRI Guidelines.[145]

Other disclosure obligations

Another UK legislative development which appears to be having an impact on CSR reporting by UK companies is the amendment to the Occupational Pension Schemes (Investment) Regulations 1996 which now requires pension fund managers to include, in their Statement of Investment Principles, information regarding 'the extent (if at all) to which social, environmental or ethical considerations are taken into account in the selection, retention and realisation of investments . . . and . . . their policy (if any) in relation to the exercise of the rights (including voting rights) attaching to investments'.[146] While this provision does not impose any obligations on fund managers to comply with 'socially responsible investment' (or 'SRI') policies, it does help provide greater transparency for investors. And this rather innocuous-looking provision appears to be having far-reaching consequences. Credited by many researchers as being a key factor (if not *the* key factor) in the 'explosion' of interest in SRI since it came into effect in 2000,[147] it has indirectly helped to create new market pressures for companies to operate 'socially responsible' policies and to communicate them effectively.[148] Similar 'pensions disclosure' laws have been passed in Belgium,[149] Germany[150] and Sweden,[151] and this approach was also endorsed by the European Commission's 2002 Communication on CSR when it invited all 'occupational pension schemes and retail investment funds to disclose whether and how they take account of social, environmental and ethical factors in their investment decisions'.[152]

---

[144] See http://www.accountability.org.uk.   [145] See http://www.globalreporting.org.

[146] The Occupational Pension Schemes (Investment, and Assignment, Forfeiture, Bankruptcy etc.) Amendment Regulations (SI 1999 No. 1849), Regulation 2(4).

[147] According to research by the UK Socially Responsible Investment Forum, 'the total value of SRI assets in the UK increased from £23 billion in 1997 to £225 billion in 2001 – that is an increase of over £200 billion across four years'; http://www.uksif.org.

[148] S. Miles, K. Hammond and A. Friedman, 'Social and Environmental Reporting and Ethical Investment', ACCA, Research Report No. 77 (2002), http://www.accaglobal.com/research.

[149] Occupational Pension Law (Loi Pensions Complementaires), 15th May 2003.

[150] Effective 1st August 2001.   [151] Public Pensions Act (2000:192).

[152] European Commission, 'A Business Contribution to Sustainable Development', n. 28 above, p. 16.

Freedom of information

Although freedom of information (or 'FOI') laws generally only apply to public authorities,[153] they can be used to obtain information about dealings between governments and companies, and information held by public authorities in relation to corporate activities, whether that information relates to activities taking place within the jurisdiction or elsewhere. For example, a number of applications have been made under UK FOI legislation for information relating to lobbying of government by multinationals and for information on grants to foreign projects.[154] FOI laws do not generally impose any restrictions on the eligibility of applicants,[155] only on the types of information that must be disclosed,[156] with the result that there is generally nothing to prevent applicants from other countries from seeking information under these kinds of laws.

In Europe, additional FOI rights have been created under a 2003 Directive on Public Access to Environmental Information,[157] implemented in the UK by the Environmental Information Regulations 2004.[158] These regulations apply to a wider range of entities than the Freedom of Information Act 2000, and potentially cover some companies, to the extent that they carry out 'functions of public administration' or are 'under the control' of a public authority.[159] Also significant is the fact that applications do not need to relate to activities taking place within the United Kingdom.[160]

FOI legislation is potentially an important means by which home states can confer extraterritorial rights and benefits on foreign

---

[153] See UK Freedom of Information Act 2000, sections 1 and 3; US Freedom of Information Act of 1966, 5 USC § 552 (as amended by Public Law No. 104–231, 110 Stat. 3048) which covers information held by 'agencies'.

[154] B. Allen and J. Zerk, 'Information is Power' (2005) 148 EIB 14.

[155] E.g. the UK Freedom of Information Act 2000 extends rights of access to information held by public authorities to 'any person' (section 1). See also Australian Freedom of Information Act 1982, section 11, which lays down a right of access to government documents (other than 'exempt' documents) for 'every person' regardless of 'any reasons the person gives for seeking access'.

[156] See Part II of the UK Freedom of Information Act 2000 for a list of items that are exempt from disclosure by UK public authorities.

[157] Council Directive 2003/4/EC of 28th January 2003 on public access to environmental information and repealing Council Directive 90/313/EEC, OJ L41/26, 14 February 2003.

[158] SI 2004 No. 3391.

[159] Regulation 2(2)(d). See further DEFRA, 'Guidance to the Environmental Information Regulations, 2004', http://www.defra.gov.uk/corporate/opengov/eir/guidance/index.htm, para. 2.4; R. Barnard and J. Cooper, 'The Information Age', *Utility Week*, 11 March 2005, pp. 16–18.

[160] DEFRA, 'Guidance', para. 3.2.

individuals, communities and campaigning groups, although it is worth pointing out that none of these rights is absolute. Domestic FOI laws invariably contain exemptions, sometimes far-reaching, from obligations to disclose information. The precise nature and scope of these exemptions vary from state to state, but information typically exempt from disclosure includes information pertaining to national security, 'commercially sensitive' information, information given in confidence, information relating to internal discussions and advice, information relating to law enforcement and legal proceedings, and information which, if disclosed, would undermine a person's right to privacy.[161]

Extractive Industries Transparency Initiative (EITI)

The EITI is mentioned here as an example of a novel scheme to improve international transparency in relation to payments by certain companies to foreign governments, although strictly speaking it does not amount to extraterritorial regulation by home states as such – rather an attempt by one home state to encourage and co-ordinate efforts by host states to introduce their own domestic measures.[162] Launched by UK prime minister, Tony Blair, at the WSSD in 2002, the aim of the EITI is, as its name suggests, to improve transparency in relation to payments received by governments from oil, gas and mining companies. The initiative is currently overseen, from the UK, by the DFID. Primarily an anti-corruption measure, the EITI also seeks to 'empower citizens and institutions to hold governments to account for the right use of these resources'.[163] The parties with primary responsibility for implementation are resource-rich host states, although companies also have an important supporting role to assist with 'developing and testing methods of payment and revenue disclosure and publication in the extractive industries in countries heavily dependent on natural resources, wherever the government has decided to do so' and 'working at the country level to implement reporting guidelines consistent with EITI principles'.[164] Under EITI criteria, both companies and governments are required separately to disclose details of various kinds of payments made to government authorities, including royalties, taxes, dividends and signature bonuses (referred to

---

[161] A useful summary of the FOI exemptions allowed in different jurisdictions is provided in the UK Government White Paper, Cabinet Office, 'Your Right to Know: the Government's Proposals for a Freedom of Information Act', Cm-3818, Annex D.

[162] See further p. 179 below.   [163] See http://eitransparency.org.

[164] EITI, London Conference, 17 June 2003, 'Statement of Principles and Agreed Actions', Part IV, available from http://www.dfid.gov.uk.

in EITI literature as 'benefit streams'), and these payments must be 'reconciled by a credible, independent administrator, applying international auditing standards'.[165] The exact mode of implementation of the EITI is left to host state parties to determine, which means that, although participation by companies in the overarching initiative is voluntary, their reporting obligations may still be regulated at domestic (i.e. host state) level.[166]

Obligations to share information about risks and hazards

This is a reasonably well-established method of CSR regulation, under which operators and manufacturers of potentially harmful technologies are required to share information about any risks with potentially affected communities and consumers. The EU Directive on Major Accident Hazards,[167] for example, requires operators of installations to notify local authorities of processes using certain chemicals and possible accident risks.[168] EU labour law also contains detailed requirements on consultation and information sharing with workers in relation to health and safety issues.[169]

On occasion, home states enact laws requiring the sharing of information on potential risks with people and regulatory authorities *outside* territorial boundaries.[170] For example, OPIC[171] is required, before providing financial assistance or insurance in respect of any 'environmentally sensitive' overseas investment, to notify the relevant government officials in that country, first, of any World Bank or other international guidelines relating to public health or safety or the environment relevant to the project and, second, of restrictions under US law which would

---

[165] EITI Criteria, paragraph 3, reproduced in EITI, 'Extractive Industries Sourcebook', http://www.eitransparency.org., p. 9.

[166] As the EITI Sourcebook, ibid., explains: 'Governments will need to consider how best to ensure that all companies report in a timely manner and using the agreed reporting templates. Whilst in some countries this may be achieved through voluntary agreements with the companies, in other countries this may require a legal framework to be established.'

[167] Council Directive 96/82/EEC of 9 December 1996 on the control of major accident hazards involving dangerous substances, OJ 1997 No. L10/13, 14 January 1997.

[168] Article 6.

[169] Council Directive 89/391/EEC of 12 June 1989 on the introduction of measures to encourage improvements in the safety and health of workers, OJ 1989 L183/1, 29 June 1989.

[170] There are now several treaty regimes requiring home state measures such as these. See further pp. 290–6 below.

[171] See pp. 190–1 below.

apply if a similar project were to go ahead in the USA.[172] In addition, before taking the final decision to finance or insure the project, OPIC is required to 'take into account any comments it receives' on the project involved,[173] which would include comments from overseas interests.

Obligations to warn third countries and their citizens of risks, restrictions on the export of hazardous substances and technologies, import bans and public awareness campaigns on multinational activities and social standards are all ways in which home states, directly or indirectly, can influence levels of protection enjoyed by workers, communities and consumers abroad. These can also be used to help host states with their own regulatory efforts. The impact of these extraterritorial 'benefits' will, however, depend on the extent to which information is capable of reaching those affected, which will be influenced by factors such as remoteness, education and literacy, as well as the domestic political and regulatory situation.

Social and 'eco' labels

Social and eco-labelling schemes are designed to harness consumer pressures for 'ethical' products by allowing certified companies to affix to their products a logo indicating compliance with certain social or environmental standards. Plenty of examples of voluntary schemes, operated by NGOs, already exist.[174] These kinds of schemes are largely unregulated, and their administration is left up to the sponsoring NGO. However, there are examples of government-led schemes. The Belgian government, for instance, passed a law in 2002 that entitles Belgian-based companies to apply for a social label for products produced in compliance with standards set out in 'core' ILO Conventions. The European Union, too, operates an 'eco-label' scheme[175] for products and services 'of the highest environmental quality',[176] albeit for a limited range

---

[172] See Foreign Assistance Act of 1961, 22 USC § 2197.   [173] Ibid.

[174] An established 'social label' is the 'FairTrade' label operated by the Fair Trade Foundation, which certifies that goods were purchased from producers in less developed countries for a 'fair' price. The 'Rugmark' label, operated by a German-based NGO, is designed to help consumers select rugs made without the use of child labour. An example of eco-labelling is the scheme run by the Forest Stewardship Council. Under this scheme, wood originating from producers that have demonstrated a commitment to environmentally sound forest management is marked with an 'FSC' logo at retail outlets.

[175] Established under Council Regulation 1980/2000 of 17 July 2000 on a revised Community eco-label award scheme, OJ 2000 No. L 237/1, 21 September 2000.

[176] European Commission, 'A Business Contribution to Sustainable Development', n. 28 above, p. 15.

of products.[177] However, with regard to the possibility of further EU schemes, the European Commission has expressed some reservations, mainly about their effectiveness, and reliability as a source of information for consumers.[178] The Commission seems to share the opinion of many national governments that participation in social and eco-label schemes should remain 'voluntary'. However, there is a hint of future regulation in the Commission's commitment, in its 2002 White Paper, to 'examin[e] existing private labelling schemes, such as organic labelling, fair trade and CSR measures to assess their effectiveness *and the need for further measures in achieving the objectives of transparency and information for consumers with a view to promote* [sic] *development*' (emphasis added).[179]

Protection for whistleblowers

The fact that CSR reporting remains 'voluntary' in most home states – and the lack of a universally agreed set of reporting standards – means that cases of serious corporate misconduct or negligence are unlikely to be reported with any objectivity (if indeed they are reported at all). However, 'whistleblower' legislation may help bring these cases out into the public domain. 'Whistleblower' legislation encourages employees to report instances of malpractice or abuse by their employers by protecting them from victimisation at work or dismissal as a result of their disclosures. The UK's Public Interest Disclosure Act 1998 (amending the Employment Rights Act 1996) makes it clear that employees are entitled to raise genuine concerns about issues such as possible criminal offences, failures to comply with legal obligations, or possible dangers to health and safety or the environment. Concerns may be raised with employers, appropriate regulatory authorities or even the media, provided that this action is reasonable in the circumstances and not done for personal gain.[180] Under section 47B of the Employment Rights Act 1996, employees have the right not to suffer any 'detriment' at work as a result of having made a 'protected disclosure' under the Act, and any dismissal as a result of whistleblowing activities is treated as an 'unfair' dismissal for which damages can be claimed.[181] Although this legislation

---

[177] Eco-label Regulation, n. 175 above, Article 2, paras. 4 and 5.

[178] European Commission , 'Promoting a European Framework', n. 51 above, pp. 20–1.

[179] European Commission, 'A Business Contribution to Sustainable Development', n. 28 above, p. 16.

[180] Employment Rights Act 1996 (as amended), sections 43G and 43H.

[181] Employment Rights Act 1996, section 103A.

does not provide protection to employees working outside the territory of the UK,[182] it does have an extraterritorial dimension in that 'protected disclosures' under this legislation need not relate to failures taking place only within the UK. On the contrary, the Act applies regardless of the geographical location of the relevant breaches, meaning that employees are entitled to raise concerns about health and safety and environmental problems arising from their employer's activities anywhere in the world.[183] In this legislation, what is deemed to be in the 'public interest' is not confined merely to territorial concerns, but also takes account of the interests of workers and communities beyond UK territorial boundaries.

Enforcement of standards by private individuals and interest groups

Whether or not a person has the capacity (or 'standing') to commence legal action in relation to the activities of multinationals depends on the domestic law of the state in which the action is to be brought. In some countries, and particularly the USA, civil enforcement is an important regulatory tool. However, where extraterritorial rights are not expressly provided for in the relevant legislation, foreign litigants often have to contend with a 'presumption against extraterritoriality'. In other words, it must be established that, despite the absence of provisions expressly extending enforcement rights to non-residents, this was nevertheless the intention of the legislature.[184]

Do home state laws in CSR-related areas confer any enforcement rights on non-resident private individuals or groups? Generally, home states tend not to grant rights to enforce domestic health, safety or environmental statutes to non-residents, although this varies from state to state and according to the subject matter. Employment laws, to the extent that they may be privately enforced, tend only to be enforceable by those living and working within the territory of the regulating state.[185] Similarly, domestic environmental laws are presumed (unless it is expressly stated

---

[182] See Public Interest Disclosure Act 1998, amending section 196 of the Employment Rights Act 1996.

[183] Employment Rights Act 1996, section 43B(2).

[184] *Equal Employment Opportunity Commission* v. *Arabian American Oil Co.* 499 US 244, 111 S Ct 1227, 113 L Ed 2d 274 (1991).

[185] US anti-discrimination law does contain some exceptions, however. For instance, the US Age Discrimination in Employment Act of 1976, 29 USC § 621 was amended in 1984 to extend the protection of US law on age discrimination to overseas workers employed by subsidiaries of US companies, although these rights are limited to US citizens.

otherwise) to be restricted in scope to the territory of the regulating state and surrounding territorial sea.[186] Statutory rights under domestic consumer protection laws may extend to non-residents (e.g. individuals injured by a dangerous product purchased while abroad)[187] but, generally speaking, the 'regulatory potential' of the statutory civil action, as a means of regulating multinationals abroad, is largely unexplored. There remains, however, the possibility of civil claims under domestic tort law. In addition, the US Alien Tort Claims Act[188] is thought to provide a statutory right of action to foreign litigants in respect of human rights abuses by US-based multinationals committed outside US territory. These two different types of private law claim are considered further in the next chapter.

Where a multinational has been given some form of support by its home state, it may be possible to seek remedies under home state administrative law. Under UK law, for example, a person outside the jurisdiction may be able to institute proceedings for 'judicial review' in the UK courts, provided the relevant administrative action gave rise to consequences in which he or she had a particular interest.[189] While not an everyday set of circumstances, the *Pergau Dam*

---

[186] T. Digan, 'NEPA and the Presumption against Extraterritorial Application: the Foreign Policy Exclusion' (1994) 11 *JCHL&P* 165. See *Amlon Metals* v. *FMC Corporation*, 775 F Supp 668 (SDNY 1991). But see also *Environmental Defense Fund, Inc.* v. *Massey*, 986 F 2d 538 (DC Cir. 1993) in which it was held that the US National Environmental Policy Act (NEPA) could be applied to the activities of the National Science Foundation in Antarctica. In a novel piece of litigation, a group of US environmental NGOs have recently been given permission by a Californian court to sue two US government agencies (OPIC and the US Ex-Im Bank) on the basis that they failed properly to evaluate the effects of applicant projects on global warming (and hence the environment of the USA) contrary to NEPA. The plaintiffs argue that the legislation should apply to the assessment of foreign as well as local projects. A. Buncombe, 'Washington to be Sued over Global Warming', *Independent*, 26 August 2005, p. 38.

[187] E.g. under the UK Consumer Protection Act 1987.   [188] 28 USC § 1350.

[189] See Supreme Court Act 1981, section 31(3) and Rules of the Supreme Court of England and Wales (SI 1965 No. 1776) (as amended), Order 53, rule 3 requiring that the applicant demonstrate a 'sufficient interest' in the matter to obtain leave of the court to commence an action for judicial review. Note also Article 230 of the Treaty Establishing the European Community, which provides that proceedings may be instituted in respect of a decision by the European Commission by 'any natural or legal person', provided that that issue is of 'direct and individual concern' to him or her. (See Treaty Establishing the European Community (as amended), consolidated version published at OJ 2002 No. C325/33, 24 December 2002.) However this requirement of 'direct and individual concern' was given a narrow reading in Case T-585/93, *Stichting Greenpeace Council* v. *Commission* [1999] ECR 2205 in which it was held

case[190] gives an example of the kind of administrative action that might give rise to challenge by overseas litigants based on environmental concerns. Of course, judicial review is not a method of obtaining remedies against multinationals as such. However, proceedings of this kind can provide a forum within the home state in which residents of the relevant host state can raise their concerns about the adverse effects of potentially dangerous or environmentally damaging activities.[191]

Recently, home states have been creating new, less formal, routes by which concerns about the CSR standards of multinationals can be raised with their domestic authorities. Under the national implementation arrangements for the OECD Guidelines, concerned individuals and bodies may raise issues relating to compliance with the Guidelines with an appropriate national contact point (or 'NCP'). The role of the NCP is then to 'contribute to the resolution of issues that arise relating to the implementation of the Guidelines in specific instances'.[192] This includes 'mak[ing] an initial assessment of whether the issues raised merit further examination' and, where they do, 'offer[ing] good offices to help the parties involved to resolve these issues'. Following completion of these procedures, if the parties have not reached agreement about the issues raised, the NCP is required to issue a statement containing any 'appropriate' recommendations on the implementation of the Guidelines. These recommendations are not, however, legally enforceable and are made in light of the fact that the Guidelines themselves are non-binding. While the mediation procedures are intended to be confidential, the recommendations themselves are only made public if the NCP does not take

that an NGO and concerned local residents would not have standing under this provision to challenge a funding decision by the European Commission in relation to two power stations planned for the Canary Islands. See also Case T-219/95, *Danielsson* v. *Commission* [1995] ECR II-3051.

[190] *R* v. *Secretary of State for Foreign Affairs ex parte World Development Movement Limited* [1995] 1 All ER 611.

[191] See *Danielsson* v. *Commission*, n. 189 above, in which a group of residents of Tahiti challenged a determination by the Commission that treaty commitments on public health and safety had been met by France in relation to nuclear testing in French Polynesia. Judicial review was also threatened in relation to the Ilisu Dam project, see p. 190 below. P. Brown, 'Byers Faces Court Action to Block Aid for Turkish Dam', *Guardian*, 24 December 1999, p. 3.

[192] See OECD, 'Decision of the OECD Council on the OECD Guidelines for Multinational Enterprises', C(2000)96/FINAL, adopted by the Council at its 982nd session on 26–27 June 2000, 'Procedural Guidance on Implementation Procedures of the OECD Guidelines for Multinational Enterprises', June 2000, part C.

the view that 'preserving confidentiality would be in the best interests of effective implementation of the Guidelines'.[193]

Finally, it may be possible for opponents of multinational activities abroad to make a complaint under domestic trade practices legislation. This kind of action does not, of course, address the extraterritorial standards of multinationals directly, merely statements and representations made about them. Therefore, it is only an indirect way of holding multinationals accountable for poor CSR standards abroad. Nevertheless, legal action of this kind has the potential to cause a great deal of embarrassment for companies, as the *Kasky* v. *Nike* litigation in the USA illustrates. *Kasky* v. *Nike*[194] concerned a complaint by anti-sweatshop activist Mike Kasky, alleging that Nike had misled the public in relation to the workplace standards of its foreign clothing suppliers, amounting to 'unfair competition' contrary to the Californian Business and Professions Code.[195] While this particular action (a 'private attorney general action . . . on behalf of the General Public Of California') is only available to Californian residents, private enforcement rights under the trade practices laws of other countries are not so restrictive. Under the Australian Trade Practices Act 1974, for example, 'any person' can apply to court to have legislative prohibitions on 'misleading or deceptive conduct' enforced,[196] whether or not that person is an Australian resident, and without it being necessary for the applicant to show she was personally harmed by the company's conduct.[197]

In summary, the rights of foreign individuals and communities to enforce home state public law relating to the international CSR performance of multinationals are patchy at best. These options (the availability of which depends on the geographical scope of the relevant domestic legislation as well as home state rules on standing) are generally limited to seeking remedies under administrative law (assuming there has been some governmental involvement) or complaints under trade practices legislation. Another (albeit informal) complaint mechanism is provided

---

[193] Ibid, para. 4. For further discussion on the work of different NCPs so far, see pp. 251–4 below.

[194] 539 US 654 (2003).   [195] §§ 17200–17210.

[196] Australian Trade Practices Act 1974, sections 52 (prohibition on misleading or deceptive conduct) and 80 (enforcement). Note, however, that there must still be an Australian connection: the complaint must relate either to activities by Australian corporations or to activities taking place within Australia.

[197] Ibid, section 80.

under the national implementation arrangements for the OECD Guidelines, although the confidential nature of negotiations (not to mention the 'non-binding' nature of NCP recommendations) means that many campaigners are understandably sceptical about its regulatory value. However, it is possible that more use will be made of civil enforcement in future. There is clearly a good deal of interest among CSR campaigners in this particular regulatory technique. As noted above, statutory causes of action for individuals have been a feature of several recent private member's bills aimed at addressing the problem of 'double standards' by multinationals. Under the Australian Code of Conduct Bill, 'any person . . . whether resident in Australia or elsewhere' who suffered loss or damage as a result of a contravention of its provisions could commence a legal action for recovery in the Federal Court of Australia. Civil enforcement was also proposed as part of the extraterritorial regime contemplated by the McKinney Bill. This bill sought to establish a right of action in the US District Court for any person 'aggrieved by a violation of the act'.[198] In addition, it would be open to 'any person' to file a petition requesting an investigation by the authorities into possible breaches of the legislation, together with the use of applicable sanctions.[199] Finally, the Corporate Responsibility ('CORE') Bill, introduced into the UK parliament in 2003, included a statutory obligation for UK parent companies to 'pay compensation' for 'physical or mental injury' or environmental damage caused as a result of sub-standard management practices.[200] This provision expressly applies to injury or damage occurring outside as well as inside the UK[201] (although does not specifically state whom it is to be paid to, or the procedures by which it is to be claimed).

Clearly, there are advantages in the CORE bill approach. By focusing on the role of the parent company as overall manager of the corporate group, the legislation is less prone to accusations of unlawful interference in the domestic affairs of other states.[202] Rather than regulating the health and safety and environmental standards of foreign subsidiaries directly, the idea is to empower those affected by the overseas activities of multinationals to take enforcement steps themselves. However, the value of these extraterritorial enforcement rights in practice, as with all the options for private enforcement discussed in this section, will

---

[198] McKinney Bill, n. 103 above, section 8.   [199] See sections 5 and 6.
[200] Corporate Responsibility Bill 2003, section 6(1).   [201] Ibid, section 6(2).
[202] See pp. 136–9 above.

depend on the extent to which they are publicised outside the regulating state and the resources of those to whom they are addressed. Here, alliances between affected groups and home state NGOs can be expected to play a crucial role.

Other hearings and public inquiries

The confidential nature of dispute resolution procedures under the OECD Guidelines,[203] and the possibility that the results of these procedures may never be made public, is one of the most criticised aspects of the OECD Guidelines' implementation regime. FoE has expressed concerns about the risk that complaints under the Guidelines could be 'ignored or [become] bogged down in secretive procedures leading to meaningless ambiguous statements', adding that 'too much is left to the discretion of individual NCPs in these respects, especially in the context of reporting on specific instances'.[204] The European Parliament was aiming for an altogether more challenging procedure when it floated the idea of public hearings on the social, ethical and environmental practices of European-based multinationals in poorer countries. Under its 1999 Resolution on EU Standards, the European Parliament proposed the establishment of a new 'monitoring mechanism' for multinationals to 'promote dialogue on standards met by European enterprises and the identification of best practice, *as well as being open to receiving complaints about corporate conduct from community and/or workers' representatives and the private sector in the host country, NGOs or consumer organisations, from individual victims and from any other source*'.[205]

Pending the establishment of this new mechanism, the European Parliament proposed that 'special rapporteurs are appointed for a period of one year and annual hearings are held in the European Parliament, inviting the social partners and NGOs from the South and the North . . .'[206] and, further, recommended that 'public hearings be organised regularly in the European Parliament in order to discuss specific cases, or good and bad conduct, and that all persons concerned (including enterprises) be invited to attend them'.[207]

---

[203] See further pp. 251–4 below.

[204] See FoE, 'The OECD's Revised "Guidelines for Multinational Enterprises" a Step towards Corporate Accountability?', http://www.foe.co.uk/campaigns.

[205] European Parliament Resolution on EU Standards, n. 122 above, para. 18 (emphasis added).

[206] Ibid, para. 19.   [207] Ibid, para. 20.

On the basis of its own resolution (but without any formal legal mandate) the European Parliament has so far convened several hearings on issues of topical interest. The first of these, which took place in November 2000, related to the behaviour of multinationals in the 'infant nutrition' (i.e. 'babymilk') and clothing sectors. Lacking any legal powers to compel witnesses, participants were simply 'invited' to attend. Nestlé and Adidas were selected to represent the business community, along with representatives of various interested NGOs. Neither multinational did attend the event, however, a decision which, along with the material presented at the hearing, resulted in a certain amount of adverse publicity for both of them.[208]

A second European Parliament hearing took place on 11 November 2001 and concerned the activities of oil companies in Burma.[209] On this occasion, and unlike the first hearing, representatives of the invited companies did attend. Questions were asked by MEPs of representatives of TotalFinaElf and Premier Oil, as well as the ILO and Earthrights International, an NGO. Other issues tackled in further hearings organised by the European Parliament included 'conflict diamonds' and the activities of construction companies in Lesotho.

Benefits and incentives

Export credit policies

Home state incentives to improve foreign health, safety and environmental standards come in many different guises. Most CSR campaigners consider that, as a minimum, home states should not provide investment assistance to multinationals that flout international standards relating to workplace, environmental and consumer health.[210] In 2001, the Dutch parliament approved a proposal to introduce procedures whereby investment assistance provided by the government of the Netherlands could be withdrawn from companies found not to be complying with the OECD Guidelines. Under these procedures, companies applying for investment support from the Dutch government (e.g. through export-credit guarantees) would be required to sign a 'declaration of intent' to adhere

---

[208] S. Castle, 'Adidas Boycotts EU Ethics Hearing', *Independent*, 23 November 2000, p. 19; A. Osbourn, 'Adidas Attacked for Asian Sweatshops', *Guardian*, 23 November 2000, p. 16. The hearing also received television news coverage in the UK.

[209] A. Osbourn, 'British Oil Firms Accused of Burma Abuses', *Guardian*, 12 October 2001, p. 18.

[210] A survey of web-sites and the literature produced by NGOs active in the CSR field suggests that this is a standard position.

to the OECD Guidelines in relation to the project for which support is sought. While the declaration itself is not legally binding, it was envisaged that terms conditioning support on compliance with the OECD Guidelines could potentially be placed in the investment support agreement. However, the government decided not to monitor compliance with the OECD Guidelines on an ongoing basis. Originally, it was proposed that an adverse finding by the Dutch NCP following a complaint against a company under the OECD Guidelines implementation procedures would result in a withdrawal of government assistance from that company. However, a more recent policy document states that 'sanctions are not foreseen'.[211]

While other countries have not linked the OECD Guidelines and investment assistance so directly,[212] 'social and environmental' screening is increasingly becoming a part of application procedures for export assistance. Since 2000, the UK Export Credits Guarantee Department ('ECGD') has required applicants for support from the ECGD[213] to undergo a 'social impact screening' procedure. This process includes completion by the applicant of a questionnaire on issues such as the workplace health and safety and environmental standards to be applied to the project, details of any formal environmental and social impact assessments, and a self-assessment by the applicant of environmental, social and human rights impacts associated with the relevant overseas project.

[211] European Commission, 'National Public Policies', n. 133 above, p. 29. It is worth noting that the Dutch proposals were quite controversial at the time, with many representatives of the international business community complaining that they undermined the 'non-binding' nature of the OECD Guidelines. See the statement of the OECD Business and Industry Advisory Committee, reproduced in OECD, 'The OECD Guidelines for Multinational Enterprises: Annual Report' (OECD, 2001), p. 34. Now, applicants for export assistance are merely required to state that they are aware of the OECD Guidelines 'and that they will comply with them to the best of their ability'. See 'Summary Report of the Chair of the Meeting on the Activities of NCPs, 2002, Table 1' in OECD, 'OECD Guidelines for Multinational Enterprises: Annual Report 2002: Focus on Responsible Supply Chain Management' (OECD, 2002).

[212] The French government operates a system under which French companies asking for export credits or investment assistance are 'systematically informed' about the principles of the OECD Guidelines. However, the only response required is a signature acknowledging that the company has been so informed. The German government uses the export credit process to raise awareness about the OECD Guidelines, which includes providing applicants with a brochure. However, it does not require companies to sign up to the Guidelines explicitly. See further European Commission, 'National Public Policies', n. 133 above, p. 21 (France) and p. 15 (Germany).

[213] Like most export-credit agencies, this support can include arranging political risk insurance, provision of guarantees against non-payment for goods and services, and financing packages to assist with purchases of UK goods.

Although social impact screening has been welcomed by NGOs, many are sceptical as to whether it has had any real impact on the project assessment process. In 2003, the chairman of the UK parliament's Environmental Audit Committee remarked that '[d]espite a commitment to take sustainable development into account in considering applications for support, there has been little noticeable change in the balance of ECGD's portfolio, which remains dominated by projects in unsustainable sectors'.[214] The need for scepticism is borne out by the UK government's indication that it was 'minded' to provide support for Balfour Beatty's involvement in the Ilisu Dam project, notwithstanding a sustained international campaign against the project because of environmental and human rights concerns.[215] Criticisms of the ECGD's screening process include the lack of formal criteria against which the social, environmental and human rights impacts of projects will be judged,[216] and the failure of the ECGD Business Principles[217] to provide any indication as to the consequences for a project should the social, environmental or human rights impacts ultimately turn out to be significantly worse than initially claimed. NGOs have also complained about the 'very weak' procedures for monitoring and enforcement.[218] Clearly, if it is to have any impact on the social and environmental performance of companies abroad, the ECGD has some way to go.

The US government operates several different investment assistance programmes. The US export-credit guarantee scheme is administered by the Export-Import Bank (the 'Ex-Im Bank'). In addition, political risk insurance and other financial assistance packages are available to US (and US-owned) companies through OPIC.[219] The Ex-Im Bank was

[214] Environmental Audit Committee press release, 'ECGD and Sustainable Development Report Publication', 17 July 2003, launching its report, 'Export Credits Guarantee Department and Sustainable Development', 17 July 2003.

[215] Balfour Beatty withdrew from the project in November 2001.

[216] Although the ECGD has recently been consulting on suitable performance indicators by which to measure its own contribution to sustainable development. See http://www.ecgd.gov.uk.

[217] See http://www.ecgd.gov.uk.

[218] 'Without adequate monitoring, there is a tendency for environmental impact assessments to be used merely as a rubber stamp to allow the project to go ahead, rather than to create a work-plan to maximise positive environmental impacts and to mitigate damage'; WWF-UK, 'Memorandum to the Environmental Audit Committee: the Export Credit Guarantees Department and Sustainable Development', 12 May 2003.

[219] For companies to be eligible for OPIC support they must be *either* incorporated in the USA and beneficially owned by US citizens *or* foreign corporations at least 95 per cent

created in 1934 to facilitate US imports by means including guarantees of working capital loans, loans to foreign purchasers and credit insurance. It is a government-held corporation, managed by a board of directors, the members of which are selected by the US president. Through the bank's 'Environmental Exports Programme', the US government offers an enhanced level of support to goods and services designated as 'environmentally beneficial', and to exporters participating in 'environmentally beneficial projects'.[220] In addition, the bank is required under its charter to establish environmental review procedures for projects for which assistance is requested, and is authorised to decline finance 'if the Board of Directors determines that this is appropriate in light of serious environmental impacts'. As part of these procedures, the bank requires all applicants for limited recourse project finance or long-term guarantees to participate in 'environmental screening' at application stage. A list of applications pending final approval (along with brief details) is posted on the Ex-Im Bank's web-site, and interested parties are invited to give their comments about the environmental impacts of prospective projects.

Applications for support from OPIC are also subject to social and environmental vetting. Since 1985, OPIC has been required by statute to carry out environmental impact assessment of all projects that are the subject of an application for political risk insurance or other financial assistance and to refuse applications that, in OPIC's determination, pose 'a major or unreasonable environmental, health or safety hazard'.[221] Also, as noted above, OPIC is generally prohibited from supporting projects that contribute to violations of 'internationally recognized worker rights'. 'Internationally recognized worker rights' are defined under the US Trade Act of 1974 to include 'fundamental' rights such as rights of association and collective bargaining, a prohibition on forced or compulsory labour, a minimum age for employment and acceptable working conditions, including reasonable working hours and occupational health and safety.[222] Compared with the UK, US regulatory provisions are more prescriptive as to when export assistance may and may not be granted on social or environmental grounds. Nevertheless, NGOs monitoring the activities of OPIC complain that projects continue to be approved for US government support that fail to meet OPIC's own social and

beneficially owned by US investors *or* other foreign entities that are 100 per cent US owned. See 22 USC § 2191 (2000).

[220] See http://www.exim.gov.   [221] 22 USC § 2191(n).   [222] 19 USC § 2462(a)(4).

environmental criteria.[223] Also, once export assistance is granted, it is almost never withdrawn.[224] With this knowledge, and given the general lack of ongoing monitoring by export assistance agencies, what are the incentives for recipients of export assistance packages to comply with their previous social and environmental commitments? The McKinney Bill and 1999 European Parliament Resolution, discussed above, contain a number of suggestions as to how links between access to export assistance and CSR could be strengthened.[225] Home state governments, however, have yet to be convinced.[226]

One CSR-related area of government policy in which campaigners are making progress, however, is public procurement – the idea being that governments can provide additional incentives for companies to be 'socially responsible' by including CSR-related standards in the selection process for government contracts. The European Commission has suggested that this is an issue best left to individual member states, while recognising that some 'awareness raising' activities may be useful.[227] This issue was subsequently debated before the EMSF, which reported strong support (particularly among NGOs and trade union representatives) for the idea of linking public procurement contracts to CSR performance.[228] (Revealingly, though, opponents of the idea were concerned that including social and environmental criteria in public procurement

---

[223] FoE cites OPIC's 1999 decision to support a loan to Enron and Shell in relation to a proposed pipeline from Bolivia to Brazil which it says 'directly violates' OPIC's own environmental guidelines. See
http://www.foe.org/camps/intl/institutions/boliviabrazil.html.

[224] The UK ECGD has never withdrawn investment support on human rights or environmental grounds. However, environmental considerations were thought to have played a significant part in the decision by OPIC in 1995 to withdraw political risk insurance for a copper mining project in Indonesia operated by a subsidiary of Freeport McMoRan. See K. Gooding, 'OPIC Withdraws Mine Cover: Irian Jaya Waste is Degrading Rainforest says US Insurance Corporation', *Financial Times*, 8 November 1995, p. 6.

[225] The McKinney Bill, n. 103 above, uses export assistance as one of the main methods of 'enforcing' compliance with a 'code of conduct' for US companies operating overseas. See also the European Parliament, Resolution on EU Standards, n. 122 above, para. 28.

[226] The European Commission did not address the issue at all in its 2002 White Paper, European Commission, 'A Business Contribution to Sustainable Development', n. 28 above.

[227] European Commission, 'A Business Contribution to Sustainable Development', n. 28 above, p. 22.

[228] EMSF, 'Final Report and Recommendations', 29 June 2004, esp. annexed 'Final Report of the Roundtable on Improving Knowledge about CSR and Facilitating the Exchange of Experience and Good Practice', p. 10.

procedures might undermine the 'voluntary' nature of CSR.[229]) In any case, a number of EU member states have pressed ahead with changes to their own procurement policies. The UK government announced that from 1 November 2003 all new contracts entered into by central government departments must apply 'minimum environmental standards' as well as value for money. Other states that have introduced social and environmental criteria into their public procurement decisions include Belgium, Denmark and France.[230]

Tax incentives

One of the more obvious ways a state can deliver financial benefits to a company is, of course, through its taxation system. In the past few years, European states have introduced a raft of new tax incentives designed to encourage companies to invest more in local communities, environmental protection and other social projects.[231] Potentially, tax incentives could also be designed to deliver benefits further afield. Home states are in a position to encourage greater corporate philanthropy or social or environmental investments in other states through the taxation treatment given to dividends remitted from foreign subsidiaries back to the parent. In theory, the home state of a multinational could, for example, establish a preferential rate of taxation in relation to dividends remitted from foreign subsidiaries that could demonstrate compliance with 'socially and environmentally responsible' corporate policies.[232] Alternatively, a home state could put CSR conditions on the availability, to the parent company, of home state tax credits in relation to taxation paid on foreign earnings or on the treatment of certain payments and receipts for the purposes of calculating foreign earnings.[233] The home state may also move to address possible tax *dis*advantages to the parent company of pursuing 'socially responsible' policies.

However, this method of 'extraterritorial regulation' has its limitations. The lack of taxation jurisdiction by the home state over the foreign

---

[229] Ibid.   [230] European Commission, 'National Public Policies', n. 133 above.

[231] See, for example, the UK 'Community Investment Tax Relief', introduced pursuant to the Finance Act 2002.

[232] Although note that the practice by home states of granting tax credits or tax exemptions in relation to home state taxation of foreign subsidiary income means that a preferential taxation of dividend income by the home state would only be of benefit to the parent company if the preferential rates of home state taxation were *equal to or higher than* rates of taxation imposed in the host state.

[233] See OECD, 'Recommendation on the Tax Deductibility of Bribes to Foreign Public Officials', adopted by the Council, 11 April 1996, C(96)27(FINAL); (1996) 35 ILM 760.

subsidiary itself means that the home state's ability to influence foreign social standards in this way will depend upon the extent to which the profits of the subsidiary actually become part of the parent company's income stream.[234] While well established as a domestic regulatory technique, the use of tax incentives as a means of improving the CSR performance of multinationals on a global scale is an underexplored area. However, this may well form an important part of future home state regulation,[235] not least because of its essential compatibility with the idea that CSR should be 'voluntary', and that the role of home states should be primarily to facilitate and encourage – rather than enforce – best practice.

Awards

Numerous government-sponsored awards already exist to recognise corporate contributions to sustainability and human rights issues. For instance, national awards are given by the Dutch government (for CSR initiatives by companies in agricultural and food industries), by the Danish government (for efforts to integrate ethnic minorities into the workforce), by the Spanish government (for companies that maintain policies to promote work–life balance).[236] The UK government is a major supporter of BITC, a UK-based organisation which each year presents a series of highly sought-after awards for contributions to workplace, community and environmental issues including a special award for 'companies that can demonstrate the impact of an *international* corporate social responsibility programme or partnership'.[237]

Home state CSR initiatives under international law

Home state governments are not unconcerned about the way in which their multinationals conduct their operations overseas. On the contrary, there has lately been a flourishing of regulatory initiatives of the 'softer' kind – and some substantive legislative changes too – all with the aim of causing multinationals to focus upon, and hopefully improve, their CSR standards in other countries.

---

[234] See further F. Beveridge, *The Treatment and Taxation of Foreign Investment under International Law* (Manchester: Juris Publishing/Manchester University Press, 2000).

[235] DTI, 'International Strategic Framework', n. 49 above.

[236] See further European Union, 'National Public Policies', n. 133 above.

[237] See http://www.bitc.org.uk/awards/entering/categories/index.html.

It was suggested in the previous chapter that, in assessing the legitimacy of extraterritorial initiatives in the CSR field (as opposed to the more 'state-centred' areas of competition regulation or national security), a different set of considerations may come into play to reflect, first, the different types of regulatory methods used and, second, the 'universality' of human rights principles.[238] As it turns out, none of the home state initiatives discussed above poses a direct challenge to traditional jurisdictional principles. Even the most ambitious campaigners (with the exception of the Australian Democrats[239]) have avoided the use of 'foreign-prescriptive' legislation in favour of 'parent-based' methods of control. Home states are clearly entitled, under traditional principles of 'nationality' and 'territory', to impose 'group' reporting requirements on a parent company, and to develop their own (territorial) social and eco-labelling schemes. As discussed above, a number of home states have done just that. The home state is also entitled (subject to its human rights obligations[240]) to regulate access to its own courts as it sees fit (e.g. to enable litigants to raise concerns about projects abroad or to enforce other statutory rights), to attach such conditions to its overseas investment assistance schemes as it chooses, to devise its own group taxation schemes, and (subject to its obligations under international trade law) to regulate imports and exports into and out of its territory.

But, as discussed in the previous chapter, there is more to the question of the *legitimacy* of home state initiatives such as these than the threshold issues of 'territoriality' (i.e. of the relevant activities) and 'nationality' (i.e. of the person to whom the initiative is addressed). To stay within the international rules on extraterritorial regulation, the home state would also need to ensure that the regulatory initiative does not amount to a violation of the duty of non-intervention. This obligation applies whether or not the initiative is 'extraterritorial' in the traditional sense. Unfortunately, international law still provides only very vague guidance as to how this duty is to be interpreted in the context of workplace, environmental and consumer regulation. As a general rule, however, the more 'internationally accepted' the standards imposed on the multinational, the less likely it is that the extraterritorial regulation will amount to a breach of the duty of non-intervention in the domestic affairs of other states. *Genuine* initiatives designed to give effect to

---

[238] See pp. 133–6 above.
[239] See pp. 165–7 above.   [240] See further pp. 83–91 above.

established principles of human rights should not *automatically* be regarded as interference. Even where an initiative goes beyond that which is strictly necessary to give effect to human rights, it is arguable that the extraterritorial regulation would not usually be 'unreasonable' where there is a significant degree of international consensus as to the content of those obligations, the need for regulation and the form that regulation should take.

But while the duty of non-intervention may not pose a significant problem for less direct forms of extraterritorial CSR regulation, it will certainly limit the scope for compliance monitoring by the home state (e.g. of commitments made under social labelling schemes) or for verification of social and environmental information published by the parent (e.g. under home state reporting requirements) or for checking the accuracy of claims made in the support of an application for benefits under an incentive scheme. If foreign activities are to be monitored effectively – and in many cases this will be vital for a regime's credibility – the co-operation of the host state will be needed to assist with information gathering and to facilitate (and in some cases compel) access to commercial facilities. In any event, the legal powers of home state authorities would be limited. However, even with this co-operation, regulatory conflicts could still arise, for example, where the parent company was obliged under home state law to disclose matters the foreign affiliate was required (or even permitted) under domestic law to keep confidential.

Conclusion

Does the state practice discussed above represent the beginnings of a sustained commitment by home states to improving the CSR performance of multinationals abroad, or a half-hearted response to pressure from an active and very vocal group of NGOs? From the point of view of most campaigning NGOs, the pace of reform so far has been frustratingly slow. Nevertheless, the fact that home state governments are now starting to sign up to public commitments with respect to their CSR policies[241] is a promising new development.

At present, there is no real evidence to suggest that extraterritorial CSR initiatives are being introduced out of any sense of legal compulsion; rather it is a result of a mixture of political and economic self-interest,

---

[241] See WSSD Plan of Implementation, n. 47 above, paragraph 18. See further pp. 267–8 below.

and arguably, ethical and moral concerns. To these ends, home states are taking steps to encourage and facilitate good practice, at home and abroad, while continuing to stress that CSR is, and should remain, a 'voluntary' concept. A variety of different regulatory methods are being experimented with. So far, the most developed of these is CSR reporting, and some states have legislated to make this a legal requirement in relation to the activities of not only the locally incorporated parent, but foreign subsidiaries as well. Other, though less developed, methods of regulating multinationals extraterritorially include the use of incentive schemes, such as linking access to government assistance to CSR performance. Although these regulatory methods do not prescribe any binding standards for multinationals, they add to the pressure on multinationals to develop and conform to non-binding codes. In addition, extraterritorial 'benefits' – e.g. the right to complain about the behaviour of multinationals or their planned projects – already exist, to a limited extent, under the laws of some home states, including administrative, consumer protection and trade practices laws.

Ultimately, developing state practice on CSR has the potential to contribute to the development of a more flexible set of rules on international jurisdiction, more in tune with the needs of a 'globalising' international society. In any event, the more home states seek to regulate the extraterritorial impacts of multinational activity, the more likely it will be that multinationals will find themselves subject to conflicting or overlapping regulatory requirements (at least in relation to procedural matters if not the underlying principles). Ultimately, some degree of harmonisation of laws may be needed to simplify regulatory requirements and to reduce the overall regulatory burden associated with home state CSR initiatives. The prospects for an 'international law on CSR' are taken up again in chapter 6. First, though, it is necessary to consider how home state courts are currently responding to private claims against multinationals under domestic law.

5   Private claims for personal injury and environmental harm

To what extent does domestic law, as enforced by domestic courts, provide a means of obtaining redress against multinationals for loss or damage arising from poor health, safety or environmental standards overseas? Until recently, the experiences of plaintiffs in national courts had not been very encouraging. However, a series of pro-plaintiff decisions (of which the House of Lords decision in *Lubbe* v. *Cape plc*[1] is a good example) have re-ignited interest in the regulatory possibilities afforded by private claims.

Cases like *Re Bhopal*[2] and *Lubbe* v. *Cape plc* dramatise very clearly the potential dangers of an 'unregulated' international system, in which multinationals can dump their most hazardous activities and processes on poorer countries, safe in the knowledge that they are unlikely to be required to compensate their victims fully, if at all. Given the lack of enforcement machinery at international level, it is not surprising that plaintiffs are now exploring the potential of private claims under domestic laws to hold multinationals to account. The past decade or so has seen a sharp increase in the number of 'foreign direct liability' ('FDL') claims,[3] that is, claims brought in home state courts that target, not the subsidiary, but the parent company as the apparent 'orchestrator' of company-wide investment standards and policies. So far, a number of prominent home states have been affected – including the UK,[4] the

---

[1] [2000] 1 WLR 1545; [2000] 4 All ER 268 (HL) 277.
[2] *In Re Union Carbide Corporation Gas Plant Disaster at Bhopal, India in December, 1984*, 634 F Supp 842 (SDNY 1986).
[3] H. Ward, 'Governing Multinationals: the Role of Foreign Direct Liability', RIIA, Briefing Paper, New Series No. 18, February 2001.
[4] *Ngcobo and Others* v. *Thor Chemical Holdings Ltd*, TLR 10 November 1995; *Sithole and Others* v. *Thor Chemical Holdings Ltd*, TLR 15 February 1999; *Connelly* v. *RTZ* [1998] AC 854; *Lubbe* v. *Cape plc*, n. 1 above.

USA,[5] Australia[6] and Canada[7] – and there is no reason to expect that it will stop there. A heady mix of factors – the high profile of CSR in these countries, the current level of media interest in cases of corporate wrongdoing, the availability of public interest lawyers willing to take on such cases, the financial and procedural advantages offered by many of these home state courts over foreign ('host state') alternatives (such as contingency fee representation or the possibility of class actions),[8] the more than theoretical possibility of financial compensation,[9] and generally better prospects for enforcement – makes further FDL litigation more than likely.[10] The aim of this chapter is to explore the legal background to FDL claims, and the implications of these for international law.

FDL claims are a potentially important source of regulatory pressure on parent companies of multinationals, but this depends on two things: first, the willingness of home state courts to accept jurisdiction and, second, substantive rules of parent company liability. The question of jurisdiction has already been discussed in chapter 3 in which it was noted that home states are entitled to take jurisdiction over cases involving a locally incorporated parent company as a defendant, including cases concerning damage or injury occurring overseas.[11] However, in some common law states (and particularly in the USA) foreign plaintiffs must still face up to the likelihood that proceedings relating to foreign damage or injury will be 'stayed' (i.e. stopped) in favour of a more 'convenient forum' (under the doctrine of forum non conveniens). Substantive issues relating to parent company liability are considered later in this chapter,

---

[5] *Re Bhopal*, n. 2 above. In addition, numerous claims have been made under the US Alien Tort Claims Act (or 'ATCA'). See further pp. 207–15 below.

[6] *Dagi v. BHP* [1997] 1 VR 428.

[7] *Recherches Internationanales Quebec v. Cambior Inc.* [1998] QJ No. 2554 [QL].

[8] See Joseph, *Transnational Human Rights Litigation*, pp. 16–17; *Connelly v. RTZ*, n. 4 above; *Lubbe* v. *Cape plc*, n. 1 above.

[9] Although none of the 'foreign direct liability' claims discussed in this chapter has gone to trial on the merits, some plaintiffs have obtained some financial compensation under settlement agreements. See further pp. 201–6 below.

[10] In June 2005, lawyers representing a group of Colombian farmers announced that they would be commencing proceedings in the English courts against BP for damages arising out of a controversial oil pipeline project. According to a press release by Leigh Day & Co., 'The farmers' claim is based on nuisance, negligence and in some cases breach of contract'; 'Colombian Farmers Start Claim against BP for Pipeline that has Ruined Lives', 18 June 2005, http://www.leighday.co.uk. See R. Verkaik, 'Farmers "Terrified out of their Homes" to Sue BP for £15m', *Independent*, 18 June 2005, pp. 18–19.

[11] See pp. 117–20 above.

after a brief survey of notable cases so far, first, under the common law of negligence (i.e. 'tort law') and, second, under the US Alien Tort Claims Act[12] (or 'ATCA' for short). Establishing the legal liability of a parent company (notwithstanding the closer involvement of a foreign subsidiary) is by no means easy, and there is little case law to go on at present. Nevertheless, a brief study of English tort law principles reveals a number of theories that might potentially be used, in relation not only to equity-based multinational structures, but to contract-based business forms as well.

This chapter then concludes with an assessment of the implications of these private law claims for international law. Although different courts deal with the underlying issues of public policy in different ways, decisions about the liability of parent companies of multinationals are not made in a vacuum. Developments at national and international level in the CSR field have the potential to influence the future role of home state courts in the adjudication of private claims against parent companies of multinationals. A difficult, and as yet unresolved, issue is the relationship between the domestic law doctrine of forum non conveniens and the rights of individuals, under international human rights law, to have access to legal remedies for harm. The approach of national courts to private claims of this kind is potentially an important source of evidence of state practice on how the competing interests of plaintiffs, corporate defendants and states are to be resolved. In addition, domestic jurisprudence on parent company liability in relation to workplace injuries and environmental harm is likely to be influential in the development of future international CSR regimes.

Tort-based claims

Tort law potentially allows CSR standards to be enforced privately by affected individuals through claims for negligence and other related causes of action. Employees injured as a result of poor workplace standards, families who have lost their livelihoods as a result of environmental damage caused by poor operating practices or consumers who have been hurt or have become ill as a result of a breach of product safety standards should all have a right of action against the responsible party for damages. As noted above, plaintiffs in large class actions against multinationals are increasingly targeting not the operating

[12] 28 USC § 1350.

subsidiaries of multinationals but the parent company. There are a number of reasons for targeting a parent company in this way: not only is the parent company likely to have a greater pool of assets with which to satisfy a judgment against it, but an action against a parent company also potentially gives plaintiffs access to the courts of home states such as the UK and the USA, with all the procedural advantages that this may entail.[13]

Despite all this, there is still a dearth of case law on the issue of parent company liability for the activities of foreign subsidiaries. There are three main reasons for this: first the enormous difficulties (financial, technical, logistical and emotional) associated with mounting such a claim in the first place; second, various procedural obstacles (particularly legal challenges on grounds of forum non conveniens); and, third, the tendency of claims to settle once a critical stage in the litigation is reached. As discussed below, decided case law on group liability is less than encouraging for plaintiffs, emphasising, as it does, the importance of the 'corporate veil'. On the other hand, there is nothing in the case law which would positively rule out the possibility of parent company liability for the health, safety and environmental failings of foreign subsidiaries in an appropriate case.

Re Bhopal[14] may have been just such a case. This was a claim for negligence by victims of the 1984 Bhopal disaster, for which the Indian government assumed responsibility (under the 1985 Bhopal Gas Leak Disaster (Processing of Claims) Act) against Union Carbide India Limited ('UCIL') and its US parent company, Union Carbide Corporation ('UCC').[15] While the negligence of the Indian subsidiary appeared to be the most direct cause of the disaster, the plaintiffs sought to argue that UCC ought also to be held responsible. Several theories were advanced in support of this, as shall be discussed below, but perhaps the most promising of the plaintiffs' arguments revolved around UCC's role in the design and construction of the Indian plant and the lack of subsequent safety monitoring. Ultimately, though, this particular set of proceedings was dismissed on grounds of forum non conveniens in favour of the Indian courts, primarily on public interest grounds.[16] In 1989 the Indian Supreme Court ratified a settlement offer by UCC of $470 million, $420 million of which

---

[13] See n. 8 above.   [14] Re Bhopal, n. 2 above.

[15] The plaintiffs also argued, in the alternative, that Union Carbide was liable on the basis of a strict duty to ensure that the Bhopal plant did not cause harm. Joseph, Transnational Human Rights Litigation, p. 72.

[16] See pp. 121–3 above.

was paid by UCC and $50 million of which was paid by UCIL. This did not, however, bring an end to the Bhopal litigation. Legal wrangling continued in the Indian courts for some time afterwards, mainly over the constitutionality of the 1985 legislation by which the Indian government had assumed responsibility for the conduct of the claims, and hence the legality of the 1989 settlement agreement.[17] Some victims of the Bhopal disaster have also tried, so far unsuccessfully, to reinstitute claims against UCC and its chairman, Warren Anderson, under ATCA. These ATCA-based proceedings were, however, dismissed on the grounds that they were barred by the settlement orders of the Supreme Court of India.[18] But while the litigation may be largely over, for many victims justice still seems a long way off. A number of charities working with victims of the disaster have complained of serious delays in distributing compensation payments. In a report to mark the twentieth anniversary of the tragedy, Amnesty notes that as of mid-2004 the Rupee equivalent of US$337.5 million was still in the custody of the Reserve Bank of India.[19]

Despite the general reluctance of US courts to entertain claims by foreign litigants,[20] US courts are still a popular starting point for international tort-based litigation.[21] Over the past two decades, at least 470 separate lawsuits (involving some twenty thousand plaintiffs) have been commenced in US courts over a single issue: injuries arising from the use by foreign banana plantation workers of pesticides banned in the USA.[22] US companies targeted in this particular series of class actions have been chemicals manufacturers (such as Dow Chemicals, Occidental

---

[17] In the end, the Act was upheld. See *Sahu* v. *Union of India* 1990 AIR (Supreme Court) 1480. Further claims were also instituted in the District Court of Texas (and subsequently transferred to the Southern District of New York). However, these too were dismissed, first on the grounds of forum non conveniens (see *In Re Union Carbide Corp. Gas Plant Disaster*; No. MDL 626, 1992 WL 36135, 1992 US Dist. LEXIS 1909 (SDNY, 18 February 1992)) and, on appeal, on the ground that the plaintiffs lacked standing (see *Bi* v. *Union Carbide Chems. and Plastics Co.*, 984 F 3d 582 (2d Cir.) cert. denied 510 US 862, 114 S Ct 179, 126 L Ed 2d 138 (1993).

[18] *Bano* v. *Union Carbide Corporation* 273 F 3d 120 (2d Cir. 2001), 122

[19] Amnesty International, 'Clouds of Injustice' (Amnesty International Publications, 2004) http://www.amnesty.org/library, p. 66.

[20] See pp. 121–4 above.

[21] There are a number of reasons for this, not least the availability of contingency fee representation, the 'substantial public interest legal sector in the US willing to take on such cases', the general requirement that defendants bear their own costs (even if the plaintiff is unsuccessful), the prospect of higher damages, and plaintiff-friendly discovery rules. Joseph, *Transnational Human Rights Litigation*, pp. 16–17.

[22] Mayer and Sable, 'Bananas', p. 136.

and Shell) and food companies (such as Dole, Del Monte and Standard Fruit). So far, the vast majority of these cases have been dismissed on grounds of forum non conveniens and all but a few of the remaining cases have settled out of court.[23] However, the willingness of judges in more recent cases to look more critically at the issue of whether there is an adequate and available alternative forum,[24] and the placing of conditions on decisions to stay actions on grounds of forum non conveniens (which may give the right to reinstitute proceedings at a later stage),[25] does suggest a more plaintiff-friendly attitude on the part of some US courts.[26]

One further series of US cases to mention here is the group of claims known as *Doe* v. *Unocal*. Although originally commenced under the ATCA (see below), parallel claims were also commenced in the California state courts alleging other torts, namely 'wrongful death, battery, false imprisonment, intentional infliction of emotional distress, negligent infliction of emotional distress, negligence per se and conversion'.[27] In 2002 the defendants applied to have the state law claims struck out on several grounds, including lack of a duty of care (in relation to the allegations of negligence) and lack of causation. After hearing the arguments, Chaney J dismissed the plaintiffs' claims based on allegations of Unocal's own actions, such as aiding and abetting and intentional torts.[28] However, it was decided that the claims based on the possible 'vicarious liability' of the Unocal companies should stand.[29] After a further unsuccessful attempt to have the tort-based claims struck out in 2004,[30] the *Doe* v. *Unocal* litigation (both

---

[23] Ibid., pp. 138–9.

[24] *Martinez* v. *Dow Chemical Company* 219 F Supp 2d 719 (ED La 2002).

[25] *Borja* v. *Dole Food Company* 2002 US Dist. LEXIS 23234 (ND Tex, 4 December 2002).

[26] See futher pp. 123–4 above.

[27] Joseph, *Transnational Human Rights Litigation*, p. 68.

[28] Although it might have been possible to revisit some of these dismissals following the decision of the Ninth Circuit Court of Appeals in relation to the ATCA-based claims (see n. 73 below). See further Joseph, *Transnational Human Rights Litigation*, p. 70.

[29] 'Ruling on the Defendants' Motion for Summary Judgment, or in the alternative, summary adjudication on each of the Plaintiffs' tort claims', Decision of the Superior Court of California, County of Los Angeles, 7 June 2002, unreported, copy available from http://www.earthrights.org/unocal/index/shtml.

[30] This time on the basis that a previous ruling by Judge Chaney of the California Superior Court that the Unocal subsidiary could not be viewed as an 'alter ego' precluded liability based on any other theories. Judge Chaney disagreed and dismissed the application. See 'Ruling on the Defendants' Motion for Judgment', Decision of the Superior Court of California, County of Los Angeles, 14 September 2004, available from http://www.earthrights.org/unocal/index/shtml.

tort-based and ATCA-based) settled out of court. Under the terms of settlement, agreed in principle on 13 December 2004, Unocal would provide funds 'to compensate plaintiffs and . . . enabl[e] plaintiffs and their representatives to develop programs to improve living conditions, health care and education and protect the rights of people from the pipeline region'.[31]

In the UK there have been four notable FDL cases in the English courts. In each case the plaintiffs (claiming damages for injuries sustained as a result of exposure to the operations of foreign subsidiaries of UK companies) have been represented by Leigh Day & Co., a London-based firm of solicitors. *Connelly* v. *RTZ*[32] concerned a claim for damages against the parent company of the operator of a mine in Namibia alleging negligent exposure to uranium dust causing cancer. Importantly, the House of Lords rejected the defendant's application to stay the proceedings on grounds of forum non conveniens, having taken the view that the inability of Mr Connelly to litigate his claim in Namibia (owing to the non-availability of legal aid) meant that Namibia was not a forum in which the action could be tried 'more suitably for the interests of all the parties and the ends of justice'.[33]

A series of similar claims have also been made against the UK-based chemicals company Thor Chemicals Holdings Limited, a manufacturer of mercury-based chemicals. Richard Meeran, one of the lawyers acting for the plaintiffs, has explained the background to the claim as follows:

Health and safety at the Margate factory came under considerable criticism over a prolonged period from the Health and Safety Executive (HSE) due to elevated levels of mercury in the blood and urine of the workers. In about 1986, the company terminated mercury-based processes in Margate and shifted its Margate mercury operations (including key personnel and plant) to Cato Ridge, Natal, South Africa. At that factory, precisely the same deficiencies which had been identified by the HSE were replicated.[34]

By 1992, a number of cases of mercury poisoning among workers at the South African plant had been noted, including three deaths. Gaining no real satisfaction from criminal proceedings (a somewhat derisory fine of

---

[31] Joint press release by the parties, 13 December 2004, http://www.laborrights.org.

[32] [1998] AC 854.

[33] See pp. 124–6 above. On the current status of the doctrine of forum non conveniens in the UK, see p. 126 above.

[34] R. Meeran, 'The Unveiling of Transnational Corporations' in M. Addo (ed.), *Human Rights and the Responsibility of Transnational Corporations* (The Hague: Kluwer, 1999), pp. 164–5.

the equivalent of £3,000 was imposed by the local magistrate's court), claims were brought in the English courts by some twenty workers.[35] Eventually, two separate group actions[36] were settled out of court after the English courts refused to stay the proceedings on grounds of forum non conveniens.[37]

The next UK case of this type, *Lubbe* v. *Cape plc*,[38] arose out of the asbestos mining and production activities of a wholly owned subsidiary of Cape plc in the Northern Cape of South Africa. These claims were originally commenced in 1997 on behalf of three mine-workers and two local residents who had contracted asbestos-related injuries and, in one case, mesothelioma (an asbestos-related cancer). Having survived an application by the defendants for a stay on grounds of forum non conveniens, further claims were commenced in the form of a class action by nearly two thousand more litigants, and the English courts were once again asked to consider the issue of the appropriate forum for the case. This time the Court of Appeal felt that 'the fact that there could be 3,000 or more plaintiffs whose individual circumstances will need to be investigated as opposed to five in the [earlier] *Lubbe* action, adds dramatically to the South African weighting'[39] and upheld the defendants' application for a stay of proceedings. The plaintiffs appealed to the House of Lords which ruled, in a landmark decision, that to remove the proceedings to South Africa would amount to a denial of justice as the plaintiffs would not be able to secure the necessary resources (financial and otherwise) to prosecute their claims.[40] Eventually, the consolidated class action was settled out of court on 21 December 2001 for approximately £27 million.

FDL claims have also been commenced in other common law home states. The Australian case of *Dagi* v. *BHP*[41] concerned a claim for damages by landowners for pollution of the Ok Tedi River in Papua New Guinea and adjoining land caused by the mining activities of a subsidiary of the Australian mining company BHP. No application to stay the proceedings on grounds of forum non conveniens was made by the defendants; as discussed above, Australian courts will only grant such an

---

[35] Ibid., p. 165.

[36] *Ngcobo* v. *Thor Chemical Holdings Ltd* and *Sithole* v. *Thor Chemical Holdings Ltd*, n. 4 above.

[37] The *Ngcobo* claim was settled in 1997 for £1.3 million. The *Sithole* claim was settled in October 2000 for £270,000. Ward, 'Governing Multinationals', p. 3.

[38] *Lubbe* v. *Cape plc* [2000] 1 WLR 1545; [2000] 4 All ER 268 (HL).

[39] *Lubbe* v. *Cape plc* [2000] 1 Lloyd's Rep. 139, 143.

[40] *Lubbe* v. *Cape plc*, n. 38 above.   [41] [1997] 1 VR 428.

application in extremely limited circumstances, meaning that such an action would have no real prospect of succeeding.[42] Following an unsuccessful attempt by the defendants to get the proceedings dismissed on other grounds,[43] *Dagi* v. *BHP* eventually settled out of court for A$150 million in 1997. There have also been examples of FDL cases in Canadian courts. *Recherches Internationales Quebec* v. *Cambior Inc.*[44] was a claim brought by a public interest group against a Canadian parent company for damage arising from a spill of cyanide-contaminated tailings into a main waterway in Guyana. The mine site was operated by a subsidiary of Cambior. In their statement of claim, the plaintiffs claimed a total of $69 million in damages (calculated on the basis of $3,000 for each of the estimated 23,000 victims). Ultimately, though, the court agreed with the defendant's arguments that Guyana, not Canada, was the appropriate forum and declined to hear the case.[45]

FDL cases appear to be on the increase, particularly in the USA. However, the lack of judicial pronouncements on the substantive points means that it is still only possible to speculate as to whether and when a parent company may be liable for the CSR failures of foreign subsidiaries. From the perspective of plaintiffs (and their lawyers), this uncertainty can be viewed as a risk – or an opportunity. On the one hand, there is the possibility that a claim, having cleared all the procedural hurdles, could still ultimately fail on the issue of liability involving potentially enormous legal costs.[46] On the other hand, the chance that a parent company may eventually be held liable by a court of law for the activities of its subsidiaries is far from remote, especially given the changing social and political context in which these cases are decided.[47] Prospective plaintiffs must surely take some encouragement from recent, generally sympathetic decisions by home state courts, such as the House of Lords in *Lubbe* v. *Cape*[48] and the US courts in *Martinez* v. *Dow*

---

[42] See pp. 126–7 above.

[43] I.e. the 'Mozambique' principle. See chapter 3, nn. 67–70 and accompanying text.

[44] [1998] QJ No. 2554 (QL).

[45] See further Seck, 'Environmental Harm'. However, in *Wilson* v. *Servier Canada* 50 OR (3d) 219 (2000), the court refused an application to dismiss a products liability class action for injuries suffered in France on grounds of forum non conveniens, on the basis that a class action in Canada offered the best option for 'the just resolution of [the plaintiffs'] claims'. Joseph, *Transnational Human Rights Litigation*, p. 127.

[46] Although these concerns are mitigated, from the plaintiffs' perspective, by access to contingency fee representation, legal aid and other financial assistance, as well as the rule, in the USA, that plaintiffs, if unsuccessful, do not need to bear defendants' costs unless the legal action was 'vexatious'.

[47] See pp. 114, 133 above.   [48] See n. 38 above.

Chemical Company[49] and *Doe* v. *Unocal* (i.e. state proceedings).[50] This, coupled with the commercial and reputational risks associated with having to defend a large-scale negligence action, means that there are substantial pressures on companies to seek out of court settlements of tort-based claims. (It is worth noting that, with only one exception,[51] each of the FDL cases discussed above was either stayed on grounds of forum non conveniens or settled – after the defendant's application for a stay was rejected.)

The US Alien Tort Claims Act ('ATCA')

The ATCA confers jurisdiction on the US District Courts in respect of 'any civil action by an alien for a tort only, committed in violation of the law of nations or a treaty of the United States'.[52] Although this provision dates back to the eighteenth century, it was the landmark case of *Filartiga* v. *Pena-Irala*[53] in 1980 that drew attention to its potential as a means of holding individuals accountable for breaches of human rights standards in other countries.[54] The past decade has seen a dramatic growth in the number of proceedings launched against US parent companies under ATCA[55] alleging violations of human rights obligations. Although its application to private individuals and entities was initially in doubt, it now seems clear that the ATCA does indeed give rise to a cause of action against private companies, even (in rare cases) where no 'state action' is involved.[56] Less clear, though, is the means by which liability under the Act would be attributed to the US parent company, rather than the foreign subsidiary with direct responsibility on the ground.

---

[49] See n. 24 above.

[50] See nn. 29 and 30 above and accompanying text.

[51] *Connelly* v. *RTZ*, n. 4 above, which was struck out on limitation grounds.

[52] 28 USC § 1350.   [53] 630 F 2d 876 (2d Cir. 1980).

[54] B. Stephens and S. Ratner, *International Human Rights Litigation in US Courts* (Irvington-on-Hudson, NY: Transnational Publishers, 1996).

[55] See *Doe* v. *Unocal*, 963 F Supp 880 (CD Cal 1997); *Beanal* v. *Freeport McMoRan*, 969 F Supp 362 (ED La 1997); *Jota* v. *Texaco*, 157 F 3d 153 (2d Cir. 1998); *Wiwa* v. *Royal Dutch Petroleum*, 226 F 3d 88 (2d Cir. 2000); *Bigio* v. *Coca-Cola*, 239 F 3d 440 (2d Cir. 2000); *Bowoto* v. *Chevron*, 312 F Supp 3d 1229 (ND Cal 2004). These cases have generated an enormous amount of literature but see, in particular, Joseph, *Transnational Human Rights Litigation*, esp. chapter 2 and Stephens and Ratner, *International Human Rights Litigation*.

[56] See *Doe I v Unocal*, 395 F 3d 932 (9th Cir. 2002). On the requirement for 'state action', see further pp. 209–11 below.

Most of the lawsuits brought under ATCA against US companies so far (presently numbering around forty)[57] have been based on allegations of 'corporate complicity' in human rights breaches by state authorities, rather than on allegations of human rights violations by companies directly.[58] *Doe* v. *Unocal*,[59] for example, concerned a claim for damages by a group of Burmese nationals for human rights abuses suffered at the hands of Burmese security forces in connection with the construction of a gas transportation pipeline. According to the plaintiffs, Unocal and Total were party to these abuses, having utilised the services of the police and military and having subsidised their activities in the region, in the knowledge that human rights abuses, including forced labour, were being employed in connection with the project.[60] *Wiwa* v. *Royal Dutch Petroleum Ltd*[61] was an action brought by members of the family of the Nigerian environmental activist, Ken Saro-Wiwa, in which Nigerian subsidiaries of the Royal Dutch Shell group were alleged to have utilised local security forces to put down opposition to their oil operations in Nigeria and, subsequently, to have instigated the imprisonment, torture and killings of the plaintiffs and their relatives. The causes of action revolved around the claim that 'while these abuses were carried out by the Nigerian government and military, they were instigated, orchestrated, planned and facilitated by Shell Nigeria under the direction of the defendants'.[62] In particular:

The Royal Dutch Shell Group allegedly provided money, weapons and logistical support to the Nigerian military, including the vehicles, ammunition used in the raids on the villages, procured at least some of these attacks, participated in the fabrication of murder charges against Saro Wiwa and [John] Kpuinen, and bribed witnesses to give false testimony against them.[63]

---

[57] B. Stephens, 'Upsetting Checks and Balances: the Bush Administration's Efforts to Limit Human Rights Litigation' (2004) 17 *Harv. HRJ* 169, 179.

[58] C. Forcese, 'ATCA's Achilles Heel: Corporate Complicity, International Law and the Alien Tort Claims Act' (2001) 26 *YJIL* 487

[59] 963 F Supp 880 (CD Cal 1997).

[60] Although note that the claims against Total were dismissed by the court for want of 'personal' jurisdiction over the French parent company, 27 F Supp 2d 1174 (CD Cal 1998) (affirmed 248 F 3d 915 (2001). See further pp. 118–19 above.

[61] 226 F 3d 88 (2d Cir. 2000).

[62] Ibid., 92. See also *Bowoto* v. *Chevron*, n. 55 above, which alleges that human rights abuses were 'inflicted by Nigerian Military and police personnel, who were acting at the behest of, and with the support, cooperation and financial assistance of . . . Chevron'; quoted in Forcese, 'ATCA's Achilles Heel', 490.

[63] Ibid., 92–3.

In *Beanal* v. *Freeport McMoRan*,[64] the plaintiffs claimed the members of the Freeport group of companies

had systematically engaged in a corporate policy both directly and indirectly through third parties which has resulted in human rights violations against the Amungme Tribe and other Indigenous tribal people. Said actions include extra-judicial killing, torture, surveillance and threats of death, severe physical pain and suffering by and through its security personnel employed in connection with its operation of the Grasberg mine.[65]

The *Doe* v. *Exxonmobil* proceedings, launched in 2001, concern allegations of complicity by Exxonmobil and its Indonesian subsidiaries in human rights abuses committed by the Indonesian military on the island of Aceh, Indonesia. Specifically, the plaintiffs allege that Exxonmobil provided 'logistical and material' support to the Indonesian military, in return for protection of its operations, in the knowledge that 'their logistical support was being used to effectuate the Indonesian military's commission of . . . human rights atrocities'.[66]

A company can be liable under ATCA either if its activities amounted to 'state action' in breach of the 'law of nations' or where the obligation alleged to have been breached is one which is applicable directly to a private individual or company under customary international law.[67] The court in *Beanal* v. *Freeport McMoRan*[68] considered four different grounds on which the activities of Freeport McMoRan might be regarded as 'state action' – the 'nexus' test,[69] the 'symbiotic relationship' test,[70] the 'joint action' test[71] and the 'public function' test[72] – before deciding

---

[64] 969 F Supp 362 (ED La 1997).

[65] Extract of plaintiff's complaint, quoted in Forcese, 'ATCA's Achilles Heel', 492.

[66] *Doe* v. *Exxonmobil*, Complaint, 11 June 2001, copy available from http://www.laborrights.org.

[67] See *Doe* v. *Unocal* 963 F Supp 880 (CD Cal 1997) and *Beanal* v. *Freeport McMoRan* 969 F Supp 362 (ED La 1997).

[68] 969 F Supp 362 (ED La 1997).

[69] 'Under the nexus test, a plaintiff must demonstrate that there is a sufficiently close nexus between the government and the challenged conduct such that the conduct may fairly be treated as the acts of the State itself'; ibid., 377.

[70] State action can be established under the symbiotic relationship test if the state 'has so far insinuated itself into a position of interdependence' with a private party that 'it must be recognized as a joint participant in the challenged activity'; ibid., 378 (citations omitted).

[71] 'State action is present where a private party is a 'wilful participant in joint action with the State or its agents'; ibid., 379 (citations omitted).

[72] '[S]tate action can exist where a private entity performs a function traditionally the exclusive prerogative of the State'; ibid., 379 (citations omitted).

in each case that the necessary relationship did not arise from the facts alleged. In *Doe* v. *Unocal*, on the other hand, in the first decision of its kind, the court at first instance was prepared to take subject matter jurisdiction over the defendants based on the 'joint action' test.[73] However, the matter eventually settled out of court in December 2004 before the issue of Unocal's liability under ATCA could be tried again.

Although the issue was never finally resolved in *Doe* v. *Unocal*, it is fair to say that the US courts tend to interpret 'state action' restrictively. State approval or acquiescence in alleged human rights violations by a private company does not necessarily mean that the company's activities can be regarded as 'state action' for the purposes of an ATCA claim.[74] Neither does the fact that operations were carried on pursuant to a concession granted by the state.[75] Absent 'state action', companies would only be liable under ATCA in very limited circumstances. To be successful, plaintiffs need to be able to establish the existence, not only of binding norms,[76] but of norms that are also directly applicable to non-state actors.[77] The types of violations which may give rise to corporate liability under ATCA in the absence of 'state action' include genocide,[78] piracy,[79]

---

[73] 963 F Supp 880 (CD Cal 1997), 891. In a subsequent hearing the case against the defendants was dismissed by Lew J on the basis that Unocal did not sufficiently control or participate in the activities of the military to be liable under ATCA for their abuses; 110 F Supp 2d 1294 (CD Cal 2000), 1303. However, this decision was then reversed on appeal by the Court of Appeals for the Ninth Circuit (with respect to allegations of forced labour, murder and rape) and the proceedings were partly reinstated; *Doe I* v. *Unocal*, 395 F 3d 932 (9th Cir. 2002). In yet another twist of fortune for the plaintiffs, the Ninth Circuit decision was vacated, and Lew J's decision was reinstated, pending a hearing by an eleven judge *en banc* panel of the Ninth Circuit; *Doe* v. *Unocal*, 2003 WL 359787 (9th Cir. 14 February 2003). The *en banc* panel's decision was then delayed, pending the outcome of a Supreme Court appeal in another ATCA case, i.e. *Sosa* v. *Alvarez-Machain*, 542 US 692 (2004), 124 S Ct 2739 (2004). See further S. Joseph, 'Corporations and Human Rights Litigation (Update on *Sosa* v. *Alvarez-Machain*)', copy available from http://www.hartpub.co.uk.

[74] *Beanal* v. *Freeport McMoRan*, 969 F Supp 362 (ED La 1997), 377–80.

[75] Ibid., 379.

[76] See *Amlon Metals* v. *FMC Corporation*, 775 F Supp 668 (SDNY 1991) in which the court refused to hold that the Stockholm Principles (from the 1972 UN Stockholm Conference on the Human Environment) would constitute part of the 'law of nations'.

[77] *Tel-Oren* v. *Libyan Arab Republic*, 726 F 2d 774 (DC Cir. 1984), 794–5.

[78] *Kadic* v. *Karadzic*, 70 F 3d 232 (2d Cir. 1995), 242–3. See also discussion in *Beanal* v. *Freeport McMoRan*, 969 F Supp 362 (ED La 1997) and *Doe I* v. *Unocal*, 395 F 3d 932 (9th Cir. 2002).

[79] *Doe* v. *Unocal*, 963 F Supp 880 (CD Cal 1997), 891.

slave trading[80] and forced labour.[81] However, claims relating to large-scale environmental damage have so far been found to be beyond the scope of ATCA, and attempts by plaintiffs to portray environmental damage as 'genocide'[82] or a violation of other human rights (such as the 'right to life, health and security of the person')[83] have not been successful. To date, no US company has been found liable under ATCA on the basis of 'directly applicable' human rights norms, although before the case settled, the Court of Appeals of the Ninth Circuit thought that Unocal, in *Doe I* v. *Unocal*, had at least a case to answer in relation to allegations of complicity in human rights abuses by the Burmese military. In particular, the Ninth Circuit thought that the Unocal companies could potentially be liable, under a test derived from international criminal law, for 'aiding and abetting' human rights abuses committed by the military by virtue of their practical assistance for security-related activities '[which] took the form of hiring the Myanmar Military to provide security and build infrastructure along the pipeline route in exchange for money or food . . . using photos, survey and maps in daily meetings to show the Myanmar Military where to provide security and build infrastructure'.[84]

Even if subject-matter jurisdiction under ATCA is held *prima facie* to exist (as was the case in *Doe* v. *Unocal*), there are, as with tort-based claims, a number of further potential hurdles for plaintiffs to overcome. First (and almost always an issue where foreign state entities are involved) there is the potential application of the doctrine of 'act of state'. Under the 'act of state' doctrine, courts 'will generally refrain from . . . sitting in judgment on . . . acts of a governmental character done by a foreign

---

[80] See *Doe I* v. *Unocal*, 395 F 3d 932 (9th Cir. 2002), 946–7, in which forced labour is described as 'a modern variant of slavery'.

[81] See *Doe* v. *Unocal*, 963 F Supp 880 (CD Cal 1997), in which the judge held that '[t]he allegations of forced labour in this case are sufficient to constitute an allegation of participation in slave trading'. He went on to hold that the allegations that the defendants knew of the use by the Burmese security forces of forced labour and its payments for their services 'are sufficient to establish subject matter jurisdiction under the ATCA', 892.

[82] See *Beanal* v. *Freeport McMoRan*, 969 F Supp 362 (ED La 1997).

[83] *Sarei* v. *Rio Tinto*, 221 F Supp 2d 1161 (CD Cal 2002). However, as Joseph points out, this case is concerned with *intra-state* environmental damage. There remains the possibility that transborder environmental damage could come within the scope of the statute on the basis that it constitutes a 'tort . . . in violation of the law of nations'; Joseph, *Transnational Human Rights Litigation*, pp. 28–30.

[84] *Doe I* v. *Unocal*, 395 F 3d 932 (9th Cir. 2002), 952.

state within its own territory and applicable there'.[85] However, this doctrine has not proved a significant block to ACTA-based litigation, mainly for the reason that the doctrine only extends to acts that are 'valid', 'public' and 'official'.[86] Acts that are universally condemned under international human rights law should not fall into this category.[87] However, ATCA-based claims have been dismissed under the doctrine of 'act of state' because of the potential foreign relations implications in allowing the proceedings to proceed. In *Sarei v. Rio Tinto*,[88] for instance, allegations of racial discrimination and breaches of UNCLOS were dismissed following a submission by the Bush administration that the proceedings would jeopardise US efforts in relation to the Bougainville peace process.[89]

A related basis on which a court may decline jurisdiction is where the proceedings raise a non-justiciable 'political question'. This doctrine 'directs the courts to decline to decide a case otherwise properly presented for resolution because the dispute presents issues constitutionally assigned to the political branches of government'.[90] Unlike the 'act of state' doctrine, the 'political question' doctrine can be invoked in relation to very serious human rights violations where, for instance, a judicial pronouncement on a subject could conflict with or undermine a political settlement.[91] However, the circumstances in which this doctrine would oblige a court to decline jurisdiction are 'by definition quite limited'[92] and should not generally include cases where the human

---

[85] ALI, 'Restatement of the Law, Third, Foreign Relations', 1987 § 443.

[86] Stephens, 'Upsetting Checks and Balances', 193. See esp. *Banco Nacional de Cuba v. Sabbatino*, 376 US 398 (S Ct 1964): 'the greater the degree of codification or consensus concerning a particular area of international law, the more appropriate it is for the judiciary to render decisions regarding it', 428. See also *WS Kilpatrick v. Environmental Tectronics Corp.*, 493 US 400 (1990): 'Act of state issues only arise when a court must decide – that is, the outcome of the case turns upon – the effect of *official action* by a foreign sovereign', 46 (emphasis added).

[87] *Kadic v. Karadzic*, 70 F 3d 232 (2d Cir. 1995): 'We think it would be a rare case in which the act of state doctrine precluded suit under [ATCA]', 250. For consideration of the application of the doctrine of act of state to ATCA cases see *Doe I v. Unocal*, 395 F 3d 932 (9th Cir. 2002), 958–60; *Sarei v. Rio Tinto*, 221 F Supp 2d 1116 (CD Cal 2002), 1189; *Presbyterian Church of Sudan v. Talisman Energy*, 244 F Supp 2d 289 (SDNY 2003), 345. See further Joseph, *Transnational Human Rights Litigation*, pp. 40–4.

[88] F Supp 2d 1116 (CD Cal 2002), 1192.

[89] For criticism of this decision see Joseph, *Transnational Human Rights Litigation*, p. 41. See also Stephens, 'Upsetting Checks and Balances', 192–3.

[90] Stephens, ibid., 193. For guidance on how to recognise a 'political question', see the US Supreme Court decision in *Baker v. Carr*, 369 US 186 (S Ct 1962), 217.

[91] *Iwanowa v. Ford Motor Co.*, 67 F Supp 2d 248 (DNJ 1999).

[92] Stephens, 'Upsetting Checks and Balances', 194.

rights violations complained of have already been documented and condemned by the US executive branch.[93] Even so, the political question doctrine has provided a basis for at least one decision to dismiss an ATCA-based claim. In *Sarei v. Rio Tinto*,[94] the court was moved by a State Department brief to dismiss the claim, in part because of the potential for 'embarrassment' resulting from inconsistencies between the judiciary and the executive branch on the questions raised in the proceedings.

A third potential issue arises from the international law doctrine of 'sovereign immunity' under which state entities are immune from the jurisdiction of other states, at least as far as their governmental acts are concerned. The US position is regulated by the Foreign Sovereign Immunities Act of 1976.[95] Under this Act, foreign governments and their 'agencies and instrumentalities' will generally be immune from the jurisdiction of the US courts. This means that, in cases involving joint ventures between companies and state entities, it may only be possible to proceed against the company. In *Doe v. Unocal*, for instance, the District Court held (and the Court of Appeals for the Ninth Circuit confirmed) that the Burmese military and the state Oil and Gas Enterprise could not be made subject to ATCA-based claims. The plaintiffs had argued that exceptions under the Foreign Sovereign Immunities Act applied to this case as the two state agencies were involved in 'commercial activities' outside the ambit of the Act.[96] However, the Ninth Circuit concluded that the claims did not come within the precise wording of the exceptions, as the claims neither related to acts done in the USA nor did they create a 'direct effect' within the USA.[97]

A fourth ground on which a court may be able to dismiss a claim under ATCA is that of 'international comity'. This was one of the grounds on which the US courts dismissed three claims against Texaco.[98] In these cases, the courts applied a 'balancing' test, weighing up the various competing policy interests in the subject matter of the claims, before

---

[93] Ibid., esp. 196–200. See also *Doe v. Exxonmobil*, Civ No. 01–1357 (LFO), 'Plaintiffs' Memorandum of Points and Authorities in Opposition to the Defendants' Motion to Dismiss', 4 December 2001, copy available from http://wwwlaborrights.org, pp. 35–9.

[94] 221 F Supp 2d 1116 (CD Cal 2002). For criticism of this decision see Joseph, *Transnational Human Rights Litigation*, p. 46; Stephens, 'Upsetting Checks and Balances'.

[95] 28 USC §§ 1602.   [96] See § 1605(a)(2).

[97] *Doe I v. Unocal*, 395 F 3d 932 (9th Cir. 2002), 956–8.

[98] *Aguinda v. Texaco*, 945 F Supp 625 (SDNY 1996); *Jota v. Texaco* 157 F 3d 153 (2d ED La 1997); *Sequilhua v. Texaco*, 847 F Supp 61 (SD Tex 1994). Although note that, of these, only *Jota v. Texaco* was an ATCA-based claim.

concluding that an exercise of jurisdiction would not be appropriate.[99] 'Comity' was also given as a reason for the dismissal of racial discrimination and environmental claims in *Sarei* v. *Rio Tinto*.[100] However, it is not a justification for dismissal of claims relating to war crimes, crimes against humanity or genocide, all of which are regarded as 'particularly odious'.[101]

A further potential obstacle for plaintiffs in ATCA-based cases is, of course, the doctrine of forum non conveniens. The proposition that forum non conveniens provides grounds for dismissal in ATCA-related cases has been confirmed in a succession of cases.[102] But this was by no means a foregone conclusion. In *Jota* v. *Texaco*, the Court of Appeals asked the District Court to reconsider a decision to dismiss on these grounds, finding that the District Court had failed to take proper account of the plaintiff's arguments that such a dismissal would 'frustrate Congress's intent to provide a federal forum for aliens suing domestic entities for violations of the law of nations'.[103] The matter was remanded back to the District Court (although this did not make any difference to the outcome in that particular case).[104]

The test used for forum non conveniens is the same as that used in non-ATCA cases: the court must first establish whether there is an adequate alternative forum and then weigh up the competing private and public interests to determine which forum is most 'convenient'.[105] The doctrine of forum non conveniens has proved a real problem for plaintiffs in ATCA-based cases, and a good many cases against corporations have been dismissed for this reason.[106] However, in line with developments in relation to tort-based cases, there are indications that courts are now taking a more sympathetic approach towards plaintiffs on this issue. First of all, as noted in chapter 3, courts are adopting a more critical approach to the question of the 'adequacy' of the alternative forum for the purposes of the first part of the forum non conveniens test.[107] Second, courts seem to be more willing to recognise and give weight to the 'US policy interest in providing a forum for the adjudication of

---

[99] Note, however, that the Ecuadorian government had made clear its opposition to the jurisdiction of the US courts in those cases. See Ward, 'Governing Multinationals'.

[100] 221 F Supp 2d 1116 (CD Cal 2002), 1208.

[101] Joseph, *Transnational Human Rights Litigation*, p. 47.

[102] K. Boyd, 'The Inconvenience of Victims: Abolishing Forum Non Conveniens in US Human Rights Litigation' (1998) 39 *VJIL* 41.

[103] *Jota* v. *Texaco*, 157 F 3d 153 (2d Cir. 1998), 159.

[104] *Aguinda* v. *Texaco*, 945 F Supp 625 (SDNY 1996).   [105] See pp. 120–4 above.

[106] Stephens, 'Upsetting Checks and Balances', 180.   [107] See p. 123 above.

international human rights abuses'.[108] There is some uncertainty about how far this particular policy interest extends; in *Aguinda* v. *Texaco*, the Court of Appeals of the Second Circuit sought to limit it to cases involving torture and extra-judicial killing.[109] However, in *Presbyterian Church* v. *Talisman*, the court thought that US policy interests in providing a forum for human rights litigation would extend to all human rights violations with jus cogens status, i.e. genocide, war crimes, torture and slavery.[110]

So far, none of the ATCA cases launched against US multinationals has been heard on the merits. A large proportion of these cases[111] have already been dismissed, mostly on grounds of forum non conveniens[112] or failure to state a proper claim under ATCA.[113] A further case has been dismissed under the act of state doctrine.[114] Of the few cases that have survived motions to dismiss, the *Doe* v. *Unocal* claim progressed the furthest through the courts,[115] although as noted above, it was settled out of court before proceeding to trial on the substantive issues. Nevertheless, the Court of Appeals of the Ninth Circuit gave a firm steer as to the test of liability that it thought *ought* to apply in that case, as shall be discussed in the next section.

Theories of parent company liability

In what circumstances will a parent company of a multinational be liable for damage or harm arising out of the activities of its foreign affiliates?

---

[108] *Wiwa* v. *Royal Dutch Petroleum Co.*, 226 F 3d 88 (2d Cir. 2000), 103–7. See also *Bowoto* v. *Chevron*, Case no. C 99–2506, unreported decision of Legge J (ND Cal, 16 June 2000). See p. 124 above, n. 92.

[109] 142 F Supp 2d 534 (SDNY 2001), 554.

[110] *Presbyterian Church* v. *Talisman*, 244 F Supp 2d 289 (SDNY 2003), 340. See further Joseph, *Transnational Human Rights Litigation*, p. 94.

[111] By spring 2004, twenty-three out of a total of thirty-eight cases against corporations had been dismissed. Stephens, 'Upsetting Checks and Balances', 179.

[112] E.g. *Aguinda* v. *Texaco*, 303 F 3d 470 (2d 2002); *Flores* v. *Southern Peru Copper*, 343 F 3d 140 (2d Cir. 2003).

[113] E.g. *Beanal* v. *Freeport-McMoRan*, 969 F Supp 362 (ED La 1997); *Aguinda* v. *Texaco*, 142 F Supp 2d 534 (SDNY 2001) (re. environmental claims); *Flores* v. *Southern Peru Copper*, 343 F 3d 140 (2d Cir. 2003).

[114] *Sarei* v. *Rio Tinto*, 221 F Supp 2d 1116 (CD Cal 2002). See also *Roe* v. *Unocal*, 70 F Supp 2d 1073 (CD Cal 1999) and *National Coalition Government of the Union of Myanmar* v. *Unocal*, 176 FRD 329 (CD Cal 1997) in which the act of state doctrine was also used to dismiss claims although, as Joseph points out, in neither case were the relevant claims capable of activating ATCA. Joseph, *Transnational Human Rights Litigation*, p. 43.

[115] At the time of writing, both the *Presbyterian Church* v. *Talisman* and *Bowoto* v. *Chevron* cases were still at the discovery stages and no trial date had been set. Parties in *Wiwa* v. *Royal Dutch Petroleum Limited* were still awaiting the outcome of various pre-trial actions and discovery-related disputes; again, no trial date had been set.

In law, as noted above, a parent and its subsidiaries are separate legal persons, which means that a parent will not be liable for the acts of a subsidiary merely by virtue of its equity interest. But the doctrine of separate corporate personality does not act as a general exclusion of liability. On the contrary, there are various legal theories on which a tort-based case against a parent company might conceivably be built. These can be grouped under the headings of 'primary' liability (the liability of a party for the consequences of its own conduct or activities), 'vicarious' liability (the liability of a party for the conduct of those deemed to have been acting on its behalf), 'secondary' liability (the liability of a party for its participation in, or a contribution towards, a tort committed by another) and finally (and most controversially), 'enterprise' liability (the liability of a party for the activities of another on the basis that together they are involved in a single commercial enterprise).

'Primary' liability

Under English law, the parent company may be a 'primary tortfeasor'[116] on the basis that it owed a 'duty of care' to those affected by the activities of its foreign affiliate and that duty of care was breached, resulting in harm. This is straightforward enough, although in practice the legal position is complicated by the role of the foreign affiliate in the circumstances leading up to the claim. First, given that the parent and subsidiary are separate companies, was the parent company sufficiently involved in the day-to-day management of the subsidiary to justify the imposition of liability? To what extent does a parent company have duties of ongoing supervision? And is there a point at which the subsidiary's own negligence is such that the parent can no longer be said to have 'caused' the harm?

Establishing a duty of care is the first difficulty, but, depending on the facts, there are two lines of argument a plaintiff could potentially use, one focusing on the role of the parent company as the 'creator' or 'orchestrator' of hazardous operations carried on by its subsidiaries, the other focusing on the overall duty of a parent company to control its subsidiaries effectively. However, neither of these has been properly tested in court in the context of an FDL claim. There would, in principle, be a duty of care between the parent company of a multinational and those affected by the activities of its affiliates where the possibility of injury or harm is (or ought to have been) foreseeable by the parent company

---

[116] I.e. the party primarily responsible for a tort.

and the plaintiffs are sufficiently 'proximate' to the parent company to justify the imposition of liability.[117] This ought to be the case where the parent company is familiar with the activities of the affiliate and the health and environmental risks they may pose *and* that parent exercises a degree of control over the activities of the affiliate sufficient to influence the way in which (and the standards to which) those activities are carried out. If the harm was foreseeable, the fact that the foreign affiliate may have played a more direct role in the circumstances leading to the harm than the parent company itself would not, of itself, prevent a duty of care from arising. In the Western Australian case of *Barrow and Heys* v. *CSR Ltd*,[118] the parent company of a subsidiary was held to have owed a duty of care to two employees of that subsidiary, on the basis of its managerial control over mining operations carried on by the subsidiary, its control over the subsidiary's budget, and (crucially) the fact that employees of the parent were involved in the supervision of operations at the mine.[119] Similarly, in the case of *CSR Ltd* v. *Wren*,[120] the New South Wales Court of Appeal held that a parent company owed a duty of care to an employee of a subsidiary on the basis that the asbestos-related injuries suffered by the claimant were foreseeable, and that the parent company was in a sufficiently proximate relationship to the employee to make the imposition of a duty of care reasonable in the circumstances. In that case, 'proximity' was based on the fact that the management staff in charge of the subsidiary's activities were actually employees of the parent and, thus, had 'assumed responsibility' for the working conditions of the subsidiary.[121] Another Australian case in which a parent company was held to owe a duty of care to a subsidiary was *CSR Ltd* v. *Young*, in that case because the parent had been appointed the subsidiary's managing agent 'with full and absolute authority to do all things necessary for the proper management and control of the business and undertaking of the subsidiary'.[122] It is important

---

[117] *Donoghue* v. *Stevenson* [1932] AC 562. 'Proximity . . . [should] . . . not be confined to mere physical proximity but be used . . . to extend to such close and direct relations that the act complained of directly affects a person', 581. It has been suggested, in light of *Williams* v. *Natural Life Health Foods* [1998] 1 WLR 830 (HL), that the appropriate test to use is whether the parent had 'assumed responsibility' for the subsidiary's operations. However, this actually adds little, if anything, to the traditional test. See *Phelps* v. *Hillingdon LBC* [2000] 3 WLR 776, 791.

[118] Unreported, Supreme Court of WA, 4 August 1988, Library No. 7231.

[119] See further R. Carroll, 'Corporate Parents and Tort Liability' in M. Gillooly (ed), *The Law Relating to Corporate Groups* (Sydney: Federation Press, 1993).

[120] (1997) 44 NSWLR 463; [1998] Aust Tort Rep 81–461.   [121] Ibid., p. 486.

[122] [1998] Aust Tort Rep 81–468, 64952.

to note, however, that the duty of care found to exist in each of these three cases rested on particular (and perhaps rather unusual) situations. In other words, these cases do not support the idea that parent companies owe a general duty of care to employees of foreign subsidiaries. Nevertheless a duty of care may be found in cases where there is an unusually high degree of involvement by a parent in its subsidiaries' activities.[123]

This was a key aspect of the plaintiffs' case against Cape plc in *Lubbe v. Cape plc*,[124] i.e.

Whether a parent company which is proved to exercise *de facto* control over the operations of a (foreign) subsidiary and which knows, through its directors, that those operations involve risks to the health of workers employed by the subsidiary and/or persons in the vicinity of the factory or other business premises owes a duty of care to those workers and/or other persons in relation to the control which it exercises over and the advice which it gives to the subsidiary.[125]

It is impossible to say for sure how the issue of liability would have been determined, had the case proceeded to trial. It is likely, though, that the judges would have been extremely careful not to create any precedent that might look like 'piercing the corporate veil'. If Cape plc had been found liable, this would have been on the basis that the particular facts of the case supported Cape plc's *primary* liability.

Claims against a parent company may also be based on its role in the design, testing and manufacture of substances, such as pharmaceuticals and pesticides.[126] Analogising from this, it is possible, too, that a creator

---

[123] See further *Bowoto v. Chevron*, 312 F Supp 2d 1229 (ND Cal 2004).

[124] *Lubbe v. Cape plc* [2000] 1 WLR 1545; [2000] 4 All ER 268 (HL) 277.

[125] *Lubbe v. Cape plc* [2000] 1 Lloyds Law Reports 139 (Court of Appeal), 146.

[126] For a US statement on the circumstances in which a parent company may be liable based on its role in the research and development (R & D) of a product see ALI, 'Restatement of the Law, Second, Torts', 1965, § 354A: 'One who undertakes, gratuitously or for consideration, to render services to another which he should recognize as necessary for the protection of a third person or his things, is subject to liability to the third person for physical harm resulting from his failure to exercise reasonable care to protect his undertaking, if (a) his failure to exercise reasonable care increases the risk of such harm, or (b) he has undertaken to perform a duty owed by the other to the third person, or (c) the harm is suffered because of reliance of the other or the third person upon the undertaking.' See also *The Amoco Cadiz* [1984] 2 Lloyds Rep. 304, 338, in which the parent company's role in the design of the vessel the *Amoco Cadiz* is given as one of the reasons why the parent company should be liable for the damage resulting from the grounding of the tanker, along with its subsidiaries.

of a hazardous technology or 'process' could owe a duty of care to workers or communities that might come into contact with it, regardless of the level of control exercised over the way that technology is subsequently applied. In relation to workplace hazards, therefore, a duty of care might extend not only to employees of subsidiaries of a parent company, but to employees of its contractors, franchisees and licensees as well. Meeran writes:

> there seems no logical reason why, in principle, damage arising from the design and transfer of hazardous technology overseas should be regarded as any less foreseeable than damage from defective products. Consequently, I would suggest that 'process' liability should be regarded as analogous to 'product' liability and a comparable duty of care should be recognised.[127]

In *Re Bhopal*[128] the plaintiffs based their claim against the parent company, UCC, partly on UCC's role in the design and construction of the Indian plant and subsequent safety monitoring. However, these arguments, effectively an attempt to mount a case for 'process liability', were never properly tested in a US trial.

A third possible argument can be made in favour of a duty of care owed by parent companies – this time based on the proposition that, in certain, limited cases, it is entirely appropriate for one party to be held liable for the acts of another. It is well established that there is no general obligation to prevent a third party from causing damage or injury. But the position may be different in cases where there is a 'special relationship' between the defendant and the third party, under which the third party could (and should) have been prevented or restrained by the defendant from causing the harm.[129] The US Second Restatement of the Law of Torts states that liability for the acts of third parties may potentially arise where either '(a) a special relation exists between the actor and the third person which imposes a duty upon the actor to control the third person's conduct, or (b) a special relation exists between the actor and the other [i.e. the plaintiff] which gives the other a right to protection'.[130] This clearly is of relevance to relationships between members of multinational groups. The point was considered in a 2002 decision by Chaney J in *Doe* v.

---

[127] R. Meeran, '"Process Liability" of Multinationals: Overcoming the Forum Hurdle' [1995] *JPIL* 170, p. 170.

[128] 634 F Supp 842 (SDNY 1986).   [129] *Home Office* v. *Dorset Yacht Club* [1970] AC 1004.

[130] See n. 126 above, § 315. See further D. Howarth, 'My Brother's Keeper? Liability for Acts of Third Parties' (1994) 14 *Legal Studies* 88.

Unocal[131] (although not, at that point in time, in relation to the parent's control over its subsidiaries, but the Unocal group's alleged control over a third party). In that case, the judge decided that as Unocal did not 'control' the Burmese military[132] there was no 'special relationship' between Unocal and the Burmese military (and therefore Unocal owed no general duty to protect the plaintiffs from them). But this was not the end of the matter. There would still exist a legal duty 'not to place another person in a situation in which the other person is exposed to an unreasonable risk of harm through the reasonably foreseeable conduct . . . of a third person'.[133] As Chaney J put it, 'Where the "defendant has made plaintiffs' position worse and has created a foreseeable risk of harm from the third person" such conduct "which contributes to, increases or changes the risk of harm that would otherwise existed" [*sic*] creates a duty to prevent foreseeable harm.'[134] However, in the end, Chaney J held that, although the plaintiffs' case raised a possibility that Unocal's investment in Burma may have 'perpetuated the risk', this would not satisfy the legal requirements for a duty of care.

Assuming that a duty of care can be established – and this is by no means straightforward – the second major element of a plaintiff's case against the parent company of a multinational is that the parent company's conduct has fallen short of legal standards. The proper standard of care is determined in accordance with a 'reasonableness' test; in this context, what precautions would a reasonable parent company have taken in the circumstances to guard against the risk of damage or injury posed by its subsidiary's operations? In *Lubbe* v. *Cape plc*, 'the negligence alleged . . . consists of instructions and advice which [the parent company] gave, or failed to give, to their South African employees and to the South African subsidiaries who operated the mines and mills, in the course of carrying out business internationally there and elsewhere . . .'[135] In identifying the substantive obligations of the parent company, the courts will take account of the general state of knowledge about the risks posed by the particular industry, processes or technology,

---

[131] 'Ruling on the Defendants' Motion for Summary Judgment, or in the alternative, Summary Adjudication on Each of the Plaintiffs' Tort Claims', Decision of the Superior Court of California, County of Los Angeles, 7 June 2002, unreported, copy available from http://www.earthrights.org/unocal/index/shtml, p. 12.

[132] The plaintiffs argued that the Burmese military was effectively a contractor to the project. See *Doe I* v. *Unocal*, 395 F 3d 932 (9th Cir. 2002), 938.

[133] Chaney J, 'Ruling on Defendants' Motion, 7 June 2002', n. 131 above, p. 12.

[134] Ibid., pp. 12–13.   [135] [2000] 1 Lloyd's Rep 139, 146.

and how to minimise them. To this end, home state regulatory requirements, codes of conduct, industry 'best practice', safety cases and risk
control manuals are likely to be important sources of evidence.

The third element of a tort-based case against a parent company of a
multinational is causation. The plaintiff would have to prove that 'but
for' the parent company's negligence, the harm complained of would not
have occurred. Crucially, the court would have to be satisfied that the
chain of causation was not broken by any independent conduct on the
part of the affiliate.[136] It is usual, therefore, for defendants in FDL cases
to emphasise the autonomy of the foreign subsidiary, as this passage
from Re Bhopal illustrates:

On the liability question Union Carbide asserts that the Bhopal plant was managed and operated entirely by Indian nationals who were employed by UCIL [the
Indian subsidiary] . . . Defendant asserts that the Bhopal plant is part of UCIL's
Agricultural Products Division, which has been a separate division of UCIL for
at least 15 years and that the plant had 'limited contact' with UCIL's Bombay
headquarters and almost no contact with the United States.[137]

In the UK case of Connelly v. RTZ,[138] the causal relationship between the
parent company and the injuries suffered by Mr Connelly was based on
the following allegations:

Key strategic technical and policy decisions relating to Rossing [i.e. the uranium
mine at which the claimant was employed] were taken by the English-based
RTP [i.e. Rio Tinto plc] companies. For example, in order to meet contractual
deadlines for the supply of uranium internationally by RTP companies, directors
of their English companies were directly responsible on the ground, for substantially
increasing the output of uranium – and the consequent dust levels – without
ensuring that effective precautions were taken to protect workers against the
hazards of uranium dust exposure. (emphasis added)[139]

In many cases, 'causation' will be based on the same facts used to establish a duty of care, e.g. the level of knowledge within the parent company
about the risks associated with the subsidiary's activities ('foreseeability') and the level of control actually exercised by the parent over day-
to-day operations. However, even if the foreign affiliate can be regarded
as truly 'independent' of the parent company, the parent company may
not escape liability for damage that was foreseeable if its own negligence

---

[136] See Smith v. Littlewoods [1987] AC 241, 259. See further Howarth, 'My Brother's Keeper?'
[137] Re Bhopal, 634 F Supp 842 (SDNY 1986), 853.   [138] [1998] AC 854.
[139] Meeran, 'The Unveiling of Transnational Corporations', pp. 166–7.

'played a part in causing the damage'.[140] In other words, where harm resulting from acts of third parties was foreseeable, and the parent company's conduct has increased the likelihood of that harm occurring, it is arguable that the actions of the foreign affiliate should not be regarded as an 'intervening act' (novus actus).[141] This could conceivably be a basis for liability in relation to a negligently designed process (see comments on 'process liability' above), which was then utilised by a subsidiary in accordance with the parent's instructions. However, if it could be shown that the subsidiary was itself negligent, there is still a risk that this could break the chain of causation.

In summary, to succeed in a 'primary liability' claim against a parent company for damage arising from the activities of its foreign affiliates, it seems that the foreign plaintiffs would need to be able to show, at a minimum, (a) that the parent had detailed knowledge of the health and environmental risks posed by the relevant activities, processes or technology; (b) that the parent had had particularly close involvement in the day-to-day operations of the foreign affiliate; (c) that the parent failed to exercise the level of due diligence that would have been appropriate given all the circumstances; and (d) those failures were a direct cause of the injury or damage, even if they were not the only cause.

The possibility that the parent could be liable for the consequences of the activities of its affiliates as a *primary* tortfeasor gives rise to an important policy issue. Will an increase in FDL claims against parent companies of multinationals cause parent companies generally to take greater responsibility for the CSR standards of their foreign subsidiaries, in line with commitments given in their CSR reports?[142] Or will parent companies conclude that the best way to minimise the legal risks will be to adopt a 'hands-off' approach? Reacting to *Re Bhopal*, it has been suggested that parent companies can help to reduce their legal liabilities by delegating 'as much autonomy as possible

---

[140] Howarth, 'My Brother's Keeper?', 94–6. See also 'Second Restatement on the Law of Torts', n. 126 above, § 354A. This is not, however, to be confused with 'secondary' liability, under which a party may be liable for the torts committed by a third party on the basis that it *knowingly* contributed to the commission of a tort by the primary wrongdoer. See further pp. 225–8 below.

[141] See also 'Second Restatement on the Law of Torts', n. 126 above: 'An act or omission may be negligent if the actor realizes or should realize that it involves an unreasonable risk of harm to another through the negligent or reckless conduct of the other or a third person,' § 302A.

[142] Zerk, 'Legal Aspects of Corporate Responsibility Reporting'.

concerning operational matters'[143] to their foreign affiliates. Cassels adds: 'the advice to multinationals, then, is to maintain strategic control from afar, but to leave operations in the hands of local managers and safety in the hands of the host government. Control can thus be maintained, and responsibility avoided. Arguably, this is precisely what happened in Bhopal.'[144]

But would parent companies really allow the risk of FDL claims to dictate their global CSR strategies to this extent? Other considerations – long-term profitability, commercial and governmental relations, corporate reputation ('licence to operate') and insurance issues – are likely to feature at least as prominently in the development of global policies on CSR, if not more so. Whatever the legal pros and cons, attempts by parent companies to distance themselves from dangerous or controversial activities of subsidiaries are no longer politically or socially acceptable.

Vicarious liability

Could a parent company be held vicariously liable for the negligence of a foreign affiliate on the basis that the affiliate was an 'agent' of the parent company? Under English law, the subsidiary will be regarded as acting as an 'agent' of the parent company only in very limited circumstances. Essentially, the control relationship would have to be so close that the subsidiary could not really be regarded as carrying on its own business. The issue was considered in *Adams* v. *Cape Industries*,[145] in which the Court of Appeal found that, while the subsidiaries' activities were no doubt of assistance to the multinational group as a whole, they were carried out by the subsidiaries as their own businesses on their own account. Crucially, they did not have the authority to bind any other members of the group to any contractual obligation, nor was there any evidence that any such transaction was entered into.[146]

A much more common source of vicarious liability for companies derives from the company's role as an employer. There are good policy reasons why a company should be vicariously liable for the acts of employees conducted in the course of their employment. One justification is that, as the employer has the ability to control how its employees carry out their work, it ought to bear the consequences of its

[143] Seward, 'After Bhopal', 706.   [144] Cassels, *The Uncertain Promise of Law*, p. 145.
[145] [1990] Ch 433.   [146] Ibid., 545–9.

employees' negligence. Another is that the employee is engaged in an economic enterprise established by the employer, and therefore there is a causal relationship between the employer and any harm brought about by the employee in the course of his employment. A further justification is the 'deep pocket' argument:

the employer is richer so he should pay; which also suits the victim since the employer is invariably in a better position to pay than his employee. Economic and moral considerations also seem to be satisfied by those who advocate that the person who derives a benefit from the activity of another should also bear the risk of damage inflicted by those acts. Yet another economic variant is that the employer is in a better position to spread the loss through insurance or the price of his products.[147]

These comments could also be applied to other contexts, including the 'control' relationships that exist within a multinational group. Nevertheless, the English courts remain generally unconvinced by the policy justifications in favour of more flexible use of vicarious liability concepts, preferring to limit their use to narrowly defined 'agency' situations. The idea that parent companies can be 'vicariously' liable for the acts of their foreign subsidiaries is better established in US jurisprudence and has been raised in several ATCA-based cases. In *Doe v. Unocal*, Chaney J was prepared to allow the matter to go to trial on the basis of the possible vicarious liability of the Unocal parent. Having previously discounted the idea that Unocal's local subsidiary in Burma was the 'alter ego' of its US parent, the defendants filed a motion to dismiss on the basis that the court's decision to disallow the alter ego arguments would dispose of the agency arguments as well. Chaney J disagreed, holding that '[t]o establish liability under an agency or enterprise theory . . . plaintiffs must prove, among other things, only a lesser degree of control'.[148] Similarly, in a 2004 ruling in *Bowoto v. Chevron*,[149] although the judge was not satisfied that Chevron's Nigerian subsidiary was the 'alter ego' of its parent, she thought the US parent could still be liable for its foreign subsidiary's acts on the basis of an agency relationship. According to Illston

---

[147] B. Markesinis and S. Deakin, *Tort Law*, 4th edition (Oxford: Clarendon Press, 1999), p. 532.

[148] 'Ruling on the Defendants' Motion for Judgment', Decision of the Superior Court of California, County of Los Angeles, 14 September 2004, unreported, copy available from http://www.earthrights.org/unocal/index/shtml, p. 7. Although note that the issue of Unocal's vicarious liability was not finally determined as the matter settled out of court.

[149] 312 F Supp 2d 1229 (ND Cal 2004).

J, the test for an agency relationship which would give rise to liability under ATCA was, first, a 'close relationship or domination between the parent and subsidiary' and, second, 'a finding that the injury allegedly inflicted by the subsidiary . . . was within the subsidiary's authority as agent'.[150] Taking particular account of

(1) the degree and content of communications between CNL [the Nigerian subsidiary] and defendants, particularly including the communications during the incidents at issue; (2) the degree to which defendants set or participated in setting policy, particularly security policy, for CNL; (3) the officers and directors which CNL had in common; (4) the reliance on CNL for revenue production and acknowledgment of the importance of CNL and other international operations to the overall success of defendants' operations; and (5) the extent to which CNL, if acting as defendants' agent, was acting within the scope of its authority during the events at issue. . .[151]

the judge concluded that a reasonable juror could find that the relationship was sufficiently close to constitute an agency, with the result that the US parent could potentially be held liable under ATCA for the behaviour of its subsidiaries. Illston J also held that, even if the plaintiffs failed to establish that an agency existed at the time of the incidents complained of, they might still be entitled to proceed against Chevron on the basis that Chevron had subsequently 'ratified' its subsidiary's acts. Ratification involves 'knowing acceptance after the fact by the principal of an agent's actions', but in some cases evidence of a cover-up by the parent of its subsidiary's 'misdeeds' may be sufficient.[152] While neither the fact of this alleged agency nor its consequences has been established in a trial on the merits, judicial pronouncements on corporate liability under ATCA so far suggest a rather more flexible approach to the question of 'agency' than that used by the English courts.

'Secondary' liability

Could a parent company be liable for the negligence of a foreign affiliate on the grounds that it has 'aided and abetted' the commission of a tort? This was the basis of the allegations made by the plaintiffs in *Dagi v. BHP*[153] although, as the matter was ultimately settled out of court, the 'secondary' liability of the defendant, BHP, was not adjudicated.

---

[150] Ibid., 1239.   [151] Ibid., 1243.   [152] Ibid., 1247.
[153] [1997] 1 VR 428. See further Seck, 'Environmental Harm', 172.

English law recognises at least four possible bases of secondary liability for tort.[154] These are 'assistance' (i.e. supply of the means to commit the primary wrong), 'inducement' (i.e. the exercise of influence over the primary wrongdoer to commit the wrong), 'encouragement and authorisation' (which may include support and approval given after the primary wrong has been commenced) and 'conspiracy' (i.e. an agreement to commit the primary wrong, which is then committed pursuant to the agreement).

There are a number of important distinctions between 'primary' and 'secondary' liability for tort. First of all, and crucially for parent company liability, 'secondary' liability does not require proof of a duty of care on the part of the 'secondary' party (i.e. the parent company) towards the victim of the tort, or that the acts or omissions of the parent company were the primary cause of the tort. Instead, liability is based on a *knowing contribution* to the commission of a tort. Except in the case of 'assistance', a key determinant of secondary liability for tort is the amount of *control* enjoyed by the secondary party over the primary wrongdoer. Secondary liability on grounds of 'assistance', on the other hand, is based on the idea of a causal relationship between the assistance given by the secondary party and the tort itself.[155] However, in each case there is a requirement that the secondary party play an effective role in the commission of the tort. The 'intent' or 'knowledge' of a corporate entity for legal purposes is normally established by reference to the intent or state of knowledge of its directors and key officers. In English law, attribution of knowledge for the purposes of tort is similar to the attribution of criminal intent, that is, based on identification of the entity's 'directing mind and will'.[156]

Where a foreign affiliate is the primary 'tortfeasor', there are a number of ways in which the parent company could also be liable under theories of secondary liability. First, it might be argued that the parent company had knowingly assisted in the commission of the tort, for example by supplying the necessary technology and resources. However, as noted above, the plaintiff would need to be able to establish both that the

---

[154] D. Cooper, 'Secondary Liability for Civil Wrongs', PhD thesis, University of Cambridge (1995). Note the distinction between 'secondary' liability and 'vicarious' liability. As Cooper explains, vicarious liability arises by virtue of the relationship between the tortfeasor and the 'secondary' party, whereas 'secondary' liability arises because the secondary party 'has knowingly *participated* in the primary wrong', p. 3.

[155] Ibid., pp. 6–8.

[156] *Leonard's Carrying Company Ltd* v. *Asiatic Petroleum Company Ltd* [1915] AC 705; *Meridian Global Funds Management Asia Ltd* v. *Securities Commission* [1995] 3 All ER 918.

parent company knew of the affiliate's wrongful behaviour and that the tort would not have been committed but for the parent company's assistance.[157] In other words, the connection between the parent company and the wrongful acts of the subsidiary must be a real one.[158] Second, it might be argued that the parent company had induced, authorised or encouraged the commission of the tort by the foreign affiliate. This may be relevant in cases of social and environmental 'dumping', e.g. where foreign affiliates are established or utilised specifically to take advantage of lower health and safety or environmental standards.[159] While failing to prevent harm by a third party is not generally accepted as a basis for tortious liability in most common law jurisdictions,[160] it has been suggested that, where a secondary party has sufficient *control* over the activities of the primary wrongdoer, a failure to take steps to prevent the commission of the tort may be tantamount to 'authorisation'.[161] Finally, it might be argued that the parent company was party to a conspiracy, with its foreign affiliate, to commit a tort.[162] This would require demonstration by the plaintiffs of some agreement between the parent company and the affiliate reflecting a 'common purpose' to commit the wrong.[163]

These arguments are, however, largely untested in the courts in the context of FDL claims. There may well be strategic reasons for this; in many cases, primary liability and secondary liability will rest on the same or similar facts, but the danger that the defendant might successfully apply for a stay of the proceedings on grounds of forum non conveniens has meant that plaintiffs have tended to favour arguments that emphasise the responsibility of the parent company for the tort over that of the subsidiary.[164] However, the possibility of parent

---

[157] Cooper, 'Secondary Liability', p. 8.

[158] *Sanyo Corp.* v. *Universal City Studios*, 464 US 417 (1986).

[159] See, for example, Meeran's comments on the background to the 'Thor' cases at p. 204 above.

[160] But see pp. 219–20 above.   [161] Cooper, 'Secondary Liability', pp. 10–11.

[162] A company can be party to a conspiracy to commit a tort, see *Belmont Finance* v. *Williams Furniture (No. 2)* [1980] 1 All ER 393. 'Conspiracy' is the basis of a series of class actions commenced in the US courts against multinationals, most recently against several banks and companies by South African plaintiffs claiming damages for death and injury inflicted under the apartheid regime. See *In re South African Apartheid Litigation* 346 F Supp 2d 538 (SDNY 2004).

[163] Cooper, 'Secondary Liability', pp. 11–12.

[164] See Seck, 'Environmental Harm', 151–2. See also Blumberg, 'Asserting Human Rights', in which the author claims that US cases that concern negligence *in the USA* are less likely to be dismissed on grounds of forum non conveniens.

company liability for 'aiding and abetting' foreign human rights abuses was considered by the 2002 decision of the Court of Appeals of the Ninth Circuit in *Doe I v. Unocal*.[165] Reversing an earlier decision to dismiss the proceedings, the Ninth Circuit found that there were 'genuine issues of material fact whether Unocal's conduct met the actus reus and mens rea requirements for liability under ATCA for aiding and abetting forced labour'.[166] Importantly, the Ninth Circuit felt that the applicable law for determining liability should be *international* law, rather than US federal law.[167] After reviewing international criminal case law, the Ninth Circuit defined 'aiding and abetting' for their purposes as 'knowing practical assistance or encouragement which has a substantial effect on the perpetration of the crime'.[168] More recently, in a 2004 ruling in the ATCA-based case of *Bowoto* v. *Chevron*, the court held that, based on the facts pleaded in support of agency arguments,[169] the plaintiffs would also be entitled to proceed against Chevron on the basis that Chevron had 'aided and abetted' human rights violations committed by its subsidiaries in Nigeria.[170]

'Enterprise' liability

Occasionally, courts have been persuaded to 'lift the corporate veil' and disregard the legal separation between parent company and subsidiary. This may be done in cases of 'fraud', i.e. where the corporate form has been misused by its owners to avoid liability, or to defeat a third party's existing legal rights.[171] However, to structure a group of companies with a view to minimising legal liability is not of itself regarded as a misuse of the corporate form. On the contrary, such a right is 'inherent in our [i.e. English] corporate law'.[172]

While limited liability is well protected in law, it is not uncontroversial. Bakan writes:

The corporation's unique structure is largely to blame for the fact that illegalities are endemic in the corporate world. By design, the corporate form generally protects the human beings who own and run corporations from legal liability, leaving the corporation, a 'person' with psychopathic contempt for legal constraints, the main target of criminal prosecution. Shareholders cannot be held

---

[165] 395 F 3d 932 (9th Cir. 2002).
[166] Ibid., 953. Note that references to 'Unocal' in the judgment are collective references to Unocal Corporation *and* its wholly owned subsidiary Union Oil Company of California (both US companies), 937.
[167] Ibid., 948–53.   [168] Ibid., 951.   [169] See pp. 224–5 above.
[170] 312 F Supp 2d 1229 (ND Cal 2004), 1247–8.
[171] *Jones v. Lipman* [1962] 1 All ER 442; *Gilford Motor Co.* v. *Horne* [1933] Ch 935.
[172] *Adams v. Cape Industries* [1990] Ch 433, 544.

liable for the crimes committed by corporations because of limited liability, the sole purpose of which is to shield them from legal responsibility for the corporation's actions. Directors are traditionally protected by the fact that they have no direct involvement with decisions that may lead to a corporation's committing a crime. Executives are protected by the law's unwillingness to find them liable for their companies' illegal actions unless they can be proven to have been 'directing minds' behind those actions. Such proof is difficult if not impossible to produce in most cases, because corporate decisions normally result from numerous and diffuse individuals' inputs, and because courts tend to attribute conduct to the corporate 'person' rather than the actual people who run the corporations.[173]

In academic writing too, there has been extensive criticism of the twin principles of 'limited liability' and 'separate corporate personality', mainly for the injustice these can inflict on victims of tort (the so-called 'involuntary creditors').[174] Although there may be a solid claim for negligence against a subsidiary, the subsidiary may not be sufficiently capitalised to allow full recovery, especially in the case of a mass catastrophe, leaving the victims under-compensated and the parent company largely immune. While the parent company could theoretically also be liable in its own right,[175] tracing and proving a chain of responsibility leading back to the parent can be extremely difficult for an outsider, no matter how generous the discovery rules. In the meantime, a claimant faces the distinct possibility, in most common law jurisdictions, that any lawsuit brought in the parent company's home state will be dismissed on grounds of forum non conveniens. For both economic and moral reasons, it is argued, courts ought to be much bolder about 'piercing the corporate veil' and holding the parent company responsible in tort-based cases.[176]

Under 'enterprise' liability, parent and subsidiary would be treated as one enterprise instead of two separate companies, and there would be no question of the foreign subsidiary 'breaking the chain of causation'. What this amounts to, in practical terms, is that a parent company would be held strictly liable for the activities of a foreign subsidiary by virtue of the 'control relationship' that exists between parent and

---

[173] Bakan, *The Corporation*, p. 79.

[174] See H. Hansmann and R. Kraakman, 'Towards Unlimited Shareholder Liability for Corporate Torts' (1991) 100 *Yale LJ* 1879; B. Pettet, 'Limited Liability – A Principle for the 21st Century?' (1995) 48 *Current Legal Problems* 125; F. Easterbrook and D. Fischel, 'Limited Liability and the Corporation' (1985) 52 *UCLR* 89; P. Halpern, M. Trebilcock and S. Turnbull, 'An Economic Analysis of Limited Liability in Corporation Law' (1980) 30 *UTLJ* 117; Blumberg, 'Limited Liability'.

[175] See pp. 216–23 above.

[176] See U. Baxi and T. Paul, *Mass Disasters and Multinational Liability: the Bhopal Case* (Bombay: NM Tripathi, 1986).

subsidiary. But when would an 'enterprise' approach to corporate groups be justified? In *DHN Ltd* v. *Tower Hamlets LBC*,[177] Lord Denning had this to say:

> We all know that in many respects a group of companies are treated together for the purpose of general accounts, balance sheet and profit and loss account. They are treated as one concern. Professor Gower . . . says: 'there is evidence of a general tendency to ignore the separate legal entities of various companies within a group, and to look instead at the economic entity of the whole group.' This is especially the case when a parent company owns all the shares of the subsidiaries – so much so that it can control every movement of the subsidiaries. These subsidiaries are bound hand and foot to the parent company and must do what the parent company says . . . So here. . . [the members of the group] should not be treated separately so as to be defeated on a technical point . . . These three companies should, for present purposes, be treated as one . . .[178]

In *Adams* v. *Cape Industries*, however, the judges of the Court of Appeal were careful to restrict Lord Denning's comments in *DHN Ltd* to their statutory context.[179] A key issue in the *Adams* case was whether a judgment secured in a Texan court against South African subsidiaries of a UK-based multinational could be enforced against the UK parent. The court held that in that case they did not have 'discretion to reject the distinction between members of the group as a technical point'.[180] The court then went on to quote with approval the following comments of Goff LJ in *Bank of Tokyo* v. *Karoon*: '[Counsel] suggested beguilingly that it would be technical for us to distinguish between parent and subsidiary company in this context; economically, he said, they were one. But we are concerned not with economics but with law. The distinction between the two is, in law, fundamental and cannot here be bridged.'[181]

But while 'enterprise theory' appears to be losing ground in English law,[182] the ECJ has been willing to accept the idea of the 'single economic unit' as a basis on which liability can be imposed on foreign (i.e. non-EC) companies under EU competition law. In competition law, 'groups' of companies have been held to form one 'undertaking' for the purposes of

---

[177] [1976] 1 WLR 852.   [178] Ibid., 860.
[179] *Adams* v. *Cape Industries* [1990] Ch 433, 536.   [180] Ibid., p. 538.
[181] [1987] AC 45, 64. For a similar statement from an Australian court see *Briggs* v. *James Hardie & Co. Pty Ltd* (1989) 16 NSWLR 549: 'The law pays scant regard to the commercial reality that every holding company has the potential and, more often than not, in fact, does, exercise complete control over the subsidiary', 557.
[182] Dine, *Corporate Groups*, p. 46.

establishing liability under European anti-trust provisions[183] 'even if in law that economic unit consists of several persons, natural or legal'.[184] Even so, the use of 'enterprise' concepts in this particular regulatory context does not necessarily translate to other areas of law.

'Enterprise' theories have been raised in litigation in the USA, both as grounds for establishing jurisdiction over a foreign company and as grounds for holding a parent company liable for the actions of foreign subsidiaries. In *Doe* v. *Unocal*, the plaintiffs argued that the District Court was entitled to take jurisdiction in an ATCA-based claim against Total, a French company, on the basis that its Californian subsidiaries were effectively agents of their French parent, or, alternatively, its alter ego. In other words, notwithstanding that Total was a foreign company, it was nevertheless 'present' in the jurisdiction by virtue of the presence of its subsidiaries.[185] Under Californian law, the court could disregard the legal barriers between parent and subsidiary if '(1) there is such unity of interest and ownership that the separate personalities no longer exist and (2) failure to disregard [the separate personalities] would result in fraud or injustice'.[186] However, while the French parent was an 'active parent corporation involved directly in decision-making about its subsidiaries holdings', this was not sufficient to found jurisdiction based on the alter ego doctrine,[187] and proceedings against the French company were dismissed. The alter ego doctrine would be discussed again, this time in the context of tort-based claims against the Unocal parents under Californian state law for the activities of their Burmese subsidiaries.[188] Applying the criteria laid down in *Associated Vendors, Inc.* v. *Oakland Meat Co.*,[189] Chaney J made a number of observations about corporate arrangements within the Unocal group, some of which pointed in the direction of the alter ego doctrine, and some of which did not, i.e.

(1) [t]here was some commingling of funds among defendants and their subsidiaries. . . (2) the subsidiaries controlled their own assets . . . (3) corporate formalities were observed . . . (4) four out of five subsidiaries were wholly owned by

---

[183] Treaty Establishing the European Community (as amended), consolidated version published at OJ 2002 No. C325/33, 24 December 2002, Article 82.

[184] Case 170/83, *Hydrotherm Geratebau* v. *Andreoli* [1984] ECR 2999, 3016.

[185] See pp. 118–19 above.   [186] *Doe* v. *Unocal*, 248 F 3d 915 (9th Cir. 2001), 926.

[187] Ibid., at 927, noting that Total had observed 'all of the formalities necessary to maintain corporate separateness'.

[188] Preliminary arguments were made in the context of a motion to dismiss by the defendants for want of a cause of action. See 'Ruling on the Defendants' Motion for Judgment', 7 June 2002, n. 131 above.

[189] 210 Cal. App 2d 825 (1962), 838–40.

their parents . . . (5) the parents did not inappropriately control the subsidiaries' daily operations . . . (6) the corporations shared officers, directors, employees and offices . . . (7) the subsidiaries were adequately capitalized . . . (8) none of the subsidiaries was a shell . . . (9) ownership was not concealed . . . (10) defendants maintained appropriate arm's-length relationships with the subsidiaries . . . (11) there was no wrongful diversion of assets . . .and (12) the corporations were not created to transfer existing liability.[190]

After finding also that 'the plaintiffs had not proven that disregarding the corporate entities at issue would sanction a fraud or promote an injustice',[191] the court held that the plaintiffs would be unable to rely on the alter ego doctrine to establish the liability of the Unocal parents in this case (although it would still be open to the plaintiffs to proceed against the Unocal parents on the basis of agency theory).[192]

There have been isolated cases in which courts have been prepared to apply 'enterprise' concepts to hold a parent company liable for the acts or omissions of its subsidiaries.[193] In *Amoco Cadiz*, Judge McGarr, of the US District Court, said:

As an integrated multinational corporation which is engaged through a system of subsidiaries in the exploitation, production, refining, transportation and sale of petroleum products throughout the world, Standard is responsible for the tortious acts of its wholly owned subsidiaries and instrumentalities . . . Standard exercised such control over its subsidiaries . . . that those entities would be considered to be mere instrumentalities of Standard. Furthermore, Standard itself was initially involved in and controlled the design, construction, operation and management of Amoco Cadiz and treated that vessel as if it were its own.[194]

'Enterprise' concepts have also been endorsed by the Indian courts in litigation arising out of the disaster at Bhopal. In *Union Carbide* v. *Union of India*, Judge Seth felt that 'there is no reason why . . . the corporate veil . . . cannot be lifted on purely equitable considerations in a case of a tort which has resulted in a mass disaster and in which on the face of it the assets of the alleged subsidiary are utterly insufficient to meet the just claims of multitude [*sic*] of disaster victims.'[195]

---

[190] 'Ruling on the Defendants' Motion for Judgment', 14 September 2004, n. 148 above, pp. 2–3.

[191] Ibid., p. 3.   [192] On the outcome of this case see pp. 203–4 above.

[193] Muchlinski, *Multinational Enterprises and the Law*, pp. 323–7.

[194] [1984] 2 Lloyd's Rep 304, 338. (The reference to 'Standard' in this quote refers to Standard Oil Co. (now Amoco Corporation), the parent company of the owners of the *Amoco Cadiz*.)

[195] Decision of the Madhya Pradesh High Court at Jabalpur, Civil Revision No. 26 of 88, 4 April 1988.

Clearly, enterprise theory does have some supporters among the judiciary, but it would be overstating the significance of these decisions to suggest that they point to a general trend.[196] If proving the 'direct' liability of parent companies is already difficult, the circumstances in which a court would be prepared to pierce the corporate veil and hold a parent company liable for a subsidiary's torts, merely because of its shareholding in that subsidiary, would be rarer still. However, enterprise theories may yet have their uses in future FDL claims, 'where the direct liability of the parent is doubtful in light of established legal rules, but where, for reasons of policy, it may be desirable for the parent to be answerable for losses suffered by the plaintiff'.[197]

Summary

Although 'parent company liability' and 'piercing the corporate veil' are often spoken of as if they are the same thing, it is actually only 'enterprise theory' that asks the courts to disregard the legal separation that exists between different companies. Theories of 'direct', 'secondary' and 'vicarious' liability all respect the doctrine of 'separate corporate personality' – indeed, the idea that parent and subsidiary are separate is the very foundation of theories based on agency or liability for acts of 'third parties'. However, in deference to the principle of 'separate corporate personality', courts are, and are likely to continue to be, extremely careful about how these various theories of parent company liability are applied in practice. To be successful, plaintiffs must be able to show a very clear connection between the parent's activities and policies and the failings of its subsidiary; in other words, a level of involvement in the circumstances leading up to the tort of a different order from that which would normally be expected in a parent–subsidiary relationship.

But while prosecuting an FDL claim may be difficult, it is by no means an impossibility. Contrary to popular belief, the doctrine of 'separate corporate personality' does not give the parent company general immunity from the consequences of the activities of foreign affiliates over which it has control. Domestic civil law already suggests several different bases for liability, even though these are still largely untested in court as a means of allocating liability among members of corporate

---

[196] Muchlinski describes Judge McGarr's comments in *The Amoco Cadiz* (quoted above) as 'difficult to reconcile with authority'; Muchlinski, *Multinational Enterprises and the Law*, p. 325.
[197] Ibid., p. 323.

groups. Depending on the particular facts of the case, a plaintiff may try to establish that the parent was *primarily* responsible, based on its involvement in the development or design of products or processes, or on a general obligation to control, and protect others from, the activities of its subsidiaries. Second, a plaintiff may be able to mount a claim that the parent was *vicariously* liable on the basis that its subsidiary was actually its agent, although the circumstances in which a court will hold a subsidiary to be an 'agent' of its parent are very limited, especially in English law. Third, a plaintiff may seek to argue that the parent was liable under theories of *secondary* liability, e.g. that it intentionally aided and abetted a tort, although, as noted above, proving that the parent company had the necessary mens rea can be difficult in practice. Finally, a plaintiff could argue that the case is an appropriate one for 'lifting of the corporate veil' on the basis that to maintain corporate separation between the parent and subsidiary would result in grave injustice. However, as noted above, there is only scant support for 'enterprise principles' in the case law, and therefore, in practice, this particular theory would only ever be used as a last resort.

Of course, there may be strategic considerations in deciding which of these theories to use. As noted above, plaintiffs have tended to emphasise the 'primary' liability of the parent in FDL claims because this was thought to lessen the chances of dismissal for forum non conveniens. (In theory, the defendants ought to have a more difficult job persuading a domestic court that the chosen forum is unsuitable if the key defendant is a locally incorporated company and there is a chance that the case is governed by the law of the forum state.) On the other hand, the way courts have approached the question of forum non conveniens in foreign direct liability cases so far gives reason to wonder whether some judges have fully grasped the nature of primary liability in this context.[198]

Parent company liability and the relevance of the organisational form

None of the conventional theories of tort-based liability discussed above – primary, vicarious, secondary or 'enterprise' liability – is associated with any particular organisational form.[199] In other words, there is

---

[198] Seck, 'Environmental Harm', 162. See also pp. 122–3 above.

[199] While theories of 'enterprise' liability have been developed largely in response to the 'artificiality' of corporate structures within *equity*-linked groups, there is nothing in principle to prevent the extension of these theories to contract-linked groups.

nothing inherent in these theories that would necessarily yield different results depending on whether the relevant control relationships were 'contract' or 'equity' based. What is crucial in each case is the presence of a 'control' relationship between parent and foreign affiliate (however related) that is sufficient to justify the imposition of liability on the parent in the particular case. As noted above, to establish 'primary' liability, the plaintiffs would need to demonstrate the parent company's familiarity with the risks associated with the relevant activities and close involvement with the day-to-day operations of its foreign affiliate. These may be attributes of an equity relationship or, equally, a franchise or a licence or distribution arrangement. Although there may be contractual disclaimers of liability and indemnities, this should not affect the allocation of liability in tort towards a third party. Alternatively, even though the parent company may not have been the *primary* wrongdoer, it might be possible to establish that it ought nevertheless to be held responsible on the basis of 'secondary' theories of liability, such as aiding and abetting, authorisation, encouragement or conspiracy. To be successful on this basis, it would be necessary to establish not only the parent company's knowledge of the wrongdoing, but that its own behaviour materially assisted in or encouraged the commission of the wrong. Theories of 'vicarious' and 'enterprise' liability both reflect the idea that an entity ought in principle to be liable for the torts committed by another in the course of that entity's commercial enterprise although, as noted above, the courts are likely to prefer theories based on 'actual fault' to theories that appear to 'pierce the corporate veil'.

But how much weight should be given to the principle of 'separate corporate personality' relative to other factors relevant to establishing liability, such as the level of knowledge held by the parent company of operational risks, or the level of involvement by a parent in its subsidiaries' activities? As shown above, the fact that victims may have had a closer connection with the foreign affiliate – as employees or neighbours – does not necessarily preclude the liability of the parent company. But the doctrine of 'separate corporate personality' does create an added complication for claimants against 'equity-based' groups, as courts are likely to be extremely wary of creating precedents that might lead to unlimited parent company liability 'by the back door'. On the other hand, courts should be wary, too, of placing too much weight on the corporate form, and thus perpetuating meaningless distinctions between 'corporate' and 'contract-based' groups for liability purposes. Clearly, liability should depend upon the consistent application of theories to determine who within the multinational was at fault, not on the form of its internal relationships.

Unfortunately, though, this tendency to focus on form over substance has also proved a problem for claimants against contract-based groups. In the ATCA-based claim of *Sinaltrain* v. *Coca-Cola*,[200] the court dismissed claims against two Coca-Cola companies on the basis that its franchise agreement did not give it any duty to control the labour practices of its Colombian franchisee. Although the defendant's involvement with its Colombian franchisees and their operations may have been greater than this, the court refused to look behind the words of the contract, which obviously places plaintiffs in cases such as these at something of a disadvantage vis-à-vis their corporate adversaries.[201]

Private claims as 'regulation'

It will be clear by now that the circumstances in which a plaintiff will be able to claim successfully – under the common law of tort – against the parent company of a multinational in relation to the activities of foreign subsidiaries are fairly limited. Plaintiffs seeking to bring a tort-based claim against a parent company in a foreign home state face huge hurdles: financial, practical and legal. Furthermore, while conditions will vary from industry to industry, it may be possible (and in some cases, relatively easy) for parent companies to head off tort-based claims for damages through adjustments to group structure and management systems.[202]

But the regulatory impact of private actions does not depend entirely on positive determinations of liability by the courts. According to business observers, litigation risk is emerging as a real source of regulatory pressure on US companies.[203] Private claims for personal injury or environmental damage against multinationals now attract significant media interest. Whether or not the matter proceeds to trial on the merits, allegations of poor CSR standards generate 'reputational risk' for multinationals.[204] For this reason, CSR campaigners see lawsuits against parent companies as a useful way of applying pressure to multinationals to

[200] 265 F Supp 2d 1345 (SD Fla 2003).

[201] Joseph, *Transnational Human Rights Litigation*, p. 143.

[202] H. Ward, 'Corporate Accountability in Search of a Treaty?: Some Insights from Foreign Direct Liability', RIIA Briefing Paper No. 4, May 2002.

[203] 'The People v. America Inc.', *The Economist*, 24 March 2001, p. 85; R. Cowe, 'Blooming Liabilities', *Green Futures*, No. 51, March–April 2005, p. 34.

[204] US-based clothing multinationals have been quick to settle these kinds of claims; 'Go Global, Sue Local', *The Economist*, 14 August 1999, p. 54.

improve their global social and environmental standards. In the USA, human rights organisations are actively involved in the identification and preparation of ATCA-based claims for trial.[205] The claims against Cape plc in the English courts received campaign support from a number of notable charities and NGOs, including Amnesty International, the Transport and General Workers Union and the Anti-Apartheid movement.[206] Although that litigation ended in late 2001 with an out of court settlement it was, according to the plaintiffs' solicitors, 'a salutary warning to multinationals generally against "double standards"'.[207]

Implications for international law

What do these FDL decisions mean for the development of international law? Although ensuring access to effective legal remedies is part of the human rights obligations of every state, the use by some states of the doctrine of forum non conveniens is inconsistent with the idea that home states of multinationals are required to provide rights of access to their domestic courts to foreign litigants *in every case*. In *Re Bhopal*,[208] a US court held that respect for the regulatory interests of India justified a stay of the proceedings. In *Cambior*,[209] the Canadian Supreme Court refused to accept that a stay of the proceedings in favour of the alternative forum (Guyana) would amount to a denial of justice. When the question was considered in *Lubbe* v. *Cape plc*, the House of Lords considered the English approach to the doctrine of forum non conveniens to be consistent with the UK's obligations under the ECHR.[210] Of course, this could all change. As noted above, forum non conveniens is a doctrine no longer available to UK courts, following a recent decision of the ECJ,[211] but, even before this, there were signs that the English

---

[205] See, for example, the work of the International Labor Rights Fund, http://www.laborrights.org. The Centre for Constitutional Rights, based in New York, and Earthrights International, a human rights charity based in Washington and Thailand, have also been closely involved in a number of ATCA-based claims.

[206] Press release issued by Leigh Day & Co., 22 December 2001.

[207] Ibid.   [208] 634 F Supp 842 (SDNY 1986).   [209] [1998] QJ No. 2554 [QL].

[210] *Lubbe* v. *Cape plc* [2000] 1 WLR 1545; [2000] 4 All ER 268 (HL) 277. Article 6 of the ECHR provides that '[i]n the determination of his civil rights . . . everyone is entitled to a fair and public hearing within a reasonable time by an independent and impartial tribunal established by law'.

[211] See p. 126 above. Although note that this conclusion was based on the wording of the Brussels Regulation, which binds all EU member states, not because of any restrictions under customary law.

courts were taking a more 'humanitarian stance' towards foreign litigants 'in dismissing FNC [forum non conveniens] applications . . . on
the grounds that alternative forums were simply unable to offer a just
resolution to the cases'.[212] In US courts, too, there are signs of a more
plaintiff-friendly approach to procedural issues such as forum non conveniens, both in ATCA-based claims and in more conventional tort-based
litigation.[213]

But judicial decisions are not the only source of state practice in this
area, and it should not be assumed that this apparent 'softening' in
attitude by some home state courts towards FDL claims will necessarily
be mirrored in other branches of government, as recent practice from
the USA shows. There, the Bush administration has filed a succession of
amicus briefs in the preliminary stages of ATCA cases, objecting not only
to the jurisdiction of the court in particular cases, but to the constitutionality of judicial interpretations of ATCA in general.[214] In at least one
case, interventions by the US government, pleading the adverse impact
of the proceedings on foreign policy objectives, have proved influential
in decisions to dismiss ATCA-based claims.[215] Of more concern to plaintiffs' groups, their attorneys and campaigners, however, have been the
Bush administration's attacks on the constitutionality of judicial interpretations of ATCA post-*Filartiga*.[216] The administration gave its support
to a Supreme Court appeal which sought to overturn the line of cases
on which litigation against private individuals and companies has been
based, on the basis that the judiciary has 'unconstitutionally misinter-
preted the ATCA, thereby exceeding the executive branch's constitutionally assigned control over foreign affairs'.[217] However, this intervention
proved unsuccessful, and in a 2004 ruling by the US Supreme Court, the
prevailing interpretation of ATCA was confirmed.[218] In the meantime,
business groups continue to petition the US government to repeal, or
at least constrain, ATCA by further legislation.[219] But executive branch

---

[212] Joseph, *Transnational Human Rights Litigation*, p. 147.

[213] See pp. 123–4 above.

[214] See Joseph, *Transnational Human Rights Litigation*, pp. 55–61; Stephens, 'Upsetting
Checks and Balances'.

[215] See, for example, *Sarei v. Rio Tinto*, 221 F Supp 2d 1116 (CD Cal 2002).

[216] See p. 207 above.

[217] Stephens, 'Upsetting Checks and Balances', 182. See further 'Brief for the United
States in Support of the Petition for Writ of Certiorari, *Sosa v. Alvarez Machain* (No.
03–339)'.

[218] *Sosa v. Alvarez-Machain*, 542 US 692 (2004), 124 S Ct 2739 (2004).

[219] Joseph, *Transnational Human Rights Litigation*, p. 60.

attacks on 'foreign direct liability' litigation have not been confined to the USA. In 1998, litigation against UK companies in the English courts provoked a restricted consultation letter from the Lord Chancellor's Department, expressing concern about the implications of FDL cases and arguing that exposing multinational companies to actions that would 'more appropriately be conducted abroad' could be bad for British business.[220] As Ward points out, 'the threat of relocation is a potent political force'.[221]

This, of course, further undermines the idea that the home states of multinationals must, as a matter of customary international law, ensure that remedies are available under their own laws for those injured or harmed as a result of multinational activities abroad. But international lawyers need to keep an eye on developments in domestic litigation against multinationals for other reasons. Not only may domestic case law help shed light on the substantive human rights obligations of multinationals, it is also likely to prove crucial in the development of theories to help explain when and why different elements within a multinational group should be held liable for breaches of international law. Although technically discrete, domestic and international legal systems regularly borrow from one another, and this exchange of ideas is helping to shape legal responses to multinationals at both levels. Furthermore, ideas taken up at international level are also capable of cross-fertilising into other domestic systems, as illustrated by the decision of the US Court of Appeals of the Ninth Circuit, in *Doe I v. Unocal*, to apply an *international law* test to determine the liability of members of the Unocal group under ATCA.[222] Even if not expressly referred to, the developing international law on multinationals, human rights and CSR is likely to be highly influential in the way domestic courts approach future FDL claims.

Conclusion

Private claims are a potentially vital source of regulatory pressure on multinationals. They also highlight the possibilities for international regulation from a domestic source. This is, however, an area in its infancy. There is little case law to go on and much will depend, going forward, on the attitudes of judges to questions such as the role of the

---

[220] Ward, 'Governing Multinationals', p. 4.   [221] Ibid.
[222] 395 F 3d 932 (9th Cir. 2002). See p. 228 above.

domestic courts in international litigation of this kind, the role and responsibilities of parent companies as co-ordinators, and beneficiaries, of international commercial activities, and the rights of those affected. While it is impossible to predict for certain how the law on parent company liability will unfold, it is important to remember that these kinds of claims, though private, still have a public dimension. Growing pressure on home states to take action in relation to the CSR standards of multinationals, from below and above, should have an impact on the way the competing interests of states and individuals are weighed up in court. The law is often criticised for changing too slowly, and for failing to keep pace with social change. But it is just possible that judges are now starting to take account of the 'new regulatory agenda' for CSR in FDL cases involving multinational groups.

What does this mean for the liability of parent companies of multinational groups? As noted above, there are a number of existing theories of tort-based liability that could potentially be applied to FDL-type cases. And multinationals, especially those with a high public profile, take this new litigation threat very seriously indeed. But the principle of 'separate corporate personality' is deep-rooted in company law. Although theories of primary, vicarious and secondary liability do not challenge this principle head on, courts will inevitably be concerned about the possible legal and commercial fall-out from any decision that appears to undermine it. This only adds to the mountain that plaintiffs must already climb in order to be successful. The financial, emotional, practical and most of all legal obstacles faced by plaintiffs in private claims means that, as a form of regulation, FDL will never be systematic. Many argue that a more comprehensive, international regulatory solution is called for. How realistic is this? What are the prospects for an international law on CSR? These questions form the focus of the next chapter.

PART III · INTERNATIONAL
REGULATION OF MULTINATIONALS

6   Towards an international law of CSR?

Based on developments so far, what are the prospects of a new body of law emerging, an 'international law of corporate social responsibility'? How would it be structured? What form would it take? To whom would it be addressed? What would the primary obligations be? Would it focus primarily on human rights, or would it encompass wider concerns?

This chapter is a preliminary attempt to answer these questions. As discussed in previous chapters, international law on CSR could be based on customary law, or could be regulated by treaty, or both. It could be addressed to multinationals themselves, or home states, or host states, or all three. While the regulatory methods are still very much open to negotiation, considerable effort has already been invested at international level in devising 'soft law' standards for multinationals. This chapter begins with a brief history of the various different international regulatory projects aimed at multinationals and CSR, some of which have been discussed in earlier chapters. None of these involves any formal enforcement measures as yet, but this does not mean that they are not legally significant. On the contrary, these various 'codes of conduct', 'guidelines' and 'principles' contain a number of recurring themes which, if given sufficient support by the international community, could eventually develop into binding obligations. The second part of this chapter is an attempt to draw out some of these key themes.

While these so-called 'voluntary' initiatives undoubtedly have 'regulatory value', regulation which relies on activism for enforcement will inevitably be 'piecemeal and inconsistent' in its impact.[1] Many

---

[1] R. McCorquodale, 'Human Rights and Global Business' in S. Bottomley and D. Kinley (eds.), *Commercial Law and Human Rights* (Aldershot: Ashgate, 2002), pp. 111–13.

campaigners argue that it is now time for something more formal and systematic: an international treaty on CSR, perhaps?[2] While this would be a daunting task, there are a number of precedents in international CSR regulation that could prove useful. These are considered in the final part of this chapter, together with some other recent regulatory proposals.

International CSR standards for multinationals: a brief history

The search to find an international regulatory solution for the social and environmental problems posed by multinationals began in earnest in the mid-1970s. As discussed in chapter 1, this was a time of growing disquiet, at both national and international level, about 'big business' and its implications for national sovereignty, democracy and cultural diversity. The period between 1975 and 1980 saw the unveiling of no fewer than three separate initiatives relating to the social regulation of multinationals: the Draft UN Code of Conduct on Transnational Corporations (the 'Draft UN Code'),[3] the 1976 OECD Guidelines on Multinational Enterprises (the 'OECD Guidelines')[4] and the 1977 ILO Tripartite Declaration Concerning Multinational Enterprises and Social Policy (the 'ILO Tripartite Declaration').[5]

Negotiations on the Draft UN Code were abandoned in 1992. Nevertheless, the UN has continued to monitor multinational activities closely, through UNCTAD. If anything, work within the UN agencies on issues relating to multinationals and CSR has intensified of late. The role of multinationals in helping to deliver UN environmental and development goals is recognised in a number of significant policy statements from Agenda 21 (adopted at the 1992 UNCED)[6] to the Political Declaration made at the WSSD in 2002.[7] The Global Compact, launched by UN Secretary General Kofi Annan in 1999,[8] has become a major forum for

---

[2] FoE, 'Towards Binding Corporate Accountability', http://www.foei.org.

[3] UN Doc. E/1990/94, 12 June 1990.

[4] Annexed to the 1976 OECD Declaration on International Investment and Multinational Enterprises, 21 June 1976; (1976) 15 ILM 967. (The Guidelines are reproduced at (1976) 15 ILM 969.)

[5] (1978) 17 ILM 422.

[6] 'Agenda 21: Programme of Action for Sustainable Development', adopted by the UNGA at its 46th session, UN Doc. A/CONF.151/26.

[7] 2002 'Declaration on Sustainable Development' of the WSSD, in UN, 'Report of the World Summit on Sustainable Development' UN Doc. A/CONF.199/20, Sales No. E.03.II.A.1.

[8] UN Press Release SG/SM/6881, 1 February 1999.

discussion on CSR-related issues. Separately from this, a working group of the UN Sub-Commission on the Promotion and Protection of Human Rights (the 'UN Sub-Commission') has, since 1998, been engaged in a project to define the human rights obligations of business enterprises. The product of its work, the 'UN Norms on the Responsibilities of Transnational Corporations and other Business Enterprises with Regard to Human Rights' ('the UN Norms')[9] was adopted by the UN Sub-Commission on 13 August 2003. There are also a number of longer-standing initiatives operated by UN agencies, dating back to the 1980s, in relation to specific issues connected to multinationals and CSR, such as consumer protection,[10] marketing of baby-milk substitutes,[11] and pesticides.[12] The first part of this chapter will, however, focus on the more general initiatives.

The Draft UN Code

As discussed in chapter 1, the Draft UN Code arose out of the political and economic concerns about multinationals that were prevalent in the 1970s. These may be summarised as concerns about sovereignty, independence and economic development on the part of less developed countries and concerns about stability in international investment conditions on the part of home states. When the UN's working group delivered its report in 1974,[13] it recommended, as a long-term goal for the new UN Commission on Transnational Corporations (the 'UNCTC'), 'the conclusion of a general agreement on multinational corporations having the force of an international treaty and containing provisions for machinery and sanctions'.[14] As a first step it recommended that work should commence on the negotiation and drafting of a comprehensive 'code of conduct' for multinationals. With regard to the legal status of such a code, the 1974 report contemplated 'a consistent set of recommendations which are gradually evolved and which may be revised as experience or circumstances require. Although they are not compulsory in character, they act as an instrument of moral persuasion,

---

[9] E/CN.4/Sub.2/2003/12/Rev.2.

[10] UN, 'Guidelines for Consumer Protection', UN Doc. A/RES/39/248 (1986).

[11] 'WHO International Code on Marketing of Breast Milk Substitutes', adopted by the WHA, Res. WHA34.2, 21 May 1981.

[12] FAO, 'Code of Conduct on the Distribution and Use of Pesticides', adopted at the 25th session of the FAO Conference, Rome, 19 November 1985.

[13] See pp. 10–11 above.

[14] UN, Department of Economic and Social Affairs, 'The Impact of Multinational Corporations', p. 54.

strengthened by the authority of international organizations and the support of public opinion.'[15]

A specially appointed inter-governmental working group began work on the code in January 1977. The code was to be addressed not only to multinationals, but to states as well, and would cover a range of issues from general political, social, economic and development issues to investment protection standards. Ultimately, though, the scope of the project was to prove over-ambitious. Negotiating parties became deadlocked over issues of minimum standards of treatment for investors, the question of 'national treatment', rights of host states to expropriate assets and compensation for expropriation.[16] Moreover, by the 1990s the economic and political background had changed and enthusiasm for the project, even within the UNCTC, had waned.[17] It is interesting to note, however, that despite fierce disagreements over other issues, the provisions on what we would now refer to as 'CSR issues' – human rights, environmental and consumer protection obligations – were, by 1990, largely agreed.[18]

In relation to human rights, the Draft UN Code stated that 'Transnational Corporations shall respect human rights and fundamental freedoms in the countries in which they operate . . .'[19] In relation to consumer protection, the draft code provided as follows:

Transnational corporations shall carry out their operations, in particular production and marketing, in accordance with national laws, regulations, administrative practices and policies concerning consumer protection of the countries in which they operate. Transnational corporations shall also perform their activities with due regard to relevant international standards, so that they do not cause injury to the health or endanger the safety of consumers or bring about variations in the quality of products in each market which would have detrimental effects on consumers.[20]

In addition, multinationals would be required to supply to national authorities 'on request or on a regular basis as specified', information on characteristics of products or services 'which may be injurious to the

[15] Ibid., p. 55.
[16] W. Feld, *Multinational Corporations and UN Politics: the Quest for a Code of Conduct* (New York: Pergamon Press, 1980); P. Muchlinski, 'Attempts to Extend the Accountability of Transnational Corporations: the Role of UNCTAD' in M. Kamminga and S. Zia-Zarifi (eds.), *Liability of Multinational Corporations under International Law* (The Hague: Kluwer, 2000).
[17] Ibid., pp. 102–5.
[18] UNCTC, 'Transnational Corporations, Services and the Uruguay Round', UN Doc. ST/CTC/103 (New York: UN, 1990), pp. 175, 177.
[19] Draft UN Code, n. 3 above, para. 14.   [20] Ibid., para. 37.

health and safety of consumers' and 'prohibitions, restrictions, warnings and other public regulatory measures imposed in other countries on grounds of health or safety protection of these products or services'.[21] Multinationals would also be required to disclose information on the possible hazards associated with their products 'by means of proper labelling, informative and accurate advertising or other appropriate methods'.[22]

On environmental protection, the Draft UN Code provided as follows:

Transnational Corporations shall carry out their activities in accordance with national laws, regulations, administrative practices and policies relating to the preservation of the environment of the countries in which they operate and with due regard to international standards. Transnational corporations should, in performing their activities, take steps to protect the environment and where damaged to rehabilitate it and should make efforts to develop and apply adequate technologies for this purpose.[23]

Similar to their obligations on consumer protection, multinationals would also be required to supply national authorities with information concerning environmental risks relating to their products, processes and activities, and 'prohibitions, restrictions, warnings and other public regulatory measures imposed in other countries on grounds of protection of the environment . . .'[24]

With regard to issues relating to employment conditions and industrial relations, the UNCTC decided not to duplicate the work of the ILO. Instead, the principles of the ILO Tripartite Declaration are incorporated by reference into the UN Draft Code.

Compared with other aspects of the code, these health, safety and environmental provisions were uncontroversial. There were no substantial amendments to provisions relating to these issues between the 1984 draft and the 1990 draft, other than the decision to cast the most basic obligations of multinationals in terms of the word 'shall' (rather than the softer 'should').[25] This does not, however, imply any expectation on the part of the UNCTC that the code would become mandatory. On the contrary, while the legal status of the code was never finally settled, the UNCTC had by 1990 accepted the likelihood that the code would remain 'a voluntary instrument',[26] while at the same time noting that

---

[21] Ibid., para. 38.   [22] Ibid., para. 3.   [23] Ibid., para. 41.   [24] Ibid., para. 42.

[25] Although some provisions retain the softer wording. See, for instance, paras. 40 and 43. The 1984 draft, UN Doc. E/C.10/1984/S/5 of 29 May 1984, is reproduced at (1984) 23 ILM 602.

[26] UNCTC, 'Transnational Corporations, Services and the Uruguay Round', n. 18 above, p. 185.

the effectiveness of an international instrument does not necessarily depend on its legal form. The pertinent question is: does the instrument effectively influence the decision makers – governmental or corporate – in applying the prescribed standards? The answer to this question will depend not so much on the legal characterization of the instrument as on the extent to which its provisions are acceptable to Member States, transnational corporations, trade unions and other relevant groups.[27]

Although the code was never finalised, it would be wrong to dismiss it altogether. In relation to social, environmental and consumer issues, it provides evidence of international consensus on the responsibilities of multinationals dating back to the 1980s. This is of some significance, given the divergent interests of different groups of negotiating states. Also, despite its formal lack of status, the code continued to be used by UNCTAD as a 'source of examples and ideas' in the context of ongoing work on international investment law and policy.[28]

The OECD Guidelines for Multinational Enterprises

By the time negotiations on the UNCTC Draft Code were underway, the OECD was already working on its own set of 'Guidelines' for multinationals, albeit from a very different political and economic perspective. OECD governing bodies saw the greater harmonisation of social standards as part of a wider package of measures aimed at greater stability and liberalisation of investment conditions between OECD states. However, it had been recognised within the OECD that some kind of regulatory gesture was required to help defuse mounting public concern about the lack of accountability of multinationals within the international economic system.[29]

Negotiations on the first version of the OECD Guidelines took place between March 1975 and May 1976. The Guidelines were eventually issued in the form of an annex to the 1976 Declaration on International Investment and Multinational Enterprises[30] and were presented as a series of 'recommendations' addressed 'jointly' to OECD member states and multinationals operating in their respective territories. The Declaration was accompanied by three Decisions of the Council 'promulgated simultaneously as they are complementary and interconnected'[31]:

---

[27] Ibid., p. 186.   [28] See Muchlinski, 'The Role of UNCTAD', p. 111.

[29] T. Vogelaar, 'The OECD Guidelines: Their Philosophy, History, Negotiation, Form, Legal Nature, Follow-Up Procedures and Review' in N. Horn (ed.), *Legal Problems of Codes of Conduct for Multinational Enterprises* (The Hague: Kluwer, 1980), p. 128.

[30] See n. 4 above.   [31] Ibid., paragraph 5.

on consultation between member states on the Guidelines (the 'follow-up procedures'), on 'national treatment' for investments and on international investment incentives and disincentives.

Since the Guidelines were issued in 1976, there have been several revisions and clarifications of the provisions relating to the health, safety and environmental responsibilities of multinationals. A new section on consumer protection was included in 1984 and a new chapter on environmental protection added following the 1991 review. In 1998, the OECD commenced a detailed review of the Guidelines as a whole, 'to ensure their continued relevance and effectiveness in the rapidly changing global economy'.[32] This review culminated in the launch in June 2000 of a revamped set of Guidelines known as 'Revision 2000'.[33]

In an important change of emphasis, Revision 2000 gives much greater prominence than previous versions of the Guidelines to the existence of *international* as well as national regulatory standards, especially in relation to labour issues.[34] For example, whereas provisions on employment and industrial relations previously applied to multinationals 'within the framework of law, regulations and prevailing labour relations and employment practices, in each of the countries in which they operate', the new version subjects multinationals to the framework of '*applicable* law, regulations and prevailing labour relations and employment practices'.[35] In addition, certain international statements are referred to explicitly in the OECD's commentary,[36] such as the UDHR, the 1998 ILO Declaration on Fundamental Principles and Rights at Work,[37] the 1992 Rio Declaration on Environment and Development[38] and Agenda 21.[39] As

---

[32] Statement by the Chair of the Ministerial, Peter Costello MP, June 2001.

[33] (2001) 40 ILM 237. The 2000 Guidelines are annexed to the 'Declaration on International Investment and Multinational Enterprises', Paris, 27 June 2000, DAFFE/IME(2000)/20, Annex I.

[34] J. Murray, 'A New Phase in the Regulation of Multinational Enterprises: the Role of the OECD' (2001) 30 *Ind LJ* 255.

[35] OECD Guidelines, Revision 2000, n. 33 above, Part IV (Employment and Industrial Relations) (emphasis added). See further Murray, 'A New Phase'.

[36] OECD, 'Commentary on the OECD Guidelines for Multinational Enterprises', in OECD, 'The OECD Guidelines for Multinationals: Revision 2000' (OECD, 2000).

[37] Adopted at the 86th session of the International Labour Conference, Geneva, 18 June 1998.

[38] 1992 Declaration of the UN Conference on Environment and Development, Report of the UN Conference on the Environment and Development, Rio de Janeiro, 13 June 1992, UN Doc. A/CONF.151/26/Rev. 1, Vol. 1, Annex I; (1992) 31 ILM 874.

[39] See n. 6 above.

Murray observes, 'the Guidelines no longer take the integrity of national jurisdictions for granted in the way that the original instrument did'.[40]

Revision 2000 also introduced many significant substantive changes to the Guidelines. New provisions were included in relation to the use of child labour[41] and forced labour,[42] two issues that had been the subject of sustained media attention and high-profile campaigns by NGOs. In addition to new provisions on employer–worker consultation,[43] multinationals are also asked to 'take adequate steps to ensure occupational health and safety in their operations'.[44]

As regards human rights, multinationals are requested, in a new addition to the Guidelines, to '[r]espect the human rights of those affected by their activities', although this is qualified by the proviso that this be 'consistent with the host government's international obligations and commitments'.[45] On environmental protection, chapter V provides that

Enterprises should, within the framework of laws, regulations and administrative practices in the countries in which they operate, and in consideration of relevant international agreements, principles, objectives, and standards, take due account of the need to protect the environment, public health and safety, and generally to conduct their activities in a manner contributing to the wider goal of sustainable development.[46]

This provision gives lower priority to international standards than the provision on employment policy quoted above, although 'international agreements, principles, objectives and standards' must still be taken into account. More specific recommendations include environmental information-gathering, target-setting, monitoring and disclosure.[47] The Guidelines also emphasise the importance of sharing information with employees, local communities and the public at large about the potential environmental impacts of operations. The 'precautionary principle'[48] and the principle of 'continuous improvement' are included to guide multinational behaviour.[49] Finally, it is recommended that multinationals '[p]rovide adequate education and training to employees in environmental health and safety matters'[50] and '[c]ontribute to the

---

[40] Murray, 'A New Phase', 264.
[41] OECD Guidelines, Revision 2000, n. 33 above, Part IV (Employment and Industrial Relations), para. 1(b).
[42] Ibid., para. 1(c).   [43] Ibid., para. 2(c).   [44] Ibid., para. 4(b).
[45] OECD Guidelines, Revision 2000, n. 33 above, Part II (General Policies), para. 2.
[46] Ibid., Part V (Environment).
[47] Ibid., paras. 1 and 2. See also Part III (Disclosure).
[48] Ibid., para. 4. See further pp. 271–2 below.   [49] Ibid., para. 6.   [50] Ibid., para. 7.

development of environmentally meaningful and economically efficient public policy'.[51]

Consumer protection is also covered in Revision 2000. In this area, multinationals appear to have been given greater latitude, without explicit reference to international standards. According to Revision 2000, 'when dealing with consumers, enterprises should act in accordance with fair business, marketing and advertising practices and should take reasonable steps to ensure the safety and quality of the goods and services they provide'. This includes, however, '[e]nsur[ing] that the goods and services they provide meet all agreed or legally required standards for consumer health and safety, including health warnings and product safety and information labels'.[52] In addition, multinationals are required to 'provide accurate and clear information regarding their content, safe use, maintenance, storage and disposal sufficient to enable consumers to make informed decisions',[53] to '[p]rovide transparent and effective procedures that address customer complaints and contribute to a fair and timely resolution of consumer disputes without undue cost or burden'[54] and, finally, to '[c]o-operate fully and in a transparent manner with public authorities in the prevention or removal of serious threats to public health and safety deriving from the consumption or use of their products'.[55]

It was never the intention that the OECD Guidelines would be 'binding' (i.e. in the sense that non-compliance would lead to the imposition of formal sanctions by the OECD or its member states). However, it was recognised that some oversight of implementation would be needed if the Guidelines were to be credible. Originally, the only follow-up contemplated was a periodic 'exchange of views' convened by the OECD's Committee on International Investment and Multinational Enterprises, the results of which would be reported to the Council.[56] One of the aims of Revision 2000 was to improve the transparency and effectiveness of implementation within OECD member states. Under the revised arrangements,[57] each adhering country agrees to establish a National Contact Point (or 'NCP') 'for undertaking promotional activities, handling inquiries and for discussions with the parties concerned

---

[51] Ibid., para. 8.   [52] Ibid., Part VII (Consumer Interests), para. 1.
[53] Ibid., para. 2.   [54] Ibid., para. 3.   [55] Ibid., para 6.
[56] OECD, 'Decision of the Council on Inter-Governmental Consultation Procedures on the Guidelines for Multinational Enterprises', 21 June 1976, para. 1; (1976) 15 ILM 977.
[57] See 'Decision of the OECD Council on the OECD Guidelines for Multinational Enterprises', C(2000)96/FINAL, 19 June 2000.

on all matters covered by the Guidelines'.[58] The NCP need not be a single individual or government department.[59] The summary of the first annual meeting of NCPs, held in June 2001, notes a wide range of implementing arrangements, including multi-departmental consultative bodies and, in some cases, 'tripartite' consultative groups (involving government, business and union representatives).[60] However the NCP is structured, its key role is to 'raise awareness' about the Guidelines within the business community, employee organisations, NGOs and the wider public. In addition, the NCP is charged with 'contribut[ing] to the resolution of issues that arise relating to implementation of the Guidelines in specific circumstances',[61] effectively a dispute resolution function.

In terms of geographical coverage, the Guidelines were originally limited to the territory of OECD member states. The reasons for this were both legal (i.e. concerns about the extent of the OECD's mandate in relation to the subject matter covered by the Guidelines) and political (i.e. concerns about the propriety of extending the standards set out in the Guidelines to areas 'where different socio-economic and political circumstances might prevail').[62] The decision was made to extend the scope of the Guidelines to non-adhering countries as part of Revision 2000. Whereas the Guidelines were previously addressed to multinationals operating *in* the territories of member states,[63] Revision 2000 has removed this reference to a territorial connection, adding that

[s]ince the operations of multinational enterprises extend throughout the world, international co-operation in this field should extend to all countries. Governments adhering to the Guidelines should encourage the enterprise operating on their territories *to observe the Guidelines wherever they operate*, while taking into account the particular circumstances of each host country.[64]

There is, however, a lack of clarity as to how the complaint procedures should operate in practice, when the behaviour complained of takes

---

[58] Ibid., Part I, para. 1.   [59] Ibid., 'Procedural Guidance', Part I, section A.

[60] See OECD, 'Summary Report of the Chair of the Meeting on the Activities of National Contact Points', 21 September 2001, Part I (and tables).

[61] OECD, 'Decision of the OECD Council', n. 57 above, 'Procedural Guidance', Part I, section C.

[62] Vogelaar, 'The OECD Guidelines', p. 131.

[63] OECD Guidelines; (1976) 15 ILM 969, para. 6.

[64] OECD Guidelines, Revision 2000, n. 33 above, Part I (Concepts and Principles), para. 2 (emphasis added).

place in a non-adhering state.[65] At present, the NCP is merely directed to 'take steps to develop an understanding of the issues involved, and to follow [the usual procedures] where relevant and practicable'.[66] The commentary to this section anticipates some of the difficulties that may arise, such as lack of access to relevant information or individuals.[67] To assist, the OECD has launched an 'outreach' programme to raise awareness of the Guidelines among non-OECD countries and to promote dialogue on Guidelines issues.[68] Alternatively, non-member states can put their relationship with the OECD on a more formal footing by adopting the Guidelines themselves. This would entail establishment of their own NCPs to administer the Guidelines within their respective jurisdictions. So far, seven non-member states of the OECD – Brazil, Argentina, Chile, Israel, Estonia, Lithuania and Slovenia – have adopted the Guidelines and have been given observer status at NCP meetings.

Because of the confidentiality of the dispute resolution procedures, it is difficult for outsiders to obtain a complete picture of their use to date. However, it is possible to gain an idea of the kinds of cases that have been brought to the attention of NCPs so far from information posted on the OECD web-site, in particular, the reports on annual meetings of NCPs, and the OECD's own annual reports. The UK NCP, for instance, had had three 'instances' involving compliance by multinationals with the Guidelines bought to its attention by the time of the publication of the 2001 Annual Report,[69] one referred from another NCP and two by NGOs. Two of these were reported to involve the activities of UK-based multinationals in non-adhering countries. The OECD's 2002 Annual Report mentions a further two cases then under consideration by the UK NCP in 2002[70] and, according to a UK government report, a further four

---

[65] See 'NGO Statement on the OECD Guidelines for Multinational Enterprises', reproduced in OECD, 'OECD Guidelines for Multinational Enterprises: Annual Report 2001: Global Instruments for Corporate Responsibility' (OECD, 2001), http://www.oecd.org, p. 47.

[66] See OECD, 'Decision of the OECD Council', n. 57 above, 'Procedural Guidance', Part I, section C, para. 5.

[67] See OECD, 'Commentary on the Implementation Procedures of the OECD Guidelines for Multinational Enterprises', in OECD, 'The OECD Guidelines for Multinationals: Revision 2000' (OECD, 2000), para. 20.

[68] See OECD, 'Non-member Economies and the OECD Guidelines for Multinational Enterprises', Proceedings of Meeting, Paris, 12 December 2000, http://www.oecd.org.

[69] OECD, 'OECD Guidelines for Multinational Enterprises: Annual Report 2001: Global Instruments for Corporate Responsibility' (OECD, 2001), http://www.oecd.org.

[70] OECD, 'OECD Guidelines for Multinational Enterprises: Annual Report 2002: Focus on Responsible Supply Chain Management' (OECD, 2002), http://www.oecd.org.

cases were referred to the UK NCP during 2003.[71] By 2005, the UK NCP had a total of seven cases on its books, all of which involved activities of UK-based multinationals in 'non-adhering countries'.[72] The UK NCP does not disclose the details of cases lodged under the OECD Guidelines' implementation procedures, but the complaints made to other NCPs so far have covered subjects as diverse as resettlement of communities in the Zambian copper belt, child labour, human rights standards in Burma, allegations of interference with union rights in Guatemala, and workplace standards in Malaysia.[73] So far, complaints and queries about possible non-compliance of companies with the Guidelines are usually 'resolved' (at least as far as NCPs are concerned) through meetings and dialogue, although NCPs have also issued recommendations to companies working in a particular sector or country,[74] and occasionally have been known to issue a public statement setting out, in broad terms, whether or not, in their opinion, the Guidelines have been complied with in the particular case.[75]

The ILO 'Tripartite Declaration'

The impact of multinationals on employment conditions has long been an issue of concern within the ILO. The ILO began examining the relationship between multinationals and social policy in earnest in the early 1970s.[76] In 1976 a 'Tripartite Advisory Meeting on Multinational Enterprises and Social Policy' recommended the preparation of a set of 'non-mandatory principles for multinationals in the area of social policy', and the ILO Tripartite Declaration was adopted by the Governing Body of the

---

[71] DTI, 'Corporate Social Responsibility: a Government Update' (DTI, May 2004), http://www.societyandbusiness.gov.uk, p. 9.

[72] See DTI, 'UK NCP Report for 2005', http://www.dti.gov.uk/ewt/ukncp.htm.

[73] OECD, 'OECD Guidelines for Multinational Enterprises: Annual Report 2002', n. 70 above, pp. 18–19.

[74] E.g. 'Recommendations of the French National Contact Point to Companies on the Issue of Forced Labour in Burma', 28 March 2002. (An English translation is reproduced as Annex VI of Part I of OECD 'OECD Guidelines for Multinational Enterprises: Annual Report 2002', n. 70 above, p. 45.)

[75] OECD, 'OECD Guidelines for Multinational Enterprises: Annual Report 2002', n. 70 above, p. 19. According to OECD Watch, a coalition of NGOs, of the thirty-two complaints under the Guidelines monitored, 'only two resulted in a joint statement of outcome between the complainant and the multinational'; R. Stancich, 'Why Mandatory Reporting has Fallen from the EU Agenda', *Ethical Corporation*, September 2005, p. 11.

[76] A short history of the background to the ILO's work in this area can be found on the ILO's web-site at http://www.ilo.org/public/english/employment/multi/history.htm.

ILO in November 1977. The stated aim of the ILO Tripartite Declaration is practically identical to that of the OECD Guidelines, i.e. 'to encourage the positive contribution which multinational enterprises can make to economic and social progress and to minimise and resolve the difficulties to which their various operations give rise'.[77]

The ILO Tripartite Declaration has been amended on only one occasion since its adoption, in March 2001. The purpose of this amendment was to incorporate a reference to the ILO's 1998 Declaration on Fundamental Principles and Rights at Work.[78] This 1998 Declaration identifies four 'fundamental' rights arising from principles embodied in the ILO Constitution and certain ILO Conventions, namely:

(a) freedom of association and the effective recognition of the right to collective bargaining;
(b) the elimination of all forms of forced or compulsory labour;
(c) the effective abolition of child labour; and
(d) the elimination of discrimination in respect of employment and occupation.

The 2001 amendments to the ILO Tripartite Declaration make it clear that multinationals, too, have a role in the implementation of these 'fundamental' rights. Under paragraph 8, multinationals are to 'contribute to the realization of the ILO Declaration on Fundamental Principles and Rights of Work and its Follow-up, adopted in 1998'. This is in addition to the requirement, present in the original version, that multinationals 'respect the Universal Declaration of Human Rights and the corresponding International Covenants adopted by the General Assembly of the United Nations'.

The ILO Tripartite Declaration is addressed ('commended') 'to the governments, the employers' and workers' organizations of home and host countries and to the multinational enterprises themselves'.[79] The substantive obligations addressed to multinationals concern a range of employment-related issues such as industrial relations, security of employment, non-discrimination, workplace conditions and, following the 2001 amendments, child labour. While the right to a safe and healthy workplace environment is not identified as a 'fundamental' right in the 1998 ILO Declaration on Fundamental Principles and Rights at Work, it is covered in the ILO Tripartite Declaration:

---

[77] ILO Tripartite Declaration, n. 5 above, para. 2.   [78] See p. 81 above.
[79] ILO Tripartite Declaration, n. 5 above, para. 4.

Multinational enterprises should maintain the highest standards of safety and health, in conformity with national requirements, bearing in mind their relevant experience within the enterprise as a whole, including any knowledge of special hazards. They should also make available to the representatives of workers in the enterprise, and upon request, to the competent authorities and the workers' and employers' organizations in all countries in which they operate, information on the safety and health standards relevant to their local operations, which they observe in other countries. In particular, they should make known to those concerned any special hazards and related protective measures associated with new products and processes. They, like comparable domestic enterprises, should be expected to play a leading role in the examination of causes of industrial safety and health hazards and in the application of resulting improvements within the enterprise as a whole.[80]

This italicised section points to *international* (rather than national) health and safety standards and effectively prohibits multinationals from lowering their own standards in countries where domestic regulatory requirements may be low or non-existent. In addition, the ILO Tripartite Declaration requires multinationals to '[c]ooperate in the work of international organizations concerned with the preparation and adoption of international health and safety standards',[81] and

In accordance with national practice . . . [to] . . . cooperate fully with the competent health and safety authorities, the representatives of the workers and their organizations, and established health and safety organizations. Where appropriate, matters relating to safety and health should be incorporated in agreements with the representatives of the workers and their organizations.[82]

There are no limitations on the geographical scope of the Tripartite Declaration. According to paragraph 4, 'the principles . . . are commended to the governments, employers' and workers organizations of home and host countries and to the multinational enterprises themselves'.[83]

Like the OECD Guidelines, the ILO Tripartite Declaration was always intended to be a 'non-binding' set of standards. Accordingly, the ILO does not take any steps to enforce these standards, nor does it engage in any systematic compliance monitoring. However, the ILO has developed a 'follow-up' procedure that takes the form of a periodic survey. In this survey, interested parties are invited to give their comments on their 'experiences' in implementing the principles set out in the Declaration. Originally, questionnaires were issued only to governments, but in 1985

---

[80] Ibid., para. 38 (emphasis added).   [81] Ibid., para. 39.   [82] Ibid., para. 40.
[83] Although note that the 'follow-up procedure' (see below) is confined to ILO member states.

the procedure was opened up to enable employers' and workers' organisations to submit their own reports directly to the ILO. The periodic survey procedure is not, however, to identify cases of non-compliance by multinationals, but to gain feedback on attitudes to the Tripartite Declaration generally, and guidance as to where future resources should be concentrated.

Cases of alleged breaches by individual multinationals of provisions of the Tripartite Declaration have been brought to the ILO's attention under a 'dispute procedure' established by the Governing Body in 1980.[84] Under this procedure, governments or (in cases where a government has failed or declined to act) national or international employers' or workers' organisations can apply to the ILO for an 'interpretation' of the provisions of the Tripartite Declaration in relation to 'an actual situation'.[85] However, surprisingly little use has been made of these procedures so far. As of mid-2004, the ILO had considered only four formal requests for interpretations of the Tripartite Declaration relating to issues of compliance by multinationals with it (a fifth request was found not to be receivable). Two of these requests were submitted by the Belgian government, and three by workers' organisations. While NGOs do not have access to the 'dispute procedure',[86] they have nevertheless presented the ILO with 'a number of communications and requests for assistance relating to the alleged wrongdoings of MNEs' which have been 'handled outside the scope of the Procedure for interpretation of the MNE Declaration'.[87]

Agenda 21

Agenda 21,[88] a key UN strategy document on sustainable development, was adopted by the governments of more than 178 states at the United Nations Conference on Environment and Development held at Rio de Janeiro in June 1992. Its provisions are claimed to reflect 'a global consensus and political commitment at the highest level on

[84] A consolidated version of the 'disputes procedure' is reproduced at http://www.ilo.org/public/english/ employment/multi/dispute.htm.

[85] For a more detailed discussion of the procedure, see J. Diller, 'Social Conduct in Transnational Enterprise Operations: the Role of the International Labour Organization' in R. Blanpain (ed.), *Multinationals and the Social Challenges of the XXIst Century* (The Hague: Kluwer, 2000), p. 21.

[86] Under the 'receivability criteria', interpretation requests may only be made by governments of member states of the ILO, or workers' organisations (national or international).

[87] See further http://www.ilo.org/public/english/employment/multi/ dispute.htm.

[88] See n. 6 above.

development and environmental cooperation[89] and have been highly influential in the development of international environmental policy.[90] Although aimed at wider concerns than the activities of multinationals, Agenda 21 included a number of provisions addressed directly to business ('including transnational corporations'). Noting that '[b]usiness and industry play a crucial role in the social and economic development of a country',[91] Agenda 21 goes on to set out a number of basic principles regarding the responsibilities of multinationals, e.g. 'Business and industry, including transnational corporations, should recognise environmental management as among the highest corporate priorities and as a key determinant to sustainable development,'[92] and

Business and industry, including transnational corporations, should ensure responsible ethical management of products and processes from the point of view of health, safety and environmental aspects. Towards this end, business and industry should increase self-regulation, guided by appropriate codes, charters and initiatives integrated into all elements of business planning and decision-making and fostering openness and dialogue with employees and the public.[93]

The UN's Commission on Sustainable Development, set up in December 1992 to oversee the Rio Conference follow-up, does not directly monitor compliance by multinationals with these provisions of Agenda 21. It focuses instead on the co-ordination of national policies in environment-related areas. However, as noted above, Agenda 21 is mentioned in the OECD's commentary on the OECD Guidelines as a source of environmental principles for multinationals which it is claimed are 'broadly reflect[ed]' in the Guidelines.[94]

The UN Global Compact

The UN Global Compact is an initiative of Kofi Annan, in his capacity as UN Secretary General. Launched in 1999, its core aim was to establish a framework to facilitate dialogue between the UN and 'world business' in relation to the social issues arising from 'globalisation'. This programme revolves around ten core 'principles' relating to human rights, labour,

---

[89] Ibid., Preamble, para. 1.3.
[90] Birnie and Boyle, *International Law and the Environment*, pp. 69–70.
[91] Agenda 21, n. 6 above, para. 30.1.   [92] Ibid., para. 30.3.   [93] Ibid., para. 30.26.
[94] OECD, 'Commentary on the OECD Guidelines for Multinational Enterprises', in OECD, 'The OECD Guidelines for Multinationals: Revision 2000' (OECD, 2000), para. 30.

the environment and anti-corruption measures.[95] These 'principles' are essentially a set of objectives, said to have been distilled from international law, which, it is suggested, should be implemented as part of corporate policy. They include:

> ... the protection of international human rights within their sphere of influence [Principle 1];
> ... the elimination of all forms of forced and compulsory labour [Principle 3];
> ... the effective abolition of child labour [Principle 4];
> ... a precautionary approach to environmental challenges [Principle 7];
> ... initiatives to promote greater environmental responsibility [Principle 8].[96]

The Global Compact is not intended as a 'code of conduct' as such. Obligations are expressed in the widest possible terms and there are no plans for any formal programme of external monitoring. Instead, the aim is that the ten principles set out in the 'Compact' will provide a flexible framework for ongoing co-operation or 'partnership' between multinationals and the UN. Companies are asked to signify their intention to 'sign on' to the 'Global Compact' by a letter – but '[t]he letter is a first step towards full engagement with the Global Compact, not a binding commitment associated with specific performance criteria'.[97] Companies taking this step are referred to as 'participants'. After this, each participant is asked to publish a 'Communication on Progress' in its annual report or CSR reports describing the different ways in which the company is supporting the Global Compact and its ten principles.

The Global Compact project is supported by an Advisory Council (the 'GCAC'), the first meeting of which was held in January 2002. The role of the GCAC is to advise the Global Compact office on strategy, recruitment and participation standards and, generally, 'to think creatively about measures that might enhance the quality and concrete impact of participation in the Compact'.[98] The defining characteristic of this initiative,

---

[95] The introduction of a 'tenth' principle, on corruption, was announced at the Global Compact Leaders Summit, held in New York in June 2004.

[96] See http://www.unglobalcompact.org.

[97] UN, 'Twenty Questions on the UN Global Compact: What Companies Need to Know', http://www.unglobalcompact.org/gc/unweb.nsf/ content/questions.htm.

[98] UN Press Release, 'Secretary-General Convenes First Meeting of Global Compact Advisory Council', 8 January 2002.

however, is its flexibility and general informality. A key communication tool has been the Global Compact web-site which, it is hoped, will provide a databank of 'good practice' accessible by other companies, NGOs and the public at large.[99]

While the flexibility and informality of the Global Compact initiative are regarded by many of its participants as an advantage, concerns have been expressed, particularly by NGOs, about the possibility that its credibility, and the credibility of the UN, could be undermined by participants who consistently flout the principles, or who fail to live up to their commitments under the scheme. This has led to the introduction of a set of 'integrity measures', under which companies can be removed as participants if they fail to comply with guidelines about the use of the Global Compact logo, or fail to provide regular 'Communications on Progress', or for behaviour which threatens to undermine the credibility of the project as a whole.[100]

The non-prescriptive nature of the Global Compact standards themselves has meant that the initiative has been able to appeal to companies and governments from developing as well as industrialised states.[101] Although states have only had a peripheral role in the development of this initiative to date,[102] most seem broadly supportive of it. Many governments have already formally expressed their support for the core aims and principles, and newsletters issued by the Global Compact office give many examples of involvement by states in outreach and promotional activities.[103] Participants at the Global Compact Leaders Summit held in New York in June 2004 included governmental representatives from a diverse group of states including the USA, Norway, Sweden, Brazil, China, Senegal, Qatar and Egypt. The UK government has recorded its own support of the Global Compact on numerous occasions, including in its 2000 White Paper on international development policy in which

---

[99] 'Twenty Questions', n. 97 above.
[100] The Global Compact 'Integrity Measures' can be viewed at the Global Compact web-site, http://www.unglobalcompact.org.
[101] Calder and Culverwell, 'Following Up the World Summit'. A report into the impact of the Global Compact by McKinsey & Co. found that 'The Compact had established a relatively strong presence in developing countries with more than half of the Compact's formal participants headquartered outside the OECD'; McKinsey & Co., 'Assessing the Global Compact's Impact', 11 May 2004, http://www.globalcompact.org, p. 11. However, the same report noted that there was a 'noticeable shortfall' in US membership, p. 11.
[102] Calder and Culverwell, 'Following Up the World Summit', p. 54.
[103] UN, Global Compact Newsletter, December 2001, at http://www.unglobalcompact.org. See also UNGA Res. No. 56/76 of 24 January 2002 ('Towards Global Partnerships').

the Global Compact is described as a set of 'key principles for the conduct of multinational enterprises'.[104]

The UN Norms on the Responsibilities of Transnational Corporations

Since 1998, the UN Sub-Commission on the Protection and Promotion of Human Rights, through a specially created Working Group, has been working on a project to examine, identify and elaborate upon the responsibilities of multinationals under human rights law.[105] The UN Norms,[106] adopted by the Sub-Commission on 13 August 2003, are essentially an attempt to translate existing human rights principles (traditionally addressed to states) to the corporate context. In addition to the more traditional human rights concerns, such as rights to life and security of the person, they also cover many of the key issues associated with CSR, such as workplace health and safety, environmental protection and consumer safety. In 2004, the UN's Commission on Human Rights decided, at its sixtieth session, to continue the process (while noting that the Sub-Commission's norms were merely 'a draft proposal' with 'no legal standing of their own') by proposing further consultation and a report by the UN High Commissioner for Human Rights.[107] This report was handed down at the Commission's sixty-first session in April 2005, following which the Commission issued a resolution requesting that the Secretary General appoint a 'special representative on the issue of human rights and transnational corporations and other business enterprises, for an initial period of two years . . . with the following mandate':

(a) To identify and clarify standards of corporate responsibility and accountability for transnational corporations and other business enterprises with regard to human rights;

(b) To elaborate on the role of States in effectively regulating and adjudicating the role of transnational corporations and other business enterprises with regard to human rights, including through international cooperation;

---

[104] DFID, White Paper, 'Eliminating World Poverty: Making Globalisation Work for the Poor', Cm 5006 (2000), pp. 59–60.

[105] UN Sub-Commission, Res. 1998/9, 20 August 1998. For further background to this project, see D. Weissbrodt, 'The Beginning of a Sessional Working Group on Transnational Corporations within the UN Sub-Commission on Prevention of Discrimination and Protection of Minorities' in M. Kamminga and S. Zia-Zarifi (eds.), *Liability of Multinational Corporations under International Law* (The Hague: Kluwer, 2000).

[106] See n. 9 above.   [107] UN Doc. E/CN.4/RES/2004/116.

(c) To research and clarify the implications for transnational corporations
     and other business enterprises of concepts such as 'complicity' and
     'sphere of influence';

(d) To develop materials and methodologies for undertaking human
     rights impact assessments of the activities of transnational
     corporations and other business enterprises;

(e) To compile a compendium of best practices of states and transnational
     corporations and other business enterprises.[108]

Summary

There are several general international CSR regimes already in existence,
and several other international instruments touching on CSR. All of
these regimes (with the exception of the UN Norms) are explicitly stated
to be 'voluntary'. However, although a particular initiative is described as
'voluntary', it by no means follows that compliance with its underlying
principles is optional too. Could these 'soft law' initiatives eventually
provide the basis of 'an international law of CSR', applicable directly to
companies? If so, what are the key principles likely to be?

Emerging legal principles

It is at least a theoretical possibility that new international law principles, directly applicable to multinationals, could emerge from current
'soft law' CSR-related initiatives. As discussed in chapter 2, for a new customary principle to emerge, there must be both consistent state practice,
evidencing a high degree of consensus around the desirability of the new
principle, and evidence of a conviction on the part of states that the new
principle is legally binding. Although it is states that ultimately *make* the
law, they are not the only possible *subjects* of international law. Therefore,
it is open to states to allocate certain international law responsibilities
directly to companies, whether as a matter of custom or by treaty.

Although most of the 'soft law' initiatives discussed above are explicitly 'non-binding', they are still legally significant, as discussed in chapter
2, as a way of testing attitudes, developing consensus around an issue
and shaping future norms. Already, a number of themes are emerging from international 'soft law' initiatives, which could well form the
foundations of future international rules on CSR. Some of these could

---

[108] UN Doc. E/CN.4/2005/L.87. Professor John Ruggie was appointed to this post on 28 July
2005.

possibly emerge as customary principles, though others are more likely to be features of treaty-based regimes.

Minimum international health, safety and environmental standards

The CSR-related work of UN agencies and other international organisations, discussed in the previous section, suggests that the idea that multinationals are subject to *international* (as well as national) standards is already widely accepted. This appears to be most strongly felt in relation to labour standards. In this area, both the ILO and the UN Secretary General (through the UN Global Compact) have referred to the existence of 'core' or 'fundamental' principles, said to derive from international consensus. These 'core' or 'fundamental' principles do not include workplace health and safety. However, the provisions of the ILO Tripartite Declaration make it clear that compliance with *national* workplace health and safety standards will not necessarily be sufficient.[109] Workplace health and safety is also covered in the OECD Guidelines, imposed on multinationals 'within the framework of *applicable* [i.e. including international] law'.[110] However, its provisions give greater flexibility to multinationals than the ILO Tripartite Declaration, requiring merely that multinationals should 'take *adequate* steps to ensure occupational health and safety in their operations'.[111] In addition, the minimum general standards that must be observed by multinationals in relation to employment and industrial relations are only 'those observed by *comparable employers in the host country*'.[112] It would appear, therefore, that a multinational could fulfil its obligations under the OECD Guidelines without necessarily applying the 'highest' standards. These inconsistencies would tend to contradict the idea of a customary prohibition on 'double standards' in relation to workplace health and safety, although, given the restricted membership of the OECD, the ILO Tripartite Declaration is arguably a better indication of international consensus on this point.

The UN Sub-Commission regards the provision of a safe and healthy workplace as part of the human rights obligations of companies. In its Commentary on paragraph 7 of the UN Norms, it refers to both national *and* international standards, i.e., 'Transnational corporations and other business enterprises bear responsibility for the occupational health and

---

[109] See ILO Tripartite Declaration, n. 5 above, Article 37, quoted at p. 256 above.
[110] OECD Guidelines, Revision 2000, n. 33 above, Part IV (Employment and Industrial Relations).
[111] Ibid., para. 4(a) (emphasis added).   [112] Ibid. (emphasis added).

safety of their workers and shall provide a working environment in accordance with the national requirements of the countries in which they are located *and with international standards . . .*'[113]

Environmental protection is included in the 'core' principles listed in the Global Compact. Both the Draft UN Code and the OECD Guidelines have alluded to the presence of 'international' standards for multinationals in relation to environmental protection. However, the OECD Guidelines downplay the significance of international standards in this area, casting the obligations of multinationals 'within the framework of laws, regulations and administrative practices *in the countries in which they operate* and *in consideration of* relevant international agreements, principles, objectives and standards . . .' (emphasis added). On the other hand, Agenda 21 refers to environmental management as 'among the highest corporate priorities'. The language of the UN Norms is stronger still, under which multinationals '*shall* carry out their activities . . . in accordance with nationals laws, regulations, administrative practices and policies . . . *as well as in accordance with the relevant international agreements, principles, objectives, responsibilities and standards with regard to the environment*'.[114] However, unlike the provisions on workplace health and safety, no further guidance is provided in the Commentary as to where the relevant international standards may be found.

Overall, of the three key health and safety issues related to CSR, it is in relation to consumer protection that international standards receive the least prominence. The Draft UN Code included a provision stating that multinationals 'shall perform their activities *with due regard to international standards* and so that they do not cause injury to the health or endanger the safety of consumers'.[115] However, the OECD Guidelines merely refer to 'fair' practices and the need to take 'all reasonable steps to ensure the safety and quality of the goods or services they provide'. On the other hand, all goods or services are required to meet 'legally required standards' in relation to consumer health and safety, which

---

[113] UN Norms, n. 9 above, Commentary, to para. 7, sub-para (a) (emphasis added). The Commentary then goes on to list a number of ILO Conventions in which the relevant international standards are said to be found, including the 1981 Occupational Safety and Health Convention (No. 155) and the 1993 Prevention of Major Industrial Accidents Convention (No. 174). Although, given the 'variable level of normative content' of these treaties, it is questionable whether many of their provisions are actually reflective of customary law as yet. Calder and Culverwell, 'Following Up the World Summit', p. 62.

[114] UN Norms, n. 9 above, para. 14 (emphasis added).

[115] Draft UN Code, n. 3 above, para. 37.

could encompass international standards (though perhaps not those set out in 'voluntary' codes).[116] The UN Norms, too, refer to the standard of 'fair business, marketing, advertising practices' and require also that multinationals 'take all necessary steps to ensure the safety and quality of the goods and services they provide'.[117] However, the Commentary makes it clear that this does involve observance of 'the relevant international standards for the protection of consumers, such as the United Nations Guidelines for Consumer Protection, and relevant international standards for the promotion of specific products, such as the International Code of Marketing of Breast-milk Substitutes . . . and the Ethical Criteria for Medical Drug Promotion'.[118]

As well as referring to 'international standards', the Draft UN Code included an express prohibition on 'double standards' in relation to consumer safety.[119] The standards relating to consumer protection under the OECD Guidelines, on the other hand, are less explicit on this point and allow for a greater degree of subjectivity as to what will constitute 'fair' business and marketing.

Supply chain responsibility

As discussed in previous chapters, the fact that multinationals are composed of different legal entities inevitably raises the question of how international law responsibilities are to be allocated as between members of the group. The OECD Guidelines provide only limited guidance in this respect.[120] However, in recognition of the fact that many multinationals now operate through non-equity forms, the OECD Guidelines also contain provisions relating to the management of the 'supply chain', in which multinationals are asked to '[e]ncourage, where practicable, business partners, including suppliers and sub-contractors, to apply principles of corporate conduct compatible with the Guidelines'.[121]

Recent statements on the CSR responsibilities of multinationals show growing acceptance of the principle of 'supply chain responsibility', that is, the idea that multinationals have responsibilities to promote good

---

[116] OECD Guidelines, Revision 2000, n. 33 above, Part VII (Consumer Interests), para. 1 and Commentary.

[117] UN Norms, n. 9 above, para. 13.   [118] Ibid., Commentary on para. 13, sub-para (b).

[119] I.e. multinationals should not 'bring about variations in the quality of products in each market which would have detrimental effects on consumers'; Draft UN Code, n. 3 above, para. 37.

[120] See OECD Guidelines, Revision 2000, n. 33 above, Part I (Concepts and Principles), para. 4.

[121] Ibid., Part II (General Policies), para. 10.

business practices amongst their suppliers and contractors. As Amnesty explains:

The performance of a company's contractors, suppliers and partners . . . is perceived to reflect the performance of the company. The general public does not draw a distinction between them and the transnational corporations to whom they are contracted. Companies should therefore promote similar standards through all third parties who act with them or on their behalf.[122]

Compared with the soft language used in the OECD Guidelines, the Commentary to the UN Norms sets the bar very high indeed:

Transnational Corporations and other business enterprises shall *ensure* that they only do business with (including purchasing from and selling to) contractors, subcontractors, suppliers, licensees, distributors, and natural or other legal persons that follow these or substantially similar Norms. Transnational corporations and other business enterprises using or considering entering into business relationships with contractors, subcontractors, suppliers, licensees, distributors, or natural or other legal persons that do not comply with the Norms shall initially work with them to reform or decrease violations, but if they will not change, *the enterprise shall cease doing business with them.*[123]

Similarly, the Base Code of the UK's ETI[124] commits its members:

on the basis of knowledge gained from monitoring to: (a) negotiate and implement agreed schedules for corrective actions with suppliers failing to observe the terms of the code, i.e. a continuous improvement approach; (b) require the immediate cessation of serious breaches of the code; and (c) where serious breaches of the code persist, to terminate any business relationship with the supplier concerned.[125]

This effectively requires multinationals to police compliance by their contractors with the Base Code and to use termination of contractual relationships as a sanction. Whether this actually happens in practice, the principle of 'supply chain responsibility' has developed into a key

---

[122] Amnesty International, 'Human Rights Guidelines for Companies', 1998 (Personnel policies and practices).

[123] UN Norms, n. 9 above, Commentary to para 15, sub-para (c) (emphasis added).

[124] See pp. 96, 99 above.

[125] ETI, Base Code, Principles of Implementation, para. 4., http://www.ethicaltrade.org. Note, however, that this provision draws back from the position set out in a previous version of the Base Code, which provided that 'member companies must *require* that suppliers meet agreed standards within a reasonable timeframe and that performance in this regard is measured, transparent and, ultimately, a precondition to further business'.

concept in the international CSR debate, and is now widely referred to in corporate policy statements and reports on CSR.[126]

These developments point to an emerging principle that the obligations of multinationals in relation to workplace, environmental and consumer health are owed not only to those immediately affected by their *own* operations (e.g. workers, communities and consumers), but also to those affected by the operations of their contractors, suppliers and distributors as well. While the limits of 'supply chain responsibility' are not clear, this could potentially extend, as the UN Norms suggest, to all those entities involved in the supply, production and marketing of a particular brand or product, both upstream (e.g. suppliers) and downstream (e.g. distributors). As far as *downstream* obligations are concerned, the responsibility of parent companies is already recognised, in theory at least, in the area of product liability. Overall, though, the allocation of international law responsibilities within multinationals is an issue that urgently needs clarification. It is a pity, therefore, that this issue is not directly referred to as an item for further study in the mandate given to the UN's special representative on business and human rights,[127] although, as noted in chapter 5, it is quite possible that domestic jurisprudence on 'parent company liability', if allowed to develop, will have a bearing on how international law on this question develops in future.

Sustainable development

An interesting feature of the more recent statements on CSR is the extension of concepts derived from international environmental law to the corporate context. Under the OECD Guidelines, for example, multinationals are required to have respect for the 'wider goal of sustainable development'[128] and to 'assess, and address' the environmental impacts of processes and products over their 'full life cycle'.[129] According to the Commentary on the UN Norms:

Transnational corporations and other business enterprises shall respect the right to a clean and healthy environment in the light of the relationship between the

---

[126] K. Gordon and M. Miyake, 'Deciphering Codes of Conduct: a Review of their Contents', OECD Working Papers on International Investment, No. 1992/2, 1999, p. 14; OECD, 'Codes of Conduct – Explaining their Economic Significance', p. 15.

[127] See n. 108 above and accompanying text.

[128] OECD Guidelines, Revision 2000, n. 33 above, Part V (Environment).

[129] Ibid., para. 3.

environment and human rights; concerns for intergenerational equity; internationally recognised environmental standards, for example with regard to air pollution, water pollution, land use, biodiversity and hazardous wastes; and the wider goal of sustainable development, that is, development that meets the needs of the present without compromising the ability of future generations to meet their own needs.[130]

The role of business in achieving sustainable development goals was one of the central themes of the WSSD held in Johannesburg in September 2002 and is mentioned specifically in the final Political Declaration, i.e. 'We agree that in pursuit of its legitimate activities the private sector, including both large and small companies, *has a duty* to contribute to the evolution of equitable and sustainable communities and societies.'[131] The connection between CSR and sustainable development is also recognised in the WSSD Plan of Implementation in which governments express their commitment to step up their efforts in relation to the promotion of CSR within their own jurisdictions, and in particular to

Enhance corporate environmental and social responsibility and accountability . . . [including] . . . action at all levels to:

(a) Encourage industry to improve social and environmental performance through voluntary initiatives, including environmental management systems, codes of conduct, certification and public reporting on environmental and social issues . . .

(b) Encourage dialogue between enterprises and the communities in which they operate and other stakeholders;

(c) Encourage financial institutions to incorporate sustainable development into their decision-making processes;

(d) Develop workplace-based partnerships and programmes including training and education programmes.[132]

Sustainable development ideals are clearly having a significant impact on the development of national and international policy towards multinationals. Despite the reference to the 'duty' of multinationals to

---

[130] UN Norms, n. 9 above, Commentary to para. 14, para. (c).

[131] WSSD 2002 Declaration on Sustainable Development, n. 7 above.

[132] WSSD 2002, 'Plan of Implementation of the World Summit on Sustainable Development', in UN, 'Report of the World Summit on Sustainable Development', UN Doc. A/CONF.199/20, Sales No. E.03.II.A.1, para. 18. See also the UNGA Millennium Declaration, UN Doc. A/RES/55/2, para. 30, in which members of the UN resolve to 'give greater opportunities to the private sector, non-governmental organisations and civil society, in general' to contribute to the realisation of the UN's 'Millennium Development Goals'.

contribute to sustainable development in the WSSD Declaration, there is no real evidence that this amounts to a positive legal obligation as yet.[133] Nevertheless, the involvement of the private sector is now seen as crucial to the fulfilment of key sustainable development objectives set by the international community, including the Millennium Development Goals.[134] This, in turn, has led to the establishment of a number of new 'enabling' initiatives designed to help connect multinational businesses with international development policy.[135]

Obligations to warn of dangers; obligations to consult

Obligations to warn of dangers, and to consult with those affected by potential risks, are already part of the customary international law that applies between states.[136] To what extent might multinationals be subject to similar obligations under international law? Provisions to this effect already appear in key 'soft law' instruments on CSR and, as shall be discussed further below,[137] are also a prominent feature of treaties relating to hazardous wastes and chemicals. Under the OECD Guidelines, multinationals are asked also to 'provide information to employee representatives which is needed for meaningful negotiations on conditions of employment'[138] and to 'promote consultation and co-operation between employers and employees on matters of mutual concern'.[139] In relation to the environment, multinationals are asked to

provide the public and employees with adequate and timely information on the potential environment, health and safety impacts of the activities of the enterprise, which could include reporting on progress in improving environmental performance ... and ... engage in adequate and timely communication and consultation with the communities directly effected by the environmental, health and safety policies of the enterprise and by their implementation.[140]

---

[133] On the legal status of the principle of 'sustainable development' in international law generally, see Birnie and Boyle, *International Law and the Environment*, p. 95.

[134] See Calder and Culverwell, 'Following Up the World Summit'; IBLF, 'Business and the Millennium Development Goals: a Framework for Action' (IBLF, 2003), http://www.undp.org/business/docs/mdg_business.pdf.

[135] E.g. the UNDP 'Growing Sustainable Business' Initiative, http://www.undp.org/business/gsb/; GRI, 'Communicating Business Contributions to the Millennium Development Goals', November 2004, http://www.globalreporting/org.

[136] See p. 66 above.   [137] See pp. 290–6 below.

[138] OECD Guidelines, Revision 2000, n. 33 above, Chapter IV (Employment and Industrial Relations), para. 2(b).

[139] Ibid., para.2(c).

[140] Ibid., Chapter V (Environment), para. 2(a) and (b). This is a stricter obligation than that which previously appeared in the Draft UN Code, which merely required

As far as consumers are concerned, multinationals are asked, 'as appropriate to the goods or services', to 'provide accurate and clear information regarding their content, safe use, maintenance, storage and disposal, sufficient to enable consumers to make informed decisions',[141] and to '[p]rovide transparent and effective procedures that address consumer complaints and contribute to fair and timely resolution of consumer disputes without undue cost or burden'.[142]

The ILO Tripartite Declaration, in addition to requiring 'the highest standards of safety and health', requires that multinationals:

> make available to the representatives of the workers in the enterprise, and upon request, to the competent authorities and the workers' and employers' organizations in all countries in which they operate, information on the safety and health standards relevant to their local operations, which they observe in other countries. In particular, they should make known to those concerned any special hazards and related protective measures associated with new products and processes.[143]

Provisions on information-sharing about risks also feature prominently in the UN Norms. On the issue of workplace health and safety, the Commentary to the Norms provides that:

> Transnational Corporations and other business enterprises shall consult and cooperate fully with health, safety and labour authorities, workers' representatives and their organizations and established safety and health organizations on matters of occupational health and safety . . . [and] . . . shall investigate work-related accidents, keep records of incidents stating their cause and remedial measures taken to prevent similar accidents [and] ensure the provision of remedies for the injured.[144]

In relation to environmental issues, multinationals are required to 'take appropriate measures in their activities to reduce the risk of accidents and damage to the environment by adopting best management practices and technologies' including 'sharing of technology, knowledge and

---

disclosure to national authorities 'on request or on a regular basis, as specified by those authorities'; Draft UN Code, n. 3 above, para. 38.

[141] OECD Guidelines, Revision 2000, n. 33 above, Chapter VII (Consumer Interests), para. 2. Compare with the Draft UN Code which required, in addition, disclosure of general information about product risks, information relating to regulatory restrictions or warnings required under the laws of other countries. Draft UN Code, n. 3 above, para. 38.

[142] OECD Guidelines, Revision 2000, n. 33 above, para. 3.

[143] ILO Tripartite Declaration, n. 5 above, para. 37.

[144] UN Norms, n. 9 above, Commentary on para. 7, sub-para (d).

assistance, as well as through environmental management systems, sustainability reporting, and reporting of anticipated or actual releases of hazardous and toxic substances'.[145]

On consumer protection, the UN Norms provide that:

Any information provided by a transnational corporation or other business enterprise with regard to the purchase, use, content, maintenance, storage and disposal of its products and services shall be provided in a clear, comprehensible and prominently visible manner in the language officially recognized by the country in which such products or services are provided.[146]

As noted above, rules on warnings, information-sharing and consultation are already part of customary international law obligations of states. Of course, it does not automatically follow from this that these obligations can or should be extended to apply to multinationals directly. However, the fact that these principles have been repeatedly endorsed in a series of instruments relating to multinationals,[147] plus their relative lack of ambiguity, makes it quite possible that they will emerge as part of the customary law of CSR. At the very least, it is likely that these kinds of provisions will play an important part in any future treaty-based solutions.

Precautionary principle

The 'precautionary principle', already an important principle in international environmental law,[148] is also becoming influential as a way of defining the scope of multinationals' obligations in relation to health, safety and environmental issues, as evidenced by its adoption by the Global Compact as one of the ten core 'principles' to be observed by companies.[149] The OECD Guidelines explain the 'precautionary principle' in the following terms: '[c]onsistent with the scientific and technical understanding of the risks, where there are threats of serious damage to the environment, taking also into account human health and safety, not to use the lack of full scientific certainty as a reason for postponing cost-effective measures to prevent or minimise such damage'.[150]

---

[145] Ibid., Commentary on para. 14, sub-para. (g).
[146] Ibid., Commentary on para. 13, sub-para (d).
[147] See pp. 292–5 below on the use of the principle of 'prior informed consent' in existing treaty regimes.
[148] See pp. 66–7 above.
[149] 'Businesses should support a precautionary approach to environmental challenges'; Global Compact, Principle 7, http://www.globalcompact.org.
[150] OECD Guidelines, Revision 2000, n. 33 above, Part V (Environment), para. 4.

The UN Norms contain a number of references to the 'precautionary principle'. According to the paragraph on environmental protection,
business enterprises are obliged to 'conduct their activities . . . in accordance with . . . the precautionary principle'.[151] The Commentary adds:

Transnational Corporations . . . shall . . . respect the precautionary principle
when dealing, for example, with preliminary risk assessments that may indicate
unacceptable effects on health or the environment. Further, they shall not use
the lack of full scientific certainty as a reason to delay the introduction of cost-
effective measures to prevent such effects.[152]

The UN Norms also propose the 'precautionary principle' as the standard
of care that should apply in relation to consumers.[153]

Present uncertainty about the meaning and application of the 'precautionary principle' makes suggestions that it has already achieved customary status somewhat premature.[154] However, it does, as Birnie and
Boyle point out, have a 'legally significant core'[155] which is helping to
give substance to the standard of care required from multinationals in
relation to their international operations and, as such, is likely to be
an important guiding principle in any future customary or treaty-based
CSR regimes.

Environmental impact assessment

Environmental impact or 'risk' assessment goes hand in hand with good
environmental management. Over the past few decades, environmental impact assessments have become an important regulatory tool in
national environmental law.[156] Not surprisingly, therefore, the need for
environmental impact assessments for certain projects is also frequently
mentioned in international 'soft law' instruments on CSR. The OECD
Guidelines recommend, for example, that all multinationals

Assess, and address in decision-making, the foreseeable environmental, health
and safety-related impacts associated with the processes, goods and services of
the enterprise over their full life cycle. Where these proposed activities may have
significant environmental, health or safety impacts, and where they are subject
to a decision of a competent authority, prepare an appropriate environmental
impact assessment.[157]

---

[151] UN Norms, n. 9 above, para. 14.   [152] Ibid., Commentary on para. 14, sub-para. (c).
[153] Ibid., para 3, and Commentary on para. 13, sub-para. (c).
[154] Birnie and Boyle, *International Law and the Environment*, pp. 118–21
[155] Ibid., p. 120.   [156] Ibid., p. 131.
[157] OECD Guidelines, Revision 2000, n. 33 above, Chapter V (Environment), para 3.

The UN Norms contain the suggestion that environmental impact assessment is part and parcel of compliance by companies of their human rights obligations, i.e.:

transnational corporations and other business enterprises shall assess the impact of their activities on the environment and human health, including impacts from siting decisions, natural resource extraction activities, the production and sale of products or services, and the generation, storage, transport and disposal of hazardous and toxic substances.[158]

There is clearly a fair amount of support, in international 'soft law' instruments, for the idea that multinationals ought to carry out environmental impact assessments prior to undertaking activities that may pose a risk to individuals, communities or the environment at large. Although environmental impact assessments are well established in international law, and are arguably already mandatory from states in relation to projects which pose a risk of transboundary environmental damage,[159] there is no real evidence that multinationals are presently subject to any direct obligations to this effect. Nevertheless, like the 'precautionary principle', the idea that multinationals should take proper steps to assess environmental risks is likely to be an important guiding principle in future international CSR regimes.

Openness and transparency

Openness and transparency has emerged as one of the key issues in developing policies on multinational accountability, at both national and international level. As discussed above, the issue of whether CSR reporting should be 'voluntary' or 'mandatory' has been one of the more contentious issues of policy in the international CSR debate. While the approach at national level has hitherto been to encourage social and environmental disclosures on a voluntary basis, there is now, as discussed in chapter 4, a move towards greater regulation of their timing and content.

Both the Draft UN Code and the OECD Guidelines contain references to the periodic reporting of non-financial, as well as financial, information.[160] Under the Guidelines, the standards for social and

---

[158] UN Norms, n. 9 above, Commentary on para. 14, sub-para. (c).
[159] Birnie and Boyle, *International Law and the Environment*, pp. 131–2.
[160] Draft UN Code, n. 3 above, part C; OECD Guidelines, Revision 2000, n. 33 above, Chapter III (Disclosure), para. 1.

environmental reporting should be of 'high quality', where such standards exist.[161] Chapter III of the Guidelines provides:

Enterprises should ensure that timely, regular, reliable and relevant information is disclosed regarding their activities, structure, financial situation and performance. This information should be disclosed for the enterprise as a whole and, where appropriate, along business lines or geographic areas. Disclosure policies of enterprises should be tailored to the nature, size and location of the enterprise, with due regard taken of costs, business confidentiality and other competitive concerns.[162]

In addition:

Enterprises are encouraged to communicate additional information that could include . . . value statements or statements of business conduct intended for public disclosure including information on the social, ethical or environmental policies of the enterprise and other codes of conduct to which the company subscribes . . . . and information on systems for managing risk and complying with laws, and on statements or codes of business conduct.[163]

Similar, though less detailed, provisions also appear in the UN Norms, which also provide that multinationals should disclose 'the location of their offices, subsidiaries and factories, so as to facilitate measures to ensure that the enterprises, products and services are being produced under conditions that respect these Norms'.[164] Reflecting the growing interest in CSR reporting as a form of regulation of multinationals, the WSSD Plan of Implementation provisions on CSR include a commitment to provide support for 'voluntary initiatives' including 'public reporting on environmental and social issues, taking into account such initiatives as the International Organization for Standardization (ISO) standards and Global Reporting Initiative guidelines on sustainability reporting'.[165]

External monitoring

Independent and external monitoring of CSR-related disclosures by companies is obviously essential to the credibility of CSR initiatives. Amnesty's comments are representative of the position of many NGOs:

Amnesty International recommends that there be in place credible systems for monitoring compliance with corporate codes of behaviour and that their reports

---

[161] OECD Guidelines, Revision 2000, n. 33 above, Chapter III (Disclosure), para. 2.
[162] Ibid., para.1.   [163] Ibid., para. 5.
[164] UN Norms, n. 9 above, Commentary on para 15, sub-para. (d).
[165] WSSD Plan of Implementation, n. 132 above, para. 18(a).

be independently verifiable. There is an analogy with financial audits and social audits. Companies maintain their own internal accounting controls which are periodically verified by outside independent auditors in order to ensure their integrity. Similarly, while companies should have internal social auditing procedures by which they can determine the degree of compliance with the organisation's code of conduct, there should also be periodic independent verification of these procedures and the reports they generate.[166]

In the past, many CSR initiatives have settled for *internal* monitoring and verification procedures, although external monitoring is becoming more widespread, both on a voluntary basis and as a condition of participation in CSR-related schemes.[167] External monitoring organisations have also benefited from out-of-court settlements between campaigners and multinationals.[168]

The OECD Guidelines contain only scant references to independent monitoring. In relation to environmental management, it is suggested that multinationals should establish and maintain a management system 'appropriate to the enterprise', which would include 'regular monitoring and verification of progress towards environmental, health, and safety objectives or targets'. Elsewhere it is suggested that 'the transparency and effectiveness of non-financial disclosure may be enhanced by independent verification',[169] but this does not form part of the substantive provisions of the Guidelines.

The UN Norms, in contrast, propose something far more ambitious:

Transnational corporations and other business enterprises shall be subject to periodic monitoring and verification by United Nations, other international and national mechanisms already in existence or yet to be created, regarding application of Norms. This monitoring shall be transparent and independent and

---

[166] Amnesty International, 'Human Rights Guidelines for Companies', 1998 (Implementation and Monitoring).

[167] T. McCawley, 'Racing to Improve its Reputation', *Financial Times*, 21 December 2000, p. 14, reporting on Nike's decision to employ accounting firm PriceWaterhouseCoopers as external 'social auditors' in relation to the company's Asian and South American suppliers. The US-based Fair Labor Association now requires external monitoring of labour standards of participating companies. See http://www.fairlabor.org/all/companies/index.html.

[168] See, for example, the settlement reached in the case of *Kasky v. Nike*, 539 US 654 (2003) under which Nike agreed to donate US $1.5 million to the Fair Labor Association, part of which would be applied towards '[i]ncreased training and local capacity building to improve the quality of independent monitoring in manufacturing countries'; Nike, Press Release, 12 September 2003.

[169] OECD, 'Commentary on the OECD Guidelines for Multinational Enterprises', in OECD, 'The OECD Guidelines for Multinationals: Revision 2000' (OECD, 2000), Chapter III – Disclosure, paragraph 16.

take into account input from stakeholders (including non-governmental organisations) and as a result of complaints of violations of these Norms. Further, transnational corporations and other business enterprises shall conduct periodic evaluations concerning the impact of their own activities on human rights under these Norms.[170]

The proposition that independent external monitoring is usually necessary for the credibility of a multinational's CSR-related disclosures and claims is, by now, fairly uncontroversial. However, the present lack of any universally agreed monitoring and verification system makes the idea of external verification as a *legal* obligation problematic. Nevertheless, there are, as noted in chapter 1 above, several non-governmental projects now underway to develop international reporting and auditing guidelines for companies, of which the GRI is probably the best-known example. In the longer term, it is likely that external monitoring will become a standard feature of mandatory CSR regimes.

Identifying customary rules on CSR: some cautionary remarks

Although there are differences, there is also a good deal of common ground between the various international initiatives discussed above. Given enough international consensus about their meaning, application and 'bindingness', any of these principles – the need to observe international minimum standards, to consult with those affected, to take a 'precautionary' approach, to undertake proper risk assessment, to maintain policies of openness and transparency, and to engage external monitors – could potentially become legally binding on multinationals as a matter of international customary law.

However, these international initiatives do not, of themselves, provide the strong evidence of state practice needed to support the claim that their contents, and the principles they stand for, are mandatory for multinationals under international law. So far states, and particularly developing states, have had little involvement in the development of the content of these international 'codes of conduct' for multinationals. The most recent of these, the Global Compact and the UN Norms, for example, have been developed, not by states but by individuals and committees working within the UN system. (States are not, officially at least, party to the Global Compact 'network' – although, as noted above, many have shown their support for the initiative in other ways – and the UN Norms are still only a set of recommendations, rather than a

---

[170] UN Norms, n. 9 above, para. 16.

finished code, and have not formally been adopted by UN members.[171])
An exception is the OECD Guidelines – an inter-governmental initiative
both addressed to, and endorsed by, OECD member states. It is the only
internationally agreed regime covering workplace, environmental *and*
consumer health, and, following an extensive overhaul in 2000, 'the only
international CSR initiative with a compliance mechanism'.[172] Although
not an international treaty, successive annual reports on the implementation of the Guidelines suggest a reasonable level of commitment by
member states. On the other hand, this is an initiative to which developing states have made little or no contribution, although a number
of non-member states have chosen to adopt the Guidelines and thereby
become involved in follow-up meetings and procedures.[173]

Of course this does not mean that the principles set out in these various initiatives cannot achieve customary status. As is often noted, international CSR regulation is only in its infancy. Although work in this field
dates back to the 1960s, it is only relatively recently that governments
of the world have recognised, as the WSSD commitments make clear,
the linkages between business and sustainable development, and the
vital role of national governments in helping to create an enabling environment for CSR, not only within national boundaries but internationally.[174] Clearly, much depends, now, on the extent to which states take up
these key principles and incorporate them in their national policies. This
is already happening to a limited extent, in the practice of some home
states, discussed in chapter 4, of making export-credit assistance condi-
tional upon some form of acknowledgement of the OECD Guidelines,
or in enacting legislation requiring greater transparency from companies about social and environmental issues or in their support for international CSR initiatives. While many campaigning NGOs complain that
they do not go nearly far enough, these experimental measures may well
lead to more ambitious forms of home state regulation in the future.
With enough conviction and consistency, the regulatory initiatives of
home states have the potential to bring about new legal responsibilities
under international law, not just for states, but also for multinationals
themselves.

---

[171] Note also that the UN Norms themselves have been criticised for the failure to
distinguish between customary obligations, 'soft law' obligations and implementing
arrangements. 'Though it was apparently intended that they should be binding, it
would be difficult to make them so given the imprecision surrounding the source of
their authority, and the lack of clarity as to exactly what was being prescribed and
proscribed'; Calder and Culverwell, 'Following Up the World Summit', p. 62.
[172] Ibid., p. 47.   [173] See pp. 252–3 above.
[174] Calder and Culverwell, 'Following Up the World Summit', p. 35.

International CSR regulation: proposals, precedents and possibilities

Customary law clearly has an important role to play as a source of future international rules on CSR. But customary law-making can be an uncertain and lengthy process. How, in the shorter term, can states strengthen the international regulatory framework for CSR? This section looks at some recent proposals, together with some international regulatory initiatives, relevant to workplace, environmental and consumer health, which are already in place.

Recent international regulatory proposals

A Framework Convention on Corporate Social Responsibility?

The WSSD Plan of Implementation includes a provision under which state parties commit to

Actively promote corporate responsibility and accountability, based on Rio Principles, *including through the full development and effective implementation of intergovernmental agreements and measures*, international initiatives and public–private partnerships, appropriate national regulations, and continuous improvement in corporate practices in all countries.[175]

This could be read as a commitment to develop new international agreements relating to CSR. However, interpretative statements issued by states since the wording was finalised suggest that it was only intended to cover existing agreements.[176] No doubt, this was a disappointment to NGOs such as FoE, which had used the WSSD as a forum to present a set of proposals for an 'effective legally binding international framework on corporate accountability and liability'.[177] In its position paper, released prior to the summit, FoE had proposed a number of legal reforms including new corporate and directors' duties to report on social and environmental impacts, imposition of new liabilities on corporations and directors for corporate activity in breach of international agreements, private rights of action for 'affected people' (including a right to challenge 'company decisions'), the obligation of states to provide legal aid to foreign litigants, and minimum standards of corporate behaviour in relation to environmental, social, labour and human rights issues.[178] A number of innovative sanctions were also proposed, including

---

[175] WSSD Plan of Implementation, n. 132 above, para. 49 (emphasis added).
[176] Calder and Culverwell, 'Following Up the World Summit', p. 14.
[177] FoE, 'Towards Binding Corporate Accountability', http://www.foei.org.   [178] Ibid.

suspension of stock exchange listings, withholding access to public subsidies and ('in extreme cases') the withdrawal of limited liability status. Under these proposals, the onus would be on state parties to implement the necessary reforms under national legislation.

The FoE proposals are notable as an early attempt by an NGO to give some legislative substance and direction to the campaign for internationally binding CSR standards for multinationals. It is, however, difficult to imagine that many states (especially industrialised ones) would agree to such fundamental changes to company law, such as the removal of limited liability in certain circumstances, and even the less controversial proposals (such as the removal of public subsidies for companies found to be in breach of international CSR standards) would still require a considerable amount of negotiation on the detail. An overarching treaty on CSR is an unlikely prospect at present.

Human rights bodies as international regulators

One disadvantage of the FoE proposals is that they rely on states (and primarily home states) for their detailed implementation. Alternatively, a mechanism could conceivably be devised whereby multinationals would be regulated directly by an international institution. As noted above, the UN Norms propose a system of 'periodic monitoring and verification by United Nations, other international and national mechanisms already in existence or yet to be created'.[179] The Commentary adds:

United Nations human rights treaty bodies should monitor implementation of these Norms through the creation of additional reporting requirements for States and the adoption of general comments and recommendations interpreting treaty obligations . . . The Commission on Human Rights should consider establishing a group of experts, a special rapporteur, or working group of the Commission to receive information and take effective action when enterprises fail to comply with the Norms.[180]

These proposals do not necessarily require the negotiation of new international treaties for their implementation. There are various measures that states could take, one of which would be to extend existing Human Rights Commission complaints procedures[181] (which would require a resolution of the Economic and Social Council). Depending on the particular international instrument concerned, reporting

---

[179] UN Norms, n. 9 above, para. 16.   [180] Ibid., Commentary on para. 16, sub-para. (b).
[181] E.g. The '1503 procedure', established under Economic and Social Council Resolution 1503 (XLVII).

obligations of states could be expanded to cover CSR-related topics under interpretative 'General Comments' issued by the relevant supervising body. Complaints procedures under individual treaties could also be expanded (e.g. to provide standing for NGOs and individuals, where this is not already the case,[182] or to cover cases of human rights abuses by multinationals expressly) under additional agreements, known as 'Optional Protocols'.[183] As noted above, the response of the Commission on Human Rights, for the time being, has been to request the appointment of a 'special representative' to investigate a number of general legal and managerial issues relating to business and human rights. The Special Representative's terms of reference do not expressly extend to the identification of suitable international regulatory mechanisms for multinationals. However, this is perhaps indirectly covered by the request in the mandate to examine the potential regulatory roles of states ('including through international cooperation'). [184]

Investor responsibilities under IIAs

Despite the failure of the MAI,[185] there is still broad support, among developed nations and within international organisations such as the WTO and the OECD, for the idea of a multilateral treaty on FDI. But the tone of the discussion has changed. For one thing, there seems to be a greater appreciation that, if such a treaty is to get off the ground, there must be a better 'balance' between the rights and responsibilities of investors,[186] suggesting that one of the key messages of the anti-MAI campaign – 'no rights without responsibilities' – has had some impact.

With this in mind, NGOs have been busy developing proposals for a more balanced and 'people-friendly' MAI.[187] Central to these is the idea

---

[182] Note that while the ICCPR permits complaints by individuals, the ICECSR does not as yet. For a useful overview of enforcement procedures applied by the various UN Treaty bodies see Mertus, *The United Nations and Human Rights*, esp. chapter 4.

[183] Although note that such additional agreements would only be binding upon states that had signed up to them.

[184] UN Doc. E/CN.4/2005/L.87, para. 1(b).   [185] See pp. 19–20 above.

[186] See UNCTAD, 'World Investment Report 1996: Investment, Trade and International Policy Arrangements' (New York and Geneva: UN, 1996), UN Sales No. E.96.II.A.14; World Commission on the Social Dimension of Globalization, 'A Fair Globalization: Creating Opportunities for All' (ILO, February 2004), p. xiii.

[187] T. Clarke, 'Towards a Citizen's MAI: an Alternative to Developing a Global Investment Treaty based on Citizen's Rights and Democratic Control' (Ottawa: Polaris Institute, 1998); K. von Moltke, 'A Model International Investment Agreement for the Promotion of Sustainable Development', IISD, November 2004, http://www.iisd.org.

that multinationals (as 'investors') ought to be subject to social and environmental obligations, as well as the beneficiaries of rights. But investors are not parties to IIAs, which are agreements *between states*. What, then, is the best way of incorporating these social and environmental obligations into a multilateral investment treaty framework? The idea that investor protection rights[188] under international investment agreements may be conditioned upon the investor's 'corporate social responsibility' is a significant departure from standard practice. However, there are scattered precedents to be found in bilateral and regional investment treaties that provide an indication as to how this might be achieved. For instance, there are cases in which a failure by an investor to fulfil development-related obligations imposed by the host state can result in the loss by that investor of preferential status under investment promotion agreements.[189] Under other international investment agreements, development of local employment opportunities has been made a 'condition or advantage for the grant of incentives'.[190] However, for the large part, health, safety and environmental issues tend to be referred to in only 'horatory [i.e. aspirational] language', one state to another, if they are referred to at all.[191] Only in very rare instances do international investment agreements seek to regulate the behaviour of multinationals directly.

Nevertheless, by 1996, according to UNCTAD, 'issues relating to corporate behaviour' were increasingly being raised in the context of international discussions on FDI.[192] The question of 'investor responsibilities' under FDI arrangements was subsequently taken up by the WTO's Working Group on Trade and Investment, the 1998 progress report of which includes 'the rights and obligations of home and host countries and of investors and host countries' in its list of items for further study.[193] Further discussions on the issue of investor responsibilities took place within the WTO's Working Group during 1999, with the European

---

[188] E.g. access to the treaty's dispute resolution procedures. See von Moltke, 'A Model International Investment Agreement', p. 17.

[189] UNCTAD, 'Social Responsibility', UNCTAD Series on issues in international investment agreements (New York and Geneva: UN, 2001), UNCTAD/ITE/IIT/22, p. 19. (Note, though, that the examples supplied by UNTACD all relate to investment promotion agreements between developing countries.)

[190] UNCTAD, 'Employment', UNCTAD Series on Issues in International Investment Agreements (New York and Geneva: UN, 2000), UNCTAD/ITE/IIT/19, p. 14.

[191] Ibid. See also UNCTAD, 'Environment', UNCTAD Series on Issues in International Investment Agreements (New York and Geneva: UN, 2001), UNCTAD/ITE/IIT/23.

[192] UNCTAD, 'World Investment Report 1996', n. 186 above.   [193] Ibid., Annex 1.

Community submitting a short paper on the issue.[194] The Working Group's 1999 report, however, expresses the view that, while some CSR issues (such as restrictive business practices and transfer of technology) were issues that should be considered in this context, 'social and human rights issues . . . were not within the mandate of the Working Group and were not relevant to the WTO'.[195] Moreover:

it was difficult to see how the concept of a balance between the rights and obligations of foreign investors could in practice be translated into international rules. Thus, the approach that had evolved over the years was to rely on instruments of a voluntary nature which were complementary to the basic obligation of firms to respect the rules and regulations of host countries.[196]

The 2001 Doha Ministerial Declaration sought to pave the way for international negotiations, under the auspices of the WTO, 'on a multilateral framework to secure transparent, stable and predictable conditions for long-term cross-border investment'.[197] According to the Declaration, 'any framework should reflect in a balanced manner the interests of home and host countries, and take due account of the development policies and objectives of host governments as well as their right to regulate in the public interest'.[198] However, there was no express mention of the issue of 'investor responsibilities' in the 'Doha mandate' to the WTO working group. As it turned out, no further progress was made on international investment policy at the Cancun Ministerial Conference in 2003, with many developing states opposing the links made between investment and competition policy, and the inclusion of these issues in the WTO agenda generally. As a result, work on this particular part of the WTO's Doha work programme has been suspended.

New international institutions?

Concerns have been expressed by a range of different groups – companies, NGOs and governments – about the present lack of co-ordination at

---

[194] See Communication from European Community and its Member States, 'Where Are We on Foreign Investors' Behaviour?', 16 September 1999.

[195] WTO, 'Report (1999) of the Working Group on the Relationship between Trade and Investment to the General Council', WT/WGTI/3, 22 October 1999, para. 102.

[196] Ibid., para. 103.

[197] Declaration of the 2001 Ministerial Conference in Doha, WT/MIN(01)/DEC1, adopted 14 November 2001, para. 20.

[198] Ibid., para. 22.

international level on CSR. Not only has there been an 'over-proliferation of CSR initiatives at international level and a general lack of clarity about how these relate to each other',[199] there is also a perceived lack of 'policy coherence' between different international bodies on issues and policies with a CSR dimension.[200] The 2004 Report of the ILO's World Commission on the Social Dimension of Globalization proposes: 'the creation of a Parliamentary Group concerned with the coherence and consistency between global economic, social and environmental policies, which should develop an integrated oversight of major international institutions'.[201] And, in addition:

a new operational tool for upgrading the quality of policy coordination between international organizations on issues in which the implementation of their mandates intersect and their policies interact. Policy Coherence Initiatives should be launched by the relevant international organizations to develop more balanced policies for achieving a fair and inclusive globalization. The objective would be to progressively develop integrated policy proposals that appropriately balance economic, social and environmental concerns on specific issues.[202]

With respect to CSR specifically, the World Commission recommended that the ILO 'convene a Forum to develop a practical agenda around the contribution of business to the social dimension of globalization'.[203] However, while there is clearly a need for a more 'strategic approach', care must be taken to ensure that new international initiatives do not add a further, unproductive level of complexity to an already fragmented international regulatory system. At this stage, instead of developing new institutions, many of those working within civil society campaigns for CSR would prefer to see a concerted effort towards

strengthening and rationalizing key initiatives in order to improve their performance in ensuring that businesses adhere to international norms on issues such as human rights, corruption and environmental protection and on engaging business in the delivery of international goals for sustainable development such as the Millennium Development Goals.[204]

---

[199] Calder and Culverwell, 'Following Up the World Summit', p. 7.
[200] 'Negotiations on global governance take place in compartmentalized sectors such as trade, finance, health, social affairs, and development assistance. International organizations focus on their specific mandates and, as a result, the impact of their actions on other important objectives is often lost sight of'; World Commission on the Social Dimension of Globalization, 'A Fair Globalization', n. 186 above, p. 78.
[201] Ibid., p. xiv.   [202] Ibid., p. xiv.   [203] Ibid., p. 123.
[204] Calder and Culverwell, 'Following Up the World Summit', pp. 9–10.

Precedents in international CSR regulation

The regulatory debate surrounding CSR has reached a crossroads. Clearly, there is a case for further, stronger international regulation of multinationals in relation to health, safety and environmental issues. While soft law standards and 'corporate codes of conduct' may have improved the CSR performance of some multinationals, pressures on production costs, as well as fierce competition between countries for inward investment, mean that workers and communities, particularly in developing countries, will continue to suffer.[205] It seems reasonable to expect home states to take a greater role (and it is argued in chapter 3 above that the jurisdictional problems, while real, are often overstated). However, the structural complexity of many multinationals, and the difficulties in defining their boundaries (particularly for 'contract-based' forms),[206] means that gaps and inconsistencies will inevitably result. Even if home state politicians could be persuaded to put aside fears of 'migration' of industry to other states, unilateral home state action is hardly the basis for a comprehensive and systematic system of international regulation. Clearly, an effective *international* solution to the social and environmental problems posed by multinationals requires *international co-operation*. But what form should this co-operation take? What kinds of international strategies are needed? While an overarching CSR treaty would be extremely difficult to negotiate, devising international regimes to tackle specific CSR-related issues may be less problematic. This section briefly outlines some potentially useful precedents. The selection of CSR-related treaties discussed below is by no means comprehensive, but is designed to illustrate some of the various regulatory options available, and to give a flavour of what is possible in the CSR field – given enough political will.

Pollution from ships: the 1969 Civil Liability Convention and the 1971 Fund Convention

The many obstacles faced by anyone seeking to bring a private tort-based claim against a multinational are discussed in earlier chapters (and particularly chapter 5). The unfortunate result is that there will be cases where victims go uncompensated, and the multinational's operating practices go unchallenged. In the field of oil pollution, however,

---

[205] See Dine, *Companies, International Trade and Human Rights*, esp. chapters 1 and 2.
[206] See pp. 49–52 above.

states have sought to overcome these problems through a special compensation scheme set up under an international treaty.

Following the *Torrey Canyon* disaster of 1967, the International Maritime Organisation ('IMO') called an international conference in 1969, the aim of which was to develop an international convention to govern liability for oil pollution from ships. The main aim of the 1969 Civil Liability Convention,[207] together with the 1971 Fund Convention,[208] was to create a scheme whereby victims of pollution damage would be properly and fairly compensated 'in an internationally uniform manner'.[209] The 1969 Convention established 'strict' liability for the vessel owner, although some exceptions are allowed where the damage was caused by events over which the owner would have had no control, such as war or 'acts of God'. Liability under the 1969 Convention is capped by an amount linked to the tonnage of the vessel (although the cap will not apply where it can be proved that the vessel owner was at fault). To ensure that funds are available, vessel owners are required under the Convention to obtain and maintain insurance to cover the maximum amount of liability. Jurisdiction over pollution claims is given to the courts of the state (or states) in which the damage occurred, and no claims may be made otherwise than in accordance with the Convention.

The compensation scheme under the 1969 Convention is supplemented by the 1971 Fund Convention, which provided for the establishment of a special compensation fund, which can be called upon in circumstances where a claimant is unable to obtain any or sufficient compensation from the vessel owner under the civil liability scheme. This Fund comprises contributions by oil importers of contracting states on the basis that they, as cargo owners, ought to bear at least some of the financial responsibility for oil spills. Both Conventions were amended by 1992 Protocols, which raised liability and compensation limits. A further Protocol to the Fund Convention was adopted in 2003, which provided for the establishment of an additional 'supplementary'

---

[207] International Convention on Civil Liability for Oil Pollution Damage, Brussels, 29 November 1969, in force 19 June 1975, 973 UNTS 3; UKTS (1975) 106.

[208] Convention on the Establishment of an International Fund for Compensation of Oil Pollution Damage, Brussels, 18 December 1971, in force 16 October 1978; UKTS (1978) 95; (1972) 11 ILM 284 (n.b. replaced by the 1992 Protocol, 27 November 1992, in force 30 May 1996).

[209] W. Oosterveen, 'Some Recent Developments Regarding Liability for Damage Resulting from Oil Pollution – From the Perspective of an EU Member State' (2004) 6 *ELR* 223, 224.

compensation fund. The periodic raising of liability and compensation amounts reflects state parties' concerns that there may not be sufficient compensation, under the regime, to cover the more serious pollution incidents. Where insufficient funds are available, the obligation to treat all established claims equally means that compensation is 'pro-rated' among those claimants.

As a scheme for compensating victims of pollution damage, this regime is generally regarded as a success.[210] Although the limitation of liability is controversial, it contains a number of 'plaintiff-friendly' features – the imposition of strict liability, the requirement to carry insurance, the availability of further 'top-up' funds – making it 'an important precedent for international regulation of other forms of hazardous activities'.[211] Furthermore, as contributions from the oil industry of one state party will go towards the settlement of claims for pollution damage suffered elsewhere, states and companies all have a vested interest in ensuring that claims are dealt with efficiently and consistently, wherever that particular pollution incident has taken place.[212] It ought in theory to be possible to devise similar regimes for other corporate activities carrying a similar pollution risk, where the production or transportation methods used (and hence the risks involved) do not vary greatly from corporate group to corporate group (i.e. there is no unfair subsidisation by one group of another's activities).

Bribery and corruption: the 1997 OECD Convention

The 1997 OECD Bribery Convention[213] is a good example of co-ordinated 'parent-based' regulation by capital-exporting home states. Although the Convention requires regulation of individuals as well as companies ('legal persons'), the regime is clearly designed with international corporate activity in mind. Under the Convention, which came into effect in 1999, state parties are required to ensure that bribery of a foreign public official is punishable by 'effective, proportionate and dissuasive criminal penalties'.[214] Given that the regime is designed to address activities

---

[210] Birnie and Boyle, *International Law and the Environment*, pp. 388–9.   [211] Ibid., p. 389.

[212] Oosterveen, 'Liability for Damage Resulting from Oil Pollution', 228.

[213] OECD Convention on Combating Bribery of Foreign Public Officials in International Business Transactions, Paris, 27 November 1997, in force 15 February 1999; (1998) 37 ILM 1.

[214] Ibid., Article 3(1). Note, however, that this is not an absolute requirement in relation to 'legal persons'. In jurisdictions where 'legal persons' (i.e. companies) cannot be held criminally responsible, state parties are required nevertheless to ensure that

taking place outside the territorial jurisdiction of state parties, countries which take a predominantly or exclusively 'territorial' approach to jurisdictional matters are required to make greater use of other bases of jurisdiction, particularly nationality jurisdiction.[215] While this would not permit home states to prosecute foreign subsidiaries directly,[216] theories of aiding and abetting make parent companies vulnerable to prosecution, even if they were not the party that actually paid the illegal bribe.[217] In addition, parent companies may be liable for offences under book-keeping and disclosure provisions, designed to aid detection of foreign bribes.[218]

The OECD anti-bribery regime contains strong implementation and follow-up procedures, a notable feature of which is the system of 'peer review'. This involves periodic evaluations by experts appointed from two different 'examining' states (which are chosen from a rota). The first phase of the process involves an initial assessment of the 'standard of implementation', based on the examined state's answers to a questionnaire. The second phase involves an examination of how national anti-bribery laws are implemented and enforced in practice.[219] In this phase, a role for NGOs is anticipated, although 'because peer review is an intergovernmental process',[220] this role is not defined in advance. Instead, the scope and method of engagement with civil society groups is subject to agreement with the state party under review.[221]

This Convention is notable for the 'unprecedented'[222] speed with which it has been ratified and implemented by states, as well as its monitoring and reporting procedures.[223] Initially, the main push for such an international agreement came from the USA which, having taken tough

'legal persons are subject to effective, proportionate and dissuasive non-criminal sanctions, including monetary sanctions, for bribery of foreign officials', Article 3(2).

[215] Ibid., Article 4(4).   [216] See pp. 106–9 above.

[217] Note that under the terms of the Convention, state parties are 'required to take any measures necessary to establish that complicity in, including incitement, aiding and abetting, or authorisation of an act of bribery of a foreign public official shall be a criminal offence', Article 1(2).

[218] See Article 8.

[219] See further G. Aiolfi and M. Pieth, 'How to Make a Convention Work: the Organisation for Economic Co-operation and Development Recommendation and Convention on Bribery as an Example of a New Horizon in International Law' in C. Fijnaut and L. Huberts (eds.), *Corruption, Integrity and Law Enforcement* (The Hague: Kluwer, 2002).

[220] OECD, 'OECD Bribery Convention: Procedure of Self- and Mutual Evaluation, Phase 2', http://www.oecd.org.

[221] Ibid.   [222] Aiolfi and Pieth, 'How to Make a Convention Work', p. 351.

[223] By the end of 1998, all OECD member states were signatories to the Convention. Six non-member states have also become parties.

unilateral steps to curb the making of bribes to foreign officials under its own Foreign Corrupt Practices Act,[224] was concerned that US-based industry not be placed at a competitive disadvantage as a result. For the same reasons, the state parties (which 'account for over 70 per cent of world trade and around 90 percent of international investment'[225]) take a keen interest in the compliance record of other state parties, which makes peer review a particularly apt form of compliance monitoring.

The problem of international corruption has galvanised the richer nations into action in a way that other social and environmental issues have not, as yet. Clearly, corruption does a great deal of harm: it 'undermines confidence in democratic government . . . fosters criminal elements; wastes public resources; slows economic development and distorts trade'.[226] But these comments could equally be made in relation to other criminal or socially irresponsible practices too, such as serious environmental degradation or human rights abuses of employees. For the purposes of designing regulatory responses to other CSR-related issues it is instructive to consider what makes this Convention a particularly promising international regime. As noted above, each state party has a particular interest in ensuring that other states meet their commitments under the Convention. The creation of a more level playing field for companies may also bring about, in the longer term, changes in business behaviour.[227] Although the Convention only tackles the 'supply side' of international bribery, host states may also find themselves, indirectly, under pressure to prosecute bribe takers, to reassure investors which would otherwise be concerned about falling foul of anti-bribery legislation operating from their home states. Other notable features include the required use of criminal and other sanctions by the home state, and the role of NGOs (albeit limited and subject to negotiation) in the peer review process. Finally, it is worth noting the use of the principle of 'functional equivalence' which requires, not unification of laws, but a concerted

---

[224] 15 USC § 78dd-1.

[225] P. Pierros and C. Hudson, 'The Hard Graft of Tackling Corruption in International Business Transactions: Progress in International Cooperation and the OECD Convention' (1998) 32(2) *Journal of World Trade* 77, 92.

[226] Ibid., 78.

[227] 'If . . . the competitive disadvantage of obeying the law is reduced, or is perceived to be reduced, this acts to remind decision makers of the individual benefit of obeying the law as namely that of reduced corruption for all parties in international trade'; ibid., 96.

effort, 'tailored to local legal traditions and fundamental concepts',[228] towards a particular set of anti-corruption goals. Obviously – as experience with the OECD Bribery Convention shows – the more flexibility given to states in choosing their particular mode of implementation, the easier the treaty will be to negotiate and the quicker it will be ratified.

Child labour: the 1999 ILO Child Labour Convention[229]

This Convention has been ratified, so far, by 156 states, comprising some of the poorest as well as the richest nations. It is also regarded, along with seven other ILO Conventions, as a 'fundamental' Convention of the ILO which means that, according to the ILO's 1998 Declaration on Fundamental Principles and Rights at Work, 'even if they have not ratified the Conventions in question', ILO member states 'have an obligation arising from the very fact of membership in the Organization to respect, to promote and to realize, in good faith and in accordance with the Constitution, the principles concerning the fundamental rights' set out in this Convention.[230]

Under Article 1 of the Convention, states are required to take 'immediate and effective measures to secure the prohibition and elimination of the worst forms of child labour as a matter of urgency'. These are defined as child slavery (or similar practices, such as child prostitution or use of children in illicit activities, such as drug trafficking) and 'work which, by its nature or the circumstances in which it is carried out, is likely to harm the health, safety or morals of children'. However, the precise nature of this work is undefined in the treaty itself, and is left, instead, for determination by 'national laws or regulations or by the competent authority'.[231] State parties' enforcement obligations are

---

[228] Aiolfi and Pieth, 'How to Make a Convention Work', p. 351.

[229] ILO Convention concerning the Prohibition and Immediate Elimination of the Worst Forms of Child Labour, Geneva, 17 June 1999, in force 10 November 2000 (No. 182); (1999) 38 ILM 1207.

[230] 1998 ILO Declaration on Fundamental Principles and Rights at Work, adopted at the 86th session of the International Labour Conference, Geneva, 18 June 1998, paragraph 2.

[231] Article 4. Although further guidance is given in the 1999 ILO Recommendation Concerning the Prohibition and Immediate Action for the Elimination of the Worst Forms of Child Labour (No. 190), which includes, in this category, 'work with dangerous machinery, equipment and tools, or which involves the manual handling or transport of heavy loads', or 'work in an unhealthy environment which may, for example, expose children to hazardous substances, agents, or processes, or to temperatures, noise levels, or vibrations damaging to health', or 'work under

cast in similarly general terms. Article 5 refers only to 'necessary measures to ensure effective implementation and enforcement'. There is an
explicit reference to penal sanctions, although this is not an absolute
requirement. Unlike the OECD Bribery Convention,[232] there is no express
requirement on state parties to take steps with respect to extraterritorial
activities of nationals, apart from a general obligation to 'take appropriate steps to assist one another in giving effect to the provisions of this
Convention through enhanced international cooperation and/or assistance'.[233] A number of state parties have introduced extraterritorial measures relating to child sex tourism, and have reported on these in their
implementation reports to the ILO. However, national initiatives taken
under the Convention to address other issues, such as workplace conditions, have so far focused on activities taking place within territorial
boundaries.

As with other 'fundamental' Conventions of the ILO, state parties are
required, under the ILO Constitution, to submit reports on their implementation measures every two years[234] to a Committee of Experts whose
role is 'to provide an impartial and technical evaluation of the state of
application of international labour standards'.[235] So far, the reporting
record under the Convention has been relatively good, with 125 implementation reports received and processed by mid-2005, although the
quality of reporting can be variable.

Consumer health: the 2003 Framework Convention on Tobacco Control[236]

The 2003 Framework Convention on Tobacco Control, 'the world's first
public health treaty',[237] entered into force in February 2005. Negotiated
and drafted under the auspices of the WHO, it has been ratified, so far,
by 78 out of 168 signatories.[238] As its name suggests, the Convention is
designed to provide a 'framework' for future international co-operation

---

particularly difficult conditions such as work for long hours or during the night or
work where the child is unreasonably confined to the premises of the employer'
(paragraph 3).

[232] See n. 213 above.   [233] ILO Child Labour Convention, n. 229 above, Article 8.

[234] This obligation commences one year after ratification by the relevant state party.

[235] ILO, 'Committee of Experts on the Application of Conventions and
Recommendations',
http://www.ilo.org/public/english/standards/norm/applying/committee.htm.

[236] WHO Framework Convention on Tobacco Control, Geneva, 21 May 2003, in force 27
February 2005.

[237] WHO, 'An International Treaty for Tobacco Control', 12 August 2003,
http://www.who.int/features/2003/08/en/index.html.

[238] As of 5 September 2005. See www.whoint/tabacco/en/.

on tobacco regulation and the obligations of state parties are set out in very general terms. For instance, on protection from exposure to tobacco smoke, parties are required to 'adopt and implement . . . effective legislative, executive, administrative and/or other measures'.[239] The most detailed provisions in the treaty relate to the regulation of tobacco product disclosures, packaging and labelling, and advertising. State parties are required, for instance, to take 'effective measures' to ensure that 'tobacco product packaging and labelling do not promote a tobacco product by any means that are false, misleading, deceptive or likely to create an erroneous impression about its characteristics, health effects, hazards or emissions', and that each unit package carries a health warning of the prescribed size and visibility.[240] In addition, state parties are required (unless they are constitutionally prevented from doing so) to 'undertake a comprehensive ban on tobacco advertising, promotion and sponsorship', not only within their own territory', but also *originating from* their territory.[241] However, in contrast to the CSR-related treaties discussed above, the Convention is vague on enforcement issues, stating only that parties '*shall consider* taking legislative action or promoting their existing laws, where necessary, to deal with criminal and civil liability, including compensation where appropriate'.[242] With regard to technical and financial assistance, it is acknowledged, throughout the Convention, that some countries, particularly developing countries, will need extra help in order to meet their treaty commitments, but little detail is provided on when and how this assistance is to be delivered.[243]

Nevertheless, this treaty regime is only in its early stages. It remains to be seen how it will operate in practice and whether, most importantly, it is capable of bringing about measurable improvements in public health. Detailed provisions on implementation and compliance monitoring have yet to be established.[244] The first Conference of the Parties was scheduled to take place in February 2006.[245]

---

[239] Framework Convention, n. 236 above, Article 8.   [240] Ibid., Article 11.
[241] Ibid., Article 13.   [242] Ibid., Article 19 (emphasis added).
[243] The Conference of the Parties is due to consider 'existing and potential sources and mechanisms of assistance' at its first session in February 2006. See Article 26(5)(c).
[244] Framework Convention, n. 236 above, Articles 21 and 23.
[245] For the time being, each party is required to submit an initial report of its implementation of obligations under the Convention within two years of its entry into force for that party. The frequency and format of subsequent reports is to be determined by the Conference of the Parties (Article 21).

International trade in hazardous substances: the 1989 Basel Convention and the 1998 Rotterdam 'PIC' Convention

The aim of the 1989 Basel Convention[246] is, as its full title suggests, to regulate international trade in hazardous wastes and, in particular, to provide a system of protection for importing states. The Convention, negotiated under the auspices of UNEP, arose out of concerns about the environmental implications of the international waste trade (including illegal 'trafficking' of hazardous waste) and fears of possible exploitation by richer countries of the poorer, by using them as convenient dumping grounds for hazards they were not prepared to dispose of themselves. The Basel Convention operates on a principle of 'prior informed consent' ('PIC'), under which exporting states may only export wastes to another country (or through another country) once the importing country (and the country of transit), having been informed of the nature of the waste and the risks to human health and the environment, has given its express consent. Moreover, under the terms of the Convention, hazardous wastes are to be disposed of at source, and transboundary movement of wastes therefore kept to a minimum, 'consistent with the environmentally sound management and efficient management of such wastes'.[247] In addition, exporting states are required to take measures to ensure that hazardous wastes are not exported to another state if they have reason to believe that 'the wastes in question will not be managed in an environmentally sound manner'.[248]

The Convention also imposes a number of specific regulatory obligations, namely, to:

(a) Prohibit all persons under its national jurisdiction from transporting or disposing of hazardous wastes or other wastes unless such persons are authorised or allowed to perform such types of operations;

(b) Require that hazardous wastes and other wastes that are to be the subject of a transboundary movement be packaged, labelled, and transported in conformity with generally accepted and recognized international rules and standards in the field of packaging, labelling and transport, and that due account is taken of relevant internationally recognized practices; and

---

[246] Convention on the Control of Transboundary Movements of Hazardous Wastes and their Disposal, Basel, 22 March 1989, in force 24 May 1992, 1673 UNTS 126; (1989) 28 ILM 657.

[247] Ibid., Article 4(2)(d).

[248] See ibid., Article 2(8) for the Convention's definition of 'environmentally sound management' of hazardous and other wastes.

    (c) Require that hazardous wastes and other wastes be accompanied by a movement document from the point at which a transboundary movement commences to the point of disposal.[249]

With respect to enforcement, the Convention states simply that illegal traffic in hazardous wastes is 'criminal'[250] and obliges all state parties to 'take appropriate legal, administrative and other measures to implement and enforce the provisions of this Convention, including measures to prevent and punish conduct in contravention of the Convention'.[251] In theory, enforcement measures could be taken by either the importing or the exporting state, provided that a suitable basis of jurisdiction exists.[252] In addition, hazardous wastes which have been exported illegally are required to be returned to the exporting state – to the exporter, the generator or, if necessary, the state itself – for disposal.[253]

Compliance monitoring is carried out through the Conference of the Parties. Before the end of each calendar year, each state party is required to submit a report on its performance during the previous year, which is required to include details of hazardous wastes exported and imported, their efforts to achieve a reduction of the amount of hazardous wastes exported, information relating to effects on human health of practices relating to hazardous waste production and disposal, and on any accidents occurring during transportation.[254] However, the failure of the drafters of the treaty to provide for any independent verification procedures has been criticised.[255]

In 1999, a further Protocol on Liability and Compensation (not yet in force) was adopted by the parties, the aim of which is to define who is liable in the event of an accident involving hazardous wastes, and to provide for a system of compensation for those affected. Under the Protocol regime, generators, exporters, shippers, importers and disposers of waste are all potentially liable for the health and environmental consequences

---

[249] Ibid., Article 4(7).

[250] Ibid., Article 4(3). 'Illegal traffic' is defined in Article 9 of the Convention, in essence, as transboundary movements of hazardous wastes that do not conform with the provisions of the Convention.

[251] Ibid., Article 4(4).

[252] E.g. 'nationality' jurisdiction in the case of the exporting state, or 'protective' jurisdiction in the case of the importing state. Birnie and Boyle, *International Law and the Environment*, p. 432.

[253] Basel Convention, n. 246 above, Article 9(2)(a). Where the importing state is at fault, disposal of the wastes becomes its responsibility (Article 9(3)).

[254] Basel Convention, n. 246 above, Article 13(3)(b).

[255] Birnie and Boyle, *International Law and the Environment*, p. 434.

of accidents involving transboundary movements of hazardous waste,[256] depending on the point at which the accident took place. Liability for these parties is strict[257] (and capped), but other persons may also be liable under the regime if their lack of compliance with the Convention (or their own intentional, reckless or negligent behaviour) caused or contributed to the accident.[258] Those potentially liable under the strict liability provisions are required to obtain a minimum amount of security in the form of 'insurance, bonds or other financial guarantee'.[259] In addition, a supplementary compensation fund has been established, funded by voluntary contributions from state parties.[260]

Of course, many dispute the idea that trade in hazardous wastes should take place at all.[261] Nevertheless, the principle of 'prior informed consent', supported by the administrative arrangements laid down in the Basel Convention, provides a strong basis for co-operation between states in relation to the export of hazards and, as such, 'offers a model for regulating other problems of transboundary trade, whether in hazardous chemicals or technologies'.[262] The influence of the Basel regime can be seen in the 1998 Rotterdam 'PIC' Convention.[263] This Convention, which entered into force in February 2004, emerged out of a voluntary set of procedures developed by the FAO and UNEP. Its primary objective is to ensure that countries which import hazardous chemicals, particularly developing countries which may lack the necessary monitoring infrastructure, do so with knowledge of the risks involved, and of the regulatory restrictions that apply in the exporting state. Under the terms of the Convention, parties must notify the Secretariat of bans or 'severe' regulatory restrictions that apply within their jurisdictions, and this information is communicated in summary form to all the other parties.[264] A 'prior informed consent' procedure applies to certain

---

[256] This includes loss of income, costs of measures; of reinstatement and the costs of preventative measures; 1999 Protocol on Liability and Compensation for Damage Resulting from Transboundary Movements of Hazardous Wastes and their Disposal, Article 2(2)(c).

[257] Ibid., Article 4.   [258] Ibid., Article 5.   [259] Ibid., Article 14(1).

[260] This contrasts with the arrangements under the 1971 Convention on the Establishment of an International Fund for the Compensation of Oil Pollution Damage, n. 208 above, which is funded by mandatory contributions from industry. See further Birnie and Boyle, *International Law and the Environment*, pp. 435–6.

[261] Ibid., pp. 428–31, 436–7.   [262] Ibid., p. 437.

[263] Convention on the Prior Informed Consent Procedure for Certain Hazardous Chemicals and Pesticides in International Trade, Rotterdam, 10 September 1998, in force 24 February 2004; (1999) 38 ILM 1.

[264] Ibid., Article 5.

designated chemicals and pesticides.[265] Importing countries are given the opportunity formally to state whether they are prepared to import the chemical (including subject to restrictions) or not,[266] and each exporting state must then take the necessary steps to ensure that exporters 'within its jurisdiction' comply with those decisions.[267] In addition, exporting countries are required to provide periodic export notifications in relation to any chemicals 'banned or severely restricted' under their own laws. Finally, there are general obligations regarding the provision of technical assistance to developing countries.[268] Of course, much depends on how compliance with the terms of the Convention, especially by exporting states, is monitored and enforced in practice. The Convention instructs the Conference of the Parties to develop and approve the necessary procedures and institutional mechanisms 'as soon as practicable'.[269] A Working Group has been established to take this forward, and more concrete proposals are expected to emerge following the second Conference of the Parties in September 2005.

Hazardous industrial activity: the 1993 ILO Convention on the Prevention of Major Industrial Accidents

The 1993 ILO Convention on the Prevention of Major Industrial Accidents[270] was developed in the aftermath of the Bhopal disaster and eventually came into force in 1997. The aim of this Convention is to encourage state parties to take steps to prepare for the possibility of a 'major accident', including the development of 'a coherent national policy concerning the protection of workers, the public and the environment against the risk of major accidents'[271] and a system for the identification of 'major hazard installations'.[272] Article 16 imposes obligations on the 'competent authority' to disseminate information on emergency response procedures to 'members of the public liable to be affected'. The Convention also lays down a series of obligations for employers, including notification of hazards[273] and accidents,[274] training,[275] the

---

[265] Ibid.; see Annex III. At present there are forty-one pesticides listed, although there is a procedure in the Convention for inclusion of further chemical formulations from time to time. See Article 5(6) and Article 6.

[266] Ibid., Article 10.   [267] Ibid., Article 11(1)(b).   [268] Ibid., Article 16.

[269] Ibid., Article 17.

[270] ILO Convention Concerning the Prevention of Major Industrial Accidents, Geneva, 22 June 1993, in force 3 January 1997 (No. 174).

[271] Ibid., Article 4.   [272] Ibid., Article 5.   [273] Ibid., Article 8.   [274] Ibid., Article 13.

[275] Ibid., Article 9(c).

development of emergency plans and procedures,[276] and the preparation of 'safety reports'.[277] Although falling short of 'prior informed consent', Article 22 obliges each 'exporting member state' to notify states importing hazardous 'substances, technologies or processes' of any prohibitions on their use in the exporting state, and the reasons for these. However, the Convention has not been widely ratified, its parties including only three Western European states.[278]

Summary

As this short survey shows, there is a range of tactics that could be adopted by states – and have been used in the past – to develop international solutions to CSR-related problems. Importantly, these tactics do not rely on the 'host states' of multinationals for their implementation. In many cases, 'home states' take on a crucial role, for example, in notifying receiving countries and their industries about environmental and health risks of products or technologies (e.g. Basel Convention, Rotterdam PIC Convention, ILO Major Accidents Convention), in enforcing packaging regulations for harmful substances and consumer products (e.g. WHO Framework Convention on Tobacco Control, Rotterdam PIC Convention) or in providing technical or financial assistance (e.g. Framework Convention on Tobacco Control, Rotterdam PIC Convention, ILO Child Labour Convention). Through their jurisdiction over parent companies, home states have the capacity to influence the behaviour of other entities within the group, including those operating in other countries. The OECD Bribery Convention is a good example of an attempt by states to harness this regulatory power to tackle a particular international problem that has become endemic to multinational activity. States can agree specific liability regimes for corporate entities and/or individuals (e.g. the 'strict' liability of vessel owners under the Civil Liability Convention, or the liability of generators, transporters or disposers of hazardous waste under the 1992 Protocol to the Basel Convention (not yet in force)) and the defences that will be applicable in certain circumstances. Moreover, where activities by multinationals carry a risk of environmental harm or personal injury, there are a number of steps that states can take to make sure that financial resources are available to compensate potential future victims, such as statutory requirements to carry insurance (e.g. Civil Liability Convention, 1992 Protocol to the Basel Convention) and the creation of special purpose funds for the

---

[276] Ibid., Article 9(d).   [277] Ibid., Article 10.   [278] Netherlands, Sweden and Belgium.

compensation of victims (e.g. the Fund Convention, 1992 Protocol to the Basel Convention).

Obviously, though, developing a treaty regime on paper is not enough. States need to be committed to seeing their obligations through, to establishing the necessary legal and administrative mechanisms and resourcing them properly, to ensuring that requirements imposed on companies are properly enforced and to ensuring that their commitments vis-à-vis technical assistance for other states parties are met. This requires strong supervisory mechanisms, ideally with independent powers of inspection, together with a defined role for interested NGOs and civil society groups.

Conclusion

An overarching multilateral treaty on CSR seems an unlikely prospect at present. As observed above, this is an area still in its infancy. States are only just beginning to develop their policies on international CSR regulation and most of these have yet to be tested properly, even at national level. More time is needed for states to experiment with different kinds of regulatory strategies and to observe their effects. Even if broad agreement could be reached about what such a treaty should contain, reconciling the competing interests of different states (particularly as between developed and developing countries) would be extremely difficult. It would be surprising, for instance, if the same concerns that have dogged discussions about the appropriateness of a 'social' clause in international trading agreements (i.e. 'disguised protectionism')[279] did not also come to dominate any negotiations on a treaty on CSR. In the meantime, the best that NGOs can hope for in this regard is that ways can be found to strengthen existing 'soft law' initiatives on CSR.[280]

On the other hand, the practice by multinationals of 'double standards' in relation to social, environmental and consumer issues is a pressing problem and, many would argue, not adequately regulated by soft law instruments alone. Justice for those workers, communities and consumers adversely affected by the activities of multinationals requires

[279] J. Jackson, *The World Trading System: Law and Policy of Economic Relations*, 4th edition (Cambridge, MA: MIT Press, 2000), p. 245; Dine, *Companies, International Trade and Human Rights*, p. 198. See further pp. 306–9 below.

[280] See Calder and Culverwell, 'Following up the World Summit', for some suggestions as to how this might be done.

a much firmer international response, particularly from home states. Of course, soft law instruments can help to galvanise support for new legal principles. And, while the idea of direct obligations for multinationals under international law is still controversial, there is nothing in principle that would prevent this from happening, given enough commitment from states. As discussed in earlier chapters, companies are arguably already subject to some direct prohibitions under international law in the field of human rights (e.g. relating to genocide, slavery and forced labour). It is also possible that, given time, more general or procedural obligations for multinationals could emerge, such as a prohibition on 'double standards' (which may include an obligation to apply international minimum standards), an obligation to carry out environmental impact assessments and to apply a 'precautionary' approach, and an obligation to warn affected employees, communities and consumers of health, safety and environmental risks.

Whether or not these soft law initiatives do eventually give rise to obligations for multinationals as a matter of *customary* law, there is an emerging consensus as to the regulatory tactics most likely to prove useful in regulating multinationals, which will undoubtedly play an important part in future, *treaty-based*, regimes on CSR. Of course, mobilising support for, drafting and negotiating new treaty regimes is never easy, but it should be reassuring to know that we are not in entirely new territory here. Many of the key issues in the regulation of multinationals – problems of extraterritorial jurisdiction, defining liability, 'double standards' and compensating victims – have been considered before in the context of negotiations for treaties on a range of specific issues, from toxic chemicals to bribery. While some of these regimes are only in their very early stages, it is important to be aware of precedents in international CSR regulation, and to learn from them.

7 Multinationals and CSR: limitations and opportunities in international law

Can international law provide a framework for the effective regulation of the health, safety and environmental standards of multinationals on an international scale? This book suggests it can, although clarification is needed on a number of key issues before real progress can be made. First of all, who is primarily responsible for regulating multinationals? It is suggested in the previous chapters that the home states of multinationals have a significant role to play. Lately, home states seem to have become more willing to take this task on, although they have generally shied away from the more 'binding' forms of regulation, seeing themselves as facilitators (rather than enforcers) of CSR standards. On the other hand, the few international treaty regimes that have been developed so far to address the conduct of multinationals rely heavily on home state action for their effectiveness, and illustrate the many regulatory possibilities that exist. A second issue that needs clarification concerns the extent to which direct obligations apply to multinationals under international law and how, in practice, these are to be fulfilled. In particular, which of the various components of the multinational enterprise are responsible for ensuring these obligations are met, and on what basis? Although there is growing speculation that some direct obligations may exist, they are still only vaguely defined, and their substance largely speculative. Nevertheless, jurisprudence at national level – if allowed to develop – should help, not only to shed light on the norms themselves, but also with the elaboration of theories of liability appropriate to the international CSR context.

It is quite possible that new customary obligations could emerge from current international activities on CSR – for both multinationals and states. However, before new customary obligations can be said to exist, there needs to be much more evidence of real commitment from states on CSR-related principles. Also, despite the increasing levels of activity in this field, the development of international CSR policy continues to be dominated by the richer nations. Clearly, this must be taken into account when assessing the implications of recent state practice. Although initiatives like the OECD Guidelines may have, among their aims, the improvement of standards in developing host countries, it should not be assumed that they will necessarily be welcomed, nor should a lack of response be taken as 'acquiescence' at this stage. More engagement with developing countries on CSR issues and policy is needed, but the lack of an obvious international forum – not to mention a lack of resources – means that it can be difficult for some states to get their views heard.

The aim of this concluding chapter is an overall assessment of the capacity of international law, as it currently stands, to support two key ambitions of the CSR movement – greater accountability of multinationals for their international social and environmental performance, and an end to the practice of 'double standards'. After examining the potential roles and responsibilities of two key groups of actors – home states and multinationals themselves – this chapter then turns to consider the implications of unfolding international CSR policy for developing states. The chapter then concludes with some general comments about the future of international law, as it relates to CSR, and its potential as a framework for regulating multinational activity.

The developing role of home states

Home states have a potentially pivotal role to play in the regulation of multinationals. This is illustrated by the regulatory techniques employed in several treaty-based regimes, discussed in the previous chapter, which have placed home states under obligations, for example, to ensure that insurance against certain risks is in place, or to ensure that certain information is conveyed to foreign regulatory authorities and, generally, to take steps to ensure that companies operating under their respective jurisdictions observe the relevant standards. Without resorting to extraterritorial legislation in the traditional sense, home state regulation can still have a good deal of extraterritorial impact, based on the relationships of control that exist between the parent company and its foreign affiliates (whether equity-linked or not). 'Prior informed consent' procedures, for example, can indirectly provide host state authorities and communities with some of the benefits of home state regimes relating to industrial hazards, or, at the very least, potentially valuable know-how concerning the home state's regulatory approach. When it comes to exerting regulatory pressure on parent companies themselves, theories of 'aiding and abetting' provide a legal basis on which companies can be held responsible for the misdemeanours of foreign entities over which they have – or ought reasonably to have – control.

There are, however, limitations to this approach. First, treaty-based obligations will only apply to those states which are party to them. Even where states have elected to become parties to a treaty, this does not guarantee that obligations will be implemented effectively. As always, much depends on the quality of monitoring, supervisory and dispute resolution arrangements agreed between the states. Second, there are inherent definitional problems with home state regulation, as it is not always easy to say in advance which 'control relationships' between a parent company and a foreign company should come within the ambit of a home state regime. For instance, how far up the supply chain should a prohibition on the use of child labour extend? Also, the prevalence of inter-firm collaboration (e.g. joint ventures between subsidiaries from two different multinational groups) can make it difficult to identify which state is, in fact, the 'home state', exposing companies to the possibility of overlapping and potentially conflicting regulatory requirements (although, as has been seen, the problem of conflicting regulatory standards can be reduced by the harmonisation of standards through treaty regimes).

The third, and probably most important, limitation on home state regulation is, of course, jurisdiction. As discussed in chapter 3, home states do not have the right under international law to prescribe standards for foreign companies directly, although, as noted above, there are regulatory steps that can be taken, relying on the jurisdiction of the home state over the parent company of a multinational group (and the control enjoyed by that parent over its subsidiaries). It is important to remember, though, that 'parent-based' methods of regulation are also subject to limitations, generally cast in terms of 'reasonableness' or the 'duty of non-intervention' in the affairs of other states. These rather vague criteria make it difficult to be clear about what kinds of 'parent-based' regulation are and are not permitted.

It is usually taken for granted that CSR-related areas, like workplace and environmental health, will be governed by the same rules on extraterritorial jurisdiction that have been developed for other, more 'state-centred' areas of regulation, such as competition law or economic sanctions. But is this the right approach? It is suggested in chapter 3 that, where human rights are at stake, a more flexible set of jurisdictional rules is justified to take account of the human interests involved. Where there is a high level of international agreement about the need for regulation, and the basic principles (the right of employees to safe working conditions, for example), arguments that a home state has somehow infringed the host state's sovereignty through extraterritorial social regulation ought to be treated as less strong. But that may not be the end of the matter. Home states and host states may agree on a basic principle (e.g. the need to eliminate child labour) and disagree on the best mode of implementation (e.g. an outright ban on the employment of children versus no ban, but a requirement that employers identify the children in their workforce and provide special, e.g. educational, facilities for them). Clearly, it is only by testing different extraterritorial regulatory strategies and considering the responses of affected states that the scope of these jurisdictional principles, and their application to the CSR field, will become clearer.

In any event, when designing extraterritorial regulatory regimes there are still a number of practical problems to consider, including in relation to the softer, 'parent-based' forms of regulation. Imposing supervisory obligations on a parent company is one thing; monitoring and enforcing those obligations is quite another. In practice, it will be difficult – without the co-operation of host state authorities – to ensure that a parent company has honoured its commitments with respect to the health and safety performance of its subsidiaries (e.g. to assess its eligibility for certain tax incentives, or for the purposes of deciding whether it has infringed home state trade practices laws with respect to corporate communications).

While the *rights* of home states to regulate extraterritorially remain unclear, it is difficult to be certain of the scope of their regulatory *obligations*. Still, some general observations can be made. First, although states do in limited circumstances have obligations to prevent human rights abuses in other countries, it seems unlikely that home states have any positive obligations to ensure that multinationals falling under their jurisdiction (i.e. by virtue of their jurisdiction over the parent company) do not violate human rights in other jurisdictions. Neither does it seem to be the case, for the time being, that states could be held liable for the foreign activities of multinationals under international law prohibitions on transboundary harm. However, there is sufficient support for the principle of 'prior informed consent' in international treaties,[1] and

---

[1] See pp. 292–5 above.

in the practice of individual states,[2] to make new customary obligations based on this principle a real possibility, at least in relation to hazardous wastes and chemicals. This would mean that parent-based controls to ensure that multinationals did not export wastes or chemicals without the 'prior informed consent' of foreign regulatory authorities would be part of the customary regulatory responsibilities of states in relation to multinationals. It would not be too great a conceptual leap to extend these obligations to other forms of industrial hazard – such as hazardous technologies and processes.

Governments of home states are taking a much greater interest in the foreign social and environmental standards of multinationals than ever before. As discussed in chapter 4, there are several reasons for this – political, economic, developmental and ethical – although pressure from NGOs has clearly been a major factor. Inter-governmental organisations and institutions have also been influential, with both the OECD and the EU playing a significant role in the co-ordination and development of home state policies. Interestingly, the survey of state practice in chapter 5 suggests a broadly similar response by home states to the international dimension of CSR, and also a certain amount of cross-fertilisation of regulatory ideas and tactics, as different home states watch and learn from each other. However (and at least partially as a result of pressure from the business lobby), home states have a distinct preference for extraterritorial initiatives that 'facilitate' (rather than compel) better CSR standards abroad. At present, regulatory efforts are being concentrated on initiatives to enhance transparency, the idea being that this will create its own pressures on companies to be more 'socially responsible', at home and abroad. The second key area of regulatory activity concerns access to investment assistance, where the growing prevalence of environmental and human rights screening of projects seeking investment assistance suggests that home states are beginning to take on more responsibility for the quality of investments originating from their jurisdictions, not only in economic but also in ethical terms.

---

[2] See, for example, legislative requirements on OPIC prior to providing support in relation to 'environmentally sensitive' foreign projects under the US Foreign Assistance Act of 1961, 22 USC § 2191, at § 2197. See pp. 179–80 above. See also Council Regulation 2455/92/EEC of 23 July 1992 concerning the export and import of certain dangerous chemicals, OJ 1992 No. L251/13, 29 August 1992 which introduced a PIC procedure for banned or severely restricted chemicals for the European Community. Now repealed and replaced by Council Regulation 304/2003 of 28 January 2003 concerning the export and import of dangerous chemicals, OJ 2003 No. L63/1, 6 March 2003.

Whether this growing sense of moral responsibility eventually translates into new *legal* responsibilities for home states under international law remains to be seen. While there is an emerging consensus at present as to regulatory strategies, there is little, if any, evidence that home states, in their approach to international CSR issues thus far, are acting out of a sense of legal obligation. There is, however, another area of state practice with perhaps more immediate significance for the regulatory obligations of home states. This is, of course, the case law emerging from national courts in relation to private lawsuits brought by foreign litigants against parent companies of multinational groups (the so-called 'FDL' cases). As discussed in chapter 5, these cases are potentially significant, not only to the question of whether home states have particular responsibilities to these litigants under human rights law (e.g. as regards 'access to justice'), but also in relation to difficult questions concerning the allocation of liability within multinational groups. Although these cases concern 'private' claims for damages, it is reasonable to expect that they will, in turn, be influenced by wider developments in CSR policy. So far, plaintiffs have faced an uphill struggle, but some observers have suggested that we are now witnessing the beginning of a more 'plaintiff-friendly' trend in judicial decision-making in these kinds of cases. It will be interesting to see whether the case law bears this out.

Direct obligations for multinationals?

Lawyers are fond of definitions. Frustratingly, multinationals seem to defy any general legal definition although, as discussed in chapter 1, it is still possible to define multinationals in legal terms. However, for the purposes of understanding the direct obligations of multinationals, legal definitions of the 'enterprise' are of limited use. Practically speaking, it is not so important to define what is meant by a 'multinational' as to explain which components of the enterprise are responsible and why.

The issue of whether companies (and, by extension, multinationals) can be subject to direct obligations under international law has generated a huge amount of literature of late. The general view is that such obligations not only are a theoretical possibility, but are justified by the enormous economic and political influence of multinationals, and their clear capacity to affect the enjoyment of human rights. For the time being, though, there is little in the way of jurisprudence on the *substance* of those rights, and a lack of proper enforcement mechanisms.

As discussed in chapter 6, it would be possible to deal with the latter problem, through an international treaty or through amendments to the complaints procedures of existing human rights bodies. The greater challenge, though, is 'developing jurisprudence which refines and makes precise the vague aspirational statements which we see, at present, in the CSR debate'.[3] Here there is, as Dine points out, much work to be done, and it is to be hoped that the work begun by the UN Sub-Commission on the Promotion and Protection of Human Rights, to be carried on by the UN's Special Representative, will help to shed some further light on the human rights standards expected of companies and, particularly, the supervisory responsibilities of parent companies in respect of their subsidiaries, suppliers, distributors and other entities with which they have close relationships. It is relevant to note, again, that there are theories of liability under the domestic law of tort that could be of assistance here, although the precise implications of these for the liability of parent companies of multinational groups is (despite a recent surge in FDL litigation in the USA) still unclear. Other sources of information on the potential responsibilities of multinationals are the different international 'codes of conduct', as well as the numerous other statements of principles that have been developed at national and corporate level. As discussed in chapter 6, these suggest a number of possible procedural obligations, such as observance of the precautionary principle in corporate decision-making, or the obligation to carry out environmental assessments, or obligations of transparency. While it would be premature to claim customary status for these principles at present (at least in so far as they apply directly to multinationals), it is likely that they will play an important part in future treaty regimes.

In the meantime, the most promising avenue for enforcement of human rights obligations of multinationals remains the national courts. Of course, it is not entirely correct to describe tort-based litigation as human rights litigation, as plaintiffs must show, not a breach of human rights under international law, but a cause of action under the domestic law of negligence. It is, however, possible to view some cases of negligence involving multinationals as a breach of human rights as well and, to many, *Re Bhopal* is a good example of just such a case. In the USA, parallel actions have been brought under the ATCA[4] (which, uniquely, does appear to offer a cause of action to foreign nationals against companies for human rights abuses abroad) and state tort law. Just as domestic decisions on the responsibility of parent companies can be expected to have an influence on the developing international law of CSR, it is to

---

[3] Dine, *Companies, International Trade and Human Rights*, p. 234.
[4] Alien Tort Claims Act of 1789, 28 USC § 1350.

be hoped that the developing international standards, as set out in the various codes of conduct discussed in this book, will also have a bearing on the way 'foreign direct liability' litigation is approached at national level.

Clarifying the direct responsibilities of multinationals under international law is in everyone's interests (not least multinationals themselves). As noted above, it is likely that responsibility for compliance with human rights obligations would fall, primarily, on the parent company. But the detail to which these obligations must be defined would depend on the regulatory methods chosen. As discussed in chapter 1, the more adversarial and less consensual a regulatory process becomes (and the more serious the legal sanctions) the greater the requirements for legal certainty.

On the outside looking in: implications for less developed host states

As noted in chapter 3, the 'principle of non-intervention' represents the outer limit of the rights of home states to regulate CSR standards extraterritorially. This is the point at which the interests of a host state in relation to certain issues and outcomes outweigh the interests of other states in relation to the same and, specifically, the rights of the home state to impose its own requirements. Over the past few decades there has been a huge expansion of international law into areas traditionally regarded as part of the domestic affairs of states, particularly in the fields of human rights and environmental law.[5] Once an issue becomes regulated by international law, there is a corresponding shrinkage of 'reserved domain', meaning, simply, that states no longer have complete freedom to determine whether and how the issue is regulated within their respective territories. Instead, these decisions must be taken in light of that state's international obligations, and the fact that other states may have an interest, too, in how the matter is dealt with. Clearly, this makes it more difficult to argue, in the case of a dispute between two states over the scope of a regulatory regime, that the principle of non-intervention ought to apply.

As discussed in chapter 6, a significant amount of effort has been devoted at the international level to defining the CSR-related obligations of multinationals, particularly as regards their practices in poorer

---

[5] Ratner, 'The Trials of Global Norms', 66.

'developing' host states. While nearly all of the instruments that have resulted from this work are expressly 'non-binding' (at least, in legal terms), there is no guarantee that they will remain this way, especially in light of the linkages now being made between CSR and human rights. Increasingly, these statements refer to 'international', 'core' or 'fundamental' standards, particularly in relation to labour issues. This has important implications for host states, because if these standards are indeed 'international', 'core' or 'fundamental' (even if they create no positive *obligations* for home states), it becomes all the more difficult to argue that the standards to which a multinational operates within the territory of a state is solely a matter for that state's domestic jurisdiction. In other words, a high level of consensus around a particular CSR-related issue (e.g. a prohibition on forced or child labour) serves to validate and authorise (even if it does not yet require) greater use of extraterritorial regulation by home states of that particular problem.[6]

But how much support is there, really, for the idea that the performance of multinationals in key CSR areas ought to be a matter for international, rather than national, law? Within the WTO, the concept of international minimum environmental and labour standards has been a source of tension between developing and more industrialised states. Attempts to link trading rights to labour and environmental standards have generally been resisted by the poorer states, which argue that this would amount to 'hidden protectionism'. Instead, they argue that they should have the freedom to determine their own labour and environmental standards, in accordance with their own economic and developmental goals. Less developed countries have also expressed concerns about the potential impact of IIAs on their autonomy in these areas. While ongoing CSR activities at national and international level do not yet appear to have attracted any real opposition from governments of poorer states, their 'acquiescence' should not necessarily be assumed at this stage. Indeed, in so far as their objective is the development of international minimum standards for multinationals, CSR initiatives have the potential to head off the debate about a 'social clause' in international trading arrangements, particularly if these standards are extended (under the principle of 'supply chain responsibility') to suppliers and contractors based in poorer countries. The economic implications of the current CSR agenda for the less developed countries may not be fully appreciated as yet.

---

[6] See pp. 138–9 above.

The general lack of opposition of developing host states to international CSR-related activities may be because, superficially, home state regulation does not involve any direct costs to host states and, moreover, does not demand that host states take any action that would tend to limit their existing sources of 'comparative advantage'. Instead, the costs of regulation (political and economic) are borne largely by the home state. On the other hand, any home state initiative directed at enhancing the CSR performance of multinationals abroad which has the potential to alter patterns of outward investment could still undermine the development objectives of some poorer host states. Where the development of policy has been dominated by one particular group of states with broadly similar interests (as has been the case in the field of CSR), it is necessary to look at the small print. For example, as noted in chapter 6, it is in the field of labour law that the existence of international minimum standards seems most widely accepted, followed by environmental law and then consumer standards. The fact that this prioritisation is also the one capable of delivering the greatest economic advantages to the wealthier home states (i.e. in terms of preservation of local jobs on the one hand, and preservation of foreign markets on the other) is unlikely to be entirely coincidental.

So far, though, where less developed countries have had the opportunity to contribute to international CSR initiatives, they have generally been supportive of them. As was noted in chapter 6, a consensus on the health, safety and environmental provisions of the Draft UN Code was achieved relatively quickly. The ILO Tripartite Declaration reflects an understanding reached among a wide range of states, worker and employer organisations on the basic obligations of multinationals in relation to labour issues. Even the potentially controversial step by the OECD of extending its own Guidelines to the territories of non-adhering states seems so far not to have been opposed, although general concerns have been expressed within the context of the OECD's 'outreach' programme as to whether the interests of less developed countries are adequately reflected.[7]

While NGOs have been successful at linking up with campaigning organisations within developing countries, there has so far been only limited and scattered input into the CSR debate by developing countries themselves. Clearly, much greater effort needs to be made to encourage

---

[7] See comments of the representatives of Egypt and Vietnam at the OECD's 'outreach' meeting of December 2000 in OECD, 'Non-member Economies and the OECD Guidelines for Multinational Enterprises', Proceedings of Meeting, Paris, 12 December 2000, http://www.oecd.org., pp. 54–5, pp. 56–7.

the contribution of all states, and particularly developing states, to the development of future international policy on CSR.

Conclusion

Rather than inhibiting regulatory solutions, international law offers a potentially vital response to the problem of 'double standards' in relation to workplace, environmental and consumer health. Through international dialogue and co-operation, states are able to develop regulatory frameworks capable of transcending national boundaries, which should, in turn, help to reduce downward pressures on standards at national level caused by international competition for inward investment. Of course, international law has inherent limitations, none of which is peculiar to the CSR field. First, the 'state-centredness' of international law-making gives an in-built bias in favour of state interests. Second, home state initiatives are restricted by jurisdictional rules that continue to give priority to *territorial* connections between commercial activities and the state (emphasising, again, 'state-centred' interests) rather than to the interests of affected individuals and groups. Third, on a purely practical level, international policy-making can become dominated by states with the most resources to devote to the issue in question, making it difficult, in some cases, for the views of poorer states to be heard.

On the other hand, international developments in the CSR field demonstrate the capacity of international law to respond to new problems and novel actors. While state practice is the key to the formation of new custom, non-state actors such as NGOs and multinationals have been able to exert considerable influence over the CSR agenda at international level and will, in all likelihood, continue to do so.

CSR can no longer be dismissed as a passing trend. As this book shows, the process of 'socialisation' of these new principles is well underway. For the time being, most home states seem determined to keep CSR on a 'voluntary' footing. Nevertheless, regulatory changes are beginning to appear which are designed to 'facilitate' and 'encourage' (if not actually require) higher standards of CSR at home and abroad. Depending on how states respond, existing 'soft law' instruments have the potential to help create new, customary obligations – for home states as well as multinationals themselves. It would not, for example, be a huge conceptual leap from the existing law on state responsibility for transboundary harm to require that home states also bear some responsibility for the foreign activities of companies controlled by parent companies operating within their jurisdiction. Neither does it seem particularly fair to limit the human rights responsibilities of home states to those within their (primarily territorial) 'jurisdiction', in cases where they have the capacity to influence the standards of multinationals abroad, but fail to do so. While it is important not to confuse CSR and human rights, it is likely that any *direct* obligations for multinationals will emerge primarily from human rights law. However, much more work is needed on the standards that companies must observe, and the allocation of legal responsibilities, not only between multinationals and states, but between the various components of the multinationals themselves.

Ultimately, it is more than likely that new international institutions will emerge to promote – and enforce – the CSR standards of multinationals. There are many possibilities to consider, such as extending the mandates of existing human rights supervisory bodies, or negotiating new treaty-based regimes to authorise and co-ordinate better the regulatory potential of home states, and to compensate more effectively those whose lives are damaged as a result of corporate negligence or wrongdoing. Of course there are no easy solutions to the social and environmental problems posed by multinational activity and, more fundamentally, the gross imbalances of power that exist in society today.[8] But hopefully this book has managed to show that international law, despite its fundamental 'state-centredness', offers more regulatory opportunities in the CSR field than many people assume. International law is not a solution in itself, but a set of tools. It may not be a perfect framework for regulating multinationals, but at the moment we are not even making the best of what we have. In many ways, a negative view of international law is part of the problem – by blaming 'the system' we can deflect responsibility from ourselves. But there is much we can do, and justice demands that we now find ways to ensure that there is nowhere in the world where it is regarded as acceptable – morally or commercially – to sacrifice the lives or health of people, or the integrity of the environment, for the sake of profit.

---

[8] Dine, *Companies, International Trade and Human Rights*.

Bibliography

Accountability, 'Responsible Competitiveness', Briefing Paper (2004), http://www.accountability.org.uk.

Addo, M., 'The Corporation as a Victim of Human Rights Violations' in M. Addo (ed.), *Human Rights Standards and the Responsibility of Transnational Corporations* (The Hague: Kluwer, 1999).

(ed.), *Human Rights Standards and the Responsibility of Transnational Corporations* (The Hague: Kluwer, 1999).

Aiolfi, G. and Pieth, M., 'How to Make a Convention Work: the Organisation for Economic Co-operation and Development Recommendation and Convention on Bribery as an Example of a New Horizon in International Law' in C. Fijnaut and L. Huberts (eds.), *Corruption, Integrity and Law Enforcement* (The Hague: Kluwer, 2002).

Akehurst, M., 'The Hierarchy of the Sources of International Law' (1974–5) 47 *British Yearbook of International Law* 273.

Allen, B. and Zerk, J., 'Information is Power' (2005) 148 *Environment Information Bulletin* 14.

'A Partnership of Equals?' (2005) 154 *Environment Information Bulletin*, 14.

Alston, P., 'Labour Rights Provisions in US Trade Law: "Aggressive Unilateralism?"' in L. Compa and S. Diamond (eds.), *Human Rights, Labour Rights and International Trade* (Philadelphia: University of Pennsylvania Press, 1996).

'The Myopia of the Handmaidens: International Lawyers and Globalisation' (1987) 80 *European Journal of International Law* 435.

Alston, P. and Quinn, G., 'The Nature and Scope of State Parties' Obligations under the International Covenant on Economic, Social and Cultural Rights' (1987) 9 *Human Rights Quarterly* 156.

Amnesty International, 'Clouds of Injustice', Amnesty International Publications, 2004, http://www.amnesty.org/library.

Asante, S., 'International Law and Investments' in M. Bedjaoui (ed.), *International Law: Achievements and Prospects* (Dordrecht: Martinus Nijhoff, 1991).

Baade, H., 'Legal Effects of Codes of Conduct' in N. Horn (ed.), *Legal Problems of Codes of Conduct for Multinational Enterprises* (The Hague: Kluwer, 1980).

Bakan, J., *The Corporation: the Pathological Pursuit of Profit and Power* (New York: Free Press, 2004).

Baldwin, R. and Cave, M., *Understanding Regulation: Theory, Strategy and Practice* (Oxford: Oxford University Press, 1999).

Bantekas, I., 'Corporate Social Responsibility in International Law' (2004) 22 *Boston University International Law Journal* 309.

Barnet, R. and Muller, R., *Global Reach: the Power of the Multinational Corporations* (New York: Simon & Schuster, 1974).

Baxi, U. and Paul, T., *Mass Disasters and Multinational Liability: the Bhopal Case* (Bombay: NM Tripathi, 1986).

Bevan, S., Isles, N., Emery, P. and Hoskins, T., 'Achieving High Performance: CSR at the Heart of Business' (London: The Work Foundation (in partnership with Virtuous Circle), March 2004).

Beveridge, F., *The Treatment and Taxation of Foreign Investment under International Law* (Manchester: Juris Publishing/Manchester University Press, 2000).

Birkinshaw, J. 'Multinational Corporate Strategy and Organisation: an Internal Market Perspective' in N. Hood and S. Young (eds.), *The Globalisation of Multinational Enterprise Activity and Economic Development* (London: Macmillan, 2000).

Birnie, P. and Boyle, A., *International Law and the Environment*, 2nd edition (Oxford: Oxford University Press, 2002).

Blumberg, P., 'The American Law of Corporate Groups' in J. McCahery, S. Picciotto and C. Scott (eds.), *Corporate Control and Accountability: Changing Structures and the Dynamics of Regulation* (Oxford: Clarendon Press, 1993).

'Asserting Human Rights against Multinational Corporations under United States Law: Conceptual and Procedural Problems' (2002) 50 *American Journal of Comparative Law* 493.

'Limited Liability and Corporate Groups' (1986) 11 *Journal of Corporations Law* 573.

The Multinational Challenge to Corporation Law: the Search for a New Corporate Personality (Oxford: Oxford University Press, 1993).

Born, G., *International Civil Litigation in the United States Courts*, 3rd edition (The Hague, Kluwer, 1996).

Bothe, M., 'Legal and Non-Legal Norms – a Meaningful Distinction in International Law?' (1980) 11 *Netherlands Yearbook of International Law* 65.

'The Responsibility of Exporting States' in G. Handl and R. Lutz (eds.), *Transferring Hazardous Technologies and Substances* (London: Graham & Trotman, 1989).

Bowett, D., 'International Law and Economic Coercion' (1976) 16 *Virginia Journal of International Law* 245.

Boyd, K., 'The Inconvenience of Victims: Abolishing Forum Non Conveniens in US Human Rights Litigation' (1998) 39 *Virginia Journal of International Law* 41.

Braithwaite, J., 'Rewards and Regulation' in S. Picciotto and D. Campbell (eds.), *New Directions in Regulatory Theory* (Oxford: Blackwell, 2002).

Braithwaite, J. and Drahos, P., *Global Business Regulation* (Cambridge: Cambridge University Press, 2000).

Brereton, P., 'Forum Non Conveniens in Australia: a Case Note on Voth v. Manildra Flour Mills' (1991) 40 *International and Comparative Law Quarterly* 895.

Brewer, T. and Young, S., *The Multilateral Investment System and Multinational Enterprises* (Oxford: Oxford University Press, 1998).

Brown, H., 'The Extraterritorial Reach of the US Government's Campaign against International Bribery' (1999) 22 *Hastings International and Comparative Law Review* 407.

Brownlie, I., *Principles of Public International Law*, 5th edition (Oxford: Clarendon Press, 1998).

Buckley, P. and Casson, M., *The Future of the Multinational Enterprise*, 2nd edition (London: Macmillan, 1976).

Burke, J. 'The Reporting Implications of South Africa's King Code on Corporate Governance' in Accountability (ed.), *Accountability Quarterly, Does Reporting Work?: The Effect of Regulation* (September 2003) AQ21.

Buys, C., 'United States Economic Sanctions: the Fairness of Targeting Persons from Third Countries' (1999) 17 *Boston University International Law Journal* 214.

Calder, F. and Culverwell, M., 'Following Up the World Summit on Sustainable Development Commitments on Corporate Social Responsibility' (Royal Institute of International Affairs, Final Report, February 2005).

Cantwell, J., 'A Survey of Theories of International Production' in C. Pitelis and R. Sugden (eds.), *The Nature of the Transnational Firm* (London: Routledge, 1991).

Carroll, R., 'Corporate Parents and Tort Liability' in M. Gillooly (ed.), *The Law Relating to Corporate Groups* (Sydney: Federation Press, 1993).

Carter, B., *International Economic Sanctions: Improving the Haphazard US Regime* (Cambridge: Cambridge University Press, 1988).

Carter, P., 'The Role of Public Policy in English Private International Law' (1993) 42 *International and Comparative Law Quarterly* 1.

Cassels, J., *The Uncertain Promise of Law: Lessons of Bhopal* (Toronto: University of Toronto Press, 1993).

Cassese, A., *International Law in a Divided World* (Oxford: Clarendon Press, 1986).

Castleman, B., 'Workplace Health Standards and Multinational Corporations in Developing Countries' in C. Pearson (ed.), *Multinational Corporations, Environment and the Third World* (Durham, NC: Duke University Press, 1987).

Caves, R., *Multinational Enterprise and Economic Analysis* (Cambridge: Cambridge University Press, 1996).

Charlesworth, H. and Chinkin, C., *The Boundaries of International Law* (Manchester: Juris Publishing/Manchester University Press, 2000).

Charney, J., 'The Persistent Objector Rule and the Development of Customary International Law' (1985) 56 *British Yearbook of International Law* 1.

Cheng, B., 'United Nations Resolutions on Outer Space: "Instant" International Customary Law?' (1965) 5 *Indian Journal of International Law* 23.

Chinkin, C., 'The Challenge of Soft Law: Development and Change in International Law' (1989) 38 *International and Comparative Law Quarterly* 850.

Christian Aid, 'Behind the Mask: the Real Face of Corporate Social Responsibility' (Christian Aid, 21 January 2004).

Clapham, A., *Human Rights in the Private Sphere* (Oxford: Oxford University Press, 1996).

   'The Question of Jurisdiction under International Criminal Law over Legal Persons' in M. Kamminga and S. Zia-Zarifi (eds.), *Liability of Multinational Corporations under International Law* (The Hague: Kluwer, 2000).

   'Revisiting Human Rights in the Private Sphere: Using the European Convention on Human Rights to Protect the Right of Access to the Civil Courts' in C. Scott (ed.), *Torture as Tort: Comparative Perspectives on the Development of Transnational Human Rights Litigation* (Oxford: Hart Publishing, 2001).

Clapham, A. and Jerbi, S., 'Categories of Corporate Complicity in Human Rights Abuses' (2001) 24 *Hastings International and Comparative Law Review* 339.

Clarke, T., 'Towards a Citizen's MAI: an Alternative to Developing a Global Investment Treaty based on Citizen's Rights and Democratic Control' (Ottawa: Polaris Institute, 1998).

Clough, J., 'Not-so Innocents Abroad: Corporate Criminal Liability for Human Rights Abuses' (2005) 11 *Australian Journal of Human Rights* 1.

Collier, J., *Conflict of Laws*, 3rd edition (Cambridge: Cambridge University Press, 2001).

Coomans, F., 'The *Ongoni* Case before the African Commission on Human and People's Rights' (2003) 52 *International and Comparative Law Quarterly* 749.

Cooper, D., 'Secondary Liability for Civil Wrongs', PhD thesis, University of Cambridge (1995).

Craven, M., *The International Covenant on Economic, Social and Cultural Rights* (Oxford: Clarendon Press, 1995).

D'Amato, A., *The Concept of Custom in International Law* (Ithaca, NY: Cornell University Press, 1971).

Damrosch, L., 'Politics across Borders: Non-Intervention and Non-Forcible Influence over Domestic Affairs' (1989) 83 *American Journal of International Law* 1.

Danailov, S., 'The Accountability of Non-State Actors for Human Rights Violations: the Special Case of Transnational Corporations' (October, 1998) downloadable from http://www.humanrights.ch/cms/pdf/ 000303_danailov_ studie.pdf.

Dhooge, L., 'Beyond Voluntarism: Social Disclosure and France's Nouvelles Regulations Economiques' (2004) 21 *Arizona Journal of International and Comparative Law* 441.

Dicken, P., *Global Shift: Transforming the World Economy*, 3rd edition (London: Paul Chapman, 1998).

Digan, T., 'NEPA and the Presumption against Extraterritorial Application: the Foreign Policy Exclusion' (1994) 11 *Journal of Contemporary Health Law and Policy* 165.

Diller, J., 'Social Conduct in Transnational Enterprise Operations: the Role of the International Labour Organization' in R. Blanpain (ed.), *Multinationals and the Social Challenges of the XXIst Century* (The Hague: Kluwer, 2000).

Dine, J., *Companies, International Trade and Human Rights* (Cambridge: Cambridge University Press, 2005).

 The Governance of Corporate Groups (Cambridge: Cambridge University Press, 2000).

Dinham, B. and Sarangi, S., 'The Bhopal Gas Tragedy 1984 to ?: the Evasion of Corporate Responsibility' (2002) 14(1) *Environment and Urbanisation* 89.

Doane, D., 'From Red Tape to Road Signs: Redefining Regulation and its Purpose', CORE pamphlet, 2004, http://www.corporate-responsibility.org.

Dunning, J., *Multinationals and the Global Economy* (Wokingham: Addison Wesley, 1993).

 'Non-equity Forms of Foreign Economic Involvement and the Theory of International Production" in J. Dunning (ed.), *Explaining International Production* (London: Unwin Hyman, 1988).

Easterbrook, F. and Fischel, D., 'Limited Liability and the Corporation' (1985) 52 *University of Chicago Law Review* 89.

Elagab, O.,'Coercive Economic Measures against Developing Countries' (1982) 41 *International and Comparative Law Quarterly* 682.

Elias, O., 'The Nature of the Subjective Element in Customary International Law' (1995) 44 *International and Comparative Law Quarterly* 501.

European Commission, 'Communication from the Commission concerning Corporate Social Responsibility: a Business Contribution to Sustainable Development', COM (2002) 347, final, Brussels, 2 July 2002.

European Commission, Employment and Social Affairs, 'Corporate Social Responsibility: National Public Policies in the European Union', January 2004.

Farar, T., 'Political and Economic Coercion in Contemporary International Law' (1985) 79 *American Journal of International Law* 405.

Fatouros, A., 'National Legal Persons in International Law' in R. Bernhardt (ed.), *Encyclopaedia of Public International Law*, 5 vols. (Amsterdam: North Holland, 1997), vol. III, p. 495.

Feld, W., *Multinational Corporations and UN Politics: the Quest for a Code of Conduct* (New York: Pergamon Press, 1980).

Fentiman, R., 'Stays and the European Conventions – End Game?' (2001) 60 *Cambridge Law Journal* 10.

Fieldhouse, D., 'The Multinational: a Critique of a Concept' in A. Teichova, M. Lévy-Leboyer and H. Nussbaum (eds.), *The Multinational in Historical Perspective* (Cambridge: Cambridge University Press, 1986).

Fitzmaurice, G., 'The Foundation of the Authority of International Law and the Problem of Enforcement' (1956) 19 *Modern Law Review* 1.

Francioni, F., 'Extraterritorial Application of Environmental Law' in K. Meessen (ed.), *Extraterritorial Jurisdiction in Theory and Practice* (The Hague: Kluwer, 1996).

Friedman, M., *Capitalism and Freedom* (Chicago: University of Chicago Press, 1962).

Forcese, C., 'ATCA's Achilles Heel: Corporate Complicity, International Law and the Alien Tort Claims Act' (2001) 26 *Yale Journal of International Law* 487.

Ghoshal, S. and Bartlett, C., 'The Multinational Corporation as an Inter-Organisational Network' in S. Ghoshal and D. Westney (eds.), *Organisational Theory and Multinational Corporations* (London: Macmillan, 1993).

Gilpin, R., *The Challenge of Global Capitalism: the World Economy in the 21st Century* (Princeton: Princeton University Press, 2000).

Gordon, K. and Miyake, M., 'Deciphering Codes of Conduct: a Review of their Contents', OECD Working Papers on International Investment, No. 1992/2, 1999.

Gruchella-Wesierski, T., 'A Framework for Understanding Soft Law' (1984) 30 *McGill Law Journal* 37.

Gunning, I., 'Modernising Customary International Law: the Challenge of Human Rights' (1991) 31 *Virginia Journal of International Law* 211.

Hadden, T., 'Regulating Corporate Groups: an International Perspective' in J. McCahery, S. Picciotto and C. Scott (ed.), *Corporate Control and Accountability: Changing Structures and the Dynamics of Regulation* (Oxford: Clarendon Press, 1993).

Halpern, P., Trebilcock, M. and Turnbull, S., 'An Economic Analysis of Limited Liability in Corporation Law' (1980) 30 *University of Toronto Law Journal* 117.

Handl, G., 'State Liability for Accidental Transnational Environmental Damage by Private Persons' (1980) 74 *American Journal of International Law* 525.

Hansmann, H. and Kraakman, R., 'Towards Unlimited Shareholder Liability for Corporate Torts' (1991) 100 *Yale Law Journal* 1879.

Harlow, C., '"Public" and "Private" Law: Definition without Distinction' (1980) 43 *Modern Law Review* 241.

Henkin, L., 'Keynote Address: The Universal Declaration at 50 and the Challenge of Global Markets' (1999) 25 *Brooklyn Journal of International Law* 17.

Hertz, N., *The Silent Takeover: Global Capitalism and the Death of Democracy* (London: Heinemann, 2000).

Higgins, R., *The Development of International Law through the Political Organs of the United Nations* (Oxford: Oxford University Press, 1963).

  Problems and Process: International Law and How We Use It (Oxford: Clarendon Press, 1994).

Hood, J., *The Heroic Enterprise: Business and the Common Good* (New York: Free Press, 1996)

Hood, N. and Young, S., *The Economics of the Multinational Enterprise* (London: Longman, 1979).

Hopkins, M. 'Corporate Social Responsibility around the World' (1998) 2 *Online Journal of Ethics*, No. 2, http://www.stthom.edu/cbes/onlinejournals.html.
  The Planetary Bargain: Corporate Social Responsibility Matters (London: Earthscan Publications, 2003).

Hopt, K., 'Legal Elements and Policy Decisions in Regulating Groups of Companies' in C. Schmitthoff and F. Wooldridge (eds.), *Groups of Companies* (London: Sweet & Maxwell, 1991).

Howarth, D., 'My Brother's Keeper? Liability for Acts of Third Parties' (1994) 14 *Legal Studies* 88.

ICHRP, *Beyond Voluntarism: Human Rights and the Developing International Legal Obligations of Companies* (Versoix: ICHRP, 2002).

Ives, J. (ed.) *The Export of Hazards: Transnational Corporations and Environmental Control Issues* (London: Routledge & Kegan Paul, 1985).

Jackson, J., *The World Trading System: Law and Policy of Economic Relations*, 4th edition (Cambridge, MA: MIT Press, 2000).

Jackson, J. and Sykes, A. *Implementing the Uruguay Round* (Oxford: Clarendon Press, 1997).

Jägers, N., *Corporate Human Rights Obligations: In Search of Accountability* (Antwerp: Intersentia, 2002).

Johns, F., 'The Invisibility of the Transnational Corporation: an Analysis of International Law and Theory' (1994) 19 *Melbourne University Law Review* 893.

Johnson, J., 'Public–Private Convergence: How the Private Actor Can Shape Public International Law Labour Standards' (1998) 24 *Brooklyn Journal of International Law* 291.

Joseph, S., 'Corporations and Human Rights Litigation (Update on *Sosa v. Alvarez-Machain*)', copy available from http://www.hartpub.co.uk.
  Corporations and Transnational Human Rights Litigation (Oxford: Hart Publishing, 2004).
  'Taming the Leviathans: Multinational Enterprises and Human Rights' (1999) 46 *Netherlands International Law Review* 171.

Kahn-Freud, O., 'General Problems of Private International Law' (1974) 3 *Recueil des Cours* 139.

Kamminga, M. and Zia-Zarifi, S. (eds.), *Liability of Multinational Corporations under International Law* (The Hague: Kluwer, 2000).

Keck, M. and Sikkink, K., *Activists Beyond Borders* (Ithaca, NY: Cornell University Press, 1998).

Kinley, D. and Tadaki, J., 'From Talk to Walk: the Emergence of Human Rights Responsibilities for Corporations at International Law' (2004) 44 *Virginia Journal of International Law* 931.

Kiss, A., 'Concept and Possible Implications of the Right to Environment' in K. Mahoney and P. Mahoney (eds.), *Human Rights in the Twenty-First Century: a Global Challenge* (The Hague: Kluwer, 1993).

Klein, N., *No Logo* (London: Flamingo, 2000).

Kodama, Y., 'Dispute Settlement under the Draft Multilateral Agreement on Investment' (1999) 16(3) *Journal of International Arbitration* 45.

Kokkini-Iatridou, D. and de Waart, P., 'Foreign Investments in Developing Countries: Legal Personality of Multinationals in International Law' (1983) 14 *Netherlands Yearbook of International Law* 87.

Korten, D., *When Corporations Rule the World* (London: Earthscan Publications 1995).

Lange, D. and Born, G. (eds.), *The Extraterritorial Application of National Laws* (Deventer: ICC/Kluwer, 1987).

Lauterpacht, H., 'Sovereignty over Submarine Areas' (1950) 27 *British Yearbook of International Law* 376.

Lowenfeld, A., *International Litigation and the Quest for Reasonableness: Essays in Private International Law* (Oxford: Clarendon Press, 1996).

McBeth, A., 'A Look at Corporate Code of Conduct Legislation' (2004) 3(3) *Common World Law Review* 222.

McCorquodale, R., 'Human Rights and Global Business' in S. Bottomley and D. Kinley (eds.), *Commercial Law and Human Rights* (Aldershot: Ashgate, 2002).

McDonald. J., 'The Multilateral Agreement on Investment: Heyday or Mai-Day for Ecologically Sustainable Development' (1998) 22 *Melbourne University Law Review* 617.

McGarity, T., 'Bhopal and the Export of Hazardous Technologies' (1985) 20 *Texas International Law Journal* 333.

MacGibbon, I., 'The Scope of Acquiescence in International Law' (1954) 31 *British Yearbook of International Law* 143.

McLachlan, C., 'The Influence of International Law on Civil Jurisdiction' (1993) 6 *Hague Yearbook of International Law* 125.

Madeley, J., *Big Business Poor Peoples: the Impact of Transnational Corporations on the World's Poor* (London: Zed Books, 1999).

Mandel, H., 'In Pursuit of the Missing Link: International Workers' Rights and International Trade' (1989) 27 *Columbia Journal of Transnational Law* 443.

Markesinis, B. and Deakin, S., *Tort Law*, 4th edition (Oxford: Clarendon Press, 1999).

Mayer, D. and Sable, K., 'Yes! We Have No Bananas: Forum Non Conveniens and Corporate Evasion' (2004) 4 *International Business Law Review* 130.

Meeran, R., '"Process Liability" of Multinationals: Overcoming the Forum Hurdle' (1995) *Journal of Personal Injury Litigation* 170.

   'The Unveiling of Transnational Corporations' in M. Addo (ed.), *Human Rights and the Responsibility of Transnational Corporations* (The Hague: Kluwer, 1999).

Mertus, J., 'Considering Nonstate Actors in the New Millennium: Towards Expanded Participation in Norm Creation and Norm Application' (2000) 32 *International Law and Politics* 537.

   The United Nations and Human Rights: a Guide for a New Era (New York: Routledge, 2005).

Miles, S., Hammond, K. and Friedman, A., 'Social and Environmental Reporting and Ethical Investment', ACCA, Research Report No. 77 (2002), http://www.accaglobal.com/research.

Monaghan, P., 'Impacts of Reporting: Uncovering the Voluntary vs Mandatory Myth' in Accountability (ed.), *Accountability Quarterly, Does Reporting Work?: The Effect of Regulation* (September 2003) AQ21.

Monbiot, G., *Captive State: the Corporate Takeover of Britain*, 2nd edition (London: Pan Books, 2001).

Monsma, D. and Buckley, J., 'Non-Financial Corporate Performance: the Material Edges of Social and Environmental Disclosure' (2004) 11 *University of Baltimore Journal of Environmental Law* 151.

Mosley P., Harrigan, J. and Toye, J., *Aid and Power: the World Bank and Policy-Based Lending*, 2nd edition, 2 vols. (London: Routledge, 1991).

Muchlinski, P., 'Attempts to Extend the Accountability of Transnational Corporations: the Role of UNCTAD' in M. Kamminga and S. Zia-Zarifi (eds.), *Liability of Multinational Corporations under International Law* (The Hague: Kluwer, 2000).

Multinational Enterprises and the Law (Oxford: Blackwell, 1995).

'The Rise and Fall of the Multilateral Agreement on Investment: Where Now?' (2000) 34 *International Lawyer* 1033.

Mullerat, R. (ed.), *Corporate Social Responsibility: the Corporate Governance of the 21st Century* (The Hague: Kluwer, 2005).

Murray, J., 'A New Phase in the Regulation of Multinational Enterprises: the Role of the OECD' (2001) 30 *Industrial Law Journal* 255.

OECD, 'Civil Society and the OECD', OECD Policy Brief Series, 2001.

'Codes of Conduct – Explaining their Economic Significance', Report of the Working Party of the Trade Committee, 11 May 2001, TD/TC/WP (2001)10/FINAL.

'The OECD Guidelines for Multinational Enterprises: Annual Report' (OECD, 2001).

'OECD Guidelines for Multinational Enterprises Annual Report 2002: Focus on Responsible Supply Chain Management' (OECD, 2002).

Oosterveen, W., 'Some Recent Developments Regarding Liability for Damage Resulting from Oil Pollution – From the Perspective of an EU Member State' (2004) 6 *Environmental Law Review* 223.

Paul, J., 'Comity in International Law' (1991) 32 *Harvard International Law Journal* 1.

Paust, J., 'Human Rights Responsibilities of Private Corporations' (2002) 35 *Vanderbilt Journal of Transnational Law* 801.

Pearson, C. (ed.), *Multinational Corporations, Environment and the Third World* (Durham, NC: Duke University Press, 1987).

Peattie, K., 'Research Insights into Corporate Social Responsibility (Part I)' (2002) 1(2) *New Academy Review* 33.

Peattie, K., Solomon, J., Solomon, A. and Hunt, J., 'Research Insights into Corporate Social Responsibility (Part II)' (2002) 1(3) *New Academy Review* 39.

Peninou, G., Holthus, M., Kebschull, D. and Attali, J., *Who's Afraid of the Multinationals: a Survey of European Opinion of Multinational Corporations* (Farnborough: Saxon House, 1979).

Perez-Lopez, J., 'Conditioning Trade on Foreign Labor Law: the US Approach' (1987–8) 9 *Comparative Labour Law Journal* 253.

Pettet, B., 'Limited Liability – A Principle for the 21st Century?' (1995) 48 *Current Legal Problems* 125.

Picciotto, S., 'The Regulatory Criss-Cross: Interaction between Jurisdictions and the Construction of Global Regulatory Networks' in W. Bratton (ed.), *International Regulatory Competition and Coordination* (Oxford: Clarendon Press, 1996).

'Rights, Responsibilities and Regulation of International Business' (2003) 42 *Columbia Journal of Transnational Law* 131.

Pierros, P. and Hudson, C., 'The Hard Graft of Tackling Corruption in International Business Transactions: Progress in International Cooperation and the OECD Convention' (1998) 32(2) *Journal of World Trade* 77.

Pisillo-Mazzeschi, R., 'The Due Diligence Rule and the Nature of International Responsibility of States' (1992) 35 *German Yearbook of International Law* 9.

Prentice, D., 'Some Comments on the Law of Groups' in J. McCahery, S. Picciotto and C. Scott (eds.), *Corporate Control and Accountability* (Oxford: Clarendon Press, 1993).

Prince, P., 'Bhopal, Bougainville and Ok Tedi: Why Australia's *Forum Non Conveniens* Approach is Better' (1998) 47 *International and Comparative Law Quarterly* 573.

Ratner, S., 'Corporations and Human Rights: a Theory of Legal Responsibility' (2001) 111 *Yale Law Journal* 443.

'International Law: the Trials of Global Norms' (1998) 160 *Foreign Policy* 65.

Redmond, P., 'Transnational Enterprise and Human Rights: Options for Standard Setting and Compliance' (2003) 37 *International Lawyer* 69.

Reich, R., *The Work of Nations* (New York: Alfred A. Knopf, 1991).

Risse, T. and Sikkink, K., 'The Socialization of International Human Rights Norms into Domestic Practices: Introduction' in T. Risse, S. Ropp and K. Sikkink (eds.), *The Power of Human Rights: International Norms and Domestic Change* (Cambridge: Cambridge University Press, 1999).

Rosenthal, D. and Knighton, W., *National Laws and International Commerce: the Problem of Extraterritoriality* (London: Routledge & Kegan Paul and Chatham House, 1982).

Roth, P., 'Reasonable Extraterritoriality: Correcting the Balance of Interests' (1992) 41 *International and Comparative Law Quarterly* 245.

Rudolph, P., 'The Central Role of Lawyers in Managing, Minimizing, and Responding to Social Responsibility Risks – a US Perspective' in R. Mullerat (ed.), *Corporate Social Responsibility: the Corporate Governance of the 21st Century* (The Hague: Kluwer, 2005).

Schlegelmilch, R., 'WTO: Why Still No Multilateral Rules for Foreign Direct Investment?' (2000) 6 *International Trade Law and Regulation* 78.

Schwarzenberger, G., *International Law*, 3rd edition, 4 vols. (London: Stevens & Sons, 1957).

Scott, C., 'Translating Torture into Transnational Tort: Conceptual Divides in the Debate on Corporate Accountability for Human Rights Harms' in C. Scott (ed.), *Torture as Tort: Comparative Perspectives on the Development of Transnational Human Rights Litigation* (Oxford: Hart Publishing, 2001).

Seck, S., 'Environmental Harm in Developing Countries Caused by Subsidiaries of Canadian Mining Corporations: the Interface of Public and Private International Law' (1999) 37 *Canadian Yearbook of International Law* 139.

Seidl-Hohenveldern, I., *Corporations in and under International Law* (Cambridge: Grotius Publications, 1987).

'International Economic Soft Law' (1980) 163 *Receuil des Cours* 164.

Servan-Schreiber, J., *The American Challenge* (New York: Atheneum, 1979) (first published in French as *Le Défi Américain* (Paris: Editions Denoel, 1967)).

Seward, A., 'After Bhopal: Implications for Parent Company Liability' (1987) 21 *International Lawyer* 695.

Shaw, M., *International Law*, 5th edition (Cambridge: Cambridge University Press, 2003).

Shelton, D., 'Introduction: Law, Non-Law and the Problem of Soft Law' in D. Shelton (ed.), *Commitment and Compliance: the Role of Non-Binding Norms in the International Legal System* (Oxford: Oxford University Press, 2000).

Slaughter, A., 'A Liberal Theory of International Law' (2000) 94 *American Society of International Law Proceedings* 240.

Sornorajah, M., *The International Law on Foreign Investment* (Cambridge: Cambridge University Press, 1994).

'Linking State Responsibility for Certain Harms Caused by Corporate Nationals Abroad to Civil Recourse in the Legal Systems of Home States' in C. Scott (ed.), *Torture as Tort: Comparative Perspectives on the Development of Transnational Human Rights Litigation* (Oxford: Hart Publishing, 2001).

Staker, C., 'Diplomatic Protection of Private Business Companies' (1990) 61 *British Yearbook of International Law* 155.

Steiner, H. and Alston, P., *International Human Rights in Context: Law, Politics and Morals*, 2nd edition (Oxford: Oxford University Press, 2000).

Stephens, B., 'Upsetting Checks and Balances: the Bush Administration's Efforts to Limit Human Rights Litigation' (2004) 17 *Harvard Human Rights Journal* 169.

Stephens, B. and Ratner, S., *International Human Rights Litigation in US Courts* (Irvington-on-Hudson, NY: Transnational Publishers, 1996).

Sternberg, E., *Just Business: Business Ethics in Action*, 2nd edition (Oxford: Oxford University Press, 2000).

Stopford, J. and Strange, S., *Rival States, Rival Firms: Competition for World Market Shares* (Cambridge: Cambridge University Press, 1991).

Sustainability, 'The Changing Landscape of Liability: a Director's Guide to Trends in Corporate Environmental, Social and Economic Liability', (Sustainability, December 2004).

Swaminathan, R. 'Regulating Development: Structural Adjustment and the Case for National Enforcement of Economic and Social Rights' (1998) 37 *Columbia Journal for Transnational Law* 181.

Trebilcock, M. and Howse, R. *The Regulation of International Trade*, 2nd edition (London: Routledge, 1998).

Trindade, A., 'The Domestic Jurisdiction of States in the Practice of the United Nations and Regional Organisations' (1976) 25 *International and Comparative Law Quarterly* 715.

Tugendhat, C., *The Multinationals* (London: Eyre & Spottiswoode, 1971).

UN, Department of Economic and Social Affairs, 'The Impact of Multinational Corporations on Development and on International Relations', UN Doc. E/5500/Rev. 1., ST/ESA/6 (New York: UN, 1974); (1974) 13 ILM 800.

UNCTAD, 'World Investment Report 1996: Investment, Trade and International Policy Arrangements' (New York and Geneva: UN, 1996), UN Sales No. E.96.II.A.14.

'World Investment Report 1997: Transnational Corporations, Market Structure and Competition Policy' (New York and Geneva: UN, 1997), UN Sales No. E.97.II.D.10.

'World Investment Report 1999: Investment Trade and International Policy Arrangements' (New York and Geneva: UN, 1999), UN Sales No. E.99.II.D.3.

'World Investment Report 2000: Cross Border Mergers and Acquisitions and Development' (New York and Geneva: UN, 2000), UN Sales No. E.00.II.D.20.

'World Investment Report 2001: Promoting Linkages' (New York and Geneva: UN, 2001), UN Sales No. E.01.II.D.12.

'World Investment Report 2003: FDI Policies for Development: National and International Perspectives' (New York and Geneva: UN, 2003), UN Sales No. E.03.II.D.8.

UNCTC, 'Transnational Corporations in World Development: Trends and Prospects' (New York: UN, 1988).

Vagts, D., 'The Multinational Enterprise: a New Challenge for Transnational Law' (1970) 83 *Harvard Law Review* 739.

Vernon, R., *In the Hurricane's Eye: the Troubled Prospects of Multinational Enterprises* (Cambridge, MA: Harvard University Press, 1998).

Sovereignty at Bay: the Multinational Spread of US Enterprise (New York: Basic Books, 1971).

Storm over the Multinationals: the Real Issues (London: Macmillan, 1977).

Vidal, J., *McLibel: Burger Culture on Trial* (New York: The New Press, 1997).

Vogelaar, T., 'The OECD Guidelines: Their Philosophy, History, Negotiation, Form, Legal Nature, Follow-Up Procedures and Review' in N. Horn (ed.), *Legal Problems of Codes of Conduct for Multinational Enterprises* (The Hague: Kluwer, 1980).

Von Moltke, K., 'A Model International Investment Agreement for the Promotion of Sustainable Development', IISD, November 2004, http://www.iisd.org.

Voon, T., 'Multinational Enterprises and State Sovereignty under International Law' (1999) 21 *Adelaide Law Review* 219.

Wallace, C., *The Multinational Enterprise and Legal Control: Host State Sovereignty in an Era of Economic Globalisation* (The Hague: Martinus Nijhoff, 2002).

(ed.), *Foreign Direct Investment and the Multinational Enterprise: a Bibliography* (Dordrecht: Martinus Nijhoff, 1988).

Ward, H., 'Corporate Accountability in Search of a Treaty?: Some Insights from Foreign Direct Liability', RIIA, Briefing Paper, No. 4, May 2002.

'Governing Multinationals: the Role of Foreign Direct Liability', RIIA, Briefing Paper, New Series No. 18, February 2001.

'Legal Issues in Corporate Citizenship', (International Institute for Environment and Development, February 2003).

'Securing Transnational Corporate Accountability through National Courts: Implications and Policy Options' (2001) *Hastings International and Comparative Law Review* 451.

'Transparency and Information: a Frontier Battleground' in Accountability (ed.), *Accountability Quarterly, Does Reporting Work: The Effect of Regulation* (September 2003) AQ21.

Watts, P., 'The International Petroleum Industry: Economic Actor or Social Activist?' in J. Mitchell (ed.), *Companies in a World of Conflict* (London: Royal Institute of International Affairs, Energy and Environmental Programme, 1998).

Weeramantry, C., 'Human Rights and the Global Marketplace' (1999) 25 *Brooklyn Journal of International Law* 41.

Weissbrodt, D., 'The Beginning of a Sessional Working Group on Transnational Corporations within the UN Sub-Commission on Prevention of Discrimination and Protection of Minorities' in M. Kamminga and S. Zia-Zarifi (eds.), *Liability of Multinational Corporations under International Law* (The Hague: Kluwer, 2000).

Williams, C., 'Civil Society Initiatives and "Soft Law" in the Oil and Gas Industry' (2004) 36 *New York University Journal of International Law and Politics* 457.

Zarsky, L., 'Stuck in the Mud: Nation States, Globalization and the Environment', Globalization and Environment Study, OECD Economics Division, The Hague, May 1997.

Zerk, J., 'Legal Aspects of Corporate Responsibility Reporting: Panacea, Polyfilla or Pandora's Box?' (2004) 3(3) *New Academy Review* 17.

Zimmerman, J., *Extraterritorial Employment Standards of the United States* (Westport, CT: Quorum Books, 1992).

Index

AA 1000 standards 176
abusive marketing 22
access to information 171–82
  CSR reporting 172–6
  Extractive Industries Transparency
    Initiative (EITI) 96, 163, 178–9
  freedom of information legislation 177–8
  pensions disclosure 176
  sharing information about risks/hazards
    179–80
  social and eco labelling 95, 180–1
  whistleblower protection 142, 181–2
access to justice as international law
    obligation 116–17
accountability 7
Accountability (Institute of Social and
    Ethical Accountability) 153, 176
Action Aid 33
Adidas 188
African Commission on Human and
    Peoples' Rights 92
age discrimination 182
agency 118
  vicarious liability 223–5, 234, 235
Agenda 21 244, 257–8, 264
aid programmes, preferential trading
    relationships 155
Amnesty International 33, 266, 274
Annan, Kofi 100, 258
anti-globalisation movement 18, 20,
    21
anti-terrorism measures 107, 109
Apparel Industry Partnership 99, 163
asbestosis 22
assistance, secondary liability and 226
Australia 152, 157
  Corporate Code of Conduct Bill 164,
    165–6, 174, 186
  CSR reporting 173

extraterritorial jurisdiction 110
foreign direct liability (FDL) claims 205
forum non conveniens in 126–7
parent company liability, primary
    liability 217–18
private enforcement rights 185
authorisation 226
avoidance of regulation 37
award schemes 39, 194

BabyMilk Action 95, 96
Bakan, Joel 8, 17, 18, 25, 228
Baku–Tbilisi–Ceyhan Pipeline Project 43
Balfour Beatty 190
Barclays 43
Belgium
  pensions disclosure 176
  social and eco labelling 180
  universal jurisdiction 111
Bhopal disaster 22, 96, 121–3, 130, 201–3,
    219, 221, 232, 305
Birnie, P. 70, 272
Blair, Tony 156, 171, 178
Blumberg, P. 54
Boyle, A. 70, 272
BP 42, 99
Braithwaite, J. 29, 102
bribery/corruption 108, 110, 172, 286–9
Brownlie, I. 147
Burma (Myanmar), human rights abuses
    80, 203, 208, 211, 213, 219, 224,
    228
business case for CSR 16–17, 33, 152
Business in the Community (BITC, UK) 24,
    25, 194
Business Ethics magazine 24
Business Leaders Initiative on Human
    Rights 43
Business for Social Responsibility (USA) 25

call centres 154
Canada
  Canada–US Free Trade Agreement 14
  codes of conduct 162
  foreign direct liability (FDL) claims 206
care, duty of 216–23
Cassels, J. 114, 123, 223
causation issues 221–2
child labour
  ILO Convention (1999) 289–90
  ILO Tripartite Declaration on
    Multinationals and 255
  OECD Guidelines on Multinationals and
    250
Chinkin, C. 71
choice of law 127–31
civil actions against multinationals 117–20
  see also tort-based claims
class actions 131
Clean Clothes Campaign 96
Coca-Cola 100
codes of conduct 37, 38, 94, 98, 161–5,
    305
  Australian Corporate Code of Conduct
    Bill 164, 165–6, 174, 186
  compliance with 164–5
  CSR reporting 174
  UK Corporate Responsibility Bill 164,
    168–70, 186
  UN Draft Code of Conduct on
    Transnational Corporations 12, 45,
    150, 244, 245–8, 308
    consumer protection 246–7, 264,
      265
    openness and transparency 273
  US Code of Conduct (McKinney) Bill 164,
    167–8, 175, 186
colonialism 10
comity, international 115, 126, 213
'command and control' regulation 36–7
communications 14
communism, transition to market system
    from 13
compensation schemes 39
  pollution from ships 284–6
competition law, effects doctrine and 110
competitiveness 153–4
  Responsible Competitiveness Index 153
complicity 93
Confederation of British Industry (CBI),
    definition of CSR 30
conflicts see dispute resolution
consensus-building 95
consent, prior informed consent
    procedures 294, 300, 302
conspiracy 93, 226, 227
consultation, obligation to consult 269–71

consumer activism 21
consumer protection 82, 264, 271
  enforcement of rights 183
  OECD Guidelines on Multinationals and
    251, 264, 270
  tobacco control 290–1
  UN Draft Code and 246–7, 264, 265
continental shelf 64
contractors, supply chain responsibility
    92, 265–7
CORE Coalition 33, 95, 169, 171
corporate citizenship 31
corporate governance 26, 31
corporate personality 54–5, 93, 229, 233,
    235, 240
  international legal personality 72–6
corporate responsibility 32
corporate social responsibility (CSR) 7,
    58
  definitions 29–32
  rise of CSR movement 15–29
  see also individual topics
Corporate Watch 100
corruption 108, 110, 172, 286–9
crimes
  bribery/corruption 108, 110, 172, 286–9
  crimes against humanity 75, 76–83, 214
  genocide 75, 76–93, 112, 214
  piracy 75
  sex offences 109
  slavery 75
  universal jurisdiction 105, 111–12
  war crimes 75, 76–83, 214
CSR Wire, definition of CSR 31
customary international law 63–7, 115,
    298
  identifying customary rules on CSR
    276–7
  relationship with treaties 69

Damrosch, L. 137
definition of CSR 29–32
definition of multinational corporations
    49–52, 58, 75, 304
  constructing legal definition 52–4
Denmark
  award schemes 194
  CSR reporting 172
dependency, multinational corporations
    and 11
developing countries 306–9
  attitudes to multinational corporations
    in 10, 47
  human rights regulation and 84
development assistance, preferential
    trading relationships 155
Dicken, P. 146

Dine, J. 305
diplomatic protection 148
disclosure regulation 39–40
dispute resolution
    ILO Tripartite Declaration on
        Multinationals and 257
    jurisdictional conflicts 131–2
    Multilateral Agreement on Investment
        (MAI) 19
    OECD Guidelines on Multinationals
        253–4
distribution agreements 53
Doha Declaration 282
Donham, Walter B. 15
double standards 236
Drahos, P. 29, 102
due diligence 159, 160–94
    human rights regulation and 84
Dunning, J. 50
duty of care 216–23
Dyson 154

Earthrights International 188
eco labelling 95, 180–1
economic development
    multinational corporations and 46, 48
    as reason states have interest in foreign
        CSR standards of multinationals
        156–7
economic law 74
economic liberalism 13–14, 36
economic self-interest 152–6
effects doctrine 105, 109–10, 112, 132
employment 16
    children see child labour
    enforcement of rights 182
    extraterritorial labour standards 110
    ILO Tripartite Declaration on
        Multinationals and 255
    migration of jobs 154–5
    multinational corporations and 10, 12
    OECD Guidelines on Multinationals and
        249, 250
    UN Draft Code and 247
    vicarious liability and 223
    working conditions 22
    see also health and safety at work
encouragement 226
enforcement
    human rights 91–3
    private claims for environmental harm
        and personal injury 198–200,
        239–40, 304
    implications for international law
        237–9
    parent company liability 215–37, 240
    as 'regulation' 236–7

tort-based 200–7
    US Alien Tort Claims Act 44, 123, 183,
        207–15, 224–5, 237
    private enforcement rights 40, 182–7
    regulation of multinational corporations
        57
Enron 25
enterprise liability 228–33, 234, 235
enterprise theory 56
environmental issues 22, 23, 27, 71
    Agenda 21 244, 257–8, 264
    civil jurisdiction rules 119
    customary international law and 66–7
    enforcement of rights 182
    environmental impact assessment 272–3
    environmental rights 82
    international trade in hazardous
        substances 292–5
    minimum environmental standards 264
    OECD Guidelines on Multinationals and
        250–1, 264
    pollution from ships 284–6
    precautionary principle 271
    prevention of transboundary harm
        158–60
    private claims for environmental harm
        198–200, 239–40
    implications for international law
        237–9
    parent company liability 215–37, 240
    as 'regulation' 236–7
    tort-based 200–7
    US Alien Tort Claims Act 207–15,
        224–5, 237
    UN Draft Code and 247
Esso 96
ethical concerns as reason states have
    interest in foreign CSR standards of
    multinationals 157–8
Ethical Trading Initiative (ETI) 96, 99,
    163
    supply chain management 266
Ethics in Action, definition of CSR 30
European Convention on Human Rights
    (ECHR) 87
European Economic Interest Group 56
European Multi-Stakeholder Forum (EMSF)
    89, 97, 192
European Union 14, 153
    attitudes to multinational corporations
        in 8
    choice of law 127
    civil jurisdiction rules 117
    codes of conduct 162
    EU Parliament resolution on
        voluntary code 164, 170–1
    definition of CSR in 30

Eco-Management and Audit Scheme
    (EMAS) 39
enterprise liability and 230
freedom of information legislation 177
Green Paper on CSR 89
hearings and public inquiries 187–8
public procurement 192
sharing information about risks/hazards
    179
social and eco labelling 180
Social Charter 87
transparency/access to information and
    171
exploitation, social dumping 46, 47, 48,
    227
export controls 107
export credits 188–93
export processing zones 47
external monitoring 274–6
Extractive Industries Transparency
    Initiative (EITI) 96, 163, 178–9
extraterritorial jurisdiction 105, 142
  alternative definition of
    extraterritoriality 140–2
    extraterritorial benefits 141–2
    extraterritorial responsibilities 140–1
    extraterritorial rights 141
  Australia 110
  CSR regulation of multinationals 133–40
    CSR standards and duty of
      non-intervention 136–9, 306
    definitions of 'home state' 146–51
    initiatives under international law
      194–6
    mix of state and private interests
      135–6
    new directions 145–6, 196–7
    recent state practice 159, 160–94
    regulatory techniques 134
    why home states have interest in
      foreign CSR standards of
      multinationals 151–60
  developing role of home states 300–4
  human rights and 85, 87–91
  UK 108–9, 138
  USA 106–8, 109–10, 136
  Exxon Valdez oil spill 22

Fair Labor Association (FLA) 99
Fair Trade 180
family values 17
forced labour, OECD Guidelines on
    Multinationals and 250
Ford, Henry 15
foreign direct investment (FDI) 14, 49, 50
foreign direct liability (FDL) claims 198,
    239–40, 304

implications for international law
    237–9
parent company liability 215–37, 240
  enterprise liability 228–33, 234, 235
  organisational form and 234–7
  primary liability 216–23, 234, 235
  secondary liability 225–8, 234, 235
  vicarious liability 223–5, 234, 235
tort-based 200–7
US Alien Tort Claims Act 207–15, 224–5,
    237, 305
Forest Stewardship Council 180
Forum for the Future 153
forum non conveniens 116, 119, 120–7,
    214–15, 237
  Australia 126–7
  UK 124–6
  USA 120–4
Framework Convention on CSR proposal
    278–9
Framework Convention on Tobacco
    Control 290–1
France
  CSR reporting 172
  definition of 'home state' of MNCs 148
  export credits 189
  nuclear testing in Polynesia 184
  US extraterritorial jurisdiction and 108
franchises 53
freedom of information legislation 177–8
Friedman, Milton 16
Friends of the Earth (FoE) 33, 68, 95, 96,
    278–9
functional liability 93

General Agreement on Tariffs and Trade
    (GATT) 13
General Agreement on Trade in Services
    (GATS) 19, 46
genocide 75, 76–93, 112, 214
Germany
  definition of 'home state' of MNCs 148
  export credits 189
  pensions disclosure 176
  regulation in, allocating liabilities 55
Gilpin, R. 14
Glaxo Smith Kline 43
Global Compact 70, 71, 97, 100, 153,
    258–61, 276
  Policy Dialogue on Responsible
    Competitiveness 153
  precautionary principle 271
Global Reporting Initiative (GRI) 97
  Sustainability Reporting Guidelines 44
globalisation 21, 23, 46, 146, 157
  anti-globalisation movement 18, 20, 21
  treaties and 68

government and the state 7
  creation of international law 62–3
  developing role of home states 300–4
  human rights violations by 80–1
  international law and 104
  jurisdiction over territory 78
  multinational corporations as agents
    of 9
  self-regulation oversight by 38
  sovereign immunity 213
  why states have interest in foreign CSR
    standards of multinationals 151–60
    development goals 156–7
    economic self-interest 152–6
    ethical concerns 157–8
    legal case 158–60
    political self-interest 151–2
  see also regulation
green labelling 95, 180–1
greenwash awards 100
group liability 55
Group of 77 10

Harlow, C. 114
hazards
  duty of care and 219
  hazardous wastes 158–9
  international trade in hazardous
    substances 292–5
  obligation to warn of dangers 269–71
  prevention of transboundary harm
    158–60
  sharing information about 179–80
  see also health and safety at work
health, right to 82, 88
health and safety at work 82, 263–4
  ILO Convention on Prevention of
    Major Industrial Accidents 292,
    295–6
  ILO Tripartite Declaration on
    Multinationals and 255–6, 263
  minimum standards 264
  OECD Guidelines on Multinationals and
    250, 263
  UN Draft Code and 247
hearings 187–8
Henkin, L. 77
Higgins, R. 73, 135
Hood, J. 9
Hopkins, M. 32
human rights issues 8, 24, 42–4, 48, 74,
    302, 304
  foreign direct liability (FDL) claims
    207–15, 228
  human rights bodies as international
    regulators 279–80
  international human rights law 28–9

OECD Guidelines on Multinationals and
    250
  regulation of human rights 76–93
    direct regulation 76–83
    implementation and enforcement
      91–3
    indirect regulation 83–91
  UN Norms on Responsibilities of
    Transnational Corporations with
    Regard to Human Rights 56, 81, 82,
    83, 92, 245, 261–2, 276
    environmental impact assessment 273
    external monitoring 275
    minimum
      health/safety/environmental
      standards 263, 264, 265
    obligations to warn/consult 270–1
    openness and transparency 274
    precautionary principle 272
    proposed international CSR regulation
      279
    supply chain management 266, 267
    sustainable development 267
  violation of rights by governments 80–1

Ilisu Dam project 152, 190
incentives 38–9, 41, 188–93
  award schemes 39, 194
  export credits 188–93
  MNCs bargaining for 47
  taxation 38, 193–4
India
  Bhopal disaster 22, 96, 121–3, 130, 201–3,
    219, 221, 232, 305
  enterprise liability 232
individuals, enforcement rights 40, 182–7
Indonesia, human rights abuses 209
inducement 226
information
  access to 171–82
    CSR reporting 172–6
    Extractive Industries Transparency
      Initiative (EITI) 96, 163, 178–9
    freedom of information legislation
      177–8
    pensions disclosure 176
    sharing information about
      risks/hazards 179–80
    social and eco labelling 95, 180–1
    whistleblower protection 142, 181–2
  public information/education campaigns
    40
Institute of Social and Ethical
    Accountability (Accountability) 153,
    176
insurance schemes 39
intention, secondary liability and 226

interest groups, enforcement rights 40,
        182–7
International Baby Food Action Network
        18
international comity 115, 126, 213
International Council on Human Rights
        Policy (ICHRP) 92
International Court of Justice 63
International Covenant on Civil and
        Political Rights (ICCPR) 81, 86,
        90
International Covenant on Economic,
        Social and Cultural Rights (ICESCR)
        81, 84, 87, 90
International Criminal Court 76–93
International Investment Agreements (IIAs)
        149, 307
    investor responsibilities 280
International Labour Organisation (ILO)
        81, 137
    Child Labour Convention (1999) 289–90
    Convention on Prevention of Major
        Industrial Accidents (1993) 292,
        295–6
    Declaration on Fundamental Principles
        and Rights at Work 81
    Tripartite Declaration on Multinationals
        12, 45, 70, 71, 150, 244, 254–7, 308
        health and safety at work 255–6, 263
        obligations to warn/consult 270
    World Commission on the Social
        Dimension of Globalisation 283
international law 42, 59, 103, 299–300,
        309–10
    comity and 115, 126, 213
    CSR initiatives and 194–6
    custom 63–7, 115, 298
        identifying customary rules on CSR
        276–7
        relationship with treaties 69
    developing role of home states 300–4
    direct obligations for multinationals
        304–6
    direct regulation of human rights 76–83
        implementation and enforcement
        91–3
    foreign direct liability (FDL) claims and
        237–9
    as horizontal legal system 62
    human rights law 28–9
    implications for less developed host
        states 306–9
    indirect regulation of human rights
        83–91
        implementation and enforcement
        91–3
    international legal personality 72–6

jurisdiction and 104–5
    private international law 113–32, 133
    public international law 105–13, 132,
        133, 142
    meaning 61–2
    non-state actors and 93–102
    private 61
        jurisdiction and 113–32
    public 61
        jurisdiction and 105–13, 132, 133, 142
    soft law 69–72, 262, 297, 298
    towards an international law of CSR
        243–4, 297–8
        emerging legal principles 262–77
        international CSR standards for
        multinationals 244–62
    treaties 68, 71, 301
        relationship with custom 69
    who makes international law 62–3
International Maritime Organisation
        (IMO), conventions on pollution
        from ships 284–6
International Right to Know Coalition 171
international trade 13
    export controls 107
    export credits 188–93
    export processing zones 47
    hazardous substances 292–5
    preferential trading relationships 155
    protectionism 155, 307
Internet 21
investment
    foreign direct investment (FDI) 14, 49, 50
    International Investment Agreements
        (IIAs) 149, 307
        investor responsibilities 280
    Multilateral Agreement on Investment
        (MAI) 19–20, 46, 280–2
    socially responsible investment (SRI) 24
        pensions disclosure and 176
    Trade Related Investment Measures
        (TRIMS) Agreement 19, 46

Johannesburg Stock Exchange 40, 173
Johnson, Robert Wood 16
Johnson & Johnson 16
joint ventures 147
Joseph, S. 85
jurisdiction 86, 104–5, 301–2, 310
    extraterritorial see extraterritorial
        jurisdiction
    over territory 78
    private international law and 113–2, 133
        access to justice 116–17
        choice of law 127–31
        forum non conveniens 116, 119, 120–7,
        214–15, 237

jurisdiction (*cont.*)
jurisdiction of courts in civil cases
against multinationals 117–20
relationship between private and
public international law 113–16
resolving jurisdictional conflicts
131–2
public international law and 105–13,
132, 133, 142
effects doctrine 105, 109–10, 112, 132
nationality principle 105, 106–9, 112,
139
territoriality principle 104, 105, 109–10
universal principle 105, 111–12, 132
jus cogens 62

Kimberley Process on Conflict Diamonds
96
Kinley, D. 78, 79, 92
Korten, D. 18

law-making, MNCs and 21
legal context of CSR 26, 30, 34, 35,
158–60
emerging legal principles 262–77
environmental impact assessment
272–3
external monitoring 274–6
identifying customary rules 276–7
minimum health/safety/
environmental standards 263–5
obligation to warn of dangers/consult
269–71
openness and transparency 273–4
precautionary principle 271
supply chain responsibility 265–7
sustainable development 267–9
see also international law
liberalism
economic 13–14, 36
liberal theory of international law 94
Libya, sanctions against 107
limited liability 16, 26, 228, 229
literature on CSR 25
Lowenfeld, A. 139

Maastricht Guidelines on Violations of
Economic, Social and Cultural
Rights 85
management structures, multinational
corporations 49
Marine Stewardship Council 100
market-based initiatives 41
tradable emissions permits 39
marketing, abusive 22
Meeran, R. 219
misleading statements 110

mobility of MNCs 47–8
monitoring, external 274–6
Muchlinski, P. 20
Multilateral Agreement on Investment
(MAI) 19–20, 46, 280–2
multinational corporations 7
definitions 49–52, 58, 75, 304
constructing legal definition 52–4
direct obligations 304–6
management structures 49
mobility 47–8
public concern about 7, 8–15
see also individual topics
Murray, J. 250
Myanmar *see* Burma

National Contact Points (NCPs) 97, 150,
163, 184, 186, 251–2, 253
nationality principle 105, 106–9, 112, 139
definitions of 'home state' of MNCs
146–51
Nestlé 18, 96, 188
Netherlands
award schemes 194
CSR reporting 172
export credits 188–9
new capitalism 17
New International Economic Order 10
New Zealand, regulation in, allocating
liabilities 55
Nigeria 92
Shell Oil in 23–4, 80, 208
Nike 78, 99, 185
non-governmental organisations (NGOs)
100
international law and 94–8
see also individual organisations
non-intervention principle 136–9, 306
North American Free Trade Agreement
(NAFTA) 14
Norway, CSR reporting 172
nuclear testing 184

oil pollution 284–6
Operating and Financial Review (OFR)
173–4, 175
opinio juris 63, 65, 66, 68
Organisation for Economic Cooperation
and Development (OECD)
Bribery Convention 286–9
Guidelines on Multinationals 12, 45, 52,
70, 71, 72, 93, 97, 150, 162, 184, 186,
187, 189, 244, 248–54, 277, 308
consumer protection 251, 264, 270
environmental impact assessment 272
environmental issues 250–1, 264
external monitoring 275

health and safety at work 250, 263
National Contact Points (NCPs) 97,
    150, 163, 184, 186, 251–2, 253
obligations to warn/consult 269
openness and transparency 273
precautionary principle 271
supply chain management 265
sustainable development 267
Multilateral Agreement on Investment
    (MAI) 19–20, 46, 280–2
over-regulation 37
Overseas Private Investment Corporation
    (OPIC) 179, 190, 191–2

parent company liability 93, 215–37,
    240
  enterprise liability 228–33, 234, 235
  organisational form and 234–7
  primary liability 216–23, 234, 235
  secondary liability 225–8, 234, 235
  vicarious liability 223–5, 234, 235
paternalism 157
Paul, J. 114
pensions disclosure 176
peremptory norms (*jus cogens*) 62
personal injury claims 198–200, 239–40
  implications for international law 237–9
  parent company liability 215–37, 240
    enterprise liability 228–33, 234, 235
    organisational form and 234–7
    primary liability 216–23, 234, 235
    secondary liability 225–8, 234, 235
    vicarious liability 223–5, 234, 235
  as 'regulation' 236–7
  tort-based 200–7
  US Alien Tort Claims Act 207–15, 224–5,
    237
personality, corporate 54–5, 93, 229, 233,
    235, 240
  international legal personality 72–6
pesticides 218
pharmaceuticals 218
philanthropy 15
piracy 75
political self-interest 151–2
power, multinational corporations and 11,
    18–19, 23
precautionary principle 271
preferential trading relationships 155
Premier Oil 188
prior informed consent procedures 294,
    300, 302
private enforcement rights 40, 182–7
private international law 61
  jurisdiction 113–2, 133
    access to justice 116–17
    choice of law 127–31

forum non conveniens 116, 119, 120–7,
    214–15, 237
  jurisdiction of courts in civil cases
    against multinationals 117–20
  relationship between private and
    public international law 113–16
  resolving jurisdictional conflicts 131–2
privatisation 13, 77, 156
process liability 219
product liability, resolving jurisdictional
    conflicts 131
productivity, CSR and 17
profit, CSR and 17
proposed international CSR regulation
    278–83
  Framework Convention on CSR 278–9
  human rights bodies as international
    regulators 279–80
  investor responsibilities under IIAs 280
  new international institutions 282–3
protectionism 155, 307
public concern, about multinational
    corporations 7, 8–15
public information/education campaigns
    40
public inquiries 187–8
public interest, *forum non conveniens* and
    121, 122
public international law 61
  jurisdiction and 105–13, 132, 133, 142
    effects doctrine 105, 109–10, 112, 132
    nationality principle 105, 106–9, 112,
        139
    territoriality principle 104, 105,
        109–10
    universal principle 105, 111–12, 132
  public policy, private international law
    and 115
public sector, procurement process 38,
    192–3

race to the bottom 154
reasonableness test 220
regional customary international law 64
regional trading arrangements 14
regulation 7, 34
  avoidance 37
  in deregulatory era 32–42
  goals 46
  human rights 76–93
    direct regulation 76–83
    implementation and enforcement
        91–3
    indirect regulation 83–91
  initiatives under international law 194–6
  meanings 41–2
  multinational corporations 58

regulation (*cont.*)
  administration, supervision and
    enforcement 57
  allocating liabilities 54–6
  definitions of 'home state' 146–51
  definitions of MNCs 49–54
  extraterritorial jurisdiction 133–40
  new directions 145–6, 196–7
  precedents in international CSR
    regulation 284–97
  proposals for international CSR
    regulation 278–83
  special nature of MNCs 44–9
  why home states have interest in
    foreign CSR standards of
    multinationals 151–60
over-regulation 37
private claims as 236–7
problems with 301
recent state practice 159, 160–94
regulatory lag 37
techniques 36–41, 134, 159, 160–94
  codes of conduct 37, 38, 94, 98, 161–5
  'command and control' 36–7
  disclosure regulation 39–40
  incentives 38–9, 41, 188–93
  private enforcement rights 40, 182–7
  public information/education
    campaigns 40
  self-regulation 37–8
  'voluntary vs mandatory' debate 32–6
remedies
  access to justice and 116–17
  compensation for pollution from ships
    284–6
Responsible Competitiveness Index 153
Rio Declaration (1992) 71, 156, 158–9
Rio Tinto 42, 99
Risse, T. 98
Ruggie, John 262
Rugmark scheme 95, 180
Russia/Soviet Union, US export controls
  and 107
Rwanda 80

safety issues *see* health and safety at work
Saro-Wiwa, Ken 23, 24, 112, 208
Scott, C. 138
security companies 96
self-interest
  economic 152–6
  political 151–2
self-regulation 37–8, 98, 100, 101
sex offences 109
Shell 23–4, 80, 208
Sikkink, K. 98

Slaughter, A. 94
slavery 75
social dumping 46, 47, 48, 227
social and eco labelling 95, 180–1
socialisation of norms 94, 98, 101, 309
socially responsible investment (SRI) 24
  pensions disclosure and 176
soft law 69–72, 262, 297, 298
Sornorajah, M. 86
South Africa
  choice of law 129
  codes of conduct 161, 162, 173
  CSR reporting 173
  disclosure regulation in 40
  Johannesburg Stock Exchange 40, 173
sovereign immunity 213
sovereignty, multinational corporations
  and 11
Soviet Union 13
Spain, award schemes 194
standards 244–62
  AA1000 standards 176
  Agenda 21 244, 257–8, 264
  ILO Tripartite Declaration on
    Multinationals 12, 45, 70, 71, 150,
    244, 254–7, 308
  health and safety at work 255–6, 263
  obligations to warn/consult 270
  minimum health/safety/environmental
    standards 263–5
  OECD Guidelines on Multinationals 12,
    45, 52, 70, 71, 72, 93, 97, 150, 162,
    184, 186, 187, 189, 244, 248–54, 277,
    308
  consumer protection 251, 264, 270
  environmental impact assessment 272
  environmental issues 250–1, 264
  external monitoring 275
  health and safety at work 250, 263
  National Contact Points (NCPs) 97,
    150, 163, 184, 186, 251–2, 253
  obligations to warn/consult 269
  openness and transparency 273
  precautionary principle 271
  supply chain management 265
  sustainable development 267
  UN Draft Code of Conduct on
    Transnational Corporations 12, 45,
    150, 244, 245–8, 308
  consumer protection 246–7, 264, 265
  openness and transparency 273
  UN Global Compact 70, 71, 97, 100, 153,
    244, 258–61, 276
  Policy Dialogue on Responsible
    Competitiveness 153
  precautionary principle 271

UN Norms on Responsibilities of
Transnational Corporations with
Regard to Human Rights 56, 81, 82,
83, 92, 245, 261–2, 276
environmental impact assessment 273
external monitoring 275
minimum health/safety/
environmental standards 263, 264,
265
obligations to warn/consult 270–1
openness and transparency 274
precautionary principle 272
proposed international CSR regulation
279
supply chain management 266, 267
sustainable development 267
why states have interest in foreign CSR
standards of multinationals 151–60
development goals 156–7
economic self-interest 152–6
ethical concerns 157–8
legal case 158–60
political self-interest 151–2
suppliers, supply chain responsibility 92,
265–7
supply agreements 53
sustainability 24, 46, 267–9
Agenda 21 244, 257–8, 264
management of 98
World Summit on Sustainable
Development (WSSD) 97, 157,
268–9
sweatshop labour 22
Sweden
CSR reporting 172
pensions disclosure 176

Tadaki, J. 78, 79, 92
tariffs 155
taxation, incentives and 38, 193–4
technology 14
territoriality principle 104, 105, 109–10
see also extraterritorial jurisdiction
terrorism, anti-terrorism measures 107,
109
tobacco control 290–1
tobacco industry 22
tort-based claims 200–7
implications for international law 237–9
parent company liability 215–37, 240
enterprise liability 228–33, 234, 235
organisational form and 234–7
primary liability 216–23, 234, 235
secondary liability 225–8, 234, 235
vicarious liability 223–5, 234, 235
as 'regulation' 236–7

US Alien Tort Claims Act 207–15, 224–5,
237, 305
TotalFinaElf 188
tradable emissions permits 39
trade see international trade
Trade Related Investment Measures
(TRIMS) Agreement 19, 46
trade unions 95
multinational corporations and 10
transboundary harm, prevention of
158–60
transnational corporations see
multinational corporations
transparency 171–82, 273–4
CSR reporting 172–6
Extractive Industries Transparency
Initiative (EITI) 96, 163, 178–9
freedom of information legislation
177–8
pensions disclosure 176
sharing information about risks/hazards
179–80
social and eco labelling 95, 180–1
whistleblower protection 142, 181–2
treaties 68, 71, 301
relationship with custom 69
Turkey, Ilisu Dam project 152, 190

Uganda 100
unemployment, multinational
corporations and 12
United Kingdom 152, 157
anti-terrorism measures 109
award schemes 194
codes of conduct 38, 162
Corporate Responsibility Bill 164,
168–70, 186
CSR reporting 173–4, 175
definition of CSR in 30
definition of 'home state' of MNCs 148,
150
export credits 189–90
foreign direct liability (FDL) claims
204–5, 206
freedom of information legislation 177
jurisdictional issues
choice of law 128–9
civil jurisdiction rules 117, 118
extraterritorial jurisdiction 108–9, 138
forum non conveniens 124–6
nationality principle 108–9
migration of jobs and 154
National Contact Point (NCP) 253
parent company liability
enterprise liability 228, 230
primary liability 216, 221

United Kingdom (cont.)
    secondary liability 225, 226
    vicarious liability 223, 224
pensions disclosure 176
private enforcement rights 183
public procurement 193
regulation in 36
    allocating liabilities 55
    public information/education
        campaigns 40
UN Global Compact and 260
whistleblowers 142, 181–2
United Nations 12
    Commission on Human Rights 92, 261,
        280
    Commission on Sustainable
        Development 258
    Commission on Transnational
        Corporations (UNCTC) 245, 246,
        247
    Conference on Trade and Development
        (UNCTAD) 50, 157, 281
    Draft Code of Conduct on Transnational
        Corporations 12, 45, 150, 244, 245–8,
        308
        consumer protection 246–7, 264,
            265
        openness and transparency 273
    Economic and Social Council, working
        group on multinationals 10–12
    Environment Programme 292
    Global Compact 70, 71, 97, 100, 153, 244,
        258–61, 276
        Policy Dialogue on Responsible
            Competitiveness 153
        precautionary principle 271
    Guidelines for Consumer Protection 82
    Norms on Responsibilities of
        Transnational Corporations with
        Regard to Human Rights 56, 81, 82,
        83, 92, 245, 261–2, 276
        environmental impact assessment 273
        external monitoring 275
        minimum
            health/safety/environmental
            standards 263, 264, 265
        obligations to warn/consult 270–1
        openness and transparency 274
        precautionary principle 272
        proposed international CSR regulation
            279
        supply chain management 266, 267
        sustainable development 267
    World Health Organisation (WHO) 137,
        290
United States of America 155

Alien Tort Claims Act 44, 123, 183,
    207–15, 224–5, 237, 305
anti-terrorism measures 107
attitudes to multinational corporations
    in 9, 11
bribery/corruption in 288
Canada–US Free Trade Agreement 14
codes of conduct 161, 163–4
    Code of Conduct (McKinney) Bill 164,
        167–8, 175, 186
corporate social responsibility (CSR) in
    15–16
CSR reporting 173, 175
definition of 'home state' of MNCs 148
export controls 107
export credits 190–2
foreign corruption and 108, 110
foreign direct liability (FDL) claims
    201–3, 206
    Alien Tort Claims Act 207–15, 224–5,
        237, 305
    human rights issues in 44
    jurisdictional issues 138
        choice of law 129–31
        civil jurisdiction rules 118–19
        extraterritorial jurisdiction 106–8,
            109–10, 136
        forum non conveniens 120–4
        nationality principle 106–8
        territorial principle and effects
            doctrine 109–10
    parent company liability
        enterprise liability 231–2
        primary liability 219
        vicarious liability 224–5
    private enforcement rights 40, 182, 183
    trade unions in 10
Universal Declaration of Human Rights
    (UDHR) 77
universal jurisdiction 105, 111–12, 132
Unocal 80, 203, 208, 211, 213, 219, 224,
    228, 231

Vernon, R. 12, 15
vicarious liability 223–5, 234, 235
voluntary approach to corporate social
    responsibility (CSR) 7, 26, 30, 58,
    101, 140, 273
    'voluntary vs mandatory' debate 32–6
Voluntary Principles on Security and
    Human Rights 96, 163

war crimes 75, 76–83, 214
wealth 16
whistleblower protection 142, 181–2
working conditions 22

World Commission on the Social
    Dimension of Globalisation 283
World Economic Forum (WEF), definition
    of CSR 31
World Foundation 33
World Health Organisation (WHO) 137,
    290

World Summit on Sustainable
    Development (WSSD) 97, 157,
    268–9, 277, 278
World Trade Organisation (WTO) 14, 19,
    281–2, 307
WorldCom 25
WorldWide Fund for Nature (WWF) 95

CAMBRIDGE STUDIES IN INTERNATIONAL AND COMPARATIVE LAW

Books in the series

Multinationals and Corporate Social Responsibility
Limitations and Opportunities in International Law
    Jennifer A. Zerk

Judiciaries within Europe
A Comparative Review
    John Bell

Law in Times of Crisis
Emergency Powers in Theory and Practice
    Oren Gross and Fionnuala Ní Aoláin

Vessel-Source Marine Pollution
The Law and Politics of International Regulation
    Alan Tan

Enforcing Obligations Erga Omnes *in International Law*
    Christian J. Tams

Non-Governmental Organisations in International Law
    Anna-Karin Lindblom

Democracy, Minorities and International Law
    Steven Wheatley

Prosecuting International Crimes
Selectivity and the International Law Regime
    Robert Cryer

Compensation for Personal Injury in English, German and Italian Law
A Comparative Outline
    Basil Markesinis, Michael Coester, Guido Alpa and Augustus
    Ullstein

Dispute Settlement in the UN Convention on the Law of the Sea
    Natalie Klein

The International Protection of Internally Displaced Persons
    Catherine Phuong

Imperialism, Sovereignty and the Making of International Law
    Antony Anghie

Necessity, Proportionality and the Use of Force by States
    Judith Gardam

International Legal Argument in the Permanent Court of International Justice
The Rise of the International Judiciary
    Ole Spiermann

Great Powers and Outlaw States
Unequal Sovereigns in the International Legal Order
    Gerry Simpson

Local Remedies in International Law
    C. F. Amerasinghe

Reading Humanitarian Intervention
Human Rights and the Use of Force in International Law
    Anne Orford

Conflict of Norms in Public International Law
How WTO Law Relates to Other Rules of Law
    Joost Pauwelyn

Transboundary Damage in International Law
    Hanqin Xue

European Criminal Procedures
    Edited by Mireille Delmas-Marty and John Spencer

The Accountability of Armed Opposition Groups in International Law
    Liesbeth Zegveld

Sharing Transboundary Resources
International Law and Optimal Resource Use
    Eyal Benvenisti

International Human Rights and Humanitarian Law
    René Provost

Remedies Against International Organisations
    Karel Wellens

Diversity and Self-Determination in International Law
    Karen Knop

The Law of Internal Armed Conflict
  Lindsay Moir

International Commercial Arbitration and African States
Practice, Participation and Institutional Development
  Amazu A. Asouzu

The Enforceability of Promises in European Contract Law
  James Gordley

International Law in Antiquity
  David J. Bederrman

Money Laundering
A New International Law Enforcement Model
  Guy Stessens

Good Faith in European Contract Law,
  Reinhard Zimmerrmann and Simon Whittaker

On Civil Procedure
  J. A. Jolowicz

Trusts
A Comparative Study
  Maurizio Lupoi

The Right to Property in Commonwealth Constitutions
  Tom Allen

International Organizations Before National Courts
  August Reinisch

The Changing International Law of High Seas Fisheries
  Francisco Orrego Vicuña

Trade and the Environment
A Comparative Study of EC and US Law
  Damien Geradin

Unjust Enrichment
A Study of Private Law and Public Values
  Hanoch Dagan

Religious Liberty and International Law in Europe
  Malcolm D. Evans

Ethics and Authority in International Law
Alfred P. Rubin

Sovereignty over Natural Resources
Balancing Rights and Duties
Nico Schrijver

The Polar Regions and the Development of International Law
Donald R. Rothwell

Fragmentation and the International Relations of Micro-States
Self-determination and Statehood
Jorri Duursma

Principles of the Institutional Law of International Organizations
C. F. Amerasinghe

Lightning Source UK Ltd.
Milton Keynes UK
19 March 2011

169528UK00001B/140/P